———— ○ ————

Also by Rosalynd Pflaum

MME. DE STAËL
(in Paris)

THE EMPEROR'S TALISMAN:
The Life of the Duc de Morny

BY INFLUENCE AND DESIRE:
The True Story of Three Extraordinary Women—
The Grand Duchess of Courland and Her Daughters

GRAND
OBSESSION

GRAND

OBSESSION

MADAME CURIE
AND HER WORLD

Rosalynd
Pflaum

DOUBLEDAY

New York   London   Toronto   Sydney   Auckland

BE

PUBLISHED BY DOUBLEDAY,
a division of Bantam Doubleday Dell Publishing Group, Inc.
666 Fifth Avenue, New York, New York 10103

DOUBLEDAY and the portrayal of an anchor with a dolphin
are trademarks of Doubleday, a division of
Bantam Doubleday Dell Publishing Group, Inc.

The author is grateful for permission to reprint excerpts from:

○ *The American Institute of Physics (New York City): oral history interview of Lew Kowarski by Charles Weiner.*

○ *Bibliothèque Nationale (Paris), Département des Manuscrits, Curie Archives.*

○ *Columbia University (New York City), Rare Book and Manuscript Library, Marie Curie Papers.*

○ *Laboratoire Curie (Paris), Les Archives Pierre et Marie Curie, Les Archives Irène et Frédéric Joliot-Curie (permission for the latter granted by Hélène Langevin-Joliot and Pierre Joliot).*

○ Frédéric Joliot-Curie *by Pierre Biquard. Éditions Seghers, 1961. Reprinted by permission of the author.*

○ Madame Curie *by Eve Curie, translated by Vincent Sheean. Copyright 1937 by Doubleday, Doran & Co. Reprinted by permission of the publisher, Doubleday.*

○ Frederick Joliot-Curie *by Maurice Goldsmith. Lawrence and Wishart, 1976. Reprinted by permission of the publisher.*

○ Souvenirs et Rencontres *by Camille Marbo. Éditions Grasset, 1968. Extracts reprinted by permission of the publisher.*

○ Marie Curie *by Robert Reid. Collins, 1974. Also Dutton, 1975, a division of Penguin Books USA. Reprinted by permission of the publisher.*

○ Scientists in Power *by Spencer R. Weart, Harvard University Press, 1979. Reprinted by permission of the author.*

○ Choix de Lettres de Marie Curie et Irène Joliot-Curie, *edited by Gillette Ziegler. Les Éditeurs Français Réunis, 1974. Reprinted by permission of Éditions Messidor.*

All photographs reproduced by permission of—and thanks to—the Laboratoire Curie.

Library of Congress Cataloging-in-Publication Data

Pflaum, Rosalynd.
    Grand obsession : Madame Curie and her world / Rosalynd Pflaum.—1st ed.
    p. cm.
  Bibliography: p.
  Includes index.
  ISBN 0-385-26135-7 :
  1. Curie, Marie, 1867–1934. 2. Curie, Pierre, 1859–1906. 3. Paris (France)—Social life and customs—19th century. 4. Chemists—Poland—Biography. I. Title.
QD22.C8P44 1989
540′.92—dc20
[B]   89-34230
                                                                                  CIP

Title page photograph: The Bettmann Archive
Copyright © 1989 by Rosalynd Pflaum
ALL RIGHTS RESERVED
PRINTED IN THE UNITED STATES OF AMERICA
NOVEMBER 1989
FIRST EDITION
BG

To
Bruce,
Jason,
Andrew,
and
Jeremy

Acknowledgments

Perhaps the hardest part of writing a biography is adequately thanking those who made it all happen. In this book I have naturally had recourse to the usual traditional historical sources. But I have also been fortunate enough to talk with several of the Curies' and a number of the Joliot-Curies' colleagues and contemporaries. Their kindness in agreeing to meet with me has been invaluable, and I want to take this opportunity of thanking, once more, Pierre Auger, Pierre Biquard, Lucien Desgranges, Marcel Frilley, Françqise Gilot, Mme. Gricouroff, Mme. Jeanne Laberrigue, Jean Langevin, Mme. Aline Lapicque, Roger Mayer, Francis Perrin, Angèle Pompei—who arranged a visit to Paris to coincide with one of mine— Pierre Radvanyi, Mme. Denise Van Hooren. Also, of course, Ève Curie and, especially, the Joliot children, Hélène Langevin-Joliot and Pierre Joliot, who so graciously allowed me access to their parents' unpublished correspondence.

The writing of each of my books has been greatly facilitated by the loving assistance of different, long-standing French friends who invariably knew the right person to say open sesame for whatever I needed. In this instance, it was Mme. Nicole Henriot-Schweitzer, and I shall be forever grateful for her warm introduction to Dr. Raymond Latarjet, who in turn introduced me to Mme. Monique Bordry. There are no words in my vocabulary to express my gratitude to this pair. Dr. Latarjet, the distinguished Honorary Director of the Institut de Radium in Paris (where he served as director for more than twenty years) and a member of the Institut de France (Académie des Sciences)—among his many other distinctions—as well as an author, has given unstintingly of his time with advice, counsel, and encouragement every step of the way. Busy as he always is, he managed to find time to answer my most insignificant questions and, as a final favor, he also read the manuscript to catch any mistakes. Mme. Bordry, who is not only a popular science writer but also the librarian at the Curie Institute, as well as an assistant researcher at Saturne, the national laboratory of the Centre National de Recherche Scientifique, never said no to any request—whether by mail or long-distance phone, or during the many times I was working in Paris. Whether it was documentation, missing dates or files, or pictures, Mme. Bordry was there. Her advice was invaluable and available whenever needed, although there must have been times when I sorely tested her patience.

Members of the staff at the "Curie"—Mme. Ravigot, Messieurs Pindrus, Du Bois, and Brunot—were always on hand to be of any assistance, no matter what the request.

I would especially like to thank Dr. Monique Pagès, its present director, who so kindly placed at my disposal Marie Curie's own office and permitted me to work at the desk that not only Marie Curie but subsequent directors, Irène and, then, Frédéric Joliot-Curie, used. If that did not inspire me, I don't know what else could have—even if the desk did have to be checked periodically with Geiger counters to check the level of radiation! The staff at the Bibliothèque Nationale was once again most cooperative, especially those in the Département des Manuscrits.

Dr. Bertrand Goldschmidt merits an especial thanks. As the last scientist to be hired by Marie Curie before her death and, subsequently, a French pioneer of nuclear energy, as well as one of the founders of the French Atomic Energy Commission and one of its former directors, Dr. Goldschmidt was in a unique position to answer many troublesome questions for me. This he most kindly did. He also generously took the time to read and correct my manuscript from his firsthand knowledge of many of the events described in it.

While in these pages any opinions expressed, or conclusions drawn are necessarily my own, I have tried to be as accurate as possible, not only scientifically but also historically. With this in mind, I contacted, on this side of the Atlantic, another dear friend, Dr. William Shepherd, the former vice president in charge of academic administration at the University of Minnesota. As with Nicole Henriot-Schweitzer, in France, Dr. Shepherd knew exactly the authority I needed and promptly put me in touch with Dr. Roger H. Stuewer, Professor and Director, Program in History of Science and Technology at the University of Minnesota. Dr. Stuewer took the time to go over Grand Obsession *with great care, and I am immensely endebted to him for his efforts—and suggestions. The libraries of the University of Minnesota were most cooperative, as usual, especially the Interlibrary Loan Division's Jane Rasmussen and Christopher Loring. Dr. Shepherd also introduced me to Dr. Eugene Gedgaudes of the Department of Radiology, who kindly gave me the information I needed about some of the physiological effects of radium.*

Spencer R. Weart at the American Institute of Physics in New York and Kenneth Lohf at the Rare Book and Manuscript Library of Columbia University must also be singled out for their assistance. So, too, must Cynthia Vartan for early editorial direction.

My Doubleday editor, Shaye Areheart, and her assistant, Bruce Tracy, were there when I needed them most, as was my agent, Jacques de Spoelberch, who has never failed me. Without Jim Lyon and Terri Anderson, who helped me master a computer, this manuscript might never have reached its final form.

And, without the patience, understanding, and encouragement of my husband, Grand Obsession *might never have been realized.*

Wayzata, Minnesota
1984–89

CONTENTS

GRAND
OBSESSION

I
1867–1891

Manya

THE FAINT CLATTER OF A bell—two long rings, two short—was heard in the distance. It was the secret warning that Warsaw's dreaded Russian inspector of private boarding schools had once again arrived unannounced. Ten-year-old Manya Sklodowska, who was enthusiastically answering her teacher's question about Polish history, stopped in mid-sentence. For a few seconds her classmates, too, were startled into silence. In 1877, teaching Polish history, particularly in Polish, was forbidden by the Poles' Russian masters. But this was the children's favorite class, and they had rehearsed many times what they must do to escape detection. Swiftly and silently, the twenty-five young conspirators passed the forbidden history books and their work papers from hand to hand across the rows of desks. Those sitting on the aisle stuffed them into their outstretched aprons and disappeared into the adjacent dormitory, while the others stealthily opened, then closed, the tops of their desks.

Vysokorodye Hornberg was behind in his schedule today. The school's faithful porter barely had time to send the prearranged signal. In no time, the pompous, bespectacled inspector, a heavyset man stuffed into tight yellow pants and a sky blue tunic with gold buttons, was pushing open the hall door to the twelve-year-old's classroom. Puffing at his heels was tiny, birdlike Mlle. Sikorska, directress of the Pension Sikorska, her black silk gown rustling agitatedly.

"This is one of the girls' weekly sewing hours," she explained, as the inspector looked around at the tops of twenty-five braided heads bent over squares of unhemmed material, thimbles flashing as they stitched, with spools of thread and scissors scattered around. Silently, Hornberg advanced toward their teacher, Mlle. Antonia Tupalska. "What are you reading to them?" he asked. "Tupsia," as her pupils called her, was normally ruddy-faced but now her cheeks were drained of color, with a red circle in the center of each. With her lips pressed tightly together, she showed the hated official the book—*Krylov's Fairy Tales* printed in Russian. With surprising ease for so paunchy a man, Hornberg rapidly and at random opened the lids of several desks. All were empty. The girls stopped sewing and crossed their arms to watch him. The inspector sank into the chair Tupsia offered him while Mlle. Sikorska hovered at his side. "You will call on one of your students," he commanded.

Seated near the back, Manya resolutely turned and looked out the window. She hoped that by averting her eyes she might convince Tupsia to call on someone else for a change. But Mlle. Tupalska called on her brightest pupil, the one child she could rely on to answer correctly and in perfect Russian although the diminutive girl was two years younger than the rest of the class.

Manya rose to her feet. "Your prayer," Hornberg ordered. Steeling herself, Manya shyly complied, her voice now constrained to a whisper. The questions came rapidly. "Name the Tsars who have reigned over our Holy Russia since Catherine II." Manya swallowed hard, then did so. The inspector regarded the nervous pupil and permitted himself a smile. "Who rules over us?" Silence. "Who rules over us?" The inspector's annoyance was apparent. At his repeated question the patriotic Mlle. Sikorska glanced at the floor, and the red spots burned brighter in Tupsia's ashen cheeks. Rising angrily to his feet, the inspector repeated his question a third time. "His Majesty Alexander II, Tsar of all the Russias," Manya finally managed to say. With a curt nod, Hornberg turned on his heel and left the room with Mlle. Sikorska bustling close behind.

"Come here, my little soul,"[1] Tupsia said softly. Her ordeal over, Manya approached, drained by her efforts. Without saying another word, Mlle. Tupalska kissed her on the forehead. Manya burst into tears.

That afternoon when Manya crossed the square near the Palace of Saxony with her best friend, Kazia Przyborowska, the youngsters took elaborate pains to spit at the obelisk erected there by the Tsar, on which was inscribed in Russian, "To the Poles Faithful to Their Sovereign," a euphemism for Polish quislings. Spitting thus was a local custom subject to punishment by the municipal Russian authorities. But both girls were still so incensed by Hornberg's visit that they looked neither right nor left to see who might be watching. For once they threw caution to the winds. They did not care.

— ○ —

Poland was always being fought over and divided by other nations. Russia was now the master. The most recent Polish uprising, in 1863, had been bloodily suppressed shortly after the marriage of Manya's parents. Vladislav and Bronislawa Sklodowski still had vivid memories of the five severed heads dangling from scaffolds on the hill outside the citadel and of the numerous dead bodies left hanging on the red brick battlements near their home. In 1867, the Russians tightened their grip. The segment of Poland in their hands was renamed "The Province of the Vistula," the Polish language was demoted to a dialect while Russian was imposed everywhere, and Polish officials were gradually replaced by Russians or pro-Russian Poles, who were even more odious to the citizenry. Police informers infiltrated all walks of life.

On November 7 of that year, in a small upstairs apartment on Freta Street in the city's old quarter, there was considerable activity. While on one side of the parchment-thin walls classes were being conducted for the young daughters of Warsaw's best families, on the other side two middle-aged women carried sheets, jugs of hot water, and other necessities into an improvised delivery ward. There, the school's directress, Mme. Sklodowska, gave birth to her fourth daughter. Marie Salomée, unlike her brunet mother, was an ash blond with gray eyes.

Bronislawa Boguska Sklodowska's family on both sides were impoverished members of the lesser nobility. A gifted pianist with a good voice, she had been a pupil, then a teacher, in the Freta Street School, which she now headed. She was married at twenty-four to Vladislav Sklodowski, four years her senior, who came from the same background. Vladislav's father, Josef, the first intellectual in the Sklodowski family, left the countryside to become the physics and mathematics teacher, as well as director, of a boys' gymnasium in Lublin. Vladislav took his advanced training at the University of St. Petersburg in Russia and then taught the same subjects his father had, but in Warsaw.

With the arrival of his fifth child, Professor Sklodowski had to think of supplementing the family income. Shortly after the first of the year, the family moved to a nearby gymnasium for boys, where the professor not only taught his specialties but, as the school's underinspector, received a second income and housing. Unfortunately, his wife could not continue to run the Freta Street School if she lived elsewhere but, in frail health and with five children under six to raise, she most likely had few regrets about resigning.

Their pleasant new apartment was on the ground floor of the school building and had windows veiled with stiff lace curtains, through which tiny Manya, as Marie was promptly nicknamed, could watch the carts and lazily trotting droshkies on Nowolipki Street. The bells of the nearby Church of the Virgin rang for daily vespers—in Warsaw one was never far from a church or its influence—and as soon as Manya could toddle, she went off to Mass on Sundays with her sisters, Zosia, Bronya, and Hela, their elder brother Jozio, and their parents.

Like their peers, the Sklodowski children always addressed their parents in the third person. But by the time Manya was five, her mother transformed this traditional deference into a physical formality as well. Mme. Sklodowska had developed tuberculosis. In an endeavor to spare her family—and well in advance of the general medical precepts of the day—she assumed the heartrending precaution of never again embracing any of her children; she also wisely used separate dishes. Bewildered, small Manya yearned in vain to be kissed and hugged by the thin, pale mother she adored. She had to be satisfed with pressing herself tightly against her mother's ample skirts and by the gentle strokes her mother gave her pale blond curls when she put her to bed each evening. Unquestionably this was one reason why Manya, in later years, was noticeably undemonstrative with her own children.

With the greatest of efforts, the professor managed to scrape together sufficient funds to send his ailing wife to a clinic in Nice, accompanied by their eldest daughter, Zosia. Manya was told that after her cure Mama would be well again. But when her mother returned a year later, the ravages of consumption had taken their toll, and the child hardly recognized the wraith who greeted her.

Mme. Sklodowska was determined that her family should not notice her suffering any more than she could help. Despite increasing weakness, on Saturday nights she managed to sit with her brood, listening to the professor read aloud from the classics while she mended the children's clothes and made their boots with a small cobbler's awl and knife. At the rate the five were growing, store-bought shoes were an unattainable luxury. These evenings were isolated islands of happiness for Manya, but the older children were all too frequently dragged back into the immediate present by their mother's attempt to stifle a coughing spell and by the blood-stained handkerchief she brought away from her mouth.

The Sklodowskis were thoroughly patriotic, but they were not activists. Unfortunately, M. Ivanov, the gymnasium's director, was fanatically anti-Polish. Friction between the two men was inevitable, and before long M. Sklodowski was dismissed on the grounds that he was not sufficiently pro-Russian.

Taking with them their leather canapes, the Restoration armchairs, the malachite pendulum clock, and the one Sèvres teacup that Manya recalled from her earliest days, the family made the first of a series of moves into the steadily less comfortable quarters dictated by the professor's declining fortunes.

To make ends meet in their next apartment farther down Nowolipki Street, the family was reduced to taking in boarders—the time-honored expedient of the impoverished bourgeoisie. At first they took in only two or three boys. Unfortunately, these strangers did far worse than intrude on the family's privacy; they introduced typhus into the household. Soon both Zosia and Bronya were shaking and moaning with the fever, and Manya learned of death firsthand when her eldest sister died. On a blustery, cold January day, nine-year-old Manya followed the funeral cortège in a drab black hand-me-down coat of Zosia's, clutching her father's hand, with her brother Jozio and her sister Hela. Bronya was still too weak to accompany them, and Mme. Sklodowska was too sick.

Two years later Manya escorted her mother's coffin down the same street. For the solemn-faced eleven-year-old, it was hard to reconcile these two tragic deaths with the hours her family spent on their knees praying. As Manya knelt beside the bier in the church where she used to worship so regularly with her mother, she felt anger against a pitiless and unjust God and, she later claimed, she had her first doubts about religion. The exaggerated, yearlong mourning, the black curtains, dresses, and veils dictated by Polish custom only served to prolong her misery and grief. Professor Sklodowski's already meager income dwindled perceptibly as he was forced to accept successively lower posts. The Warsaw school system was speeding up the replacement of native teachers by Russians even though the latter were, in most instances, less qualified. Such a perversion of justice convinced Manya that when she grew up she must do whatever she could to free her beloved country from its oppressors. To make ends meet, the family increased the number of boarders to ten. As the youngest Sklodowski, Manya slept rolled up in an animal skin on the divan in the dining room, and had to be up at 6 A.M. so the table could be set for the boarders' breakfast.

The crowded apartment made study a challenge for the others, but not for Manya. Able to read at four, her amazing memory was already in evidence at Mlle. Sikorska's school the day her classmates accused her of cheating when she flawlessly recited a poem they had read together in class only twice before. Conditions at home finely honed her innate power of concentration. The minute Manya bent over her books nothing could disturb her, although her brother and sisters often ganged up, whooping like Cossacks, to try and break her train of thought.

Their next apartment, on Leschno Street, lacked some of the amenities of the previous one but afforded them more privacy. Here they had four rooms of their own, away from the ubiquitous boarders. The linens might be threadbare, their clothes patched, the meals sometimes skimpy, but food for thought was never lacking. As in Mme. Sklodowska's lifetime, Saturday night was consecrated to literature and remained the high point of the week for the close-knit family.

— o —

The government gymnasiums were completely indoctrinated by Russian political thought, but they were the sole resort for a Polish girl who wanted to continue her studies and receive a diploma in order to teach. And on an afternoon so stifling that not even the cat's-tail clouds overhead moved, a flourish of trumpets and speeches marked the traditional closing ceremonies when Manya graduated. The grand master of education in Poland stepped up to the podium to award the sixteen-year-old the coveted gold medal that went with the distinction of top student. The sun's rays bounced off the glistening disk that hung on the ribbon now around her neck as the slight girl kept returning to the platform to receive yet another prize. Soon she had an armful of books, awards for excellence in mathematics, history, literature, German, English, and French. Manya's achievement was the more remarkable because the Occupation authorities resorted to strict grading in an effort to fail as many students as possible each year and minimize the number graduating; experience had proven that any intellectual element was a potential spawning ground of revolution.

Before she could fully enjoy her triumph, Manya fell sick. Since her doctor's diagnosis is unavailable, it is impossible to determine whether the problem was physical or psychological or both. Considerable pressure was undoubtedly exerted on Manya by the doting professor, anxious to develop the intellectual capacities of the brightest of his children. Certainly, it was only normal for Manya to have felt compelled to equal or better the records of Jozio and Bronya, who had each attained a similar distinction. However, since on more than one future occasion Manya would suddenly collapse physically in times of great strain, there may also have been some deeper disorder. In later years, she herself attributed this early period of ill health to the fatigue of growth and study, while the family preferred the vague catchall phrase "nervous troubles." Whatever the cause of her illness, Professor Sklodowski wisely decided that Manya needed a prolonged rest, and he shipped her off to the country for a year.

The professor and his children usually spent their summers visiting different family members; the Boguskis were widely scattered, while the cradle of the Sklody clan was a collection of farms bearing that name about one hundred kilometers north of Warsaw. This year, Manya set out on the same rounds alone. Lancet, Manya's enormous and thoroughly spoiled brown pointer, whose likeness can still be seen in a sketch she made in her notebook, accompanied her. The twelve months that followed were the most carefree and gay of Manya's life, a period in which she did nothing but enjoy herself in an atmosphere entirely different from the intellectual one at home.

Manya obeyed her father's injunction to the letter. She wrote her friend Kazia that she had forgotten school ever existed. She had no schedule, read no serious books, and had even abandoned the needlework she started. If a sad childhood and an overly studious adolescence had tempered and matured Manya beyond her years, these twelve months worked their recuperative magic. Then they were over.

In early September, Manya returned home for good. During her extended absence, poor health had forced Professor Sklodowski to stop taking boarders. The budget again needed trimming, and the family moved to an even smaller flat in a poorer section of the city. Jozio was at the Tsar's University of Warsaw, studying to be a doctor, one of the few careers open to a young Polish man, and no longer lived at home. Hela, the beauty of the family, was not the scholar the others were, but she had inherited her mother's good voice, and Warsaw's finest singing teacher was giving her free lessons. Bronya, who had developed into a prize cook, continued to run the Sklodowski household, but she, too, was determined to become a doctor, even though this meant going abroad. The universities in Geneva and Paris were the only two schools that admitted women to graduate work. The sole way for her to earn the money she needed to go was by tutoring. There was a widespread demand —and a surfeit of tutors.

Undaunted by these statistics, Manya, who had not yet decided what she wanted to do with her life but knew that she must contribute to the family income, temporarily joined forces with her elder sister. The pair ran an ad in the paper, but response was unfortunately minimal.

A friend of hers, Mlle. Piasecka, a thin, fair-haired gymnasium teacher whose fiancé had been expelled from the University of Warsaw for subversive activity, persuaded Manya to attend the illegal night school she was directing. Since admission was free, Bronya also joined. "The Floating University" was, in many ways, a forerunner of the classes conducted by dissident Polish intellectuals who formed the Workers' Self-Defense Committee KOR in 1976, and was not unlike many similar schools flourishing in Warsaw in the 1980s. Because it appealed simultaneously to her patriotism, her intellectual aspirations, and her humanitarianism, Manya was soon one of the Floating University's most enthusiastic members.

To participate required courage. Since it was a Polish school, operating outside the Russian system, both teachers and students were subject to prison terms or possible deportation to Siberia if the authorities learned of their activities. Elaborate precautions were devised to evade detection. The school met four nights a week, and those attending were divided into groups of no more than a dozen each, meeting in garrets and cellars, or in friends' living rooms. Mlle. Piasecka's auditors were mostly young women, like the Sklodowska sisters, for whom there was no other way to obtain further education, and while some of their teachers were patently less qualified than others, Manya found new horizons of knowledge open to her. There were classes in natural history and sociology, and the latest progress in physics, chemistry, and physiology was explained. Occasionally there was a lecture on unexpurgated Polish history or a discussion of some article in the banned positivist weekly *Prawda*. Listening, enthralled like the others,

Manya was filled with the idealism of youth and the fervor of patriotism, and her dream, like theirs, was to free the fatherland.

The young intellectuals of Warsaw were in a state of ferment, and Manya was swept along with them in the flood of new ideas seeping in, illegally, from the West, especially those of Auguste Comte, the founder of positivism, whose work on "Positive Philosophy" appeared between 1830 and 1842 in France. Comte rejected theoretical speculation about man and his problems in favor of positive, observable facts, and preached emancipation of women, sexual equality of education, anticlericalism, and education of the masses. His followers believed in reason and logic, and his Warsaw disciples also elevated Darwin and Pasteur to similar status because the pair applied scientific methods to human questions in an effort to solve some of mankind's ills.

Manya's group discussions did not overlook Karl Marx's *Das Kapital*, which had appeared in 1867, or the work of his friend and collaborator, Friedrich Engels, but these exhortations to overthrow the established order by violence found no common ground with her or her friends. While the predominant dream of the Floating University's idealistic positivists was to reform society and to free Poland, they preferred to go Mlle. Piasecka's route rather than follow that of another contemporary, Rosa Luxemburg. Rosa, who did not participate in their classes and probably never knew Manya, three years her junior, espoused socialism and became celebrated as a fiery revolutionary. Mlle. Piasecka took for granted a woman's right to participate in promoting change, but preferred more peaceful means. By completing the education of the Floating University's members, she hoped to build up the country's core of intellectuals and teachers, who would, in turn, develop and educate the poor and thus, by a chain reaction, free Poland.

Here was a concrete plan that Manya could endorse, and like other enthusiastic members of the group, she agreed to teach the underprivileged. Twice weekly she conducted a class in a nearby dressmaker's atelier, reading to the women while they worked. She also built up a small library, volume by volume, for their use.

In positivism Manya found a philosophy on which to build her life, for the Church and religion offered her no solace. With the passage of years, she found it increasingly difficult to understand the hold Catholicism had had on her adored mother. Manya's early experiences with the deaths of two loved ones only reinforced her innate skepticism, an attitude fostered by her father's rationalism. Now she discovered a satisfactory alternative. The Warsaw interpretation of Comte, tempered as it was by Pasteur's work and Herbert Spencer's explication of Darwin's survival-of-the-fittest theory, also endowed the exact sciences with great prestige, and Manya thought increasingly of following in her father's footsteps as a physics teacher.

Once again, Manya's immediate future was determined by the family's chronic lack of funds. She was not worried about Jozio, who had lately received a medical scholarship, or Hela, who was hesitating between a singing career and several offers of marriage. But Bronya was a different story. She had been like a mother to Manya since Mme. Sklodowska's death, and Manya felt very close to her. For over a year, Bronya had been setting aside part of the small sums she earned tutoring in order to go to Paris and study medicine, and then return to practice in Poland. But, to date, she had only been able to set aside the cost of a one-way Warsaw-to-Paris fare and enough to cover expenses for the first year of a five-year course. At that rate, Manya figured, Bronya would be old and gray before she ever set foot in France. Working as a governess in exchange for free board, lodging, and laundry was the only solution for people in their straits, a course of action taken by many of their friends. Since Bronya was already twenty, seventeen-year-old Manya made up her mind to seek a live-in job and give Bronya the bulk of her earnings. Bronya could then go to Paris, and when Bronya graduated she, in turn, would help subsidize Manya's education abroad.

Manya had a hard time persuading her sister that this was the only possible solution for them both. The October day Bronya set off with her friend Marya Rakowska in time for the Sorbonne's fall opening, the whole family trekked to the depot to say farewell.

Manya's first job, with a lawyer's family who lived not far from the Sklodowskis, proved to be a disaster. The only child refused to learn, while her mother was petty and treated Manya like a servant. Manya was miserably unhappy and left within six weeks. She was very disillusioned and had not earned enough money to compensate for the sacrifice of living away from home. So when a three-year contract with the excellent salary of 500 rubles a year was offered, she accepted, even though it meant moving to the country far from her beloved family.

The start of the new year, 1886, saw the start of a new existence for Manya and years later she still referred to that departure as one of the most vivid memories of her youth. After a three-hour train trip to the region of Plock, a little more than one hundred kilometers north of Warsaw, she had an additional five-hour ride in the sleigh that was waiting at the station to take her to Szczuki near Przasnysz. When the horses were finally reined to a halt, after a monotonous ride across vast, treeless plains hushed beneath heavy snow, Manya stepped out, dressed as befit a governess in the unadorned frock of an old maid, her hair neatly folded under a faded hat. M. and Mme. Zorawski greeted her warmly, and she was immediately served tea with them and the children, who were as handsome as their parents and consumed with curiosity about "Mlle. Manya."

Szczuki was in the heart of the sugar beet region, and M. Zorawski was the administrator of some two hundred acres, which constituted a minute part of the domains of the Czartoryski princes. Manya found him old-fashioned, like her father, and sympathetic; Madame was herself a former governess, with a temper which often showed, and it took some knowing to get along with her. The couple treated Manya as if she were a member of the family. Only a

few of their children were at home, including Manya's two pupils—
Bronka, a year her junior, whom Manya termed "delicious" and
with whom she worked four hours a day, and spoiled, ten-year-old
Andzia, who was not interested in studying and with whom she
worked three.

As the days quickly settled into an undisturbed routine, Manya
chronicled her life at Szczuki in a series of letters to family and
friends. Those to Professor Sklodowski were of course written in
the third person and always ended with the traditional "I kiss my
little father's hands." The Zorawskis were relatively cultivated, but
the dinner-table conversation was not of the stimulating variety to
which Manya had grown accustomed. Gossip, sugar beets, and the
damage caused by the latest frost (in that order) were poor substi-
tutes for a dissection of progressivist ideas or heated discussions
over higher education for women and the rights of oppressed Poland.

Manya was appalled at the wretched conditions of the peasants
clustered in hovels around the small redbrick sugar beet factory
nearby in the village of Krasiniec. They tilled the fields, sowing,
hoeing, and reaping the beets, then manned the factory machinery
that crushed the beets into sugar. Still the "positive idealist," as she
had recently inscribed a picture of herself and Bronya, Manya soon
set out to help their illiterate children by giving them two hours of
school daily in her free time. Bronka Zorawski was so anxious to
assist Manya that her father, surprisingly, gave her permission to do
so although he was as well aware as Manya that teaching peasants
anything, let alone Polish history in Polish, was treasonable in Russian eyes.

Because Manya had a room to herself that was accessible by
outside stairs, she taught the children there, using a borrowed pine
table and chairs, and copybooks and pens purchased from the small
portion of her earnings that she earmarked for herself. The number
of pupils quickly rose to eighteen, so she divided them into two
groups, and on Wednesdays and Saturdays, her free days, she gave

them five hours of work rather than two. Often their parents, unwashed and uneducated like their barefooted offspring, crowded in too, curious to see what "Mlle. Manya" was doing, and they were as delighted as she when the children started to read and write.

In order to continue sending Bronya the money she needed, Manya elected to take no time off when summer came, homesick though she was. That was how she met Casimir. The eldest Zorawski son, a few years Manya's senior and as good-looking as the rest of the family, came home on vacation sporting a dashing blond mustache and, in a time-honored scenario, the young couple fell in love. That they did so was not surprising. Manya had lost her adolescent plumpness, and her Slavic cheekbones and high round forehead were now sharply emphasized. She was slowly developing into a pretty young woman with gossamer, ash blond hair, slender wrists and ankles, and gray eyes. What a welcome, stimulating addition to the local scene she was for the Warsaw college student, who was already sought after by the mothers of all the eligible girls in the district. To Manya, Casimir was like a visitor from Mars. He was the first intellectual equal of her own generation that she had met since coming to that sterile provincial backwater and served as a most welcome link with the sorely missed capital, bringing the latest ideas in university circles to Szczuki. Casimir was also studying science.

Unquestionably, Manya's frame of mind made her ripe for this new experience and, by the time Casimir was ready to return for another school year, marriage seems to have been mentioned and she was ready to wed the Zorawski heir. There appeared to be no obstacles in their path. But even though M. and Mme. Zorawski thought the world of Manya, they saw her in a different light when it came to accepting her as a daughter-in-law. In the eyes of the well-to-do Polish landowners of the day, urban intellectuals were an inferior class and, to make matters worse for Manya, the Sklodowskis were poor. Casimir was studying to be an agricultural engineer and could not, upon graduation, receive a lucrative post at the University of Warsaw since he was a Pole. He therefore needed a rich wife who could support him, and there were at least five suitable local girls already in line, eager for the chance. Casimir lacked the courage to stand up to his parents, and returned crestfallen to Warsaw. But he refused to give up hope.

This was Manya's first experience with love, and she was crushed. Her inexperience, as well as the depth of her emotions, can be gauged by a letter she wrote her cousin Henriette Michalowska, that December. Her plans for the future were so simple that they did not bear discussion. She would get along as best she could and, when she could do no more, "say farewell to this base world. . . . Some . . . pretend that . . . I am obliged to pass through the kind of fever called love. This absolutely does not enter into my plans. If I ever had any others, they have gone up in smoke; I have buried them; locked them up; sealed and forgotten them."[2] The letter's melodramatic hints at suicide indicate how thoroughly shattered Manya was. If Henriette was astute enough to read between the lines, it was painfully clear that Manya had been, and still was, in love.

The obvious thing for her to do was to leave Szczuki. But Manya was made of sterner stuff than Casimir. She needed the job. She did not want to disturb her father, for the family budget depended to a certain degree on her earnings, and she could not let Bronya down. Manya still had two years of her three-year contract to finish. The pay was excellent, and Casimir was out of sight. Since there had been no humiliating, face-to-face showdown with his parents, it was easier to swallow her pride. The practical young woman wisely did so, and stayed on as if nothing had happened.

Not unexpectedly, her previously warm relationship with M. and Mme. Zorawski was a thing of the past. Manya's unhappiness over the love affair made everything harder to bear. She confessed to Jozio that she had lost any hope of ever becoming anybody and transferred her ambitions to Bronya and him.

The time dragged on like a jail sentence. Since her evenings were free, Manya stayed up late, furthering her own education with books borrowed from the factory library. She set out to improve her mathematics in a pseudo-correspondence course with her father and turned increasingly toward science, for which she had inherited her father's interest and for which, as a Warsaw positivist, she had the greatest respect. She considered it the most sublime manifestation of the human spirit and a perfect tool to aid humanity. Impressed by her enthusiasm, Jean Wortman, a chemist at the beet sugar factory, gave her twenty lessons in chemistry in his spare time. Although there was no place to do practical work, Manya decided this was what she wanted to study when—and if—she got to Paris.

The following spring, as early rains and thaws were turning the surrounding landscape into a sea of red mud, she stuck her last stamp on a birthday letter to her brother so full of self-pity that it barely conveyed the good wishes with which it was sent. Her depression deepened as the months dragged wearily on and the seasons changed. But Manya was getting a better hold on herself, and her second winter there she wrote to her cousin Henriette that she seemed to be coming out of a nightmare and was determined never again to be beaten down by persons or events.

Manya left Szczuki with no regrets and returned to Warsaw at Easter 1889. Her father, who was now officially retired, had been offered the position of director of a reformatory at Studziwniec, near the capital. The job was a thankless, unpleasant one, but the pay was good and together with his pension enabled him finally to send Bronya a few rubles monthly himself. Bronya immediately wrote Manya to stop sending her any more and to start saving for her own study in Paris.

After a brief visit at home Manya signed up with another family, but this time she made only a one-year commitment. As her contract drew to a close, she received an unexpected letter from Bronya announcing that she was going to marry a fellow medical student, a thirty-four-year-old Pole, Casimir Dluski. If Manya could scrape together a few hundred rubles, she must come west the following year, 1891, in time for the opening of the Sorbonne, and live with them for her first twelve months. To Bronya's astonishment Manya declined, reciting the current Sklodowski litany of woes as her excuse. An unavowed factor was also Casimir, who was still, apparently, hovering in the background.

Bronya finally prevailed. At the end of her present commitment, Manya was to spend a year with M. Sklodowski, augment her modest savings by tutoring, and then leave for Paris in the fall of 1891. In the interim, Manya had the thrill of conducting her first chemistry experiments, rather than merely reading about them. Almost every evening, she hurried to no. 66 Krakovsky Street, crossed a well-manicured courtyard, and entered a tiny one-story building at the far end. Engraved above the lintel was the purposely misleading name "Museum of Industry and Agriculture," chosen by its founder, her maternal cousin Joseph Boguski, to disguise another of the city's clandestine academies, for there was no law against teaching science to young Poles inside a museum. Here, in the empty building, after hours, Manya attempted various experiments and acquired a lifelong fascination for this type of work.

Satisfaction at success alternated with discouragement at failure and disgust with her own clumsiness when she encountered techniques that were too difficult for her to master readily or unaided. Occasionally, if her cousin Joseph was around, he regaled her with firsthand tales about the legendary Russian chemist Dmitri Mendeleev, whose assistant Joseph had once been in St. Petersburg. Napoleon Milicer, who also worked in the museum, inspired her further with stories of his teacher, the famous German chemist Robert Bunsen, the inventor of spectral analysis. More importantly still, Milicer and his aide, Ludwick Kossakowski, gave the enthusiastic neophyte a systematic course in chemistry in their free time.

Early in September, she vacationed with her father at his brother's home in the Carpathians. He returned to Warsaw alone while Manya stayed on to spend a few days with Casimir. On their long walks together among the mountains' great black pines, Casimir confessed that he did not yet have his family's permission to marry her, and Manya finally found the strength to break their ties. Dramatically referring to the "cruel trials" she had been through lately "which will have an influence on my whole life,"[3] she wrote Paris that if Bronya wanted her, she would be on her way.

Casimir belonged to the past. But he never forgot Manya. And years later, after he retired from a distinguished teaching career at Warsaw's Polytechnical School, he came daily to the Warsaw square where a statue of Manya stood and sat contemplating it.

It was time for Manya to start living for herself. To inaugurate this new era, she painted her initials, "M.S.," in bold black letters on the big old trunk that she was sending ahead, stuffed with her own mattress, sheets, and blankets, which economical Bronya had suggested she bring along to save money. Manya's emotions must have been mixed. If she was troubled to be leaving her frail, elderly father, it was comforting to know he would be well taken care of by Jozio and his family with whom the little professor was going to live. If she felt any guilt about her pleasure in finally being able to study at the Sorbonne, or any sadness at leaving her beloved Poland, her exalted patriotism masked her ambition and appeased her conscience with the knowledge that she would return in two or three years far better equipped to help her fatherland than if she had stayed at home. There may even have been some relief to have at last exorcised Casimir from her life. Now there was nothing to stop her from concentrating on her goal.

Although she only had a secondary high school degree, Manya's sights were set high, on an advanced scientific education—an extraordinary aim for any woman of that day, especially one from Poland. Eight years had passed since she graduated from the gymnasium, and she knew that if she did not go now, she never would. For she was almost twenty-four.

Shortly before her birthday, Manya kissed her father goodbye and stepped up into the third-class compartment of the transcontinental steam train. She was equipped for the three and a half days of travel with food and drink, books and a blanket. Because she was as eager to economize as most other Polish students traveling west, Manya, too, planned to switch, when she crossed the border, to a fourth-class car with a bench around it and no seats, so she also carried a chair to use for the remainder of the journey.

Manya's character and opinions were already firmly established, tempered by conditions of life in Tsarist Poland. Yet that crucible had left unscathed the two traits it was most designed to obliterate —Manya's ambition and her independence.

II
1891–1894

Marie

92 RUE D'ALLEMAGNE
CONSULTING HOURS FROM 1 TO 3 P.M.
FREE CONSULTATIONS MONDAY AND THURSDAY FROM 7 TO 8

read the heading on Bronya's stationery, and there Manya proceeded upon her arrival at Paris's Gare du Nord. Following Bronya's directions, she gave her heavy suitcase to a man with a pushcart to deliver for her and took the next double-decker omnibus that came along. She climbed the little corkscrew stairs to the top, which was known as "the Imperial," where the seats were cheapest because they were exposed to the elements.

They also had the best view and, today, the November sun was shining.

The city's remodeling, started in the Second Empire under Napoleon III's great prefect, Baron Haussmann, was finished, and the vistas in every direction were breathtaking. If the sights and sounds of that European mecca dazzled the eyes and confounded the senses of the most sophisticated contemporary travelers, Manya's excitement and amazement knew no bounds as the Percherons ambled along, and she peered eagerly from side to side. Gustave Eiffel's famed tower, the engineering marvel built as a centerpiece for the World's Fair of 1889, which marked the centenary of the French Revolution and was intended to show what scientific industry could do for a modern nation, loomed over all and was even taller than she had expected. Electric lamps were being installed along the great boulevards that traversed Paris, and the streets were crowded with the new three- and four-wheeled internal combustion vehicles.

The Dluskis' tiny second-floor flat overlooked the bare trees of the rue d'Allemagne—today the Avenue Jean-Jaurès—in the outlying district of La Villette, near the Parc des Buttes-Chaumont. Casimir's clients were the butchers of the neighboring slaughterhouses and the Polish émigrés whose modest homes clustered roundabouts, and Bronya, a gynecologist, treated their wives and attended them at childbirth. The Dluskis used one of their rooms for consultation and alternated their respective office hours, but the greater part of their day was spent in house calls, although most of their patients in that working-class district owed them money. There was a lot of unemployment, for the twenty-year-old Third Republic was riddled with labor agitation and strikes.

Casimir showed Manya to her own room at the back, and the two got along well from the start. This was fortunate since, theoretically, she was his ward. Old Professor Sklodowski, in anticipation of every possible kind of catastrophe, had taken the precaution of placing his youngest daughter legally under Casimir's care, and even sent him a formal power of attorney to this effect. A tall, handsome, heavyset man with black hair, a bushy beard, and flashing dark eyes, Manya would always refer to him as "my little brother-in-law"—no doubt to indicate affection, since her sense of humor was almost nonexistent. Twelve years her senior, Casimir was the son of a well-to-do Polish family. While he was studying law at St. Petersburg, he was suspected of participation in the assassination of Alexander II and fled abroad. Once in Paris he entered the School of Political Science, then switched to medicine. Because he was under threat of deportation if he ever again set foot in Russian Poland, Casimir's file as a political agitator was on record at the French Ministry of Foreign Affairs; therefore he was prevented from being naturalized and settling permanently in France. The most brilliant and wittiest of the Polish exiles presently in the French capital, he was also one of the most popular.

Bronya had made the Dluskis' little flat homelike with furniture picked up for a song at different auctions, including an upright piano which Casimir liked to play when the mood struck him. With Polish books on the shelves, Polish pictures on the walls, the enticing aromas of Polish cooking, a constantly bubbling samovar so they could drink tea round the clock like good Poles, and where only Polish was spoken, no. 92 rue d'Allemagne was a Polish oasis. To come home here every evening helped Manya adapt to life in a foreign city.

She had allowed herself only a couple of days in which to see Paris and get adjusted before the Sorbonne opened. Walking through the bustling, crowded streets, jostled by women attired in colors she had never seen apparently dyed by new compounds, Manya felt she was on another planet. She had never been clothes-conscious, but still could not help noticing how differently Parisians dressed. It was also hard for her to realize she no longer had to look over her shoulder to see if she was being followed by the Tsarist police as she lingered on the Left Bank in the Latin Quarter, the heart of intellectual Europe. The weather remained surprisingly mild, and paint-spattered artists and would-be artists sat at small zinc-covered tables lining the Boulevard St.-Germain nursing a "fine" and discussing heatedly the works of Renoir, Manet, and Monet; the latter of whose landscapes, almost two decades before, had been dubbed "Impressionism" by a sneering critic. It was a stimulating atmosphere.

On November 3, Manya set out, her old portfolio of worn leather under her arm, to register for fall classes at the University of Paris. The trip from the Dluskis' required a good hour, for the first omnibus took her only as far as the Gare de l'Est. There she transferred, going by way of the Boulevard Sebastopol across the Seine and up the slight hill of the Boulevard St.-Michel to the rue des Écoles, where she descended and walked the few remaining steps to the Sorbonne. Using the French version of her name, "Marie," she registered in the Faculty of Sciences to prepare for a *licence ès sciences,* the rough equivalent of a master's degree in science. What she did not know—and it would have made no difference—was that science was the weakest department in the Sorbonne and not in a class with the one at Cambridge, where the Cavendish Laboratory had been created in 1870 in an effort to counteract German supremacy in the field. There was only a single chair of theoretical physics in Paris, and the conditions for research were Spartan, even by contemporary standards.

Students had been coming here since the Middle Ages, and for the last six years the venerable institution had been undergoing a badly needed face-lift. Its ancient walls were covered with scaffolding, and its halls were full of dust, confusion, the sound of pickaxes and shovels. Classes were held wherever possible, in makeshift quarters always one jump ahead of the workmen, and some of Manya's laboratories were temporarily scheduled in empty houses in the nearby rue St.-Jacques.

For her first year Marie concentrated on physics and calculus. She was prepared to find her background knowledge skimpy but she was dismayed to discover after the first few days that, because she lacked the mathematics necessary for a basic understanding of the physical sciences on a university level, it was hard to keep up with her French peers. More alarming was the realization that her French was also inadequate. Marie was proficient in written French, but spoken and scientific French were another matter. She lost whole phrases and complete sentences when certain professors got carried away with enthusiasm for their subject and talked rapidly. Since the amphitheater where her lectures were held was also poorly lit—a serious disadvantage during the dark, dreary winter months—reading the great blackboard along the back of the stage posed another problem. So Marie was always the first to arrive in order to get a front row seat as close as possible to the lecturing professor.

Although Marie had so much catching up to do, it was impossible to study at the Dluskis' in the evening, for after working hard during the day, Casimir liked to relax at night. Like all Slavs, their hospitality was boundless, despite their slender purse. Members of the small Free Polish colony were forever dropping in, when vodka and poppy-seed cakes made fresh that day by Bronya in some rare spare moment would appear, and the little flat would resound with excited talk as they remade Poland and the world.

On those few nights when no one came by and Marie thought she might get some work done, Casimir would burst in to chat with her, or perhaps whisk her off with Bronya to a café or a *boîte de nuit* to see some attraction ballyhooed in one of the striking Toulouse-Lautrec posters plastered along the boulevards. Marie might try to resist, but Casimir would not take no for an answer. One night the trio were given free tickets and went to the Salle Érard to hear a redheaded compatriot in a threadbare coat, the pianist Ignatz Paderewski, play to a three-quarters-empty house in his Paris debut. He and his mistress, Mme. Gorska, whom he later married and who had known Mme. Sklodowska, came occasionally to the rue d'Allemagne and more than once he played Casimir's old upright.

Not only was Marie unable to do her homework at Bronya's, but the novelty of the time-consuming omnibus ride to and fro through the teeming Paris streets had long since worn off. She could put the two hours spent traveling daily to better use over her books. Furthermore, transportation was a drain on her shallow pocketbook. So in March, with a loan from the Dluskis to pay a man with a pushcart to transport her paltry possessions, Marie settled in the Latin Quarter, where cheap rents and food attracted students. She was very poor. But because Eve Curie, in her bestselling biography of her mother, made so much of these years of struggle, it is easy to forget that Marie did not have to leave the rue d'Allemagne. Bronya's finances had been equally skimpy and she had no family willing to lodge her, yet she had managed to complete five years of medical school. Professor Sklodowski was scraping forty rubles together monthly, the equivalent today of about one hundred and twenty dollars a month, to send his daughter to live on, which meant Marie had as much money as many classmates. But the necessity for quiet dictated she move. And once she was on the Left Bank, instead of sharing a room as did most students, Marie deprived herself of all but the barest necessities for the luxury of living alone.

Choosing locations within a short walk of her classes and laboratories, she rented successively at no. 3 rue Flatters; le Boulevard de Port-Royal; and no. 11 rue des Feuillantines. Her room was invariably situated on the top floor, which was the cheapest because it was never less than six flights up, and under the eaves, where it was broiling in summer and freezing in winter. Little differentiated one garret from another. They were alike in discomfort, with a single skylight or window which rarely shut tight. At the Boulevard Port-Royal she was fortunate enough to have a wood floor. The other two rooms had only cold tiles and, of course, Marie had no rug. She brought with her a small table, one kitchen chair, a washbasin and a pitcher for water, a coal scuttle, an oil lamp, as well as an iron folding bed, her mattress and bedding from Warsaw, and her old trunk, which doubled as an extra chair. She bought coal in lumps from a dealer nearby but she lit her small stove only on the coldest days and nights. For water she filled a jug from a tap on one of the lower landings. Kerosene for one lamp, which she needed to read by in those dingy quarters, and alcohol for a tiny heater about the size of a saucer for cooking rounded out the small list of monthly necessities.

Meals posed no problem. Since Marie knew virtually nothing about the culinary arts and cared less, one saucepan more than sufficed. She also had two plates—in case one broke—and three tumblers, a present from Bronya, so that when the Dluskis came to see her, Marie could offer them a glass of tea. Food was unimportant to Marie, and breakfast, lunch and dinner, as such, were virtually dispensed with. By and large she lived on tea, radishes, and buttered bread, and on rare occasions she treated herself to two boiled eggs or stopped to sip a cup of hot chocolate in a nearby creamery.

On cold nights she, like others, studied in the warm, gaslit library of St.-Geneviève on the crest of the hill across from the Panthéon, until it closed at 10 P.M. Then she scurried home, broke the ice in her pitcher to get water to make some tea and studied a little longer before jumping into bed with all her clothes on. When the thermometer dropped lower still, she piled her coat and her other dress, as well as her towels and extra sheets, on top of herself also. And there were times near the end of the month when she ran out of coal, either through absentmindedness or because she had run out of money and used up her credit with the neighborhood vendor. Then she had to shiver and shake, with hands reddened and swollen by the cold, until the first of the following month.

It is doubtful if Marie gave a second thought to her Spartan existence. Science filled every waking moment and she was doing what she wanted to do with no one to consider but herself. Of course, the inevitable happened. One day, her first spring in Paris, Casimir received an emergency call from some mutual friends who also lived at no. 3 rue Flatters, saying that Marie had fainted on the sidewalk. By the time he arrived, she had revived, and he had to resort to force to get his stubborn sister-in-law to accompany him back to the rue d'Allemagne. The Dluskis examined her separately and arrived at the same diagnosis: starvation. Casimir chided her, Bronya scolded, a beefsteak did wonders; they managed to keep Marie with them long enough to fatten her up a little.

Casimir realized that there was a certain amount of masochism entailed in Marie's solitary life of self-denial, even if so doing gave her, as she admitted later, "a very precious sense of liberty and independence."[1] He made gentle fun of what he would always refer to as his sister-in-law's "heroic period" and of her inclination to dramatize everything. But he recognized a lost cause when he saw one and knew he would be wasting his breath trying to give her any advice. Marie took everything deadly seriously, starting with herself; while this may not have been her most appealing trait, it would be a great source of her strength.

Interestingly enough, during this period of a marginal existence Marie never once complained of her former "nervous problems." If she had any, she was too stimulated and interested in what she was doing to indulge in them, and she would later claim: "This life, painful from certain points of view had, for all that, a real charm for me."[2]

Because Marie did not feel she had sufficiently caught up with her class, she did not return home for summer vacation. Instead, she stayed in sultry Paris to work on her French—only a lightly rolled "r" that stayed with her until she died would henceforth betray her Slavic origin—and to take extra mathematics courses.

Marie was now a far more winsome sight than when she first arrived in the French capital. Her stringent life-style had slimmed her down and transformed her dewy country freshness into a transparent complexion. Her shoes were worn but neatly polished. Her Warsaw dress was threadbare and old-fashioned, but it was carefully brushed and mended and showed off to perfection her new slender waistline, which her tight corset accentuated. The hat that decency required her to wear whenever she appeared in public was pinned securely atop her fine ash blond hair, emphasizing her high round brow and accentuating the gray eyes which looked out at the world with quiet composure.

Marie's shyness made her rebuff any advances from her class-mates and kept her from initiating most friendships, had she been so inclined. Nonetheless, she could not avoid meeting people daily in the course of her university work, and she drew nearer those with whom she could talk shop—and who did not try to see her outside of school. With rare exceptions, she no longer saw any of the colony of young Polish students whom she had met through the Dluskis upon her arrival, not even the one young man who unsuc-cessfully swallowed laudanum to attract her attention. When she learned what he had done, Marie's only comment was that the young man had his priorities mixed.

That second winter of 1892–93 and the following spring, her life continued to be monastic. She was studying elasticity and mechan-ics and could be found, in the fading afternoon light, with a crum-pled linen smock protecting her clothes, bent over a Bunsen burner and blowpipes in Professor Lippmann's physics laboratory, a high, wide room with two little staircases leading to an interior gallery. As examination time loomed, Marie fretted that she was not yet ready, so she continued to work at home each evening until one or two in the morning. Failure was a possibility she refused to contemplate, for it meant a return to a governess's job in Warsaw. Marie's Hercu-lean efforts were not in vain, and on July 23 she received her coveted *licence ès sciences physiques*. She was not only the first woman to pass the test and receive such a degree at the Sorbonne, but in a class of thirty, the young Polish woman was number one.

For a Pole it was traditional to return from a trip with no money left, and Marie was no exception. Spending any remaining rubles on trinkets, scarves, and similar gifts, she now set off on her first trip home. Old Professor Sklodowski felt consoled for her long absence by her academic success, but he was shocked at her pinched, tired expression when she stepped off the train, and all summer long he enjoyed fretting over her and restoring her health.

Ambition was slowly superseding family ties. Marie now realized that a solid mathematics background was essential if she was to be fully qualified to help the Polish nation when she returned home for good. But the question of financing further work in Paris to obtain this second degree posed the same old problem, and she no longer felt her father was in any position to continue sending her money. Fortunately, one of her few Sorbonne friends, Mlle. Dydynska, was able to help her get the Alexandrovitch scholarship which was given annually to assist one deserving Pole's study abroad. If Marie could still manage to live on forty rubles a month, fifteen more months in Paris were hers.

Marie arrived back six weeks ahead of time to do some advance preparation and look for new lodgings. She earned a little spare pocket money tutoring a French student who was preparing for the same tests she had recently passed. The winter was again a hard one. But her sights remained firmly fixed on her goal, and she encouraged her brother to do likewise and finish his doctor's thesis.

The following spring Marie received a paid commission from the Society for the Encouragement of National Industry to do a study of how magnetic properties of different steels varied with their chemical composition. She started the project working in the laboratory of one of her favorite teachers, Professor Lippmann, but she soon found she needed more room to house the equipment required for testing and analysis. She did not know where to turn for help. Meanwhile, a friend from Marie's Szczuki days came to Paris on her honeymoon because her husband, Professor Kowalski, who taught physics at the University of Fribourg, was asked to give some lectures there. Professor Kowalski had recently met Pierre Curie, who was one of the most promising of the young French physicists and had a reputation for works of exceptional originality, including basic research on magnetism. Since Curie was also the laboratory chief of the School of Physics and Chemistry of the City of Paris, perhaps he might be of some assistance. So the Kowalskis invited Marie to come to their boardinghouse for tea and to meet him.

III
1859–1895

Pierre

WHILE MARIE CURIE'S *curriculum vitae* is readily available on a professional level and, to a lesser degree, on a personal one, the same is not true of Pierre. Although some of France's most eminent physicists today consider him to have been a far greater scientist than Marie, his life is a biographer's nightmare. This gentle, unprepossessing man preferred to live as anonymously as possible, devoting himself to science.

His mother, Sophie-Claire Depouilly, was born in 1832 to a Savoyard family in Lyons, and grew up in Puteaux, where her father was a prominent cloth manufacturer. She was sixteen when the economic fallout from the Revolution of 1848 ruined his business. Despite the fact that she was raised for a life of ease, Sophie-Claire courageously accepted the family's altered economic circumstances. Nothing is known of her marriage to Dr. Eugène Curie. But she was reputedly a cheerful woman who retained her slight build until late in life, despite health problems associated with the birth of her two sons, Jacques, who was born in 1855, and Pierre, on May 15, 1859.

Pierre's father, Dr. Eugène Curie, five years older than his wife, was born at Mulhouse, where his father was a doctor of Alsatian-Protestant background, a sixth-generation descendant of the noted Bernouilli scientific dynasty. At the School of Medicine in Paris, Eugène worked as an assistant under Pierre Gratiollet, the well-known anatomist. An idealist who remained an unrepentant republican throughout his life, Eugène was a medical student at the Hôpital de la Pitié when the fighting broke out during the celebrated "June Days" of the 1848 Revolution. His jaw was broken when he was hit by a bullet while caring for the wounded behind the barricades. He received the Medal of Honor for "honorable and courageous conduct" from the government of the Second Republic.

By the time his second son, Pierre, was born, the Curies were living on the rue Cuvier opposite the Jardin des Plantes, the National Museum of Natural History, where comparative anatomy, geology, zoology, and other subjects were taught and where Dr. Eugène was working in a laboratory. He would have preferred to devote his life to scientific research, but he had to practice medicine in order to raise his two boys. So he moved to the 7E Arrondissement and, like other Parisian doctors, set up his office in his apartment.

Additional proof of his courage came during a cholera epidemic when he was the only doctor in the neighborhood who did not flee but remained behind to take care of those who needed him. In the spring of 1871, at the time of the Paris Commune uprising, one of the barricades erected during the fierce street fighting was so near his apartment that Dr. Curie set up a hospital in his home. Pierre, who was then twelve, and Jacques, sixteen, never forgot helping their father transport and care for wounded insurrectionists.

Still a researcher at heart, Dr. Curie was forever making excursions into the woods around Paris to find the plants, animals, and insects necessary for his modest experiments. From the time Pierre and Jacques were old enough, they accompanied him on these long rambles, especially in the charming valley of the Chevreuse, which the boys got to know and love. When the doctor perceived that the two had a natural inclination for science and enjoyed an intimate contact with nature, he taught them how to observe facts and interpret them correctly.

Pierre with his more passive nature got along with his strict, dictatorial father. Argumentative Jacques did not and, instead, found in his younger brother the intimacy he lacked with Dr. Curie. Although vastly different, both physically and temperamentally, the two boys were so close that there was often no need to speak; they understood each other without words. Nothing illustrates this more clearly than a family picture, taken when they were young men: Dark-haired Jacques gazes alertly at his brother, personifying the action-oriented extrovert; auburn-haired Pierre looks at the camera with his elbow propped on a ledge and his head balanced leisurely against his upturned palm, the introverted dreamer.

For sons of a family of the most modest means, their education was a surprising one. Jacques attended school in a hit-or-miss fashion. But Dr. Curie recognized that even that much formal education in his formative years would prove disastrous for Pierre, who did not respond when attempts were made to direct him in the usual learning patterns. From the time he was a small boy, Pierre demanded a satisfactory rather than a superficial explanation for everything, and he always wanted to examine subjects in depth—but only those that appealed to him. Rather than subject him to the straitjacket of scholastic discipline, his mother taught him to read and write, and he enjoyed an unprogrammed, unfettered childhood. Under this regime, Pierre's special gifts were able to flower unhampered. The countryside became his classroom and, by the time he was an adolescent, he satisfied his urgent need for solitude and reflection by walking the length of the tranquil Bièvre and wandering in the lovely woods between Sceaux and Versailles. Absentminded, he had no concept of time and frequently wandered outdoors all night, to return "with twenty ideas in his head."[1] Observing the symmetry in nature on every side, he was already endeavoring to understand it more fully.

Dr. Curie possessed a large library to which Pierre was allowed unlimited access and this was compensation, in part, for his lack of orthodox classical studies. The two brothers had no religious training and, in accordance with their authoritarian father's wishes, neither was ever baptized, a rare occurrence for that day in France. As he got older, Pierre could have rectified the situation, but he never did.

Pierre's first trained teacher was M.A. Bazille. Hiring him represented a considerable financial sacrifice for the Curies, but he was to prove worthy of every sou. A remarkable man, Bazille gave the fourteen-year-old Pierre an early and thorough introduction to mathematics and opened his eyes to the beauty of numbers. Later, Bazille also helped Pierre with Latin, a subject in which he was far behind for his age.

At sixteen, as if to prove that his father's theory of education had been the correct one for him, Pierre passed brilliantly the baccalaureate examinations that are normally taken when a student finishes the *lycée* and amount roughly to getting a bachelor's degree. The following year he served as a probationer at the pharmacy of M. Vigier, in the family neighborhood on the rue du Bac. He was still very young when he was introduced to formal schooling with the beginning lectures for his degree in physics at the Sorbonne.

Two years later, Pierre received his *licence ès sciences*—the midpoint en route to a doctorate—and was appointed assistant, with a modest stipend, to Professor Desains, the director of the Laboratory of Advanced Studies on the Faculty of Sciences of the University of Paris. He was placed in charge of the students' practical work in physics, and the limited time he could call his own, he devoted to research.

Unfortunately, Pierre's professional duties, which he endured for financial reasons, forced him to forsake following lectures in higher mathematics, so he was unable to advance toward his Ph.D. On the other hand, because he was considered a teacher in the public school system, he was released from military service. Whenever he could find the time, Pierre continued to take long walks in the countryside—alone or with Jacques—looking for beauty and order in a seemingly chaotic world. Even as a boy he felt a need to extend into other domains the knowledge he acquired in a specific field. Now, he tried to apply the discipline of mathematics to natural phenomena. With this original approach, nature was an exercise in symmetry. Pierre knew there was symmetry in flowers and seashells, so why not in crystals, he wondered? His remarkable ability to visualize spatially was an enormous asset, and work with crystals and their distribution according to the laws of symmetry would fascinate Pierre throughout his life.

Meanwhile, Jacques became assistant to a mineralogy professor who was studying pyroelectricity, the spontaneous electrification of certain crystals through heating. A tourmaline crystal put in hot ashes will attract ashes. This effect had been observed almost two centuries before, but an acceptable theory to explain it had only lately evolved. Their curiosity aroused, Pierre and Jacques observed, in certain types of crystals—those that have the appropriate symmetry, like quartz—the important phenomenon of piezo, or pressure electricity, whereby the crystals produce a current when subjected to pressure. In other words, tension could produce the same effect as raising the temperature. Since the quantity of electricity set free was proportionate to the pressure employed, the new effect could be used to measure pressure as well as miniscule elec-

trical charges. To carry out further experiments regarding this remarkable new phenomenon—which would be employed in the first
crystal radio sets and by Paul Langevin in his efforts to combat the
German submarine menace in World War I—Pierre and Jacques
invented and constructed a delicate precision instrument, the
piezo-quartz electrometer.

Virtually nothing else is known about Pierre's young manhood
except for a cryptic reference, in a handful of private notes, to the
death of a childhood friend whom he called "the tender companion
of all my hours."[2] He later admitted to Marie that this was his one
love before he met her. Whether similar comments he confided to
paper about this same period refer to this young woman, or to some
other, has never been determined, but the private notes are a good
indication of Pierre's one-track mind. For he was already annoyed
whenever the thousand and one distractions of everyday life diverted him from research. By 1880, when Pierre was twenty-two,
science had already become his demanding mistress and life in a
laboratory was the epitome of his desire. That same year, the brothers published their first of seven papers on piezoelectricity which,
taken together, would constitute a thorough study of the subject.

When Jacques received his doctorate, he was named head lecturer in mineralogy at Montpellier in southern France, where he
would remain the rest of his life, teaching and raising a family. His
departure was a rude blow for Pierre, who shared with his brother
an identity of thought and action he never anticipated being able to
duplicate with anyone else. Although Jacques returned to Paris regularly to spend part of his vacation working with his brother, and
Pierre went south a few times to accompany Jacques on field trips,
young Pierre lived a solitary life, absorbed in his work. Whether it
was the pattern of the day for single men of his age and financial
circumstances to live at home, or whether his decision to do so
should be interpreted as indicative of character, Pierre endured a
long daily commute in order to live with Dr. Eugène and his wife,
who had moved recently to a cottage in the Paris suburbs.

A true nonconformist in a system that subordinated research to teaching, Pierre refused to sit for the highly competitive examinations for admission to one of the two great schools of the day, the École Normale Supérieure and the École Polytechnique. These institutions were at the pinnacle of the highly structured French educational scene and graduated the intellectual, political, and administrative elite of the land. Since neither school was free and Pierre was completely disinterested in material success, finances may have played a role in his decision, as well as his lifelong hatred of competitions. Instead, in 1882, Pierre accepted an appointment as laboratory chief at the newly founded School of Industrial Physics and Chemistry of the City of Paris—EPCI, as it was popularly called.

The Franco-Prussian War of 1870–71 had taught France the value of modern industry and also cost her the only good school of chemistry in France, the École Supérieure de Chimie in the city of Mulhouse. Germany annexed this big textile center which supplied the framework of the French chemical business. To help remedy the situation created by this loss, EPCI was set up by the city of Paris with the help of two former Mulhouse professors, Paul Schützenberger and Charles Lauth. Geared for pupils from a different social level than those of the two *grandes écoles,* it was founded with the avant-garde idea that physics and chemistry should be taught as practical subjects in a laboratory. While the new school intended to educate professional engineers and technicians needed desperately by the rising industrial companies, the fact that it was only a technical school meant that none but its most exceptional students might aspire to move into the best jobs later on. Nonetheless, EPCI was not what its name would imply in another country. It was a highly intellectual institution that quickly established a fine reputation because its first director was Paul Schützenberger, who was himself a distinguished chemist. He assembled a superior staff. There was no tuition, but the students had to be French and were carefully chosen. Upon graduation, they received the diploma of a chemical or physical engineer.

EPCI was located on the grounds and in some of the buildings of the old Collège Rollin, behind the Panthéon. Because the school was new, Pierre created and organized all the classwork and demonstrations for the thirty or so students he was teaching. He conscientiously devoted the bulk of his time to these chores, and since he was scarcely older than most of his pupils, he enjoyed a close relationship with them that was unusual for the day. Because his curiosity and enthusiasm were contagious, he was a fine teacher. He often lingered long after class and would completely lose track of time if he found himself in front of the blackboard with an attentive audience.

Paul Langevin, one of his first students and a lifelong intimate of both Marie and Pierre Curie, never forgot the afternoon when he and several classmates became engrossed in an absorbing discussion with Pierre, who kept punctuating what he had to say by scribbling equations and drawing graphs and curves to illustrate the points he was making. Suddenly someone noticed the clock. Another student hastily tried the door. School was over, the building was closed, and they were locked in. Undeterred, they climbed out the second-story window and shimmied down a drainpipe running alongside, with Pierre in the lead—still talking. Such exploits, in addition to his kindliness, further endeared the soft-spoken, introspective teacher to those who worked with him and Petit (his first and only laboratory assistant at EPCI who stayed with him until he died).

Even though his overloaded EPCI schedule barely gave him time to catch his breath, Pierre was expanding his personal research to include the physical properties of crystals, while adding a fascination with magnetism to his other interests. But it would be another two years before his academic responsibilities were well enough organized so that Pierre, who was now twenty-nine, could resume his own work in any depth.

The school's director, Professor Schützenberger, whose warm nature and kind eyes won him the nickname of "Papa Schütz" from staff and students alike, felt like a father to his young assistant, whose work he respected. Pierre, in turn, would always be grateful to "Papa," who went out of his way to be helpful to his subordinate —a rare state of affairs in the hierarchical academic world of the day.

Space and funds for supplies posed a problem at EPCI. The school was already bulging at the seams and, since no laboratory or room could be placed completely at his disposal, Pierre elected to work in a corridor running between the stairs and his classroom. It was a far from ideal locale, but it did afford the students an unusual opportunity to share in his personal scientific interests. One of the first results of Pierre's efforts was a precision scale equilibrating minute forces—the Curie scale—which he invented and built and which was to prove invaluable to Marie Curie, years later, when she was determining the atomic weight of radium.

Pierre was not ambitious. He did research for its own sake, and, since he had never been interested in titles or honors, he was in no hurry to get his doctorate. It was not until 1891 that he found a suitable subject for his Ph.D. thesis, an investigation of the magnetic properties of different substances at different temperatures. This, like his studies on crystallography and symmetry, proved to be a pioneering endeavor with widespread application—notably in the development of modern telephone, telegraph, radio, and television equipment. In his diversification Pierre was a scientist of the nineteenth century, with distinguished accomplishments in several fields: piezoelectricity, symmetry in physical phenomena, magnetism, and, later, radioactivity. Any one of these was sufficient to guarantee him an outstanding scientific reputation, for everything Pierre touched was illuminated by his brilliant insights. As scientific knowledge increased by leaps and bounds, however, it would be almost impossible for a single person to be an expert in two or more aspects of scientific research. In this respect, Marie Curie would be very much a twentieth-century scientist, limiting her entire body of work to radioactivity, with the exception of her first published paper on the magnetism of steels.

During this period, Pierre's reputation was growing abroad. Lord Kelvin, the seventy-year-old doyen of British science, whose compass was standard equipment for the British Navy and who was the father of electrometers, had already written Pierre about the brothers' "magnificent experimental discovery of piezoelectric quartz."[3] Lord Kelvin had done a lot of work on crystals and quartz, himself. Toward the end of 1893, Lord Kelvin was invited to read a paper to the Academy of Sciences in Paris. He wrote ahead, asking for permission to visit Pierre's laboratory and meet him. When Kelvin saw the conditions under which Pierre was working, he was even more impressed with his achievements and asked Pierre to make a piezo-quartz electrometer for him. At a subsequent meeting of the Society of Physics, Pierre proposed an ingenious modification in the construction and use of an electrostatic measuring device which would make it easier to use. Kelvin, the acknowledged authority in the field, was present and took exception, saying he believed Pierre was in error. The next day, the elderly savant came in person to EPCI to retract what he had said and, from then on, did whatever he could to further Pierre's career. Due largely to Kelvin's invaluable friendship and the high esteem in which he held him, Pierre's achievements were appreciated in England long before they were in France.

Pierre made another new acquaintance, some months later, who would play an even more important role in his life—Marie Sklodowska.

—— o ——

Pierre was standing near the window when twenty-six-year-old Marie entered the Kowalskis' sitting room, and she remembered that first meeting until the day she died. He was younger-looking than thirty-five, and rather handsome, with the limpid brown eyes of a dreamer, a high forehead, crew-cut hair, a small auburn mustache, and a rugged pointed beard that lengthened his thin angular face. He was tall and he conveyed a slight impression of carelessness that did not detract from a certain natural elegance. Within minutes of their introduction they were conversing easily; Pierre's slow, reflective manner of speaking, his simplicity and his grave smile inspired confidence. They discussed scientific questions and she asked his advice. Later, they also talked about social and humanitarian matters in which they shared a common interest. Pierre, who was essentially democratic and socialist in his thinking but did not belong to any political party, deeply believed that science would triumph over ignorance and peace would conquer war.

It was her lack of a laboratory that brought Marie and Pierre together and, unfortunately, this was the one thing he could not offer her, although he could give her plenty of advice. Pierre subsequently encountered Marie at meetings of the Physical Society. When his paper "On Symmetry in Physical Phenomena: Symmetry of an Electric Field and of a Magnetic Field" was published, he sent her a copy of it with a scribbled personal dedication.

No gift could better sum up the pair and their budding relationship. Pierre was never the man to appreciate the sheen of her hair or the color of her dress, but Marie was not the woman to want such praise, let alone from him. For the young graduate student who had not yet published her first paper, Pierre personified her ideal of a successful scientist. He had original outstanding work to his credit in several fields; a number of his papers had already appeared in the *Comptes Rendus* of the august French Academy. And, equally important, he was pursuing science for its own sake and not for personal glory. That she should appeal to Pierre as much for the strength of her mind as for her female charms—as Marie instinctively realized she did—was the highest possible flattery. Nothing could please her more.

It is more amazing that Marie should have attracted him, for, by now, Pierre seemed a confirmed bachelor. He was convinced that the opposite sex and life in the laboratory were mutually exclusive. There were not many women with whom he could discuss the work he loved and who could understand what he was saying.

Marie had the same enthusiasm as he for science, the same desire to probe the secrets of the natural world. He had not thought it possible to find happiness through shared interests and common understanding.

While both were introverts, Marie was tough and practical, for all her self-dramatization, while the material world rarely existed for Pierre. The role physical chemistry played in their relationship is hard to estimate, but Pierre was soon in love with Marie and remained in love with her until the day he died. Surprisingly, because no one would ever think of him as a fast worker, he broached the question of marriage shortly after their first meeting. Later, he confessed to Marie that this was the only occasion in his life when he acted without hesitation and with the absolute conviction that he was doing the right thing.

Many an evening, Pierre climbed the six flights of stairs at no. 11 rue des Feuillantines, to sit on Marie's old trunk while she sat on her one chair. The two drank tea and talked for hours. While morals were admittedly free in the bohemian student quarter, to receive a man in one's bedroom was as unthinkable for a young Frenchwoman of Marie's background and upbringing as it was for a young Pole. But Marie, throughout her life, was straightforward in what she did. She and Pierre had no money, so where else should they meet? Moreover, she was sufficiently liberated to do something if she wanted to, a tendency strengthened by her independent life-style in Paris. As far as her personal morals were concerned, it seems unlikely that they were any less Victorian than her background indicates. However, Marie, if only through her work in science, was far better informed concerning the facts of life than her peers, many of whom still did not realize that their bodies could produce pleasures other than that of childbearing.

Marie was increasingly interested in Pierre, and, as the weather turned warmer and she neared the end of her classes, she relaxed her work schedule. Taking the train to the capital's outskirts, they took long walks together in the surrounding countryside. There she entered Pierre's world, and he delighted in sharing its wonders with her. Walking in the forests around Écouen as the ground underfoot turned into a brilliant carpet of blue periwinkles, he'd pick some of the lovely little flowers to demonstrate the symmetry in every form of nature.

Marie expected to get her second degree in June and, with her goal in sight, she was already looking ahead to the future. Like a man, she sought self-fulfillment in what she did and felt the need to prove her capacities. This did not mean that she forswore love or raising a family, but whether she thought of Pierre as a possible husband at this point is not clear.

After graduating *magna cum laude,* and second in her class, Marie received her second degree—*licence ès sciences mathématiques.* That early summer of 1894, Marie left once more for the East. She and her father had a happy time visiting different relatives in Crettaz, Lemberg, and Zakopane. She also stopped to solicit a post as assistant at the University of Krakow so, presumably, she was uncertain as to whether she'd return to the West. For, with a job in hand, it is extremely questionable whether she would have left Poland. But she was denied the position. Marie's plan had always been to receive an education the equal of any man's, then return to live with her father and help her countrymen regain their freedom. However, what she saw in Poland that summer made Marie realize that the problems involved with any attempt at changing the status quo were overwhelming, whereas the possibilities of her accomplishing something in science in the West were greater, and every discovery, no matter how small, represented a contribution to all humanity.

As Pierre saw the train pull out from the Gare du Nord with Marie on board, he realized he could not let her go. Like many introverts who are often able to express themselves better in writing than in person, Pierre set out to woo her by mail. Letters on cheap paper in his immature handwriting followed her everywhere. He sensed, even before her departure, that Marie's ties with family and fatherland, while still strong, might conceivably be broken by the attraction of a life devoted wholeheartedly to research. It is clear from their correspondence that, as Pierre suspected, Marie was having second thoughts about the future, and he was to persuade her that her primary duty was her obligation to science, by which Pierre, like Marie and their colleagues and contemporaries at the Sorbonne, meant pure science, not applied. All her life, the adjective "disinterested" would be the highest accolade Marie could bestow.

He reminded her of their mutual promise "to be at least great friends . . . It would be a fine thing . . . to pass our lives near each other, hypnotized by our dreams; *your* [sic] patriotic dream, *our* [sic] humanitarian dream and *our* [sic] scientific dream. Of all those dreams, the last is, I believe, the legitimate one."[4]

In another letter in which Pierre repeated how unhappy he would be should Marie not return, he concluded—dare one add pseudo-altruistically?—"It is not from a friend's selfishness that I speak . . . I simply believe that you will work better here and can do a more solid and useful job." A surprising postscript follows. Marie had failed to answer his last letter, and he wondered if she had not received it. It contained, he explains, in what might be described as the understatement of the year, "nothing in particular. I asked if you wanted to rent an apartment with me on the rue Mouffetard with windows overlooking a garden . . . [It] could be divided into two separate parts."[5]

Not much reading between the lines is required to recognize that Pierre was well aware of Marie's essential independence. The fact that she received him time and again in her bedroom also taught him that convention did not concern her. His suggestion must have meant a lot to Pierre since he took pains to repeat what he had written earlier, although he camouflaged his interest in pursuing the matter by prefacing his postscript with the statement that the unanswered letter contained "nothing of importance." It is noteworthy that he made the suggestion in the first place. Presumably, if Marie did not want to marry him, perhaps she might be willing to live with him—or share adjoining apartments. But this was not the path for Marie.

On September 17, Pierre wrote Marie to tell her how glad he was that she made the decision to return to Paris. He thanked her for her picture, which she sent him, and then pointed out, as if they had never before discussed the possibility of marriage, that if she were to become French, it would be a simple matter for her to become a professor in a *lycée* or in a girls' normal school.

Marie was not playing hard to get. No one could ever apply the adjective coquettish to her. That was not in her nature. She simply did not know her own mind, so when she got to Paris, Pierre, who knew his, stepped up his pursuit. To save money Marie was no longer in the Latin Quarter, but living in the back room of the consultation office that her sister Bronya, whose practice was growing, had taken in a dark, dreary building on the rue de Châteaudun on the Right Bank. Since Bronya was only there in the daytime, it was quiet at night and cost Marie nothing. She attended certain classes in experimental physics at the Sorbonne and could be found, the rest of the time, bent over her instruments in Professor Lippmann's laboratory, her hands already acid-stained for life as she worked on her commission. Pierre visited her regularly and, when Émile Zola's latest book, *Lourdes,* appeared and was placed on the Catholic Church's Index, amid a great hue and cry, he gave it to her. In it Zola expressed the same doubts about religion that he and Marie shared, including their need to put reason above faith.

Marie would write in the biography of Pierre she published after his death, that "this winter our friendship grew more and more precious. Each realized that he or she could find no better life companion."[6] But, at the time, Pierre must have been discouraged with his progress, for he offered to make the ultimate sacrifice: If he went to Poland and got a position, would Marie then marry him?

They could probably conduct their scientific research together there as readily as in Paris. Troubled and moved that Pierre cared enough about her to offer to transplant himself to Warsaw, Marie finally confided in Bronya. She felt she had no right to accept so great a sacrifice.

It is not exactly clear when Pierre learned that Marie had talked to Bronya. But once he found out, he went to call on Marie's sister to solicit her support. Pierre won her over, since Bronya, with her little sister's interests at heart, knew what it meant to be married to a man who shared her own intellectual interests and pursuits. At some point thereafter, Pierre invited the two out to his home, no. 13 rue des Sablons in Sceaux, a small ancient vine-covered house hidden among the trees, to meet his parents. His mother, self-effacing Sophie-Claire, who had given up ever expecting to welcome a second daughter-in-law, greeted Marie with open arms. Pierre's father still had a fighting spirit and pronounced political convictions on some subjects that were sufficiently radical to shock what remained of the "positivist" in Marie. Nevertheless, the old doctor, with his bright blue eyes peering down at her from his wrinkled face, encircled like a halo with a shock of white hair, had no trouble discovering a number of common denominators with her progressive ideas. The young foreigner who had won the heart of their son won theirs, too, and Mme. Curie, who had stretched her slender budget to prepare a savory leg of mutton, a luxury reserved for special occasions, took Bronya aside to ask her to put in a good word on Pierre's behalf with her sister. Marie's impression of the Curies was equally favorable.

While the date Pierre first brought Marie home to Sceaux is not known, in early 1895, he agreed to be a technical advisor to a Paris optical firm for a modest monthly retainer which amounted to one third of the pittance EPCI paid him. He was also to receive a minute royalty from the company's marketing of a special optical instrument he had invented. For someone disinterested in the practical side of science, to compromise his ideals even to so small a degree was a surprising step. It was comparable to Pierre's ceding the patent for his precision balance, a few years before, to the Central Chemical Products Company for a nominal 10 percent royalty, a sale which produced a derisory sum. In keeping with his philosophy, Pierre should never have entered into either negotiation but remained pure and profitless—as was the case, later, after the discovery of radium. But human nature is a web of contradictions. Impractical Pierre's mind was fuzzy when it came to monetary matters, and the fact that he was talking contracts in January seems to indicate that he had imminent marriage on his mind. Fortunately, both Marie and Pierre had the same sense of values, and money mattered little. They were bound by temperament, ideals, philosophy, interests, and, inevitably, love.

For years Dr. Curie had been after his son to finish up his doctorate and, now, Marie added her pleas to his, persuading Pierre to present the study on magnetic fields, which he had been working on intermittently as the obligatory thesis. A Ph.D. was a mandatory requirement for a professor's chair, the sole post in the sciences that normally came with a small personal laboratory where the recipient was free to pursue his personal flights of fancy. This was virtually the only way for a contemporary French researcher to procure one, unless he had adequate personal financing.

Therefore, it must have been with great relief, mixed with pride, that Marie hurried up the rue des Écoles through a raw spring rain one blustery March day to see Pierre receive his degree. She did not want to be late, because he had invited her to sit with his parents in the Sorbonne's tiny amphitheater. There they would hear him support his thesis and receive his *docteur ès sciences physiques*. She noted with approval that the examining professors, one of whom was her own Professor Lippmann, addressed Pierre with the respect due a physicist of his standing. "It seemed to me," she wrote later, "that the little room, that day, sheltered the exaltation of human thought."[7] A *chef-d'oeuvre* of experimental skill involving the measurement of minute forces, "Magnetic Properties of Bodies at Different Temperatures" was a mine of pertinent new information on the subject, and Pierre's results were, from the theoretical point of view, of fundamental importance.

Marie still had not accepted his proposal. Nothing as practical as what they might live on as M. and Mme. Curie entered into her deliberations. Marie knew that Pierre would never push himself and, even though he now had his doctorate, academic changes were slow. After twelve years at the EPCI, he still held an obscure minor post with the same salary he started with, 3,600 francs a year, a skilled workman's wage. In 1895, 77 percent of the French earned under 1,070 francs and were considered poor; 16.2 percent earned 5,340 francs and were considered comfortably well off. Since Marie herself was accustomed to living on less than a third of what Pierre was making, she knew they could get by. So it was not the financial question that was prolonging Marie's incertitude. Pierre's competition was Poland, and he knew it.

Sometime in the late spring or early summer, quite suddenly—and for reasons unknown—Marie finally acquiesced. Casimir Dluski's mother offered to give her a wedding dress from a little couturier in the neighborhood. Characteristically, the bride chose something practical that could be useful afterward in the laboratory, a navy blue wool suit that would not show dirt, with a lighter-blue-striped blouse, in place of the conventional white gown.

On July 26, 1895, their wedding day, Pierre picked Marie up and they took the long trip out to Sceaux together. Professor Sklodowski and Marie's other sister Hela, who had come for the wedding, met them at the Town Hall, together with Bronya and Casimir, Pierre's parents, and a few university friends. They had the simplest of civil ceremonies. There was no exchange of wedding rings, not even a wedding feast. So little fuss was made over the event that it is not a matter of record whether everyone returned to the little house on the rue des Sablons for a simple collation with the Curies Sr. The next morning, Pierre and Marie set off on their newly purchased bicycles (with money given Marie by a cousin for her trousseau) to explore the French countryside and their first day together as man and wife.

IV
1895–1898

An Unknown Substance

PIERRE COULD NEVER BE away from his laboratory for any length of time, even on his honeymoon. "It's a long time since we've done any work,"[1] he declared wistfully and, by early September, they were back in Paris. At no. 4 rue de la Glacière, they found a three-room apartment whose most important feature was its fine fourth-floor view of the tree-filled garden behind the old building. The interior quickly reflected their personalities. Marie refused the furniture Pierre's family offered them because it required too much maintenance, and she intended to keep housework at a minimum. They had what they needed: two chairs, a white wooden table to work on and eat at, plenty of book-shelves, and a bed. In the middle of the table was a small gas lamp and a vase which they always kept filled with fresh flowers, available on the street corners at prices they could afford. There were no bibelots, and the walls were bare. This was decorating "à la Marie," a style with no concession to true comfort or gracious living —which she would never modify but adhere to as long as she lived.

Marie was no more fond of housework or cooking after her marriage than she had been before but, like everything else she did, if she was going to do it, she wanted to do it well. She asked old Mme. Dluski and Bronya to teach her, but this was love's labor lost. Absentminded Pierre paid scant attention to the state of the apartment or to what he put in his mouth. One night at dinner Marie asked him how he enjoyed his lamb chop and he looked at her in astonishment. "But I haven't tasted it yet," he said before noticing his empty plate.

Since they decided to live, temporarily, on Pierre's miniscule earnings to enable Marie to finish her commission from the Society for the Encouragement of National Industry before seeking a post, her initial purchase as a bride was a black book stamped "Accounts" in gold, the first in a series that Marie would keep until she died. Even with the greatest of care, Pierre's salary barely stretched to meet their needs and a strict budget had to be rigidly adhered to. Marie recorded every sou spent, under either "Monsieur's Expenditures" or "Madame's."

Shortly before they were wed, a prominent physicist at the prestigious Collège de France, Professor Éleuthère Mascart, was sufficiently impressed with Pierre's ability, and the high opinion in which Lord Kelvin held him, to intervene on his behalf and secure the creation of a new chair of physics especially for him. Unfortunately, this particular promotion to professor, because it was at EPCI, did not include a laboratory and meant Pierre now had not only his original class on crystallography but also another, much larger one, for one hundred and twenty students, on general electricity. To teach a subject Pierre had never taught before entailed a lot of extra work and preliminary preparation, and the course he subsequently set up was the most modern and complete of its kind in Paris.

Perhaps to compensate, because he was unable to do more for Pierre in his new post, Director Schützenberger gave Marie permission to transfer her research on the magnetic qualities of steel from Professor Lippmann's overcrowded quarters, in the Sorbonne complex, where she had been from the start of her project, to Pierre's research space in the school's corridor. "Papa Schütz's" authorization, which gave Marie a little more breathing room, was unheard of for the day, but, then, it was also unique to have a woman in a laboratory. There were no other women at Marie's level in science, let alone one whose husband was an authority on the same field in which she was working and, therefore, in a position to assist her. Naturally Marie had to pay her own expenses, but she succeeded in procuring free scraps of metal from different metallurgical companies, and Henri LeChâtelier, an eminent professor from the School of Mines, lent a hand with the chemical analysis.

Marie was also preparing for the *Concours d'Agrégation,* a special examination which was one of the prerequisites for any teaching position in the government *lycées.* Evenings found the gas lamp burning late on the rue de la Glacière, with Marie and Pierre at opposite ends of the table, hard at work. In essence, the Curies' lives had not changed since their marriage. They saw no one outside of their immediate families. They did not have the time or inclination to do otherwise.

Meanwhile, at the University of Würzburg, Wilhelm Konrad Roentgen had been investigating the strange behavior of Crookes' discharge tubes. When electric currents were passed through gases at low pressures a luminous glow—strange lights and colors—was noted, as well as electrical discharges. Further investigation disclosed the presence of an unknown—hence the name "X"—ray, able to pass through opaque substances. He announced this discovery in December, in the *Sitzungsberichte* of the local scientific society. He quickly realized these new rays would be invaluable in locating skeletal breaks and in detecting foreign bodies before surgery. Roentgen's picture of the bones of his wife's hand, when she held it in front of a screen and the rays passed through the surrounding flesh, horrified Frau Roentgen and caused a sensation worldwide. The sky was soon the limit for punsters and versifiers, and venerable *Punch* joined the chorus:

We only crave to contemplate
Each other's usual full dress photo.
Your worse than "altogether" state,
Of portraiture we bar in toto.

Some women began bathing with all their clothes on to escape the gaze of lecherous scientists peering at them through the brick walls of their houses. Lead-lined clothes were advertised to prevent the penetration of layers of Victorian petticoats and to protect feminine modesty.

Not only did Roentgen's rays charge the air around them but he further determined that they could pass through wood and metal as well as human flesh. They could also act on photographic plates. For radiation to be present, there had to be an energy source, and scientists promptly began to search for it. Fortunately they ignored, or forgot, that J.C. Maxwell, under whose direction the plans of the Cavendish were prepared, had remarked earlier at Glasgow, in one of the greatest misstatements in the history of science, that all the discoveries in physics had been made. Pontificating like the authority he was, Maxwell maintained that the basic nature of phenomena could be explained by existing laws, and it remained only to adjust the last decimal points in various measurements. Unbeknownst to the patriarch, the revolution in physics was about to erupt.

Doctors began to use Roentgen's X rays at once, but the main interest for scientists lay in their mysterious ability to make gases at normal temperature into conductors of electricity—a revelation of something entirely unsuspected in nature that was to be of the greatest significance in pure science. Shortly after the English magazine *Nature* spread the word about Roentgen's X rays, on January 23, 1896, at the French Academy of Sciences, a talk about them, illustrated by X-ray photos taken by two Parisian doctors, aroused the interest of Professor Henri Becquerel. Four successive generations of Becquerels—all *polytechniciens,* not *académiciens*—had lived in the same house on the grounds of the Jardin des Plantes and worked in the same field, in the same laboratory of the Museum of Natural History. Like them, Henri, a balding irascible man with a fierce little Vandyke beard, occupied the chair of physics and he, too, specialized in phosphorescence and fluorescence. Using the large collection of phosphorescent and fluorescent substances which the two earlier Becquerels had collected, Henri wanted to determine whether the phenomenon of fluorescence might not also be accompanied by the production of the same invisible X rays that affected photographic plates.

Over the next few weeks, Becquerel tried putting a number of the various lumps of stone and wood that cluttered his shelves and shone in the dark on photographic paper to see if any of them would darken it the same way Roentgen's rays did. The results were negative. Then, one day, he selected some uranium salt which he knew, from past experience, glowed under ultraviolet light. Enveloping some photographic plates in black cloth, he then placed the crystalline mix, that had been previously exposed to the sun, on top. Upon development, gray smudges on the plates showed that there had been a penetrating radiation, and he presented his first paper on these results to the Academy of Sciences on the last Monday in February. The following Wednesday and Thursday, Becquerel set up a similar experiment. Because of the contemporary belief that it was essential to work in sunlight in order to get naturally fluorescent material to fluoresce, and there was no sun,

Becquerel considered the experiment a failure and set aside the plates he had used in a desk drawer.

Three days later, for whatever reason—thoroughness, curiosity, or thrift—he decided to develop the wasted plates. To his astonishment, they were fogged, indicating they had been subjected to rays capable of penetrating matter. Since there had been no sunlight, this meant that radiation was being spontaneously emitted from the uranium salts. Becquerel hurriedly wrote up a report announcing these results which he read the next day at a session of the Academy. His paper produced not so much as a ripple of response or excitement.

By one of those coincidences that are not as rare in science as people might imagine, Sylvanus P. Thompson a few days later discovered the same phenomenon while working independently in England. Meanwhile, Becquerel continued his experiments. But his rays were far less spectacular than Roentgen's, which were soon being studied at a number of different universities. Gradually Becquerel abandoned work on them.

For the newlyweds, the early summer months were devoted entirely to work. They did not even go to Warsaw when Hela married Marie's former Sorbonne comrade Stanislaw Szalay. In August, Marie was number one in the *Concours d'Agrégation,* the examination for which she had spent so long preparing, and received her certificate to teach secondary education to girls. Pierre's classes were over at about the same time, so they put their bicycles on the train and headed south. The type of holiday they had enjoyed on their honeymoon suited both their temperaments and their pocketbooks, so on this trip and subsequent ones they covered a lot of territory in similar fashion. Over the next few years, they would range from the Auvergne mountains and the Cevennes region, to the seacoast and Channel shores, enjoying some of France's great forests.

Marie was delighted to find herself enceinte the following January, although the next nine months were difficult, health-wise. She was dizzy and fatigued, plagued by morning sickness that often lasted the entire day. Unable to stand on her feet in the laboratory her customary eight hours, her work fell behind. Marie looked to Poland for help, as she was to do throughout her life and, that summer, her father came and took her to the small Brittany fishing village of Port-Blanc in les Côtes du Nord. Pierre could not leave Paris until classes were finished and continued his study of crystals in spare moments.

This was the first and one of the rare times the Curies were ever separated, and their correspondence gives a rare, intimate glimpse into their personal relationship. The last thing one might expect the head-in-the-clouds, impractical Pierre to discuss with his "dear little child whom I love so much"[2] would be a layette—let alone swaddling clothes in assorted sizes—but he did. Marie's were equally affectionate: "My dear husband. Come quickly. I am awaiting you from dawn to dusk . . . I love you with all my heart and press you in my arms. Your M."[3] To please Marie and as if to show how anxious he was to share every part of her life, Pierre even made the effort—and it was a struggle—to write her in Polish. She replied in short simple phrases that he, as a beginner, might understand.

Pierre's mother, who was dying of breast cancer, was so sad whenever he mentioned leaving Paris that it was hard for Pierre to tear himself away but, fortunately for Marie's sake, he was not tied to her apron strings, and he arrived as soon as classes were over. By then Marie was feeling more like herself and, lulled by her assurances, Pierre, who should have known better, suggested they bicycle to Brest, a considerable distance away. Not surprisingly, they had not gone very far when Marie was unable to continue and was forced to return to Paris by train.

On September 12, 1897, a scant fortnight before Mme. Curie succumbed, Dr. Curie delivered Irène, who was healthy and well in spite of it all. In Marie's account book she noted under the heading of "unusual expense": *"Champagne 3 fr. Telegrams 1 fr.10."* Under the heading of "illnesses" the young mother wrote: *"Chemist and nurse: 71 fr.50."*[4] The outlay was so large that Marie indignantly underlined the total several times.

Marie adjusted quickly to the new member of the family and, that fall, after Professor Sklodowski returned to Poland, her letters home were full of details about her "little Queen." Because she had problems nursing and regaining her strength, she had to find a wet nurse. Marie kept losing weight, and her worried brother-in-law and Dr. Vauthier, the family doctor, talked of a possible lesion in her left lung. One out of seven people still died of tuberculosis in Europe and, given Marie's family history, the two doctors prescribed a stay in a sanatorium to be on the safe side. Depressing as their diagnosis was, Marie refused to follow their recommendations.

Marie was as liberated as Bronya and equally determined to combine maternity and a husband with a career. Simply because no woman, single or married, had ever before contemplated a life devoted to science, it never entered Marie's head that this was not feasible. So, in addition to the wet nurse, she hired an inexpensive helper to do the heaviest household chores and began preparing for the next hurdle ahead.

Although there was one *Fräulein* in Germany who was well along with a thesis in chemistry, no European woman had yet completed a Ph.D. in science. Nonetheless, Marie was both determined and self-confident and expected to be treated simply as a candidate, with no concessions made for her sex. Marie knew she had to overachieve in order for men to recognize her as an equal. Generations of male prejudice had to be overcome.

The starting point was her doctoral thesis, which had to be a subject of original research, and her choice was crucial, considering the amount of time and energy it entailed. Both she and Pierre were excited about the Becquerel rays, and she decided to try to find out the source of the energy which enabled them to darken photographic plates, as well as the nature of this radiation. Jean

Perrin, the renowned physicist and Nobel laureate who knew the couple intimately, always claimed the thesis topic was Marie's idea, because Pierre's experimental research was generally guided by theoretical concepts resulting from long reflection. He never undertook anything without knowing almost exactly what he was looking for. Perrin also heard Marie state that an added selling point in favor of her ultimate choice was the lack of a bibliography to wade through. The field was so new that there was nothing to read except Becquerel's reports in the Academy's 1896 *Comptes Rendus.* This allowed Marie to plunge right into the actual laboratory work, which she preferred.

Her decision to work on the Becquerel rays was to be one of the most important of her entire life. It was to govern the rest of her career, intimately link the Curie "clan" to the development of nuclear physics, and also affect the life of the entire world. For what the cell is to biology, what the molecule is to chemistry, the atom is to physics. Until the discovery of X rays, few people were interested in studying atoms. Little was known about them, and there seemed no way of finding out anything, for it was considered impossible to analyze what one could not see. Roentgen's and Becquerel's discoveries changed all this.

Once Marie found a subject, she needed a place to work. Again "Papa Schütz" came to the rescue, although the best he could offer was an unused little glass-paneled atelier, rather like a greenhouse. It was unheated and damp, but Marie accepted gratefully. She knew she could put up with the unregulated temperature and the rain dripping from the leaky roof, despite her troublesome cough, but she also knew these conditions would pose a serious problem for the delicate instruments she must use. Later, Marie estimated that with proper equipment and an adequate laboratory she and Pierre could have accomplished in two years what would take them five. The attendant wear and tear on themselves would be inestimable.

Here, on December 16, 1897, the same year the English physicist

J.J. Thomson discovered the negatively charged electron, the first subatomic particle, Marie made her initial notations in the same small, black-bound book that Pierre had been using for work on his beloved crystals. In the beginning, everything was recorded in Marie's neat hand interspersed, here and there, with an occasional margin note, a few figures, a curve, in Pierre's tiny, immature script to indicate how closely he was following her work.

That no one found polonium and radium before the Curies is probably due to the fact that existing instruments to measure infinitesimal amounts of electricity were crude and there existed the mistaken belief that the chemical composition of uranium was correctly established. Conversely, if Pierre and Marie had not made their discovery when they did, someone else would have, shortly thereafter. The discovery of these elements was one of those things "in the air," so to speak. And, as with so many similar scientific revelations, there was a certain amount of chance and luck involved, including the fortuitous invention by the Curie brothers of their remarkable piezo-quartz electrometer.

The time frame involved in Pierre and Marie's story is also amazing. In roughly a year—starting from scratch and with no large body of work by others to build on—they found an answer to what they were seeking. In an equally brief period, relatively speaking, from 1891 to 1898, Marie was transformed from a poor Polish student entering her first year at the Sorbonne into a married woman with a child; two degrees to her credit and a well-established path toward her doctorate and her Nobel-winning discovery.

Marie's first step, once she started, was to determine whether anything else besides uranium salts produced rays similar to Becquerel's. The only known fact about his rays was that they betrayed their presence by lightly ionizing the air and making it a conductor of electricity. Therefore she decided on a quantitative analysis to tell whether radiation was being produced by the various samples she now set out to test, and, if so, how much. Since it was imperative for her to make do with whatever equipment was at hand, she decided to use the Curie brothers' piezo-quartz electrometer which was lying idle in the EPCI laboratory. It was made to order for measuring feeble electric currents with painstaking accuracy and was far superior to the instrument Becquerel had used. Pierre, who excelled at creating imaginative makeshift apparatus, fashioned her an ionization chamber out of a jelly can, and the rest of her equipment was equally crude but functionally adequate.

Marie gathered samples of minerals from different colleagues she met in the halls of the school and from the various physicists with whom she was in contact and painstakingly tested them, one by one. As the rays ionized the gas in the chamber, she then measured for infinitesimal amounts of electricity that might result by using the exacting, accurate method which Pierre and Jacques had devised earlier for other purposes.

Within a few weeks of watching the fluctuating measurements with a microscope, Marie determined that the strength of the rays' activities was in direct proportion to the amount of uranium in the specimen under examination, regardless of whether it was in a pure or compound state, solid or powdered, dry or wet, nor was the radiation affected by anything external like light or heat. She also determined that one other element, rare grayish thorium, also produced rays similar to those of uranium salts and the other uranium compounds. Marie proceeded cautiously, repeating every stage of her work two, even three times. No errors had been made.

Up to this point, Marie's work had been unexceptional, but suddenly she made a leap of genius with the disarmingly simple surmise that the emission of the rays must be a phenomenon occurring within the atom of uranium itself. Since thorium also gave off rays, this was not the property of a single element—that is to say, of uranium and its compounds—and, therefore, it had to be given a name of its own. So Marie coined the word "radioactivity," from the Latin *radius* or "ray," for this property and "radioelement" for any element possessing it. (It was a terminology vastly superior to "hyperphosphorescence," coined by Sylvanus P. Thompson, across the Channel.) From this stark hypothesis, which was to be Marie's most important single contribution to science, the mysteries of the structure of the atom were to be exposed as the twentieth century unfolded. The Nobel physicist Frederick Soddy would express it differently: "Pierre Curie's greatest discovery was Marie Sklodowska. Her greatest discovery was that radioactivity was atomic."[5]

Next, Marie borrowed samples of the remaining known elements in both pure and compound states from the rich collections of the nearby Museum of Natural History. After examining hundreds of metals, salts, oxides, and ores, she discovered that two other uranium ores, pitchblende and chacolite, were also radioactive. To her amazement, the radiation was a lot stronger in both than she expected. A piece of crude pitchblende, an oxide of uranium, had almost four times the activity of the pure uranium extracted from it; chacolite had almost as much. At first, she could not explain the results and thought she had made a mistake. The dust particles that were forever swirling around from her dirt floor might easily cause errors. Yet each time she redid her work she got the same results. During long, solitary hours in her lab, Marie mulled over the problem. One day it was so cold, she stopped to pull on an extra sweater, took time out to brew a cup of tea on the rickety, all-purpose stove, and recorded a temperature of forty-four degrees Fahrenheit in her notebook.

As she and Pierre hurried to and fro, from the rue de la Glacière to EPCI, neighborhood shopkeepers could set their clocks, in the morning and at dusk, by the plainly dressed, somber pair always deep in discussion, trying to resolve Marie's enigma. Although scientists believed that all the components of uranium oxide were known, the Curies thought they must be mistaken. Something else had to be present in so minute a quantity that it had escaped earlier detection. The only way Marie had been able to determine its presence was by measuring the radioactivity of pitchblende, which no scientist had done before. Since she could not identify the unknown substance, she reasoned that it must be a new element. By now Marie had tested everything listed in Mendeleev's famed table, the physicists' bible in which, some twenty years before, the Russian scientist had classified the known chemical elements by weight and according to their chemical analogies. She still could not pinpoint the source of so much radiation.

Marie was anxious to prove her contention as quickly as possible, but Pierre foresaw immense difficulties for her. Swept along by her contagious enthusiasm and attracted by the mystery surrounding her results to date, he temporarily set aside his study of crystals to lend a hand. For a man who was already an acknowledged authority in his own fields to efface himself in this fashion to help his wife realize a totally different project testifies amply to his feelings for her.

Forced by the birth of Irène to seek additional income, Pierre, who was constitutionally incapable of pushing himself for any sort of promotion, or honor, had lately steeled himself to pose as a candidate for the recently vacant chair of physical chemistry at the Sorbonne's Faculty of Sciences, a far more prestigious school than EPCI. No one was better qualified than he for the post, which would almost double his present salary as well as allow more time for personal research. Unfortunately, as Pierre knew, he was seriously handicapped from the outset because he was neither a *normalien,* nor a *polytechnicien*—that is to say, a graduate of one of the two top French academic institutions. Unfortunately, the "old boy" system of school ties that prevailed over scientific qualifications in similar appointments did so again. On March 18, a scant two weeks to the day after he received word of his rejection, Marie recorded with satisfaction that Pierre was working at her side.

On April 12, Marie's first report, "Radiations Emitted by Compounds of Uranium and Thorium," which was the point of departure for the discovery of radium, was presented to the French Academy on her behalf by Professor Gabriel Lippmann, as only Academy members were allowed to present papers. The following Thursday, her report automatically appeared in the Academy's

Comptes Rendus, France's most important scientific journal. It was the quickest and surest way for any scientific news to get into print in France.

The speed with which her work saw the light of day must be attributed to Marie. Under ordinary circumstances such haste on the part of a neophyte might have seemed unbecoming, or even unwise. Pierre would have been more cautious, but he was too much in love with his young wife to find any faults in her. Pierre personally preferred to go public only after long deliberation and when he was positive he had made no error. Still, in scientific circles, it was not the person who made the discovery but the one whose article appeared first who got the credit. However, Pierre never cared if someone else stole his kudos.

It is refreshing to think that Marie's excitement was responsible for her haste. And she had the added pleasure of achieving her success with an electrometer invented by her husband and his brother, and with a method they had devised. By commencing her report with the word "I," Marie unequivocally labeled the controversial contention her own, a claim she reasserted twice in her later biography of Pierre. Marie was no egotist; she only wanted to stake out her claim as an independent agent. She knew that the doubting Thomases of the scientific community, a vast majority, would try to convince the world that no woman could possibly produce original work of any caliber.

When Lippmann read her paper, its contents caused no more of a ripple in that areopagus than had Becquerel's original report on his rays, two years before. As luck would have it, despite Marie's haste, she was beaten by a foreigner. Two months earlier, unbeknownst to her, the German Gerhard Schmidt had published the bare fact that thorium also emitted rays.

Pierre and Marie reasoned that even though the unknown element responsible for the rays existed in quantities so small that it had defied chemical analysis to date, radioactivity, presently its sole established characteristic, could guide them to it like a homing pigeon. Therefore, they started breaking down pitchblende and, after each step, kept only the fragment with the radioactivity, discarding the rest, until they found what they were looking for. As their three laboratory notebooks at the Bibliothèque Nationale indicate, it is impossible to credit the ideas and work in the weeks and months ahead, as Pierre and Marie's writing commingles on every page. Here he was obviously standing beside her, setting down figures and tabulations as she checked the instruments. There it was the reverse, and Pierre, an expert with the exacting piezo-quartz elec-trometer, was reading off the various minute amounts of radioactiv-ity, while Marie was annotating the results. It is evident from the statistics recorded that they were soon dealing with infinitesimal amounts of concentrated matter.

Meanwhile, on April 29, in a paper destined to become famous, the Englishman J.J. Thomson of the Cavendish Laboratory dis-puted the accepted fact that the atom was indivisible, let alone the smallest unit of matter. His iconoclastic report gave scientists every-where new incentive for a reexamination of the structure of the atom.

Because of Marie's penchant for recording objectively, never sub-jectively, everything concerning the three Curies that could be measured quantitatively, she kept a running commentary, in a gray, linen-covered journal. It ranged from the cost of postage stamps to how many jars of gooseberry jam she got from eight pounds of fruit. Nowhere is the pleasure she was getting from baby Irène more evident. The infant was a source of great pride and amaze-ment as she learned to do the things other babies did. On July 7 Marie recorded Irène's first words: "Gogli, gogli, go" and that she could wave thanks with her hand. The appearance of her "first tooth on the lower left" was likewise meticulously entered in her journal. Every letter she sent to Poland rang with her "little Queen's" latest accomplishments.

At the same time, Marie's attention never wavered from pitch-blende. On July 18, she threw a sweater across her shoulders and rushed to the nearby laboratory of Eugène Demarçay with the day's results. The great specialist in spectography was one of the few people privileged to enter the Curies' inner sanctum from the beginning. He so admired Pierre that when he died, some years later, he willed him his beloved spectroscope. Demarçay had only one eye; the other had been lost in a laboratory explosion, a terrible catastrophe that would have overwhelmed most people working in a specialized area of expertise where vision was all-important. But he was still able to discern the characteristic rainbow-colored patterns, or "spectra," that each element shows when sparked by an electric current and which are of an entirely different nature than the rays produced by radioactive elements. By identifying these spectra, Demarçay could positively identify the various elements, for no two were alike. That afternoon, when Marie rushed in and handed him her latest specimen, there was sufficient substance in the glass container—and it was pure enough—for Demarçay to detect a spectral line he had never seen before. This was what Marie had been waiting to hear. The element in the vial was unknown.

Compte Rendu no. 127 (1898), page 175, of the French Academy carried Pierre and Marie's joint report. They had isolated from pitchblende a preparation of sulphur of bismuth that was four hundred times stronger than a specimen of uranium of similar mass. Since their testing proved that a chemically pure specimen of sulphur of bismuth was inactive, the new radioactive element must be mixed in the bismuth compound extracted from pitchblende. This discovery provided a needed lift for Marie, whose letters to Warsaw indicated just how homesick she was. The Curies decided they would name the new substance "polonium," if its existence was confirmed.

That same month Marie received a welcome windfall: the first of three Gegner prizes given to her by the French Academy. The amount of the award was 3,800 francs, a sum slightly more than

Pierre's annual EPCI salary. With more financial peace of mind, the couple shipped their bicycles at the Gare d'Orléans station and headed south with Irène to a peasant's cottage they rented at Auroux in the Auvergne. They took a few side trips to Mont Doré, Puy, and Clermont, but were too tired to travel farther. Instead, they swam in the river and mulled over the problems posed by their experiments. After three unsuccessful attempts, Irène accepted a bath in the river without crying. Daily, she chased after the peasant's cat with wild war whoops and, as Marie recorded, "She sings a great deal."[6] The trip was a success for all concerned.

When their work resumed, Marie and Pierre discovered to their amazement that there must be two unknown elements in pitchblende. Hidden in the barium, in the residue left after bismuth and polonium were removed, there was another unknown substance that was also highly radioactive. As they continued refining and purifying the barium compound to locate this unexpected dividend, Marie enjoyed the informal brainstorming sessions with Pierre. A colleague who was helping them, Gustave Bémont, a laboratory chief at EPCI whom the students nicknamed "Bichro" because his red beard matched the sodium bichromate he kept on his shelf, often took the role of devil's advocate, arguing with Pierre and offering his own solution. According to George Jaffe, a chemist who was permitted to visit the rue Lhomond, where strangers were rarely tolerated because they represented a loss of time, it was generally hard-driving Marie who led the discussions, while amiable, self-deprecatory Pierre introduced the ingenuity into the scientific concepts.

On December 26, the trio, Pierre, Marie, and Bémont, whose exact contribution has never been clarified, made it official when they announced, jointly, in the Academy's *Comptes Rendus,* the probable existence of another new element which they christened "radium," from the Latin *radius,* or "ray."

This was fast work by any standards, coming only a year after Marie had started on her thesis, and six months after the discovery of polonium. She translated the report into Polish and had the satisfaction of sending it to her cousin Joseph Boguski, in whose laboratory at the Museum of Industry and Agriculture in Warsaw she had done her initial practical work. Boguski had it published at once in the Polish review *Swiatlo.*

That same month, the New Zealander Ernest Rutherford, the most promising research student at the Cavendish, discovered that there were two types of uranium rays. One, which he named "alpha," had great ionizing powers and little ability to penetrate; the other, "beta," was just the reverse.

As the century neared its end, man's knowledge of the structure of the atom and its incredible attributes would be pieced together, not unlike a jigsaw puzzle, by the contributions of a number of scientists around the world. It was Becquerel and the Curies, in their crudely equipped laboratories, who took the first steps into this amazing new world. Some might argue that modern physics was born in November 1895, when Roentgen stumbled on X rays; others, with the revelation of the electron by J.J. Thomson in 1897. But it was Becquerel's detection of radioactivity—the first new property of matter to have been revealed since Newton established the laws of gravity—followed by Marie's revolutionary hypothesis, which upset the centuries' old, natural law that the atom was indestructible and indivisible. And it was the Curies' subsequent discovery of radium, which opened the doors to twentieth-century physics. Scientists now had a powerful source of radiation. Its study would enable them to witness for the first time the manifestation of atomic energy. Radium was the key to unlock the mystery of the composition of the universe, for it would help them explore and understand the structure of the atom, the base of all matter on earth.

V
1898–1901

A Mysterious Blue Glow

To ANNOUNCE THE probable existence of the two new elements, radium and polonium, was one thing, but to prove it was another. In order to convince skeptical scientists that she was dealing in facts, Marie had to determine radium and polonium's principal properties as well as locate their proper places in the Mendeleev Periodic Table. Although she had only uncovered imperceptible traces of the pair, Marie's results clearly indicated that not only was radium the more powerful of the two with stronger rays, but also that it would be easier to extract than polonium. Still, it had to be in its pure form before she could conduct the necessary tests; a multifaceted operation that was going to entail years of unremitting toil.

Settling on radium as her target was the first step. Marie and Pierre estimated that it must consist of probably no more than 1/100 part of pitchblende. They were to learn the hard way, by the most drudging sort of toil, that radium was less than 1/1,000,000 of a part, and that it would require about fifty tons of water and five to six tons of chemicals to treat one ton of pitchblende and obtain five to six grains of radium—about three hundred to four hundred milligrams. Even if she had known at the outset of the Herculean task involved, it would probably have made little difference, given Marie's determination and stubbornness. But Pierre might have had second thoughts. Primarily a physicist, he was satisfied with abstract proof and was more interested in the physical properties of these mysterious rays and the fascinating problems which they posed.

Pierre and Marie needed to find a cheap, abundant source of pitchblende, since they had to pay for it themselves. Uranium ore was expensive, and the chief European source was the St. Joachimsthal Mines in Bohemia, part of the Austrian Empire near Carlsbad. Its salts were separated out in a time-consuming operation and used as pigment for dyeing skins for the yellow-colored gloves then so popular, as well as for the brilliant orange, yellow, and black hues needed for glass production. Sample specimens sent from Joachimsthal confirmed Pierre and Marie's hunch that what they were searching for was in the pitchblende residue which was discarded once the uranium had been extracted. Through the timely intervention of an admirer of Pierre, Eduard Suess, a professor at the University of Vienna and a member of the Austrian Academy of Science, the Austrian government arranged for the Curies to purchase some of the waste for its transportation costs. Minimal as this was, the bill nearly depleted their slender savings.

Because of the vast quantities of pitchblende they needed to process, more room was required. Pierre and Marie had to make do with what little additional space Schützenberger's successor, Gariel, was able to offer. The tiny atelier where Marie had done her preliminary work opened onto an unkempt back courtyard where stood a ramshackle hangar which was once used by the School of Medicine as a dissecting room. Its ceiling was of shaky laths, its windows were ill-fitting and drafty, its taps dripped. The walls were of ruined plaster and partially glassed in, as was the roof, and the dust from the bituminous soil constituting its floor would pose a serious contamination problem. The only furniture was a worn pine table, but there was a blackboard—an indispensable item for Pierre, who always needed one to think with—and a cast-iron stove with a rusty pipe that gave off a little heat in the winter. The Curies were offered the shed, and they gratefully moved in.

Their working conditions were unquestionably primitive and inadequate, even for the day. When the great German chemist Wilhelm Ostwald, one of the first to recognize the significance of the Curies' research, traveled from Berlin expressly to visit them and saw the hangar, he thought someone at EPCI was playing a joke and had showed him the wrong place. He called it a cross between a stable and a potato cellar. But, in reality, other well-known laboratories of the day were not much better.

However, as with the legend that grew up about Marie placing her one chair on top of herself in bed to anchor the skimpy covers and help keep her warm, during her Sorbonne days, the legend of their deplorable quarters was augmented by Marie's repeated and outspoken bitterness about them in later years. Paradoxically, she also remarked in her biography of Pierre: ". . . it was in this miserable old shed that the best and happiest years of our life were spent, entirely consecrated to work . . . I shall never be able to express the joy of the untroubled quietness of this atmosphere of research and the excitement of actual progress with the confident hope of still better results."[1]

Once the Curies had a place to put the pitchblende, they sent for as much as they could afford. Anxiously, Marie awaited its arrival.

The day she heard the heavily laden wagon grind to a halt on the rue Lhomond, she raced out, hatless and coatless, to direct the unloading of the precious shipment. She was so excited to see the contents of the first of the grimy gunnysacks being thrown, pell-mell, to the ground that her fingers kept fumbling with the knotted cord. Impatiently she slit one side with a small pocket knife. Black ore spilled every which way. But, for once, hoarding every tiny scrap was not on Marie's mind. Eagerly she reached down, grabbed a handful that was mixed with pine needles from the forest floor where the mining company had dumped the residue after removing the uranium, and hastened back inside. Her electrometer confirmed that the waste pitchblende was highly radioactive.

As she started the mammoth task of purifying radium, Marie had almost no help. Pierre's lone assistant, the elderly Petit, who had been with him virtually since the start of Pierre's academic career, had more than enough to keep him busy every day, just supervising the practical work of Pierre's numerous students. Still, he was devoted to Pierre, as were all those who ever worked with him, and gave the Curies a hand whenever he could. A few other colleagues also assisted from time to time. They all noted that it was the slender little woman in the dark dress, covered with the acid-stained smock, who was the more assertive, stronger personality of the pair. Marie always yielded to Pierre in a scientific argument, as she had great trust in his ability. But if the stumbling block were mathematics, Pierre would look to Marie for the solution.

Scientifically, they complemented each other well. They made a lot of false starts and errors, and there were many days when nothing seemed to work, or when they appeared to be at a dead end, but they persevered. There was even one terrible day when Marie dropped a full beaker, transforming its contents, several months of painfully accumulated precipitate, into a small puddle at Pierre's feet.

Imaginative, innovative Pierre's primary preoccupation was with the delicate tests necessary to determine radium's properties, although he continued to do a great deal of chemical work as well. He either saw, at a glance, the experiment that needed to be made, or he would have an ingenious idea—some odd angle or approach—to the matter at hand. Marie, on the other hand, preferred to obtain pure salts of radium through chemical treatments, accumulating and storing, like a persistent ant.

Heretofore, she had been working with one hundred grams of pitchblende. Now the intrepid woman was faced with a ton. Undaunted, she quickly found she could handle up to twenty kilograms of raw material at a time, enough to fill one of their largest cast-iron caldrons. She was doing the work of a day laborer, keeping the fires going under these immense receptacles while she mixed the poisonous sludge with a steel rod taller than she. There were no exhaust hoods to carry off the noxious fumes emitted by hydrogen sulphide and certain other chemicals so, in order not to asphyxiate herself and Pierre, Marie had to continue the distillation process in the open courtyard.

If it snowed, she would freeze; if there was a real downpour, she had no choice but to cart everything back indoors and work with all the windows open. And, of course, when it rained, she also had to rush to move the great jars of precipitates, already produced, from this side to that, to avoid the splash of raindrops trickling down from the cracks overhead. Eventually, as the brews became increasingly concentrated and correspondingly more radioactive and pure, it was essential to keep the laboratory spotlessly clean, an almost impossible job. More than one finished batch, representing weeks of backbreaking labor—pulverizations, crystallizations, precipitations, leachings—was ruined by their woefully inadequate facilities. Finally the material was reduced to the contents of a small receptacle and set alongside other, already filled, porcelain crystallizing bowls. And Marie started the whole cycle over again with a fresh twenty kilograms of waste pitchblende. Small wonder her fingertips were red, cracking, and sore.

The Curies had other, more serious, physical ailments. Neither one was in good health. Pierre complained of pains in his legs that the family doctor attributed to rheumatism, aggravated by the dampness in the shed, so he put him on a diet eliminating red meat and red wine. The doctor was more worried about Marie. However, a new physical examination and an analysis of her sputum for tuberculosis were negative.

Financial problems loomed as large as ever for the Curies and, as soon as Marie received her doctorate, she intended to look for a job. But, at the moment, she was too busy to stop and write her thesis on her work to date and study for the required oral examination.

If research was exciting, life outside the laboratory was not. They never went anywhere and never saw anyone except Dr. Curie. They used to see the Dluskis each Sunday, and the two sisters would sit sewing identical dresses for their little girls. Sewing was one of Marie's few forms of relaxation, as well as a measure dictated by economy. Then suddenly Bronya and Casimir took advantage of a political amnesty in Poland to return home and establish their own sanatorium. The Dluskis' departure left a big void in Marie's life, and she quickly began writing her sister for advice on everything from how to water the green plants they had left behind, to what to feed Irène, who was proving a very fussy eater and wanted only milk tapioca.

If Irène made up her mind that she wanted *renettes*—a special kind of apple—tired as Marie might be at the end of the day, she would go in search of some. She dared not go home empty-handed, or a terrible tantrum would result. Irène was a little tyrant, a difficult, demanding child like many who have to share their parents with siblings. Irène's competition, however, was a laboratory, and the small girl learned at an early age how to get her mother and father's attention. Marie continued to dress and feed her in the morning, and she fed, bathed, and put her to sleep each night. But, if Irène caught a cold or had a bad tumble in the Parc de Montsouris, where the maid took her for a daily walk, the restless child gave her parents a sleepless night. And, on Sunday, the one day that Marie and Pierre did not go to EPCI, Irène was so delighted to have them at home for a change that she awakened "Mé" and "Pé" —as Irène always called them and as Ève would later—at an ungodly hour to play with her.

For vacation, that year, after Pierre's classes were over, homesick Marie took her husband and daughter to visit the Dluskis at Zakopane, a simple resort city in the Carpathian mountain district of Austrian Poland, where the masons were building their sanatorium. Marie was very proud of Pierre's attempts to speak Polish, although he was not gifted in languages, and she was deeply touched that he cared enough about her to make the effort. She confided to Bronya: "I have the best husband one could dream of . . . He is a true gift of heaven, and the more we live together the more we love each other."[2] As usual, when Pierre was away from his laboratory any length of time, he quickly got restless and wanted to return.

Together, Marie and Pierre published two articles on their most recent findings in the Academy's November *Comptes Rendus,* and then Marie published a third, alone. Now, after Irène was tucked into bed and finally asleep, Marie and Pierre often walked back to the rue Lhomond to marvel at nature's handiworks. They would push open the creaking door and allow a few moments for their eyes to grow accustomed to the hangar's darkness. Looking around at the mysterious blue glow issuing from each of the steadily increasing number of bottles and saucers lining the tables and simple plank shelves, Marie and Pierre were filled with a sense of awe. Their mutual satisfaction as they gazed together at what they had been privileged to reveal gave a new dimension to their personal relationship. Taking Pierre's arm, Marie would ease the door shut quietly, as if afraid she might break some magic spell, and they would head home. "These lights . . . suspended in the dark were always a new source of emotion and enchantment for us."[3]

It was providential, as with so many other things at this stage of Marie's career, that Dr. Curie, when he retired, opted to stay in

Paris and be a live-in grandparent, rather than move to Montpellier
to be with his elder son, Jacques, and his family. With GrandPé
there, Marie could go off each morning with her mind completely
at ease about her growing daughter. But they now needed an extra
bedroom, so they rented a small, two-story house at no. 108 Boulevard Kellermann. Located at the south of Paris, not too far from
the rue Lhomond, their new home was situated near the old city
fortifications and faced the Porte de Gentilly, through which Marie
and Pierre could quickly pedal into the suburbs and adjacent forests. It was a neighborhood of crowded streets, factory building,
wastelands, and poor tenements. Passersby before no. 108 could
only see a wall and a door, but there was a minute garden in back
for Irène's play and for Dr. Curie's cultivation of flowers. With a
whole house to furnish, Marie accepted gladly when Dr. Curie
broke up his Sceaux household and told Marie to take her pick.
Like the rue de la Glacière, the Boulevard Kellermann establishment was furnished "à la Marie"—that is to say, sparsely.

　Pierre might have been a recluse by nature, but Marie had become one by propinquity. Still, they could not shut themselves off
completely from what was transpiring in the world, especially now
that GrandPé was living with them. That fierce, unrepentant republican was still robust and interested in everything, and he was
up in arms over the undeserved fate of the Alsatian Jewish officer
Alfred Dreyfus, who had been falsely accused—and found guilty—
of spying and selling military secrets to a foreign power several
years before. The present campaign to free Dreyfus was fanned
into flames by Émile Zola, the leading author of the day, with his
celebrated letter "J'accuse." Virtually everybody in France took
sides, and the bulk of the young academics were active
Dreyfusards. Old Dr. Curie ranted nightly over the dinner table
that justice must be tendered the unfortunate captain. Pierre sat
silent, with his usual, absentminded expression while Marie, who
had never before and would never again follow a public event with
so much interest, heartily concurred with GrandPé.

Some of the various scientific prizes which Pierre and Marie won supplemented their income, but Pierre was now faced with another mouth to feed. Driven by necessity, Pierre asked for and received a post at the École Polytechnique as substitute tutor, a ludicrous position for a scientist with his already wide reputation. Perhaps because it was so lowly, Pierre did not feel the same qualms about asking for it that he did when a position more in keeping with his achievements was available. Pierre's new job was sheer drudgery with very small pay and necessitated squeezing more hours from a day already stretched well beyond the norm. Pierre was well aware of his own abilities, but his prickly character imposed needless limits on their development. His diffident nature and humble attitude did not set well with the scientific hierarchy which made the coveted appointments and considered him a nonconformist who did not wear the old school tie. As academic openings continued to bypass Pierre, his bitterness increased and Marie, who felt as wounded as he, remained resentful of his treatment until the end of her life.

The three years between 1900 and 1903 were the most creative of Marie's entire scientific life, and the Curies published more during this period than at any other time. Marie published in her own name or in collaboration with Pierre, whereas Pierre always appeared in print with someone else. If it was not Marie, it was the young chemist André Debierne. Shy almost to the point of being tongue-tied and with an unkempt hairdo, this former student of Pierre's commenced a lifetime collaboration with the pair around this time. Debierne would discover actinium, a third new radioactive substance, in the group of iron and rare earths even before polonium and radium were successfully isolated. Pierre also worked with another young physicist, George Sagnac. Increasingly, the Curies realized their need of help. They had plenty to choose from. Their titanic efforts, together with the almost religious fervor pervading the shed in the rue Lhomond, had a strong appeal for idealistic young researchers—all men, of course.

It was still very much a man's world. Should some feminist choose to take Marie as a role model, that was her business, but Marie was not a belligerent, conscious rebel. She simply had no intention of fitting her life into any prescribed mold solely to conform to society's accepted pattern. She was her own creature, doing what she wanted to do as well as she could, with no quarter given or anticipated. However, she expected to be accepted as an equal in her efforts to fulfill her potential. And nothing she did was consciously done to open the doors for women who would follow her example.

Meanwhile, GrandPé tenderly looked after his three-year-old granddaughter, taking her for long walks and acquainting her, firsthand, with the wonders of nature, as he had her father, long ago. If Marie and Pierre were too busy with their frenetic work schedule to take Irène to the nearby Parc de Montsouris for the annual fireworks display on Bastille Day, GrandPé took the child, another evening, to admire from afar the magical new illumination of the Trocadero and the Eiffel Tower. These were now lighted with tens of thousands of electric bulbs, in place of the former hissing gas, to celebrate the Paris Exposition of 1900 which opened that summer.

That twentieth of July was the hottest day Paris had seen since 1874, and there was a water shortage, to the dismay of the thousands of visitors flocking to the Fair. It was sweltering inside the hangar in the rue Lhomond, whose partially glassed-in roof produced a hothouse effect, but Marie and Pierre would remember this day for another reason. Just as Lord Kelvin had long since recognized Pierre's worth so, now, it was another foreigner, the dean of the University of Geneva, who arrived in Paris that morning, expressly to entice Pierre to join his department. The offer was so tempting that the couple went to Switzerland to inspect the situation firsthand. The 10,000 franc salary was larger than average, and numerous other lures were also included, for the school wanted Pierre badly. The dean promised a physics laboratory custom-built to his needs and even included an official post in it for

Marie who, at present, had no official status whatsoever; she was simply a doctoral candidate working toward her degree on her own time and at her own expense. Encouraged by Marie, Pierre accepted. His leg pains had become more acute of late and Marie was convinced that their increased frequency was due to their taxing schedule. A move to Geneva would give him a chance to breathe again.

However, before the summer was over, they had second thoughts about leaving France. Marie had a head start on any possible competition in her work on radium. Any break in her routine would delay her for months, maybe even a year, and she wondered if it was wise to interrupt her research at that precise moment when it looked so promising. According to her subsequent biography of Pierre, he felt the same way.

Two recent congresses in the capital—that of the Society of Chemistry, followed by the French Physics Society meeting—featured the Curies' work. This had made the Paris scientific community aware of the Curies' increasing prominence on the international scene. Thanks largely to the efforts of Henri Poincaré, the most brilliant mathematician of the day, who was not anxious to see these rising stars depart, a counterproposal was made which Pierre accepted at the last moment. He was offered an assistant professorship at the School of Physics, Chemistry, and Natural Sciences of the University of Paris. "PCN," as it was popularly known, constituted part of the Sorbonne and there, at no. 12 rue Cuvier, teaching headquarters for PCN's first-year medical students, he was given a small office, a tiny dark room, and a little work area which could serve as a laboratory. In addition, he was given two assistants! As the recipient of such bounty, Pierre was able to resign the part-time job he had taken out of desperation.

But it was one thing to teach two classes in electricity and another when the students in one, those at EPCI, were destined to be engineers and those in the second, at PCN, future doctors. Pierre had to design an entirely fresh course of lectures, as well as oversee the practical work of two large groups, each in a different location. Consequently, Pierre's workload increased at the exact moment when his research with Marie called for every ounce of their joint energy and strength.

Fortunately, the schools were near each other and in between classes, Pierre scurried to and fro, generally with a vial of Marie's latest radioactive fracturing tucked casually in his vest pocket for future experiments. He would duck into the hangar on the rue Lhomond to see what was going on, offer advice, take readings, make measurements which he was often forced to stop at a crucial moment in anticipation of the class bell at PCN. Rather than interrupt an important operation, and to save time, he might grab a bite of lunch cooked by Marie on the little stove there or else snatch something from the students' kitchen nearby. Occasionally, if there were a few extra minutes, he joined his PCN associates at an inexpensive little restaurant at the corner of the rue Monge and the rue Censier, where workers from the laboratories in the Museum of Natural History also ate.

When new facts about radium were ascertained, one of Pierre's two assistants would come to the Curies' home on Sunday and, after dinner, sit around the table with Marie, Pierre, and Debierne, editing a *Compte Rendu* for the Academy's weekly Monday meeting. These were rigidly limited to no more than two and a half large printed pages, with two columns, adequate to clearly formulate any carefully worded report.

When Poincaré found Pierre's job for him, he also located one for Marie and, with two breadwinners at last in the family, the Curies' budget was balanced for a long time to come. In October, when Pierre started to teach at PCN, Marie set off, twice a week, on the steam tramway that crossed the Seine and proceeded at a snail's pace to the suburb of Sèvres. She got off in the Grande Rue at the beginning of a long *allée* of chestnut trees leading to the beautiful grilled entryway of a lovely walled estate. Within was Mme. de Pompadour's former porcelain factory, an old building with a great rectangular facade flanked by two wings, which now served as the École Normale Supérieure de Sèvres for Girls. A government boarding school, Sèvres was established by the law of 1880 to recruit and prepare women to teach in the state-run girls' *lycées* (naturally "sèvriennes" were not considered capable of instructing young men). Upon graduation, they were obligated to ten years of teaching.

Aside from offering Marie her first salary since coming to Paris, this was a post made-to-order for the former Warsaw positivist who was a staunch believer in equal education for both sexes. Marie found the change of atmosphere from the closed, inbred world of the rue Lhomond so stimulating that she would retain her Sèvres post for a number of years, regardless of the demands it made on her time. She liked working with the bright, outgoing students in their early twenties, and she enjoyed her contacts with its outstanding staff which, during her tenure, included some of the most eminent scholars of the Sorbonne and Collège de France. Among them was a pair of scientists who, with Marie, were to dominate French science for the next thirty years—Jean Perrin and Paul Langevin. The former, whose halo of red curls earned him the nickname of the "Archangel," had once had Marie in a Sorbonne class and was already a friend of both Curies. He had begun as a lecturer in Sèvres' third form at the same time that Marie started there. The latter, Paul Langevin, an intimate of Perrin and a former pupil of Pierre, would join the staff later. Marie's former mathematics teacher Paul Appell likewise was at Sèvres.

Marie's appointment created a sensation. A woman! Imagine! And she did not even have her Ph.D. yet! But she had discovered radium, and she had her *agrégation.*

Normally, the moment a professor crossed the school's threshold, a bell rang to warn the "sèvriennes" of his arrival. But Marie established rapport so quickly with the four girls in her first class that they watched for her from the window and, as soon as they caught a glimpse of the slight, somberly clad figure they ran to take their places in the lecture hall. On warm days, the girls waited for her outside in the courtyard. The time flew in Marie's classes. The lunch bell rang and no one stirred. On more than one occasion, the supervisor herself appeared behind the glass door and cleared her throat loudly to remind them, discreetly, of the hour, but teacher and pupils were too absorbed to see or hear her. Then, suddenly, Marie realized the time. Her pupils rushed off to eat, while she swallowed a cup of tea and walked back down between the chestnut trees to await the tram, which often ran a half-hour late.

Marie was shocked by her pupils' poor scientific preparation; they had never been allowed to touch any apparatus. She deplored the school's poor laboratory and the total lack of practical work offered the girls, a situation she resolved to remedy at once. Marie took great pains to prepare her lectures. Although she was hired to teach physics for only one and a half hours, twice a week, she quickly took it upon herself to double this time without extra charge, and added differential and integral calculus, both of which she considered essential for intelligent, well-educated young women. Marie also insisted that the girls do some laboratory work, once they had been thoroughly coached in "Madame's" basic rule: Counter tops must be kept clean at all times, and not just at the end of the day. Otherwise, as Marie took pains to point out, there was a danger of contaminating, and thereby spoiling, the results of an experiment that might have taken days to set up.

Marie gradually upgraded the physics classes until Sèvres's science curriculum was the equivalent of the men's at the prestigious École Normale on the rue Ulm. She frequently brought to class a piece of equipment that Pierre had modified, or constructed, especially for her pupils. Once the girls had passed the difficult entrance examinations to enter Sèvres, they had to work very seriously to meet graduation requirements, and they considered "Madame" their role model. By her personal enthusiasm Marie attached the girls to her, and they quickly realized that her external coldness was only a mask to hide her timidity and warm heart.

Marie's normally serious expression was often transformed into a smile at some of the naive remarks. She was well aware of their potential and, one day, in order to instill in them a love for research as well as for teaching, Marie apologetically encroached on Pierre's overloaded schedule by bringing the class to visit him in his modest new installation on the rue Cuvier. They were thrilled at the prospect of meeting this famous man, the husband of their admired and beloved teacher.

Pierre came to the door to greet them with a long loping stride, his cropped head of salt and pepper, with beard to match, leaning slightly forward, as if, the girls decided later in the postmortem they conducted in their dormitory, he were pursuing some inner idea. The "sèvriennes" watched spellbound as he showed them how the Bunsen calorimeter operated. He pointed out the various apparatuses around the room and demonstrated, in several very elementary experiments, how some of them functioned, explaining everything in his grave slow voice which, like Marie, he never raised, even in anger. Then he switched off the lights so his attentive audience might watch a glass tube glow when it was filled with the gas that emanated from radium. One of the girls, Eugénie Feytis, who became a favorite of the Curie household and eventually married one of their intimates, Aimé Cotton, noted with amazement that Pierre had long thin hands that an artist or musician might envy. She would remember the dexterity with which he carried out the various manipulations.

Marie's world was enlarged and enriched through her part-time work at Sèvres. For she was brought in contact with an entirely different environment than the hermetically sealed sanctuary of the rue Lhomond. Her exuberant young "sèvriennes" helped draw her out until she was more like the young Polish girl of the Floating University days. Her engaging colleagues had a multitude of interests they were always discussing.

VI
1901–1903

Doctor of Physical Science.
<u>Summa cum Laude</u>

MARIE ALWAYS FELT BET-
ter physically after her half day at Sèvres and, in later years, when
co-workers complained of various aches and pains, a lingering tiredness, and low resistance to disease, she advocated they take time off
and spend it outdoors. She guaranteed that they would feel better
—like she used to, when she was with her girls. Her homespun
medical advice was correct, to a degree, because the poorly venti-
lated hangar at EPCI posed a lethal health danger. Marie and
Pierre's unprotected bodies were absorbing insidious gamma radiation. They were breathing the noxious gas radon, which radium

emitted, because it was capable of diffusing through cork and rubber and was escaping from the improperly stoppered glass flasks in which the new element was unwittingly stored. When Marie and Pierre snatched a bite to eat in the laboratory, they were ingesting radioactive material along with their food. And, today, these radium-related factors are acknowledged agents for a variety of human ailments ranging from fibrosis of the lungs and other respiratory problems to different cancerous blood disorders and damaged bone marrow.

Marie blamed her intermittent poor health and Pierre, his acute leg pains, on their backbreaking schedules and, certainly, overwork played a contributing role. But the notion that radiation might pose a serious problem never crossed their minds, nor would it occur to anyone for a considerable time to come. So the Curies had no reason to take special precautions other than those of an ordinary chemist. Had they been aware of this lurking threat and tested for it, the apparatus at Marie and Pierre's disposal, while sensitive, was not sufficiently adequate to reveal the small amounts of contamination that, in aggregate, could be dangerous. Even three decades later, Marie was considerably relaxed in this regard. Should concentrates get spilled on the floor of the Institut du Radium, someone mopped up the mess with any rag at hand, which was then tossed on the refuse pail. There the deadly waste remained until the next day or whenever the janitor appeared to cart away the garbage.

It will never be known how radioactive Marie and Pierre were. Their son-in-law Frédéric Joliot's last publication in 1958 was on the contamination he still found lingering in their laboratory notebooks. These have now been transferred to the Bibliothèque Nationale, and someone wishing to consult them must first sign a release absolving that institution of any possible consequences resulting from their continued radioactivity—a minimal risk, but a risk nonetheless. For the half-life of radium is 1,580 years, and anyone who has the privilege of working at the Institut du Radium and using what was Marie's and then, later, Irène's desk, chair, and office will discover, with a start, that the furniture still clicks loudly when the decontamination squad makes its periodic check with a Geiger counter.

On the other hand, radium had one physical effect of which both Curies were already painfully aware—their abnormally hardened, damaged fingertips which never completely healed. This was a minor annoyance the couple dismissed as an unavoidable but acceptable occupational hazard, the result of incessant handling of their increasingly pure products. Marie spent the rest of her life unconsciously rubbing her fingertips together, over and over again, as if to relieve their tenderness. Marie and Pierre were surprised when two Germans, Walkhoff and F. Giesel, reported other physiological effects as well. Pierre decided to test their experiments and, some time later, when Charles Edward Guillaume, a fellow physicist, met him on the busy Boulevard St.-Germain one noon and asked for news of his work, Pierre replied, "I have something interesting to show you." Taking off his coat, which he handed to the surprised Guillaume to hold, Pierre rolled up his sleeve, startling passersby hurrying home for their midday meal. On Pierre's lower arm was a bandage containing a small amount of impure radium salts. "Look how this is beginning to redden," Pierre commented, peeling back the adhesive.[1] A few days later, the sore was open. Pierre had kept the salts there only a few hours, yet it would take several months for the resultant wound to heal. Another time Marie was burned inadvertently, and Henri Becquerel got a burn on his stomach when he forgot he had tucked a vial of the salts which the Curies loaned him into his vest pocket.

In early June 1901, Pierre and Becquerel issued a joint *Compte Rendu* on "The Physiological Effects of Rays," in which Becquerel noted that a protection of lead rendered them harmless. The next question to resolve was whether radium's rays affected unhealthy as well as healthy tissue. In an effort to find out, Dr. Danlus treated several of his patients at the St.-Louis hospital with some radioactive material borrowed from the Curies. Pierre did similar research with two other high-ranking medical men, Professors C. Bouchard and V. Balthazard, and began studying similar effects on rabbits and living organisms. It was soon apparent that radium destroyed the sick cells in skin cancer, but when the skin reformed it was healthy.

These various experiments on therapeutic methods using radium and its derivatives pointed up certain advantages of this new form of treatment. While its early applications were more dramatic than conclusive, and it was quickly evident that only certain types of tumors were affected, this marked the beginning of radiotherapy. "Curietherapy," as it was soon called in France, was to develop into an important branch of medicine and was the first step toward modern radiation treatment of cancer.

More and more doctors started borrowing infinitesimal amounts of radium and its derivative, the gas radon, for use on their patients. The preliminary beneficial results made radium the miracle drug of the day, the subject of conversation on the streets and even in the salons of *tout* Paris, and the Academy of Sciences gave Pierre and Marie a 20,000 franc credit for the extraction of additional radioactive substances.

Tremendously radioactive and frighteningly scarce, radium caught the public's eye and replaced X rays as the sensation of the moment. Reflected glory made the Curies better known. Cartoons about radium flooded the press, and one popular boulevard cabaret, quick to flair the wind, put on an hilarious, *lèse-majesté* skit featuring Marie and Pierre, on their hands and knees hunting for some spilled radium. As might be expected, what little of these goings-on filtered through to the Boulevard Kellermann profoundly shocked the modest couple.

Even today, toward the close of the twentieth century, the name Curie connotes to the average person only one thing, radium—and its use as a treatment for cancer. Most are still not aware that Marie and Pierre's discovery of polonium and radium and, even more important, Marie's daring hypothesis that radiation was an atomic property, are two important milestones in the opening of the atomic age and nuclear physics. Their long-range significance for the future of the planet itself far outweighs radium's therapeutic value. But, in 1902, it was not so much what the Curies had accomplished, as the way Pierre and, especially, Marie, had done it that captured the popular imagination.

When the first curious journalist penetrated the hangar in the desolate back courtyard of EPCI, he uncovered a Cinderella story that exceeded his wildest dreams. He was quickly followed by a stampeding horde—or so it seemed to the distraught Curies—and the press made the most of it.

Imagine! The miraculous remedy for cancer had been found by a slender blond foreigner, working against tremendous odds. A wife and mother, this frail creature had been doing a day laborer's job, with longer hours and more abominable conditions than any self-respecting workman would tolerate—all for no pay.

Marie refused to permit her enjoyable two half days a week at Sèvres to divert her one second longer than necessary from her research, especially now that J.P.L.J. Elster and F.K. Hans Giel in Germany, Stefan Meyer in Austria, as well as Ernest Rutherford, now at McGill University in Montreal, were forging ahead in the same field. For the moment, however, these men were concentrating on a study of the rays themselves. Marie, as she approached the final stages of purification, still had no competition, because what she was doing was difficult and tedious. Ambitious Marie wanted to be the first to produce pure radium metal, not just the radium chloride and bromide she already had. She was obsessed with the erroneous idea that scientists worldwide would not believe she had found a new element until she did so. Actually, those that mattered needed no further proof but, perhaps, she also had to convince herself. In accordance with Pierre's philosophy and in the contemporary spirit of disinterested science, the pair continued to publish *Comptes Rendus* detailing their developing knowledge of the new elements, and generously loaned samples of the radioactive solutions they were so laboriously preparing to properly qualified people.

By now, Marie had reached the conclusion that not only was the purification process—up to a certain stage—something that others could do in her stead, but that the method they had developed could be put to more effective use in a factory because an efficient plant would have the capacity to handle larger amounts of pitchblende at a time. So when the Central Society of Chemical Products, with whom Pierre had had earlier dealings, offered facilities for a trial run of the first part of the extraction of radium on an industrial scale, Pierre and Marie jumped at the chance. Debierne was placed in charge of several chemists whom Marie trained expressly for the task, and the approximately ten to twenty kilograms of sulphate of barium that Debierne obtained from each ton of pitchblende then went to Marie at the rue Lhomond. Because chloride of radium is less soluble than chloride of barium, she was able by various stages of fractional crystallization to purify and extract radium chloride, which resembles ordinary kitchen salt, and start determining its atomic weight—two tasks which were, in scientific terms, routine work of secondary importance.

On March 28, 1902, a blustery spring day, Marie hastened to the laboratory of her friend Eugène Demarçay, the spectroscope authority, and excitedly thrust a tube containing about one tenth of a gram of radium chloride into his hand. Testing confirmed what Marie had been waiting impatiently to hear these many months and years. The amount of barium it contained was negligible. She returned to the rue Lhomond, weighed her specimen, and reported in the July 21 *Comptes Rendus*: "Radium = 225.93." Today it is given more accurately as "226"—an atom of radium weighs 226 times one of hydrogen, the lightest element. With Debierne's help Marie had achieved her goal. The chemical biography of radium was complete. For a considerable time, her decigram remained the sole existing specimen: "the cornerstone on which the whole edifice of radioactivity stands today."[2]

The spring of 1902 was a busy one. Haunted by her mother's history of tuberculosis and determined to keep Irène outdoors as much as possible, Marie spent her weekends bicycling around the nearby valley of the Chevreuse, looking for a little house to rent for the early summer months. The minute she found what she was looking for, they promptly moved in, although this entailed a long daily commute for the Curies. They were barely settled in this new routine when she received a telegram advising her that Professor Sklodowski, who was living with her brother Jozio, now an established doctor, had suddenly taken ill and was being operated on for gallstones.

Marie left immediately. Filled with foreboding and tortured by a *mea culpa* complex for having selfishly abandoned her father to remain in France, the two-and-a-half-day train trip was sheer agony for Marie. Upon arrival, she learned that her father was dead. Devastated, she demanded that the coffin be opened at once for a last look at that beloved face. The family acquiesced. But, instead of being relieved, she sobbed so hard and reproached herself so bitterly that Bronya had a difficult time leading her away. Marie created an equally emotional scene at the funeral, wallowing in a paroxysm of grief that was no doubt triggered by the urgent need to exorcise her guilty feelings of neglectfulness. However, she did have one consolation. Professor Sklodowski, a former teacher of physics himself, had lived long enough to have the satisfaction of knowing that his daughter had obtained pure radium at last.

While she was away, Pierre was going through the ancient, antiquated ritual demanded of candidates for the Academy of Sciences. Friends had managed to convince Pierre that the benefits of membership far outweighed his innate distaste for honors and distinctions; Pierre felt the desire to obtain them degraded the worthiest aim of man—to work for the pure love of science. However, as colleagues pointed out, an Academy seat, together with the Légion d'Honneur, constituted the highest honors that France could bestow on a scientist, and would be a big plus in the campaign devoted admirers were waging to get Pierre a chair at the prestigious Sorbonne. Since this, as he knew, would automatically assure him a higher salary, a better laboratory, and more help, he reluctantly acquiesced.

Pierre still felt the procedure was ludicrous, humiliating, and outdated. The Academy should elect its members without a candidate having to solicit, personally, the necessary votes by a mandatory series of calls on each and every academician. Basically Pierre was right, but the moment was ill-chosen to try and reform that venerable body. With this approach and his usual self-deprecatory attitude, Pierre was his own worst enemy. Fifty-eight times the reluctant man climbed innumerable flights of stairs, wondering why academicians always seemed to live on the top floor, had himself announced, told why he had come, set forth his credentials, and explained his work and why he should be honored. Unlike the usual run of candidates, he also enthusiastically sang the praises of his opponents.

Not surprisingly, Pierre lost out to a much less qualified physicist when the ballots were counted on June 9. Why he should have been deeply wounded at the outcome is impossible to say, although one authority has suggested that Pierre was more affected by the radioactivity to which he was being exposed than by the Academy failure itself or his poor physical condition. Specialists, today, consider depression or lowered morale as one of radioactivity's known consequences.

These were troubled nights in the Curie household. Marie was sleepwalking, perhaps as an aftermath of her continued emotional upheaval over her father's death, which was cruelly acerbated by the injustice she felt had been done Pierre. And, when Marie did not roam the house in her sleep—sometimes even when she did—it was Pierre who could not sleep. Or lay awake moaning with terrible leg pains and dosed himself with the strychnine which the doctor prescribed for his supposed rheumatism. Worried and frightened, Marie would watch helplessly when these attacks occurred. When the pair got up the next morning, Pierre was weak and Marie was exhausted. From the sidelines, old Dr. Curie was a concerned spectator. And what about five-year-old Irène? The house on the Boulevard Kellermann was small and, even though children sleep soundly, she must have heard what was going on or been awakened by her father's crying out. What did she make of it? Was she frightened by her mother turned somnambulist and by her father racked with pain? Her grandfather and her parents must have been hard-pressed to allay her fears.

———— o ————

Not every scientist agreed with Marie's hypothesis that radioactivity was an atomic phenomenon. There were still holdouts with other ideas. But order was beginning to appear in the mass of conflicting theories through the efforts of Ernest Rutherford and Frederick Soddy, a young chemist from Oxford, six years his junior. The two, wrestling with the problem of finding an explanation for radioactivity, worked together for eighteen months at McGill University in one of the more successful and significant scientific collaborations. Soddy's brilliance as a chemist dovetailed nicely with Rutherford's physics background. The Curies, who were in communication with the pair, read and discussed with the greatest interest the development of their theory "Cause and Nature of Radioactivity" when it appeared in the September and November issues of *Philosophical Magazine,* the English-speaking world's prime source for scientific announcements. Rutherford and Soddy, both still in their twenties, discovered that radioelements slowly and spontaneously transmute into other elements—in their case, thorium was changing into helium—and that nothing can be done to stop the process.

The emission of Becquerel's rays, which consisted of the projection at high speed of charged particles, could be compared to an explosion and signaled the breakup of the thorium atom. This confirmed Marie's original thesis that Becquerel's rays were the result of action within the atom and contradicted one of the best-established laws in physics—the immutability of chemical elements. Rutherford and Soddy's disintegration theory, which proved nature was the great alchemist that man had been seeking since the Middle Ages, became the foundation for all future discoveries relevant to the nature and behaviour of the atom. It was the most important contribution to the history of radioactivity since Marie's discovery of the existence of radium.

As was to be the case with so many important milestones in this field, Rutherford had only been able to perform his alpha ray experiments, which clinched their argument, because Marie and Pierre loaned him a radioactive source to work with. At the time, the New Zealander was disappointed that the Curies had not sent him an even more powerful solution. But when he met Marie for the first time the following year, and his attention was inadvertently called to her permanently damaged fingertips, he looked down at his own, still intact, and was thankful they had not. The most direct evidence for the Rutherford-Soddy disintegration and transmutation theory was the continuous production of helium by radium, which Soddy and William Ramsay were to prove at University College, London, the next summer. Transmutation was a reality. Out of one element a totally different one was produced.

That fall, Marie brought her Sèvres class of four home for tea. None of their other teachers had ever done such a thing, and the girls were thrilled to be asked. Giggling nervously as they walked up the Boulevard Kellermann, they wondered what she would be like at home, this small frail woman who filled them with respect and seemed so distant when she lectured to them. They were also looking forward to meeting her daughter. They had talked a lot about Irène among themselves. How did it feel to be the daughter of a famous couple? Whom would she resemble?

A week had passed since Marie had issued her invitation—seven whole days filled with speculation and anticipation—and here the "sèvriennes" were at last at no. 108, ringing the bell on "Madame's" doorstep. Marie smiled when she saw them, dressed in their Sunday best from the tips of their flower-trimmed straw boaters to the toes of their high-buttoned shoes, and ushered them through the little house out to the small yard in back. There Dr. Curie was showing off to Mme. Perrin the last of the fall blooms in the tiny garden that was the old man's pride and joy. It was not so many years since Marie had been a student herself. She could imagine the excitement as well as the uneasiness of her "sèvriennes" at being there, so to make it a less formidable occasion she had thoughtfully included Mme. Perrin, whose husband Jean was another of the girls' favorite professors. Henriette Perrin, who married Jean after the death of her older sister, his fiancée, was a delightful, cultured woman; she and Jacques Curie were the only two people outside the immediate family to ever address Marie by her first name.

But where was Irène, the girls asked politely after a few moments of conversation. Irène was inside, peering at them from the other side of the living room door and she petulantly refused to join them. Finally, one of the girls, Eugénie Feytis, who was already distinguished by a certain budding regal beauty, disappeared to try and coax her to change her mind. When the child at last ventured out, she made a beeline for her mother and hid in her skirts. From that secure vantage post, with her chubby arms tightly encircling Marie's legs, the rosy-cheeked little blonde glared at the intruders. She was not shy but on the defensive, and regarded the girls with stormy uneasiness, as if to ask what they were doing here, usurping Mé's time in Irène's very own house. She refused to let them steal her mother's attention from her and, from time to time, kept repeating in a firm grave voice that reminded the girls of her father: "You must take notice of me."[3] What a telling revelation about the child's loneliness for her mother!

Marie made a great effort to make the girls feel more comfortable, asking each of them personal questions to draw them out so she might get to know them better. At last it was time for tea. Even the little girl was interested in that, and her hostility disappeared as she skipped ahead into the modest dining room. While they drank their tea at the big oval table and nibbled on the *pain au chocolat* and *petits fours,* the girls glanced around with discreet curiosity. It was evident from the sparse furnishings that Marie took no interest in interior decorating, but her warm hospitality endeared her more than ever to her "sèvriennes," Eugénie in particular.

Eugénie was invited to return, alone and often, and became a family favorite—as well as a companion for Irène. Many was the time she curled up in a chair with the child in her lap in GrandPé's bedroom, while the old gentleman recited by heart scores of La Fontaine's fables, and then was bombarded with Irène's questions about the animals in them. How big was the crow? How tall was the heron? If the dinner-table conversation lasted late, Eugénie spent the night, proud to sleep on the bed that Marie had used as a student and that now served as a divan.

The Curies were starting to pay the price for becoming better known. There were certain official engagements that it was impossible to refuse, although these constituted one more drain on their strength. In addition, Marie was preparing, at last, to finish her doctorate: writing her thesis and doing the studying necessary to present it. In January, Pierre wrote an English colleague that Marie was always tired "without being exactly ill."[4] And Marie noted in her methodical way that, since she had started her work on radium, she had lost "15 lbs., 5 oz." Georges Sagnac, a colleague who cared about them both, was shocked at her frailty when he met Marie at a Physics Society meeting, that April; actually her appearance was misleading, for she had the constitution of a dray horse. He knew Pierre well enough to realize that a face-to-face talk would be ineffectual so, instead, when he came home, he sat down and wrote him a ten-page letter.

Sagnac pleaded with them to change before it was too late, pointing out that their regime would damage the most robust constitutions. They hardly ate at all. Marie frequently called two slices of sausage and a swallow of tea lunch. She and Pierre did not give enough time to their meals, taking them at random hours and, in the evening, eating so late that their stomachs, weakened by waiting, finally refused to do any work. Sagnac went on and on in the same vein—even anticipating Marie's responses—in such a scathing, albeit well-intentioned, indictment of their life-style that it is surprising Marie saved his letter:

> *You ought not to use the indifference or stubbornness with which she opposes you as an excuse. I can also see the following objection: "She isn't hungry! And she's big enough to know what she wants to do!"—No,* [Pierre,] *it won't do! She actually behaves like a CHILD.* [sic] . . . *It is necessary not to mix scientific preoccupations into every instant of your life . . . You must sit down in peace before your meals and swallow them slowly . . . You must let your body breath.*

The picture Sagnac paints of little Irène's homelife is poignant. "Don't you love Irène? It seems to me that I wouldn't prefer the idea of reading a paper by Rutherford to getting what my body needs and of looking at such an agreeable little girl. Give her a kiss for me. If she were a bit older, she would think as I do and she would tell you all this. Think of her a little . . ."[5]

Small wonder the child had resented the intrusion of the "sèvriennes" when they came for tea. For all the loving care doting old Dr. Curie lavished on her, GrandPé was not the same as Mé and Pé. This also explains why Irène continued to be so demanding. No one but Mé could undress her at night—when she was home. Then Marie must stay with her, like other parents from time immemorial, talking or reading, no matter how tired she might be, until the six-year-old fell asleep. Should Irène awaken, she would call "Mé! Mé!" in an imperious voice, and nothing would do but for Marie to come and sit alongside her again in the darkness until slumber once more claimed her daughter.

In May, Paul Appell, under whom Pierre presently served at

PCN, tried to persuade Pierre to let himself be proposed for the annual July 14 List of Honors, emphasizing the practical value of the Légion d'Honneur which could greatly facilitate his getting a laboratory and funds for his work. Unlike membership in the Academy, nothing further was required of him, but one rejection was daunting enough. Pierre stubbornly refused, pointing out that it was not a decoration he needed but a laboratory.

That same May Pierre did, however, accept a distinction of a different sort by agreeing to be the speaker at the Royal Institution in London at one of its famous weekly Friday lectures, a series intended to spread an understanding of science to a wide, largely uninitiated audience. Although she was again enceinte, Marie accompanied him, and it was a good thing she did. For that night, as he struggled into his tails, Pierre's hands were so cracked and raw that Marie had to button his vest over his starched shirtfront. This was the same suit he wore for his regular class lectures in the Sorbonne amphitheater and she tried in vain to remove some of its shine. She was still able to fit into the one black gown she had acquired for those functions where dress was obligatory, and which she would have remade throughout the years. Its discreetly scooped-out neck revealed her white shoulders and the stark simplicity of her attire—she did not even possess so much as a wedding band.

Pierre was intimidated by his English surroundings—both by the impressive Georgian building on Albemarle Street, which housed the prestigious Royal Institution, and by the star-studded gala audience awaiting him in its tiered hall. He was warned that he might have a hard time holding everyone's attention, an admonition which naturally did not apply to the monocled British physicists who were considered the finest in the world and were turned out, en masse. Pierre looked decidedly ill when he commenced. He spoke in his usual apologetic fashion and seemed nervous, but his low-pitched voice gradually grew stronger. Speaking slowly, in French, he gave an easy-to-follow exposition of the story of radium, and then set up a simple experiment to show how the hair-thin gold leaves of an electroscope closed when near radium. Later, demonstrating how radioactive rays made an impression on photographic plates wrapped in black cloth, Pierre accidentally spilled some solution. Over fifty years later, a decontamination squad was still able to detect radiation in the hall.

As a woman, Marie could never be invited to present her work at the Royal Institution in her own right and she was there, seated next to the venerable Lord Kelvin, Pierre's sponsor and friend, solely as an auditor. But she was unconcerned about not being on the podium alongside her husband, for Pierre, as always, gave her a full share of the credit. There was also a sprinkling of other women in attendance. For the Royal Institution's statutes encouraged women members, provided "steps were taken to preclude the possibility of any improper Female's name being found among the Subscribers."[6] "Proper" or otherwise, those present were heavily jeweled and, later, Marie and Pierre cynically amused themselves figuring out how many laboratories they could build and equip with the diamond tiaras and other similar doodads on display. Prominent in the front row was Britain's own answer to the French husband-and-wife team of physicists, Professor William Ayrton and his spouse. The brilliant Herta Ayrton, whose father was Polish and who spoke excellent French, had so deeply impressed George Eliot that the latter based the character of the young Jewess, Mirah, in *Daniel Deronda* on her. She entertained the Curies at her home during their stay and would prove a staunch friend to Marie in the years ahead.

The reception accorded the Curies afterward was a triumph, and the guests were touched at the filial respect with which Pierre helped the seventy-nine-year-old Lord Kelvin down the stairs when they left together. At lunch the next day, at His Lordship's Cadogan Place home, the host showed off with obvious satisfaction a small vial of radium salt that Pierre and Marie had brought him as a gift, thereby making Kelvin the first person in England to possess any.

Marie published more reports in the Academy's *Comptes Rendus* during the years 1899–1903, her most creative years scientifically speaking, than any other period of her life. The same May she accompanied Pierre across the Channel, her thesis in manuscript form, "Researches on Radioactive Substances," was approved by her examining committee and ordered to the printer. Containing a summary of her entire work to date on radioactivity, the document that eventually ran through five editions and their revisions ranks as her most outstanding publication and belongs among the classics of science; for it depicts the beginnings of the new field of inquiry that led ultimately to nuclear physics.

On June 25, Marie appeared in the sun-drenched Students' Hall at the Sorbonne to defend it. Old Dr. Curie was there with Pierre and Bronya, who came from Zakopane for the occasion, and Marie had invited a few family friends—Henriette and Jean Perrin and Paul Langevin. She also had seats reserved for her "sèvriennes," and got them excused from class to attend. Marie's examination, like her thesis, was on the entire body of her work and, today, it was Pierre's turn to take a back seat, a proud smile on his face.

Marie had been browbeaten by Bronya into buying a new dress. It was dark gray, not because the color happened to be stylish that season, but because, like black, the color of her other dress, it did not show the soil so she could also wear it in the laboratory. The somber shade emphasized her ash blond hair, which she had recently cropped to require less care. Bronya was more excited than Marie, who was uneasy, as usual, about speaking before a number of people, but calmness personified where the examination itself was concerned. Marie was never modest about her own work. She knew her subject better than her three examiners, a physics and a chemistry professor, and the future Nobel laureate Gabriel Lippmann, her former teacher, mentor, and friend, and replied to their questions with assurance in her characteristically low voice. At the end she was accorded the title of "Doctor of Physical Science—*summa cum laude,*" Professor Lippmann added, with a benevolent smile.

Marie was the first woman to get her doctorate in France, and she had done so with tenacity and determination. She had gotten her degree because she had to, and certainly not to blaze a trail for other women. It was the only way to success in her chosen field.

Following Marie's virtuoso performance, Paul Langevin, the youngest member of Pierre and Marie's small circle of intimates, invited the Curies over for dinner that evening to celebrate. The Langevins had recently moved to no. 29 rue Gazan to be in the same neighborhood as Pierre and Marie—and also to be near the Parc de Montsouris for their children. Also included were the Perrins. Jean Perrin was now in charge of the Sorbonne's laboratory of physical chemistry. Voluble and gay, with arms flailing like windmills when he talked, Perrin had a mischievous penetrating wit, a friendly smile, and a *"Bonjour"* for everyone. Langevin's friendship with Perrin dated from their school days together at the celebrated École Normale, where Paul went after graduating from EPCI, and Perrin subsequently served as witness at Paul's marriage to Jeanne Desfosses.

Like her husband, Jeanne came from a working-class background; she lived with her family above the small grocery store they owned and in which they all worked, and wed Paul when they were both very young. Jeanne did not feel comfortable with Paul's colleagues or their wives, nor they with her, for they had little in common. But she was a good cook and that evening she did herself proud. Dapper Paul, whose crew-cut hair, neatly trimmed mustache, and erect bearing made him look like a cavalry officer in mufti—a comparison he would perversely cultivate, for his politics were far left—did not have much money and with two children to provide for, his purse was always pinched. But he was fussy about food and drink, so the wines were well chosen and he saw that they flowed freely.

Pierre and Marie thoroughly enjoyed two last-minute guests, Ernest Rutherford and his young bride, who happened to be passing through Paris. The Curies had more than once exchanged correspondence and scientific courtesies with the big, powerfully built New Zealander, but this was the first time they met. Rutherford, a brash, exuberant man with extraordinary drive, very blue eyes, a ruddy complexion, and an untidy mustache, knew Paul—who had been the first foreigner to work at the Cavendish—when they both held research scholarships there. They had remained in contact ever since, although Paul is reputed to have remarked: "One can hardly speak of being friendly with a force of nature."[7]

Before the eight got up from the table, Rutherford announced in his loud, booming voice that he considered Paul "a thundering good fellow," a description he reserved for his intimates, and he took to the "Madame"—as he would always refer to Marie—at once. That evening witnessed the start of a lifelong friendship with the prickly, reserved Polish-French woman, four years his senior, that was unique in both their lives. He liked Marie's simplicity and no-nonsense way of dressing. And it was precisely because she did not pose a sexual threat that he was attracted to her. Similarly, his own honesty and enthusiasm struck a responsive chord in her. Marie knew he treated women as equals in his laboratory and that he was one of the few contemporary scientists to encourage them to pursue scientific careers.

Two months before, in May, Rutherford and Frederick Soddy published their enlarged and completed disintegration theory—an interpretation of the process which causes the phenomenon of natural radioactivity. It concurred with Marie's contention that this manifestation of the natural laws of matter was an atomic function. Rutherford and Soddy's revolutionary hypothesis of transmutation answered the fundamental questions posed by the Curies' experiments. Although Rutherford privately felt that the Curies were limited because they themselves never put forward any theory about the phenomenon, the group talked shop amicably and animatedly. Rutherford shouted out, "By thunder!" ferociously and banged his fist down on the table so hard that droplets of wine from the glasses Paul was forever refilling polka-dotted the white tablecloth. Marie was intent and tenacious when her ideas were questioned, and later, Pierre, in his low grave voice gave a penetrating exposition of a delicate series of experiments, which he had recently performed with a new colleague Albert Laborde, on the tremendous amounts of heat released by radium salts. One of the Curies' earliest observations had been that radium spontaneously gave off sufficient heat to be measured with relative ease. It was a natural source of power during its entire existence, even sitting untouched in a container on a laboratory shelf. A gram of radium generated about one hundred calories of heat an hour, enough to melt its weight in ice, and could give off as much heat as the combustion of three hundred kilograms of coal. While Pierre and Marie were aware of the heat radium was giving off, they had never realized that transmutation was occurring.

At one point during the evening Rutherford turned to Marie and commented that radioactivity was "a splendid subject to work on, really."[8] Marie was one of a handful who could appreciate what he meant, and she never forgot his words. Since it was warm, the group adjourned to the garden shortly before midnight. There Pierre, who always took naive delight in the wonders of nature, pulled out of his pocket a tube, coated in part with zinc sulphide, that contained radium in solution. "Look!" he exclaimed with boyish glee as the coating fluoresced white, making the radium's ejection of rays clearly visible in the summer darkness. "Here is the light of the future!" "Oh, Pierre!" Marie admonished him softly for such an uncharacteristic prediction.[9] And Rutherford, who was sitting next to them, could see Pierre rest his hand, painfully swollen with radiation burns, on top of hers in secret communion.

Marie herself was filled with a different kind of glow. The mysterious light was tangible evidence of the fulfillment of the deepest of her desires. She had achieved her goal and, in doing so, she had detected the presence of a new element and found it. She was indeed a doctor of science, *summa cum laude*—an amazing, brilliant woman, whose doggedness and stubbornness had overcome enormous handicaps.

But she was never the genius that Pierre was.

VII
1903–1904

A Member of the Establishment at Last

THOUGH THE CURIES BE-
grudged taking time from their research, an August vacation was a
sacrosanct institution for every Frenchman—even Pierre—and, at
Marie's request, Eugénie, her young "sèvrienne" friend, found a
place for them at St.-Trojan on the Île d'Oléron, in her native
district of Saintonge. Although Marie felt no better with this pregnancy than when carrying Irène, she was a firm believer in physical
exercise as the best antidote for everything. So she bicycled all over
the Île, and was crushed when she suffered a miscarriage.

A recent English biographer contends that more was involved in this tragedy than overfatigue and overexertion and, in an ingenious study, he claims that Marie was exposing herself to as high as 1 rem, the unit for measuring ionizing radiation, per week. Today, a dosage of more than 0.03 rem per week is considered dangerous for expectant mothers working in the radium industry. Since the infant only survived a few hours, there is no way of telling whether she had suffered any of radiation's fetal effects. By the end of the year, all the worst symptoms of radiation-induced ill health, if not sickness, were evident in both Marie and Pierre, but undetected by contemporary doctors. However, when Ève was born, a few years later, she was a perfectly normal, healthy baby, and she is still alive, full of vim, vigor, and charm—and none the worse for any rays she might have been subjected to before birth.

Marie was bitterly disappointed at her loss, for she had badly wanted this second child, and she was still in bed when Eugénie arrived, as planned. Afraid she might be in the way under the altered circumstances, the girl offered to leave, but Pierre begged her not to because he felt her presence would distract his wife. Marie was equally insistent that Eugénie stay to keep Irène company, especially now that she herself was laid up. In the afternoon, to encourage Pierre, whose legs sometimes trembled so that he could not leave bed, to go out for a few hours and get some exercise, Marie resorted to the subterfuge of asking him to teach Eugénie how to ride a bicycle.

Foreign mines other than the St. Joachimsthal in Bohemia were beginning to supply uranium ore, but Paris was to remain its refining center. Research on pure radium was restricted because of the element's scarcity, and it was still only available from the Curies. But for medical reasons, it was now important to manufacture certain radium preparations that doctors were starting to use as therapeutic agents on an industrial scale. In response to this demand that would soon make radium more costly than gold, the fledgling radium industry was expanding greatly.

From the start, Pierre and Marie adopted a policy of answering personally, and without reserve, any professional inquiries they received concerning their work. To do so, however, amounted to more and more of a chore, for the mail kept accumulating in a geometric progression as their detailed *Comptes Rendus* increased. In keeping with the traditional, contemporary approach to pure science and acquired knowledge, which dictated that a scientist's duty was to learn, explore, and publish without thought of profit but simply to benefit mankind, Marie and Pierre felt it unworthy to do otherwise. They were also generous in loaning samples of their precious radioactive salts to qualified people and, to date, nothing had been done to protect the detailed process and special techniques they had developed for purifying pitchblende and isolating radium.

A letter from a group of engineers in Buffalo, New York, with a sheet of specific questions about these matters, brought the issue to a head. The potential worldwide royalties in question, if Pierre and Marie did not wish to consider them as Irène's birthright, could guarantee the Curies a laboratory to exceed their wildest dreams and finance their future work for years to come. At first glance, their decision to maintain the status quo might seem in contradiction with Pierre's previous inconsistent stance regarding certain minor patents before his marriage. Now a basic discovery of science was in question and such fundamentals, Marie and Pierre agreed, should always remain free and available. So, the next Sunday, when the pair sat down to try and make a dent in the mountain of mail that spilled from their worktable into a wicker basket on the floor alongside, the first letter they wrote went to Buffalo with the detailed answers the American engineers desired.

Irène started school that fall. There was nothing in the neighborhood to satisfy her parents, who were understandably fussy about her education, so the six-year-old entered the one on the rue Cassini, near the Observatory. This was some distance away but not so far that Marie could not occasionally walk Irène there en route to the rue Lhomond. Sometimes, when she was unable to do so, she managed to catch a glimpse of the girl in the afternoon in the Parc de Montsouris, where GrandPé or the nurse took her daily to play. And when Eugénie Feytis, who was now on the best of terms with Irène, came to the Boulevard Kellermann on a Sunday afternoon, along with the Curies' circle of promising young scientists—Debierne, Langevin, Sagnac, Cotton, Urbain, and Jean Perrin and his wife—she always allowed plenty of time to play with her small friend.

In mid-November, lightning struck. Pierre and Marie received a telegram from Professor C. Aurivillius, the perpetual secretary of the Royal Swedish Academy, advising them that they and Henri Becquerel had been jointly awarded the Nobel Prize for Physics for their work on radioactivity. By involving the Swedish Royal Academy and the Royal Family in its selection and presentation, the newly established Nobel Foundation assured its laureates of worldwide prestige second to none.

The news catapulted Marie and Pierre from celebrity status to international glory and changed their lives dramatically. Earlier, radium had been the star because of its seemingly miraculous results with cancer. Now the full glare of the spotlight shone on its discoverers. The Curies became the first scientists after Roentgen to experience popular acclaim and publicity on so vast a scale.

Marie and Pierre's lives now entered a more difficult period than the preceding one, which had been characterized by overwork, inadequate professional quarters, and financial worries. Photographers and journalists from the world press took up their trail, hounding them everywhere, dogging their footsteps until they had to delegate an assistant to do nothing but sit at the door of their EPCI laboratory and keep the world at bay so they might get some work done. Marie termed their notoriety and the world's continued infatuation with radium "a disaster." In a letter to his long-standing friend Georges Gouy, who was presently teaching physics in Lyons, Pierre complains about the invasion of privacy "in the magnificent establishment in the rue Lhomond"—still another sarcastic jibe about his woefully inadequate facilities.[1]

One day, when the press descended on the Boulevard Kellermann and found that Marie and Pierre and even GrandPé were out, one of the more enterprising reporters pestered Irène and her Polish nurse with questions. The latter froze and fled to the kitchen, pleading that she did not understand French. Undaunted, he turned to Irène and asked where her parents were. "At the laboratory," the girl replied self-assuredly, staring at him with a hostile glare that said, "How stupid, where else would they be?" She ignored any further inquiries and resumed playing with Dido, her black-and-white cat. The following day, a picture of Irène and Dido made the front page of the Paris papers—as did the conversation with the child and her nurse. This onslaught was a disaster for the retiring Curies, not to mention a waste of valuable time, as was the daily mail, which swelled to a tidal wave threatening to engulf them, and even included an American's request to name his racehorse "Marie."

To go to Stockholm for the Nobel ceremonies in December took forty-eight hours by train and was too long a trip not to stay a few extra days. Unfortunately, Pierre and Marie's teaching schedules made any extended absence out of the question. Nor was their health up to travel at the moment, so Becquerel went without them, and the Curies' gold medals were received in their name by the French Minister Marchand. If there had been any lingering doubt in anyone's mind, none remained. Marie belonged on anyone's list of the world's greatest contemporary scientists, and there was no other woman scientist of equal repute in the world.

The half of the prize money they received, 70,000 francs, together with the 60,000 francs Marie was shortly awarded when the Daniel Osiris Prize was split between her and physicist Édouard Branly, removed the Curies from any further financial problems. They dispensed a small amount: a loan to Casimir and Bronya for their sanatorium; another, to Pierre's brother, Jacques; a few gifts.

Marie, being Marie, did not even buy a new hat, but she did re-paper a room, and her single indulgence was to install a modern bathroom in their home. Only one Paris house in ten had yet been connected to the city's central sewer system and, as late as 1906, two French lodgings out of three still had no lavatory. The rest of the money was prudently placed in French investments and in bonds of the city of Warsaw.

Before January was out, Émile Loubet, the President of the French Republic, and M. Chaumié, the Minister of Public Instruc-tion, visited the rue Lhomond, and Pierre had to stop work in order to deliver a brief lecture and demonstrate several experiments for them. Shortly afterward an invitation, which was tantamount to a command performance, appeared from President Loubet. Pierre, who was not in the habit of accepting invitations or developing relations with anyone who did not interest him, could not very well refuse. The evening they were at the Elysée, a woman appeared at Marie's elbow and asked if she wished to meet the Queen of Greece. Marie instinctively shook her head. Then she recognized Mme. Loubet. Good manners superseded inclination, and she ac-quiesced politely: "Of course."

The Curies' days of anonymity were over. Pierre was less resil-ient to change than his wife and had a horror of appearing in the public eye. Marie, on the other hand, had arrived in the spotlight's glare as the result of a conscious act. Once she made up her mind to succeed in science, she had to prove herself superior to be recog-nized as an equal and, consequently, she was in no position to decline honors the way Pierre did. Nor, psychologically speaking, was she so inclined. For Marie, who had once written her brother Jozio how much she wanted to be "somebody," was not insensitive to distinctions. But she respected and loved Pierre too much not to pattern her behavior after his. Unfortunately, she never outgrew an almost pathological reaction to crowds—a real handicap for some-one in her present situation. And, as her classes grew larger, she had to steel herself to face them, each time they met. But she could not have it both ways. To be well known pleased her; to be recognized terrified her. Eventually she learned to cope with this basic timidity, and when strangers approached and asked, "Aren't you Mme. Curie?", she was able to dominate a small spasm of fear and reply, impassively, like an actress, "No. You are mistaken." To spare herself similar encounters, as she traveled more she took an assumed name.

With the Curies' increased income, Pierre hired a laboratory assistant whom he paid out of his own pocket and Marie procured extra household help. She no longer needed to teach at Sèvres, but she elected to remain. She loved her students, and the money she earned was her only personal income and gave her a feeling of independence.

When Armet de Lisle, a philanthropic industrialist, installed the first French plant to manufacture radium at Nogent-sur-Marne (which employed, like the rest of the burgeoning, worldwide radium industry, the Curies' basic techniques), he offered to build them a small adjacent building according to their specifications, and pay all its operating expenses. Since Pierre and Marie's previous trial run of the first stages of extraction at the Central Society of Chemical Products, under Debierne, had been so successful, they jumped at his offer. Now that they had a place to handle larger quantities of pitchblende than before, Pierre made a deal with the Austrian government to buy twenty-five hundred kilos of the ore at the rock-bottom price of one crown a kilo.

With their financial situation happily altered, Marie and Pierre occasionally went to a concert or the theater. Pierre did so largely to please Marie; these were her interests dating back to her Warsaw days, not his. For a treat, they took Eugénie Feytis with them to see Gorki's *The Lower Depths,* starring the great Italian actress Eleonora Duse, who had come expressly from Italy for the lead. Marie loved this type of play, and Voltairean GrandPé gently mocked her choice when she came home, emotionally spent, afterward. It was a euphemism, he declared, to call any outing that left her so drained a distraction.

Tolstoy and Ibsen were the new gods of the Paris intelligentsia, and *The Wild Duck* and *Ghosts* were to have a profound influence in France. The avant-garde wanted to live life according to Ibsen's formula. His plays and other Northern literature which dealt with revolt from tyranny, in general, and were concerned, more specifically, with women rebelling against the yoke of men, exercised considerable influence on those changes mushrooming in contemporary French society, which were going to produce phenomena like the emancipated female.

During one intermission, Pierre and Marie bumped into Marguerite and Émile Borel in the foyer of the Théâtre de l'Oeuvre, where Lugné Poë was mounting Ibsen's dramas. For a couple who did not like to be recognized, Pierre, in his old, misshapen, rumpled overcoat and Marie, in a somber dress with a practical loden cape carelessly slung over one shoulder, stood out in the dressy crowd, bedecked with the haute couture's latest whimsies and furbelows. Marguerite, the twenty-one-year-old daughter of Paul Appell, dean of the Faculty of Sciences at the Sorbonne and Marie's former teacher and Sèvres colleague, had recently wed the brilliant older mathematician Borel, a commanding figure of a man with a massive head accentuated by a bushy black beard. The vivacious bride's bubbling enthusiasm for the evening's performance was so contagious that it transported Marie back to her Floating University days. In an unheard-of, spontaneous gesture, she threw her arms around the startled young woman and hugged her. "You remind me of the students of my youth. You're carried away like they were—like I was—in that far-off day."[2] That Marie, who was so intimidating and intolerant of the least attempt at familiarity, should behave this impetuously made an unforgettable impression on Marguerite, who recalled the incident, six decades later, when she was writing her memoirs. The Borels held open house for a group of some thirty "normaliens"—graduates of the elite École Normale, like her husband—who met one night weekly, alternating between the Borels' and Perrins'. The men often came directly from their laboratories, but dapper Perrin always managed to find time to don his dashing red velvet vest. The atmosphere seethed with intellectual ideas, research projects, and various, here-today/gone-tomorrow enthusiasms—not to mention practical jokes—as the group gathered around the blazing fire with bottles of beer and dry cakes. Few women were ever there, except Henriette Perrin and Marguerite; Mme. Langevin never appeared. Occasionally, especially when the group met at the Perrins', Marie and Pierre would glide in with what Marguerite described as "conspicuous unobtrusiveness" and find a protected nook from which to watch and listen. Marie, who was basically only at ease in intimate groups, occasionally entered abruptly into a scientific argument, exposing her views at length and with great conviction. Pierre was more apt to be silent and, if there was nothing in the conversation worthy of his attention, he would become lost in his thoughts.

The New York *American*, on March 20, 1904, writing about the exploits of Loïe Fuller, the American girl who descended upon Paris like a denizen from outer space, noted that this new star of the Folies-Bergère had created a "number of radium dances" in which she resembled monstrous moths, using "efflorescent salts" of radium. Unfortunately, this story comes under the heading of wishful thinking. Loïe had arrived in Paris with Buffalo Bill's *Wild West Show.* Perpetually on the lookout for something different and startling, she later made the world aware that dancing was more than trick steps and a pretty smile by capitalizing on the Europeans' excitement about new art forms, and skillfully employing the curving lines and spirals of Art Nouveau, then at its peak, in her choreography. Her dances at the Folies—the Fire Dance, the Lily Dance, the Butterfly Dance—were like nothing the jaded Continent had ever seen. She perfected a number of motions to make yards of silk swirl and, because she was gifted with a scientific turn of mind, she was the first dancer to light herself from beneath the stage with frosted glass panels, using secret chemical dyes to produce shimmering, mother-of-pearl, rainbow hues.

Having read that radium was luminous, Loïe dreamt up a sensational new costume and wrote the Curies for help in creating it. The American's naive letter so amused Pierre and Marie that they took the trouble to write and explain why her dream of radium butterfly wings was an impossibility. Appreciative that the celebrated pair had taken the time to reply at length, Loïe volunteered to give a private show for them and their friends. Marie included the Perrins, but where the select performance occurred is not known. Marie admired Loïe as a liberated woman, like herself, and an unexpected friendship blossomed between her and the brash, cheerful American; Loïe later took Marie to visit the studio of one of her admirers, the sculptor Rodin, and to other interesting places where Marie would never have ventured otherwise.

Pierre complained to his friend Georges Gouy of the many days now when he and Marie were almost too busy to breathe. Young Irène had difficulty adjusting to the new state of affairs. She did not welcome the fact that her parents went out at night more frequently, and she had a hard time recognizing Mé, in her evening dress, when she left for an official reception. The whiteness of Marie's bare shoulders and arms made her fine ash blond hair even fairer, her deep gray eyes bigger, and she seemed more beautiful than ever in her daughter's delighted eyes.

Nowadays, Eugénie came out more frequently. Sometimes she took Irène to Sèvres, where the girl wanted to see her friend's room. She also wanted to visit Mé's lecture hall and laboratory and insisted on locating in the park the sites of the different pictures the "sèvriennes" were always taking of their favorite teacher. Irène had come to realize that she must share her beloved Mé with these other big girls, and it helped to be able to visualize the settings where her mother spent her time when she was at Sèvres. Irène was equally interested in the school's Natural History Museum and was fascinated by the size of a mammoth's tooth on display there.

She asked gravely—she always spoke gravely, this small girl, as if she had never had a childhood—"Eugénie, have you seen a mammoth?"—"No. The beast lived a long time ago." Anxious for an eyewitness account of the behemoth, Irène thought a moment. "Very well. I shall ask GrandPé."[3] He was surely old enough to have seen the creature.

A serious, reserved child, Irène was not used to demonstrable affection. Marie had not been brought up with any, and consequently felt no need for it with her own offspring. So it was no wonder that the girl did not enjoy being hugged and kissed by her mother's pupils, who always made a big fuss over her whenever they saw her. Irène was never truly sociable, except with an intimate few, even in later life.

Old Dr. Curie did his best to save his son and daughter-in-law from well-meaning strangers, the press, and other importunate intruders in order to conserve their strength, especially Marie's. She was pregnant for a third time and very anxious not to lose this baby. While her idea of taking care of herself was not everyone else's, she did use an ounce of caution, for once, and wisely decided not to accompany Pierre to Stockholm that summer; he was scheduled to make the Nobel speech expected of each laureate which the Curies had been forced to postpone. At the last minute, Pierre had to cancel out a second time because a violent attack of rheumatism confined him to bed.

Interestingly, Pierre's last publication—except for one posthumous one—which was written in collaboration with Doctors C. Bouchard and V. Balthazard and appeared that year, was on the effects of radioactive emanations on mice and guinea pigs. The report presented irrefutable evidence of the deadly effects of radon but, apparently, neither Pierre nor Marie saw any reason to connect the trio's laboratory results with what was happening to themselves. The following year Pierre discovered in further experiments with guinea pigs that lead was an effective screen against direct radioactive rays, and he and Marie insisted that the staff shield themselves when working with them. This was the sole precautionary measure taken in the Curie Institute as late as 1924, and one which Marie herself routinely disregarded. She, like Pierre, shrugged off any health risks they might be running as vocational hazards. Perhaps they subconsciously thought, "It can't happen to us." To this day, Pierre's only grandson and granddaughter, both distinguished scientists, can offer no positive reasons for the many bewildering ailments from which Pierre suffered. His own father, Dr. Curie, never identified them positively, and no contemporary medical diagnoses are available.

To give Irène the fresh air that she deemed essential for good health, Marie once more rented a little house she had found, several years before, at St.-Rémy-les-Chevreuse. The pair commuted daily to Paris and, whenever they did not have a class, they worked quietly in the countryside, for they were no longer strong enough to put in the long hours of an earlier day at the laboratory. Here, on Sundays, they greeted with their usual simplicity and cordiality a handful of intimates who were grateful for a chance to flee the escalating temperature in the capital. Jean Perrin always arrived with a bouquet of flowers so, he teased, Marie would not forget she was a woman. Eugénie came out often and whenever she missed a day or two, she received a peremptory note from Irène informing her that she was expected without fail the following weekend. Under the shade trees, bold hypotheses about recent discoveries and developments in the Curie laboratory were batted to and fro like shuttlecocks while Marie sat stitching away on baby clothes or a dress for Irène. And Henriette Perrin sat off in a corner making up stories to amuse Irène and her own children about the "World of the Infinitely Small" which, not surprisingly, dealt with molecules and atoms. Years later, when Eugénie heard Marie say: "What I wish for all those I love is a simple family life and work that interests them,"[4] she would hark back to those peaceful Sunday afternoons at St.-Rémy.

Marie's letters to Warsaw reflected her continued, justified resentment that the Sorbonne still did not have a post for Pierre. This anomaly finally aroused public opinion and when Liard was appointed rector of the University of Paris, he asked the Chambre des Députés to create a special physics chair for him there. This was done. But, to Liard's consternation, Pierre declined the appointment, politely pointing out that the new chair would still not furnish him with a properly equipped laboratory. Pierre was adamant. When the Chambre finally appropriated 150,000 francs to construct a modest laboratory in the PCN courtyard, he accepted, with the understanding that he continue to use his existing quarters until the proposed unit was ready. The addition, when finally built, would give Pierre a small increase in space and meant he could also take on a few research students. But it was still a far cry from the laboratory of his dreams and lacked many essentials because some of the funds now earmarked for instruments were needed to help offset increased construction costs. All Pierre's lectures were henceforth to be held in the Sorbonne amphitheater, but he was given considerable latitude where subject matter was concerned. That meant he could return to his first love and devote part of his lectures to a study of the laws of symmetry and crystallography. With these details hammered out, on October 1, 1904, in time for the upcoming school year, Pierre was officially named professor of physics of the Faculty of Sciences of the University of Paris—a member of the establishment, at last.

This belated recognition was unexpectedly sweetened for them both when the government also gave Pierre funds for three paid workers, an assistant, a lab boy, and a laboratory chief, who, they stipulated, was to be Marie. Finally she had an official title authorizing her to work in Pierre's laboratory, and she was to receive her first pay for research.

VIII
1904–1906

Catastrophe

BY NOVEMBER, MARIE, whose pregnancies were always difficult, temporarily gave up teaching at Sèvres, and that jolly pillar of strength, her sister Bronya, arrived in Paris to be on hand to greet the new arrival. On December 6, 1904, Ève Denise was delivered at no. 108 Boulevard Kellermann by Dr. Curie, after a painful labor. She was a perfectly formed little girl but Irène, who promptly inspected her new sister, was quick to point out that the infant's dark hair and blue eyes did not resemble her own green-brown ones and lighter hair in the slightest. Marie, who had been so despondent over her previous miscarriage, was delighted to have another daughter. She had wanted a second child badly.

Marie's children and household now kept her at home in the morning, although she engaged a charwoman to do the heavy work and a maid to prepare and serve the meals. The new arrival, as was to be expected, absorbed the lion's share of her time, an arrangement which did not suit Irène. Like many firstborn children faced with adjusting to a little sister, she turned despotic and jealous. Baby Ève was equally demanding. She required very little sleep and protested vigorously if she was left in the crib. Because Marie was no stoic, as she confessed to her brother Jozio, she picked Ève up and carried her until she quieted down.

Fortunately, Irène's attention was soon distracted from the baby, for, at the Curies' suggestion, the Perrins moved in next door at no. 106 Boulevard Kellermann with six-year-old Aline and four-year-old Francis. Whereupon Irène, who knew Aline well, was at the Perrins' as much or more than she was at home. A rose-covered fence separated the two homes and, when the two girls were not in the same house together, they were on either side of the trellis, exchanging secrets, toys, even grubby, slightly soiled bits of chocolate.

In early June, the Curies went to Stockholm, for Pierre to give their twice-postponed Nobel lecture at the Swedish Academy of Science, which custom dictated should be an explanation of the laureates' work that had earned them the prestigious prize. As usual, he spoke for the two of them. Even though the past eighteen months had been difficult and scientifically unproductive for Pierre, the depressed, drained man refused to let pessimism color his point of view. His terminating remarks were prescient, and Marie attached sufficient importance to them to place them at the beginning of the short biography she wrote of him after his death:

> *One can imagine that in criminal hands radium could become very dangerous, and here one must ask oneself if humanity gains*

anything by learning the secrets of nature, if humanity is ready to profit from this or whether such knowledge may not be destructive for it. The example of the discoveries of Nobel is characteristic. The powerful explosives have enabled man to undertake some admirable works. They are also a terrible means of destruction in the hands of great criminals who drag people towards war. I am one of those who think, like Nobel, that humanity will draw more good than evil from new discoveries.[1]

Pierre and Marie's work on radioactivity constituted a vital link in the chain of scientific evolution which would lead to a crossroads similar to the one that had confronted Nobel's discovery. Just as Marie's revolutionary hypothesis that radioactivity was an atomic phenomenon had opened up the world of the atom, that same year they were in Sweden, Albert Einstein, a lowly clerk in a customs office in Switzerland, forged another part of the chain when he published his "Special Theory of Relativity" in *Annalen der Physik*. One year later, as a by-product, Einstein produced his famous equation, $E = mc^2$. "Energy = mass $\times$ the speed of light, squared" heralded the atomic age and, by providing the key to the tremendous energy locked in the atom, shortened the distance to another fork in the path of destiny. There, mankind would again be confronted with a choice, for better or worse, as Pierre had foreseen in Stockholm—for nuclear reactors capable of furnishing untold amounts of energy for the world or for the atomic bomb. And Hiroshima and Nagasaki.

In July, Pierre was elected to the physics section of the Academy of Sciences. It was surprising that Pierre, who was so obdurate when it came to the acceptance of honors, consented to pose his candidacy again. But Éleuthère Mascart, who had masterminded his unsuccessful previous attempt, insisted that this time Pierre's nomination was a foregone conclusion. Because this was a repeat performance, Mascart emphasized that, while making the required calls, Pierre could simply leave a visiting card with one corner turned down and initialed "V.P.C."—*visite par carte*— if nobody was at home, instead of having to return as before.

It is hard to believe that Marie was not the dominant factor in his decision to try again. More practical than he, she was keenly aware that as an academician, Pierre would possess far more leverage for government support for his research. Mansart's claims notwithstanding, he only won after a nerve-shattering second ballot. The narrow eight-vote margin by which he beat his opponent, Gernez, was certainly attributable, in part, to Pierre's ill-disguised contempt for the preliminaries, an attitude which prompted Henri Poincaré, the most brilliant mathematician of the day, to comment: "He rose to glory with the spirit of a whipped dog."[2] Marie took great satisfaction from his victory although Pierre obviously did not. For he confided to Georges Gouy, a short time later, that he found attendance "under the Coupole"—as the establishment referred to its weekly sessions—no more to his liking than he had anticipated, and he "still had not yet discovered what is the use of the Academy."[3]

Paris resembled a work yard in whatever direction one looked. Construction was going on everywhere, and the Métro, which had opened its first line in 1899, was having one of its main entrances in front of the Opéra completed. It was hard to get around, but Marie persuaded Pierre to accompany her to the Salon d'Automne, the shrine of modern painting. They were also observed at the Grand Palais; two silent figures, contemplating *The Thinker,* the latest work of the sculptor Rodin. They even went to the Colonne to hear Bronya and Casimir's friend Paderewski, now one of the world's most famous pianists. Rare as these extracurricular outings were, one wonders if Pierre truly enjoyed them. Or if he was as happy as Marie. In November, he wrote Gouy: "I am neither very well nor very ill. But I get tired easily and I no longer have more than a very feeble capacity for work."[4]

The Curies were still deeply in love. However, as their intimates were well aware, they were under a great strain due to their new celebrity status and Pierre's wretched health, which was far worse than Marie's. Marie accepted life and adapted to it. Pierre never could. She had gotten satisfaction and pride of accomplishment from winning the Nobel, while Pierre was forced to abandon the ivory tower most suited to him. Perhaps Marie had lost some of the gayer aspects of her character by the time she received her doctorate, as Sagnac inferred in his famous letter of reproach. By now, however, two years later, she was leading a more rounded existence that was a throwback to her positivist days, when she had varied interests, rather than the purely intellectual life that was unquestionably Pierre's preference. If there was any stress in their relationship, old Dr. Curie was in the best position to know. And he never talked.

With Pierre in so sorry a physical state, off and on, over so long a period, a biographer must also wonder what happened to that side of their marriage. For Marie was still a flesh-and-blood woman—and just thirty-eight. But this was only the turn of the twentieth century and people, in general, took a different approach to such matters. As to the contemporary rumor, still echoed today in certain academic milieus, that Pierre committed suicide, there seems to be no basis whatsoever—unless the handful of his correspondence with Gouy that still remains under seal may someday throw a different light on the matter.

By the beginning of 1906, the small courtyard annex being built for Pierre at PCN was finished, and he and Marie moved any remaining work and equipment from the hangar on the rue Lhomond to the rue Cuvier. This severed their last ties with EPCI, where Pierre had ceased teaching the previous year. On his recommendation, Paul Langevin was eventually appointed to succeed him there.

It was a wet spring. On March 4, the Seine was so high that Parisians came to gape at the western tip of the Vert Galant's garden awash in its muddy waters. But, by April, the weather had turned lovely, and for the long Easter weekend, Pierre and Marie took the two children out to the little cottage at St.-Rémy-les-

Chevreuse. Early each morning they trooped down the narrow country lane to the neighboring farm to get fresh milk. Pierre laughed to see fourteen-month-old Ève tottering along behind in the dried cart tracks. Easter morning they could hear the church bells of the old abbey of Port-Royal ringing in the nearby woods as they set out for their daily walk with Ève perched contentedly on her father's shoulders. It was hot, so Irène stripped off her jumper and started chasing butterflies—a comical figure attired in a mismatched girl's undershirt and boy's underpants with a long green-handled net in one hand bigger than she was. On the way back Pierre, who never tired of demonstrating the marvels of nature and their symmetry to his elder daughter, pointed out the delicate matching designs on the wings of the butterfly she had captured. The next day, Monday, the quartet picked periwinkles and buttercups in the swamp. Then, after a quick dinner, Pierre caught a train back to Paris, carrying the flowers with him to put in the vase on their worktable.

Wednesday evening, Marie returned with the two girls. Irène fussed about leaving because the weather was so pleasant but her mother had to be back for a meeting of the Society of Physics. After dropping the girls off at home, in GrandPé's charge, she joined Pierre at the laboratory. Together they went to Foyot's, where the society traditionally held its annual reunion and dinner. The weather had changed once more. It was drizzling but later Marie and Pierre walked home, arm in arm.

On Thursday, April 19, it was raining, dark, and gloomy. Pierre had a busy schedule and rushed off while Marie was upstairs dressing the girls. She had a number of errands to attend to but planned to be home again at noon while Pierre was to have lunch with a number of his colleagues at a restaurant, the Hôtel des Sociétés Savantes on the rue Danton. This was the kind of gathering he enjoyed, where the professors talked nothing but science. The rain was beating against the windowpanes when he left, so he unfurled his big black umbrella as he headed toward the Seine. He was due at the Academy, on the Quai Conti, but was stopping first at his editor, Gauthier-Villars, to correct proof on an article. He found the door closed because the workers in the printing shop were on strike, a forerunner of the great wave of labor disturbances to come in May. So he continued on his way, turning into the rue Dauphine to reach the Seine. The street, like others in that old section of Paris, was not wide, and it was cluttered at that hour, so Pierre followed in the wake of a fiacre ambling toward the Pont Neuf. There was the usual amount of traffic at the intersection of the quais with the bridge. A heavy, horse-drawn dray with a load of military uniforms clattered across the river, and its pair of horses broke into a trot coming down the narrow rue Dauphine, head-on toward Pierre—but on the opposite side of the street.

Suddenly Pierre decided to cross over. Absentmindedly, without looking to the right or left, he stepped out from behind the fiacre, which obstructed his view, and ran right into one of the cumbersome cart's two Percherons, who were then passing abreast of the cab. Surprised—and hindered by his unwieldy umbrella—Pierre clumsily tried to grab hold of the animal's harness as it whinnied and reared in fright at this unexpected apparition. Losing his footing on the slippery, wet cobblestones, Pierre fell to the ground. Stunned but unharmed, he lay there speechless, not moving a muscle as the horse's hooves and then the front wheel of the wagon miraculously missed him. But the momentum created by the vehicle's enormous weight prevented it from stopping immediately even though the carter reined in, with all his might, and braked frantically. The iron-rimmed, left rear wheel crushed the top of Pierre's skull—smashing it into fifteen or twenty tiny pieces, according to the testimony of horrified onlookers. Death was instantaneous.

A crowd gathered. Some started to berate the thirty-one-year-old driver, Louis Manin, who was in a state of shock. While his excited horses chomped, foaming at the bit, others spoke out in his defense and a fight was about to start when the police arrived and intervened. Someone hailed a taxi to take Pierre's poor battered remains away. But the cabbie refused. He did not want to soil his seats with a bloody, muddy corpse. Finally a stretcher-bearer was summoned and took the body to the nearest police station, on the rue des Grands Augustins. In a vest pocket, a gendarme found one of Pierre's visiting cards and called the Faculty of Sciences. When his laboratory assistant P. Clerc arrived, the old man burst into sobs at the sight of the gaping wound in the back of Pierre's head, which the doctor hastily covered with a bandage. But Pierre's face, which someone wiped clean, was intact, so he had no trouble identifying him. The police commissioner promptly notified the Minister of the Interior.

Old Dr. Curie was dozing upstairs when a representative of the President of the Republic rang the doorbell and left when he learned Marie was not in. Soon after, Jean Perrin and Dean Appell arrived. Dr. Curie was astonished to see them there at that hour. One glance at their stricken faces told him why they had come. "My son is dead." Nodding sadly, they related what had happened. "What was he dreaming of this time?" the old man murmured.[5]

Marie returned late. Perrin and Appell were waiting for her with Dr. Curie, and they immediately told her what had occurred. There was a long silence. "Pierre is dead?"[6] Are you sure? There was another long silence. Did she want an autopsy? "No." Did she want Pierre's body brought home? "Yes." As they talked, Marie noticed, with the attention to irrelevant detail common in moments of great stress, that the buttercups and periwinkles the four of them had picked the previous weekend were still fresh.

She went next door to tell Irène that Pé had been in a bad accident and would need a lot of quiet, and she asked Henriette Perrin to keep the girl there with Aline for the next few days. Like other nine-year-olds, Irène returned to her play without more ado. Marie cabled Warsaw. It had stopped raining and she sat down in the garden, unmindful of the wet seat and the dripping trees, to await Pierre. A police commissioner came with his keys, wallet, and watch and, at last, Debierne arrived in an ambulance with Pierre's body. Marie ordered him laid out in a room on the ground floor, joined him, and closed the door behind her.

During the next hours and into the early evening, callers never stopped coming, beginning with the President of the Republic and the president of the council. Within hours of the time he received word of the catastrophe, Lord Kelvin, who was vacationing on the Riviera, set off for Paris. Pierre's brother, Jacques, arrived the next morning from Montpellier and, during their review of funeral arrangements, a discussion which hammered home the finality of his death, Marie broke down for the first time. While the details of who would represent the government, who the Academy, and so forth were being discussed in the appropriate ministries, Marie purposely advanced the day to avoid any official participation. Pierre's funeral must be private, the way he had preferred to live his life. As the living room filled with people making the necessary arrangements, Marie sat mute, with the vision of Pierre lying dead in the adjacent room.

Early Saturday, Marie cradled Pierre's head in her lap as his body was taken to the mortuary. Before the coffin was sealed, she placed inside it his favorite portrait of herself—from the days when he called her "the good little student." Instead of covering the bier with the customary black cloth, she insisted on periwinkles from their garden.

Pierre was laid to rest in the countryside where he had spent a large part of his youth, in the small cemetery dominating the slopes of Sceaux. The Curie family vault where his mother was buried was alongside a wall in the shade of some newly greened chestnut trees. Only friends were present, though the Minister of Public Instruction, Aristide Briand, slipped in, discreetly and unobserved. Marie stood rigid as if in a trance, her face set in a fixed, hard stare, and she made a monumental effort to control herself. There was no priest, no sermon. At the end of the simplest of services, Marie abruptly seized a sheaf of flowers resting near the tomb and, oblivious to anything and anyone, slowly and methodically broke off the flowers, one by one, and spread them over the grave. Deeply moved, those present felt like intruders and held their breath rather than betray their presence at such a private moment. Finally, the funeral director advised Marie that it was customary to accept the condolences of those gathered there. Letting the rest of the bouquet slip from her grasp, Marie stepped back from the grave like an automaton, and silently rejoined Dr. Curie. After the others left, Marie and Jacques remained behind, alone with their memories. They watched as the earth was shovelled over the coffin and the various bouquets laid on top. Then they slowly walked away.

Late Sunday afternoon, Aline Perrin and Irène were playing together in Aline's bedroom when Marie entered with Henriette Perrin. She had come to tell her elder daughter the terrible truth. Sixty years later, Aline still remembered how pale and icy she looked—in black from head to toe. Irène acted as if she did not hear what her mother was saying, and continued to play the game she and her friend had started. Marie turned to Mme. Perrin: "She is too young to understand." And left. But Irène was not too young. She did comprehend, although the realization that she would never see Pé again had not yet penetrated. Marie was barely out the Perrins' front door when Irène burst into tears and asked to be taken home. Irène had not been back since the accident and she was startled to find Uncle Jacques. Her Warsaw relatives soon arrived. She had a good cry with them, but soon returned to the comfortable normalcy of her friend Aline.

Pierre's tragic end sparked the popular imagination. Even foreign newspapers carried large articles about the brilliant scientist cut down at the height of his experimental skills, with his intellectual faculties at their peak. Letters of condolence poured in and, on the morrow of the funeral, as family and friends worried about what was to become of Marie, a widow with two small children to support, the government suggested a national pension for the trio. But

Marie was too proud and too independent to accept favors from anyone. She was young and strong and termed the proposal "charity," an insult. She was perfectly capable of supporting herself and her family. When people came to call, Irène's Polish governess told them firmly that Madame was not at home. Marie did not see a soul, and even her few closest friends felt they were committing an indiscretion to try and share her grief. Only with Jozio, Bronya, and Jacques could she get any relief, and tears did not come easily with them, either. She could only confide her feelings to Pierre.

A few days after Pierre's death Marie opened a fresh gray-bound notebook and began a diary addressed to him. Like some of the Gouy letters, this is still unavailable at the family's request; only certain fragments have yet been published. Onto this paper Marie hurled her grief and the thoughts that were stifling her. The tear-splattered pages, the normally clear handwriting now so distorted, bespeak her feelings as she said farewell to a part of her innermost self—and to her husband of less than eleven years:

> . . . Pierre, my Pierre, you are there, calm as a poor wounded man resting in sleep, with his head bandaged . . . What a terrible shock your poor head has felt, your poor head that I so often caressed in my two hands. I kissed your eyelids which you used to close so that I could kiss them, offering me your head with a familiar movement . . . Everything is over . . . ; it is the end of everything, everything, everything.[7]

Why anyone as objective as Marie would preserve anything as intensely personal as the excerpts presently available indicate is puzzling, especially when she took pains later in life to methodically destroy most papers of an intimate nature. With Pierre's death, Marie momentarily lost her security. With him she had nothing to prove. For Pierre she had been everything, and could do no wrong. He was already an established scientist when he fell in love with Marie and married her. Pierre opened the doors to a life she might never have known. Few married couples are fortunate enough to share such a community of interests and such a love as they. Pierre had seen that Marie, the scientific neophyte, always had every bit of credit due her, when so many felt she was merely riding on his coattails.

The sight of the sun and the flowers made her suffer because Pierre was no longer there to enjoy them with her. But "I shall not kill myself," she confided.[8] For what would become of Pierre's research? What might be considered an instinctive reaction—the need to live for Irène and Ève—is never mentioned. Three weeks after his tragic demise, she still could not comprehend that she would never again see Pierre. She wanted to howl like a wild beast but she did not know how.

The day before he returned to Montpellier, her wise brother-in-law maneuvered Marie, on a pretext, back into the laboratory on the rue Cuvier. Jacques knew her work would help her to survive. Marie tried to pick up where she had last left off—to take a measurement and finish plotting a curve which she and Pierre had been doing together. It was too much for her. Nonetheless, like a rider remounting a horse which has just thrown him, Marie had taken the first steps back to a normal existence. Jacques also conferred with Georges Gouy, the Perrins, and the handful of other Curie intimates who were worried about Marie's future. The minister of public instruction and the council of the Faculty of Sciences were alerted. On May 13, tradition and custom were swept aside when the council met and unanimously decided to maintain Pierre's chair for Marie and asked the minister to offer it to her with the title of assistant professor and a 10,000 franc salary. Here was a challenge cut to Marie's measure—the first post in higher education in France to be given a woman—and based on recognition of her scientific qualifications. She would also have her own research facilities. Marie owed it to herself to accept but she did not do so without considerable inner debate. She confided in her gray notebook:

My little Pierre, I want to tell you that the laburnum is in flower, the wisteria, the hawthorne and the iris are beginning . . . I want to tell you, too, that I have been named to your chair, and that there have been some imbeciles to congratulate me on it. [9]

Jacques, Gouy, and Jozio boarded their homeward-bound trains reassured that Marie was once more in control of herself. Within a month of Pierre's death, the columns of neat figures in her laboratory workbooks resumed, and Marie was back at work, purifying radium metal.

More than a quarter of a century later, shortly after Marie's death, Bronya disclosed the final macabre scene that marked Marie's ultimate catharsis to her niece, Ève, who was writing Marie's biography and confessed to her aunt that she hardly knew her mother.

To Bronya's amazement, a roaring fire was blazing on the hearth one hot June day two months after Pierre's death when Marie called her into her bedroom. "Bronya, I need your help," she informed her and locked the door. Taking out of the armoire a heavily wrapped bundle, Marie sat down cross-legged on the floor and slit it open with a huge pair of scissors. Out tumbled a heap of muddy, blood-clotted rags which the horrified Bronya suddenly realized must be the clothes that Pierre wore when he was killed. With scientific precision, Marie methodically cut them into pieces. In some strange way, she was like an Indian widow performing suttee, consecrating herself to the flames of her departed husband as she slowly tossed each one, some with bits of Pierre's dried flesh still clinging to them, into the blaze.

Bronya watched transfixed. But when Marie passionately kissed the last grisly relics, Bronya tore them from her feverish grasp and threw them, with the wrapping paper, into the greedy fire—"I couldn't bear to have anyone else touch them, do you understand? Do you understand?" [10] Marie sobbed, as buxom, matronly Bronya wrapped her arms around her little sister's frail, shuddering figure.

She then led her to the water pitcher, washed her hands, sponged her face, and tucked her into bed.

The next morning, Marie regained her cool composure as if she had, literally, exorcised her sorrow, and once more locked the door on her inner self.

IX
1906–1911

The Illustrious Widow

SOME YEARS BEFORE, IN a fit of depression, Marie had asked Pierre how, if something happened to one of them, the other could possibly survive. Now his response, echoing in her ears, helped stabilize her: "Whatever happens, even if one should become like a body without a soul, still one must always work."[1] Marie had lost not only a husband, she had also lost her closest colleague. While the laboratory gradually resumed its dominant role in her life, she became despondent, even there, from time to time.

While Marie may have broken another barrier by accepting

Pierre's chair and thereby have opened the way in France for other equally qualified women to follow, she could not have cared less. Her sole concern was to support her family and at the same time to be worthy of Pierre. Such a formidable task was exactly what Marie needed at this point in her life, and both Perrin and Langevin gave invaluable help as she prepared for the Sorbonne's fall quarter. Since Marie was determined not to neglect the delicate isolation of radium, it was often extremely late before she hung her coarse, acid-stained smock on its wooden peg in the rue Cuvier and bicycled homeward. Dawn was breaking before she reached the Boulevard Kellermann. Once home, she would check the big stove in the vestibule, add coal, and adjust the draft before turning in, for Marie was convinced that she was the only person in the household who knew how to stoke the fire properly. Her backbreaking schedule was the best thing possible for Marie. By once again establishing a routine, the rhythm of her life was restored. She was now too busy and too tired to yield to introspection. She adored her growing daughters and took increasing pleasure in their company as they got older. She did her best, in her own way, to give them a normal home life. The tree she decorated with garlands, colored candles, and gilded nuts each Christmas was just like the one Marie remembered from her girlhood in Poland and was long remembered by a starry-eyed Irène and Ève. But the girls could never be the focal point of Marie's life.

By now, the two were beginning to show their differences. Ève was already a dark-haired extrovert, toddling around after the cat, pulling up the flowers in GrandPé's carefully tended garden, and getting into the normal mischief of a two-and-a-half-year-old. Fairheaded Irène was introspective like her father and equally shy. Irène's first childhood ended with Pé's death, which was a profound shock for her. The nine-year-old vainly sought an explanation, and it is an indictment of Marie as a mother that she was too wrapped up in her own grief to recognize this. According to Ève's biography of her, Marie never permitted anyone, not even her daughters, to mention Pierre's name in front of her again. The wound was too fresh and too open. She did not want it to bleed before them—or before the world. By her arbitrary moratorium, Marie kept her deepest feelings to herself. However, Irène, perhaps because she was older and knew her father better than Ève, was unable to follow Marie's instructions and more than once in the years when she was away from home, she would write to inquire about the flowers and shrubs growing alongside her father's grave.

A heavy black cloud of insecurity hung over Irène's world, smothering the former warmth and happiness of her home. She watched in vain for her adored mother to smile again when she looked at her, unaware of the ambiguity of her position—that for Marie she was simultaneously a precious blessing and a cruel reminder of a life that was gone forever.

Fortunately, Dr. Curie was there to help Irène surmount her misery. Because GrandPé, with his twinkling blue eyes peering down at her from underneath the tattered brim of a beat-up old straw hat, understood the sad child's need for special attention and affection, the bond between the pair tightened. When he offered to live with Jacques in Montpellier so Marie might have one less mouth to feed, she refused to hear of it. Marie was as determined as the old doctor not to be beaten down by circumstances or events, and they developed a mutual understanding that ran deeper than words. But unlike Marie, he refused to be tortured by a ghost, and the knowledge that, at eighty, he could be useful by supervising the care of Pierre's children helped to overcome his personal sense of loss. His cheerfulness was good for the whole family, and with GrandPé in charge Marie left the house daily without worry. He saved the day, and she repaid him with affection and devotion.

Marie's sister Hela Szalay came from Warsaw with her daughter Hania, who was almost Irène's age, and took Irène to the seashore. Irène kept her mother posted on her daily activities on the beach, and GrandPé, in turn, acting as Ève's secretary, wrote Irène from St.-Rémy:

Eu, eu, eu, eu

—Ève.

*My dear Irène, my dear big grand-daughter. I am sending you
Ève's letter . . . I think you will recognize her style . . .*[2]

Another elderly gentleman was equally busy. Lord Kelvin had
come to the conclusion that radium was not an element, but a
probable compound of helium. Because of the public interest in the
subject, he launched his latest theory not in the usual place, in a
prestigious science magazine, but in the famous "Letters to the
Editor" column on the front page of the renowned London *Times*.
If the patriarch of English science was correct, he would have
destroyed not only all Marie's work, including her hypothesis that
radioactivity was an atomic function, but also Rutherford and Soddy's transmutation theory, which claimed that radiation was beyond
anyone's control and the result of disintegrating atoms. A war of
words ensued, with the scientific authorities of the day sniping at
each other from the columns of the *Times* and subsequent issues of
Nature, the important science magazine. Deeply disturbed, Marie
watched from the sidelines but did not participate. Pure radium
metal could prove the old British lion wrong and, at the same time,
gainsay those who were insinuating that she had never been more
than Pierre's assistant. Her success in isolating it, with Debierne's
help, was to constitute her most important scientific work as a
widow.

With this tedious task and so many other responsibilities, Marie
was forced to give up teaching at Sèvres. Langevin took over her
classes. One other matter also needed resolution: what to do with
the gram of radium salts she and Pierre had prepared. Old Dr.
Curie, among others, felt that she should retain possession of it as
security for herself and her daughters. But Marie saw no reason
why Irène and Ève should not earn their own living, as she herself
had to do, and, in accordance with what she knew were Pierre's

own feelings, she decided to make a gift of this gram—worth more than a million francs—to her laboratory.

Early Monday morning, November 5, the first day she assumed Pierre's classes, Marie went out to Sceaux to visit his grave and get strength for the ordeal ahead. Before noon, several hundred people were already gathered on the Place de la Sorbonne before the school's closed grills, although they did not open until 1 P.M. In five minutes, the small physics amphitheater which could comfortably seat some two hundred was full, and its door closed on those still trying to push their way in. For history was being made by the "illustrious widow." Her lecture that day was the first ever given there by a woman, let alone to a class of advanced studies, and it marked "A Great Victory for Feminism," as the *Journal* trumpeted across its front page. This was a highlight of the fall season which even *tout* Paris could not afford to miss. Present also were reporters, photographers, those who made it their business to attend every "first," as well as prominent scientists, celebrities, a lot of Poles, some personal friends of Marie's—and, of course, her students, for they must attend and take notes. The front rows of that staid, time-hallowed hall resembled the parterre at the opening of a popular author's latest play.

As dean of the Faculty of Sciences, Paul Appell arose at 1:20 P.M. and announced that, in accordance with Marie's wishes, the normal installation ceremony was being waived. The new professor would not give the usual thanks to the Minister of Education and others for her appointment—or the customary eulogy of her predecessor.

Emotion mingled with curiosity, ten minutes later, when Marie entered almost furtively, and bowed her head slightly in acknowledgment of the huge ovation. The stark severity of the simple, unadorned black mourning dress made her slender body thinner and more fragile, her pale coloring more like alabaster. Her taut skin showed off the bone structure of her face to better advantage, while her abundant ash blond hair, turning gray here and there, was gathered and pulled back, accentuating her high, rounded brow—a brow "like that of a Memling virgin," one journalist reported. Another, in *Figaro,* described her face as "strange, ageless; her eyes clear and profound seem weary from having read too much and cried too much."

Marie laid out her papers, placed her watch alongside, and stood holding onto the long, apparatus-laden table with one hand, as if to steady herself, until there was silence. The constant shuffling of papers with her lips pressed tightly together betrayed the usual nervousness Marie always felt when she stood up to address a group, even a small one the size of her class at Sèvres. And, if she recognized anyone as she looked out at that sea of faces, it was her former "sèvriennes," seated in reserved seats in the front row. It had required great persistence to get authorization for the girls to attend her fall Sorbonne lectures to compensate for their spring classes which had been canceled following Pierre's tragic accident. Choked with emotion, the attentive girls felt that Marie was talking directly to them.

Marie commenced at the exact spot where Pierre had left off: "When one considers the progress that has been made in physics during the past ten years, one is surprised at how much movement there has been in our ideas concerning electricity and matter . . ."[3] Fifteen years to the day since Manya Sklodowska first crossed the inner court of the Sorbonne to register as a Polish student, her second life had begun. Marie spoke a trifle quickly at first, because of the effort she was making to control herself, but she soon slowed down. Even so, her subject matter, the ionization of gas, was probably over the heads of most of the audience. At the end she slipped out by the same rear stage door through which she had entered.

Some time that late fall or early winter, Marie met Andrew Carnegie in Paris. Touched by her lack of pretense and the burning intensity of her regard, the American millionaire, a self-made success like Marie, was impressed by her achievements as a woman and by the precision of the goals she set for herself. After his return to the States, he dumbfounded her by sending Dean Appell $50,000 with instructions that this substantial sum was to found Curie Scholarships. Carnegie specified that the foundation created to handle the details was not to be named after himself but was to be known as the Curies Foundation, "Making it plural," he explained, "will include Madame, which I am most anxious to do."[4] Carnegie also stipulated that as long as Marie lived and was competent, her wishes were to be respected regarding the recipients. His gift would finance the research staff she needed to proceed with the mission that was to occupy the rest of her life—to build a laboratory worthy of Pierre's disappointed dreams, where the new science of radioactivity could be developed. Unbeknownst to Andrew Carnegie, he gave her an even more valuable gift. For their fortuitous encounter brought home to Marie her enormous potential as a fund-raiser, provided she was willing to suffer intrusions on her privacy.

Marie reasoned that a change of scenery might do them all good and was even more motivated by health reasons when she decided to move to Sceaux. She was anxious to have Irène and Ève away from the noxious city fumes, although she herself, unwittingly, continued to breathe far more deadly ones. And she considered fresh air such an essential that she soon added a portico to the house at no. 6 rue du Chemin de Fer so the girls could exercise on the outdoor trapeze daily, rain or shine.

The lovely ancient town of Sceaux, where Pierre had lived with his family before their marriage and where he was buried, was still in open country—an ideal environment for growing youngsters—but the move meant a considerable sacrifice on Marie's part. Instead of being able to walk or bicycle to work, she must now hurry to catch a slow commuter train where she sat, in a second-class compartment, correcting a satchelful of students' papers during the half-hour ride into Paris. Marie kept the same late night hours as before and when she did get to bed, she was often a prey to hideous nightmares. Occasionally, her physical strength deserted her so fast that she did not have time to send her daughters out of the room, and one of Ève's earliest memories was of Mé fainting in the dining room at Sceaux and of how deathly pale she remained for a long time afterward.

Her children and her work saved Marie's sanity during those first years of widowhood. Irène and Ève, who without GrandPé would have been stifled in the continuing atmosphere of mourning, clung to Mé wildly the little she was at Sceaux. If Marie did not give them much time, it was because she did not have many hours to give. If there were no outward signs of warmth, an illness or birthday were never neglected.

Now that Aline Perrin was no longer her next-door neighbor, old Dr. Curie became Irène's closest comrade and was an enormous stimulant for her mentally. She loved to curl up by the hour in a chair in his bedroom. That room did not present the Spartan, sterile aspect of the rest of the house but was cluttered with various personal memorabilia, and in the place of honor stood a large, jam-packed bookcase. Here, in a cracked off-key voice, the old man taught her numerous songs from his own childhood and read from his favorite author, Victor Hugo. On their daily walks, he continued to cultivate her inherited interest in nature which Pierre had earlier aroused, and he indoctrinated her for life with his republican philosophy and lay convictions. Irène's background accentuated the reflective side of her nature and the great reserve she would maintain throughout her life.

Irène, who was going on ten, was already mad about mathematics. When she was at the seashore, Marie ended her letters to her with algebraic equations to be solved, rather than kisses. Irène was at an age when her education must be taken seriously and, like Pierre, Marie had very strong ideas on the subject. She wanted to prepare the most fertile soil possible for the girls' minds to develop in and took a dim view of the French system. The elementary schools were poorly lit and heated, the children kept long hours, learned too little, and had to bring their own lunches, which were, of necessity, cold—a regime Marie considered injurious for their health. She felt children should have plenty of time for physical exercise and reflection and should not be in class morning until night with no time outdoors. Irène and Ève must be self-reliant and learn how to think for themselves, rather than learn by rote; they must be taught to use their hands well and they must be given a good scientific education at an early stage.

These revolutionary ideas were shared by a number of her Sorbonne colleagues, so Marie and a handful of her friends with children approximately the same age as Irène decided to set up their own school. The other families involved were the Édouard Chavannes—he was the Chinese language authority at the prestigious Collège de France—the Langevins, Perrins, and the Moutons. The "Cooperative," as it came to be called, started that fall. When the afternoon class was over, there was always a *goûter*—high tea—and in came a tray laden with rolls, *pain au chocolat,* oranges, and the like. Once a week the ten privileged youngsters gathered in the Sorbonne laboratory of Jean Perrin for a class in chemistry and learned about the composition of matter. Another day, they went to the Perrins' house on the Boulevard Kellermann, where Henriette taught the group French history and literature, and Henri Mouton, the natural sciences. Paul Langevin taught them mathematics in his new home in the countryside at Fontenay-aux-Roses, next door to the Chavannes' and within walking distance of his Sèvres classes. Visits were organized to the Louvre and the Musée Carnavalet by Madame Chavannes and Henriette Perrin, or to the studio of the sculptor Magrou, who taught them modeling. Each week the group returned a second time to Fontenay so that Isabelle and Fernand Chavannes' mother could teach them English and German. And while the little local steam train chugged along from the Luxembourg station with innumerable stops, Irène entertained her friends with a sight translation of Nobel laureate Henryk Sienkiewicz's *Quo Vadis?*, which she was reading in the original Polish.

Every Thursday, it was Marie's turn to work with them in an

empty room in the physics building at PCN. And here Irène got her first glimpse of the exciting other world that was also home for Mé. One day the class dipped bicycle ball bearings in ink and then placed them on an inclined plane where, by describing a parabola, they verified the law of falling bodies. Another time, Marie gave them a lesson in common sense. She took a jug of boiling water off a small burner and asked the eager, inquisitive youngsters clustered around the best way to keep its contents hot. A wide range of ingenious suggestions were offered. "Well," replied Marie, smiling, "this is what I'd do." And she put the lid on.

With all the care and thought given to Irène's and, later, Ève's education, there were to be several gaps, namely religion and manners. In an age when baptism was almost a social obligation, neither girl was baptized. Marie told them if they later wanted to take up religion that was their decision, but Irène, who was perhaps also influenced by GrandPé in this matter, would never set foot in a church. As for manners, only intimates were received in the Curie home after Pierre's death, and they were indulgent toward Irène. She saw no children other than those in the Cooperative. With little occasion to meet people she did not already know, she never learned the proper way to greet someone and obstinately refused to say "How do you do?" to a stranger. Nor did she acquire other forms of politeness called for by everyday courtesy. When she was finally old enough to know better and did conform to these customs, it was generally with poor grace. She would never possess the art of casual conversation and grew up insensitive to the attitude of others. Ève grew up in the same environment but because she was of a different disposition, she overcame these deficiencies. In Irène, the lack of sociability that she inherited from Pierre served to emphasize them.

Attending the Cooperative in which her own mother taught meant that Irène saw more of her, and her relationship with Mé assumed deeper meaning. The following summer, when the two sisters returned to the Normandy seashore, Marie managed a short vacation with them. Nowhere is the understanding adoration with which Irène now regarded her mother so touchingly epitomized as in a snapshot taken about this time. Mother and daughter are seated side by side outdoors, and Irène is gently touching Mé's badly scarred fingertips.

At the time Marie was originally named to fill Pierre's chair, it seemed too iconoclastic to award her a full professorship, but, when the Sorbonne school year commenced in 1908, she was elevated to his full rank as professor of general physics. In addition to giving the world's first course on radioactivity, Marie was continuously updating it. She was also editing Pierre's manuscripts and notes, a mammoth task which would run to over six hundred pages when published.

Conceivably, it was because of her wish to make the Curie Laboratory into a world-renowned center of radioactivity as a fitting tribute to Pierre that the American scientist Bertram Boltwood was turned down when he tried to compare his radium solution with Marie's. Disappointed, he commented to Rutherford on the "[Madame's] constitutional unwillingness to do anything that might directly or indirectly assist any worker in radioactivity outside of her laboratory."[5] On the other hand, when Rutherford, who knew how to handle Marie, made a similar request several months later, it was granted.

The Cooperative enjoyed a great success but ended when Langevin was appointed to teach at the prestigious Collège de France and the others were equally busy. Furthermore, it was time for the children to begin a more formal education so they would have no trouble, a couple of years hence, passing their baccalaureate examinations, mandatory if they were to enter college. Sometime during the summer, Marie found time to give Irène and her friend Isabelle Chavannes algebra lessons to get the girls caught up with the *lycées* they were to attend in the fall.

One day Mé asked Irène a simple question. Her daughter had not been listening and could only reply, "I don't know."—"What do you mean, you don't know? How can you be so stupid?" Indignantly, Marie reached over and tossed Irène's notebook out the open window. If she could take the time from her busy schedule to teach the pair, Irène owed it to her mother to listen . . . "I'm sorry," the girl mumbled guiltily.[6] Abashed, she rushed downstairs to retrieve the exercise book. Her sudden, uncharacteristic loss of self-control underscored Marie's point. Never again did she have to reprimand Irène for lack of attention.

Irène was worried about GrandPé, who was suffering increasingly from lung problems and was sick in bed, when she went off to the seashore once again. Their warm relationship, as well as Irène's developing personality, shows in their correspondence. When she signed one letter "Your humble little Irène," Dr. Curie promptly replied: "No, you are not a 'humble little Irène.' You are, with the 's' of the second person singular of the Indicative Tense, [GrandPé was taking the opportunity to give his granddaughter a grammar lesson] my 'grown-up Irène' . . . who has her certificate of study . . . who writes regularly to her old grandfather, which the former 'humble little Irène' did not do often."[7]

In the fall Irène entered the Collège de Sévigné, a private school in the heart of Paris where the hours, Marie had discovered after a thorough investigation, were one half of those in the state *lycées*. Irène also needed the school's superior mathematics program. Both she and Ève, who would likewise attend Sévigné, must earn their own living when they were older, and Marie stressed, from an early age, that they should be proud of their independence and their ability to do so. This was a shocking idea for a day when most girls were expected to grow up with no other thought in mind than marriage. It was also unheard-of for eleven-year-old Irène to go unattended to her new school, but Marie did not believe in being overprotective. Irène entered Sévigné equipped with a far better scientific background than would have been possible without the Cooperative, though she was somewhat lacking in the humanities. Years later, when Ève passed judgment on Mé's ideas of education

The Sklodowski family. From left to right: Zosia, Hela, Manya (Marie), Jozio, Bronya.

Photographs courtesy of the Laboratoire Curie, Institut du Radium, Paris.

Pierre and Marie about the time of their honeymoon, in the Curie garden at Sceaux, 1895.

Dr. Eugène Curie, his wife and sons, 1878.

The outside of the famous shed on the rue Lhomond where radium
was discovered.

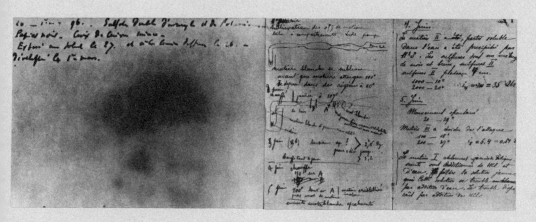

LEFT: The discovery of radioactivity: the famous Becquerel photographic plate with the marks made on it
by the uranium salts. RIGHT: Pages from the Curies' second notebook detailing their work leading to the
discovery of radium. Marie's writing is on the left, Pierre's on the right. Early June 1898.

Inside the shed.

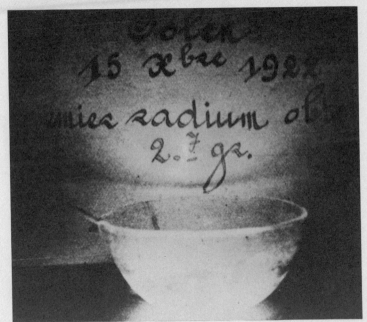

Photo taken in the dark of radium in a laboratory dish, showing its glow.

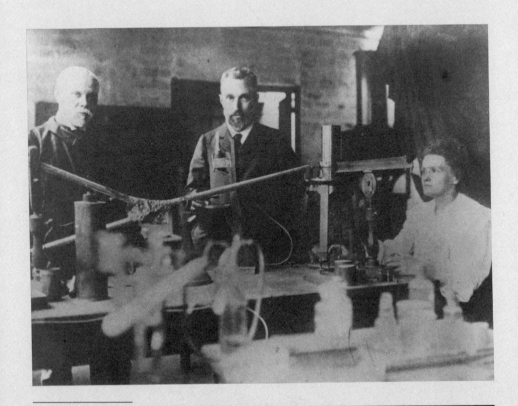

Pierre and Marie, with Pierre's assistant, Petit (left), in the hangar on the rue Lhomond.

LEFT: *Irène and Pierre at St. Rémy-les-Chevreuse, September 1904*. RIGHT: *Dr. Eugène Curie ("GrandPé") and Irène, 1903.*

Ève and Irène, March 1906.

Marie and Pierre, 1904.

Irène pointing to her mother's radium-scarred fingertips, 1909.

Marie (back row, middle) and her "sèvriennes."

Irène before one of the cars of the Army's Service of Radiology, 1916.

as exemplified by the training she gave her two daughters, she gave the best marks to the spirit of independence Marie engrained in her girls and, surprisingly, to the good health and skill in sports which she fostered.

Like Pierre, Irène had a very independent mind. On the whole, she performed admirably at Sévigné, but there were certain subjects she disliked and made no effort to learn. Naturally, she went to the head of the class immediately in science and scandalized the other girls the day she explained to them, biologically, how babies were conceived and came into the world.

Talks were beginning to take form with Dr. Roux, the head of the Pasteur Institute, concerning Marie's proposed Radium Institute. For a novice in these matters, she did very well. She felt she had found the ideal location for the new building when the University of Paris bought from the Dames de St.-Michel a vast terrain located near the Panthéon, and outlined on two sides by the rues d'Ulm and St.-Jacques. Since it seemed logical to combine an Institut du Radium, such as she proposed, with the Pasteur Institute because of radium's medical applications, talks were initiated along these lines.

Tired of the procrastination of certain University of Paris officials and afraid the long-sought-after laboratory might disappear like a mirage, Marie threatened to leave the Sorbonne and join the Pasteur Institute. This did the trick. An arrangement was worked out between Dr. Roux and Vice-Rector Liard to found, at the common expense of 400,000 gold francs each, the Institut du Radium. This was to consist of two equal parts: a laboratory of radioactivity under Marie and a laboratory of biological research and radium therapy—or curietherapy—under the eminent Professor Claude Regaud, in which would be organized studies on cancer and its treatment. These two materially independent units were to cooperate in the development of the science of radium therapy, and the two pavilions to be built on the land donated by the University of

Paris were to be known collectively as the Institut du Radium of the University of Paris.

February 1909, there was a lot of snow in Paris, and the giraffe at the Jardin des Plantes, Irène's special favorite among the animals there, died of the extreme cold. But there was a deeper sorrow in store for her, for that same month GrandPé died of pulmonary pneumonia. In the tiny Sceaux cemetery, swept bare by winter's blasts, Marie ordered Pierre's coffin removed in order to place GrandPé next to his wife. Then Pierre was put on top of them so that when Marie joined him, their two coffins would likewise lie one above the other.

This was a somber period in the Curie household and very hard on thirteen-year-old Irène, though far less so on six-year-old Ève. Twice already, in her short life, Irène had been deprived of someone close to her. For Marie, Dr. Curie's death was a grim reminder of Pierre's demise—and of her own father's. With GrandPé's passing she lost someone who had been very close to Pierre and who was an integral part of her household. However, there was no need for Marie to change into mourning black. She had never taken it off. Once more she suffered fits of depression, and her health was poor.

When Irène and Ève again spent the month of August at the seashore with their Aunt Hela and Hania, Marie put in a brief appearance. All three girls were taking piano lessons so perhaps the hubbub was more than Marie could stand. After she left, Irène's capitalized plea: "WHEN ARE YOU COMING BACK? . . . I shall be so happy when you come because I badly need someone to caress," indicates how much Irène missed Mé. "I have made a fine paper envelope to hold your letters. There is only one in it,"[8] she remonstrated.

The entire four years since Pierre's death, Marie had been plodding away at isolating radium metal. Finally, in an extremely dangerous, delicate operation which could easily have entailed a serious loss of the precious solution of radium she was working with, she condensed it by electrolysis with a cathode of mercury and got a tiny but indisputable speck of white radium metal! Soon afterward she also succeeded in preparing several samples of extremely active pure polonium.

Like a magnet attracts pieces of steel, Marie was beginning to amass honorary degrees and scientific society memberships from different countries. International cooperation among physicists and chemists was at its height, and Marie made an increasing number of window-dressing trips abroad, anxious to gain added prestige for the forthcoming new Institute. Was her presence necessary at the upcoming World Congress on Radiology scheduled for the fall of 1910 in Belgium? she wrote across the Channel to Ernest Rutherford, who was presently the leader in her field of radioactivity and had won the Nobel two years before. While a carping few grumbled that nothing new was coming out of Marie's laboratory, and Rutherford himself might privately question the originality of her experiments, Marie was the personification of radium in the public eye, so he encouraged her attendance. A correspondence between the two ensued which was to last until her death.

Concurrently, the New Zealander was also in touch with the German Otto Hahn regarding the International Radium Standard which was to be established at the Belgian meeting. Accurate, uniform measurements of radium were increasingly important in industry, research, and medicine. The pair anticipated trouble with Marie over the details. She had her own way of doing things and was not accustomed to making concessions where scientific matters were concerned, so they agreed to soften up the "Madame" with a little flattery by calling the new unit to be devised a "curie."

Jean Perrin accompanied Marie to the Hôtel du Grand Miroir in Brussels. Tempers flew when the issue of the International Radium Standard was discussed by the Steering Committee, on which Marie was the only woman. Everyone readily agreed that because of her authority in the matter she should do the laboratory work entailed in the unit's preparation, but no two present could concur on the unit itself. The tumultuous meeting dragged on. Finally Marie arose, declared she felt ill, and left the hall. When she got to her room, she spelled out her position, which was uncompromising as usual, in writing. If the unit was to be known as a "curie," then she must define it. Because radium occurs in very small amounts and is steadily disintegrating, conventional measurements were useless. She proposed measuring its radiation and suggested, as a unit, the amount of emanation in equilibrium with one gram of radium in one second. Marie returned to the fray the next morning and won out, imposing her wishes on the men who were furious with her— no doubt because they knew they would be mad at themselves afterward for yielding.

When she did not appear at the gala closing dinner that evening, claiming she had a cold, those who had not seen eye-to-eye with her earlier maintained this was a ploy to forestall any further discussion of an issue she considered closed. Marie's dictatorial manner did not set well. She was a redoubtable opponent, and many trembled at the thought of ever facing up to the slight, black-garbed woman in a scientific dispute. Detractors claimed she took excessive advantage of her fragile appearance. Perrin and Rutherford had a hard time persuading Dr. Stefan Meyer, the Austrian delegate, that her health really was poor, and she did not bring on her frequent attacks of nervous exhaustion, or use not feeling well, as an excuse to leave a meeting when she was losing ground in an argument. As the pair well knew, there was nothing devious about Marie. She placed the cards on the table and never minced words about them.

Rutherford never suffered fools gladly. He respected Marie and was one of the few who always knew how to work with her—or around her—and he was willing to make the effort to do so. He also felt genuinely sorry for her. He had been seated next to her at the Opéra the previous night, where she was in such a sorry state that he escorted her home at the first intermission and warned that she was working too hard for her own good. Marie looked so worn out and tired that she could pass for much older than her forty-three years, and he wrote his mother that "altogether she was a very pathetic figure."[9]

Some of the delegates, encountering Marie for the first time, found her glacial and insupportable. She considered the workers in her own laboratory, who adored her and to whom she gave unstintingly of herself, as her second family. But Marie could be haughty with those she did not judge sufficiently important to waste her breath on, and the honor of meeting her was stingily accorded. Needing and demanding respect at this stage of her life, she was often difficult to engage in conversation, and a young British physicist, E.N. da C. Andrade, described her as "not a very nice person."[10] It is hard to find an answer for some of the adverse criticism she aroused. Conceivably, she was still depressed by GrandPé's death earlier that year. How much of the impression of prickliness that she conveyed was due to her own timidity is hard to ascertain. Marie did not care greatly what impression she created. Like other pioneering women who knew their own worth and had a similar uphill battle to prove it and be accepted as an equal by their male peers, Marie's struggle had made her, if not belligerent, at least defiant. To some, she gave the impression of still being on the defensive and aggressively challenging the world, but never as a woman—as a scientist.

The following month, Marie published her "Treatise on Radioactivity." Nearly one thousand pages long, these two volumes included her doctoral thesis and her Sorbonne class lectures and contained everything that was known about the subject to date. Rutherford's personal fondness for Marie came up against his professional integrity when he was asked to review the work for *Nature*. He managed a properly respectful article, although his private opinion was that she had labored mightily and produced a mouse.

When Marie was asked if she would let herself be proposed for the Légion d'Honneur, she declined out of respect for Pierre's memory and the wish to follow his example. That left membership in the French Academy as the only other way for France to honor her. Marie might still be bitter that Pierre did not succeed on his first try at election to that select body and had to submit to a humiliating second attempt before ultimately becoming a member; but given her own unassailable scientific credentials, she saw no reason to assume she, in turn, would not win. Marie was woefully unaware of the antagonism her strong personality aroused in certain quarters. She also miscalculated professional jealousy, the dark counterpart of celebrity—if she thought about it at all—not to mention the horror many felt at her brazen attempt to storm the last male bastion remaining in her field. Because she was well aware of the advantages which a seat under the famous cupola conferred, she naively yielded to friends' entreaties and submitted her candidacy when a seat became vacant in the General Physics section upon the death of Désiré Gernez. In an ironic game of musical chairs, Pierre had defeated Gernez to win his own seat, and Gernez had, later, become Pierre's successor.

In mid-November, *Figaro* announced the season's novelties. The independent literary academy, the Goncourt, had recently elected its first woman member, Mme. Judith Gautier; the first Rolls-Royce was on show in the Salon d'Auto; the "illustrious widow" Mme. Curie was considering assaulting the areopagus. And it was high time, the newspaper pointed out, for Marie's absence from the Academy meant the exclusion of France's best-known physicist. Early in December, she confirmed her candidacy.

On January 4, 1911, when the Institut de France—the umbrella organization that is composed of the French Academy, the Academy of Sciences, the Academy of Inscriptions and Belles-Lettres, the Academy of Beaux-Arts, and the Academy of Moral and Political Sciences—met in plenary session, it expressed the wish that its all-male status quo be maintained. So unwarranted an intrusion into "the Sciences' " affairs played into the hands of Marie's faithful mentor and fellow Nobel laureate Professor Lippmann, who was masterminding her strategy, and he persuaded his friends to accept the principle of a woman aspirant.

The next day, the section of general physics studied the dossiers of the would-be aspirants and accepted only three—Édouard Branly, Marcel Brillouin, and Marie. The race was on. Although Brillouin was as competent as many already seated in the Assembly, his chances were negligible against this stellar competition. Whenever Marie's supporters pointed to the countless cancer victims whose lives had been prolonged or saved by the use of radium, Branly's supporters countered by listing the scores rescued at sea thanks to their candidate, who was known in France as the father of wireless telegraphy. Many felt the elderly scientist, a distinguished figure with silver hair and a pince-nez who earlier shared the lucrative Osiris Prize with Marie, had recently been unfairly treated and should have split the 1909 Nobel physics award with the Italian Guglielmo Marconi and the German K.F. Braun. This loss on the international level, coupled with two previously unsuccessful attempts to scale the French Olympus, aroused a lot of sympathy for Branly. His announcement that it was "now or never" —this was his last try—helped his cause as did the fact that Gernez, whose seat was in contention, had been his close friend. To compound the maze of swirling, conflicting interests and non sequiturs that frequently outweighed scientific qualifications in these elections, among Branly's leading champions was Émile Amagat, who had defeated Pierre on the latter's abortive first attempt there.

The next two and a half weeks, in weather so unseasonably cold that there was skating in the Bois de Boulogne, Marie, Branly, and Brillouin went through the ancient ritual of visits that Pierre had found so distasteful. Marie's partisans overplayed their hand, however, when they attempted to coerce Branly into renouncing his candidacy on chivalrous grounds. And Branly's reply, if it was ever repeated to Marie, would have pleased her: "Mme. Curie presents herself to me as a woman of science and therefore as my equal. I have no need to know anything about her except her achievements. It is not a question of gallantry in these circumstances . . ."[11] His daughter, Jeanne Terrat-Branly, discloses in her life of him that her father might have yielded had Marie been more nearly his contemporary. But she was twenty-three years his junior and had plenty of time for the sought-after honor.

Until now the Institut de France's elections had never been discussed publicly, and Marie wrote the editor of *Le Temps* that it would be painful to her should custom be modified on the present occasion. To no avail. This was the first time a woman presumed to an Academician's seat, and sides were quickly drawn, uniting liberals, feminists, and anticlericals against a coalition of right-wingers, nationalists, and religious fanatics who emphasized that Marie was a freethinker. An illustrated daily, *L'Excelsior,* devoted the whole top half of its front page to head-on and side photographs of Marie, purposely unflattering as mug shots of a wanted criminal, together with a facsimile page of one of her letters. Underneath were two reports, the first by a handwriting expert and the second by a physiognomist, giving biased interpretations of Marie's qualifications for the high honor to which she aspired. The tug-of-war for the necessary votes was quickly baptized the "War Between the Sexes," and *Figaro* ran a half-page cartoon showing a glamorous girl holding the Institut's famous cupola over her flowing locks. The accompanying caption read: "What a pretty hat the Cupola would make." For some, Marie was not only a woman but something even worse—a foreigner. Anti-Semitism was not dead, despite the happy outcome of the Dreyfus affair, and a handful insisted that anyone with the name Sklodowska must be a Jew.

On January 23, the day of the vote, a crowd of the curious gathered in the early afternoon at the Institut's gates on the Quai Conti to watch its distinguished members arrive. When the president tried to open the session, he had as much trouble establishing silence as if it were the Chambre des Députés. Finally succeeding and banging down his gavel, he announced in a loud voice, "Let everyone enter, women excepted." The vote was always public and the crowd surged in, pushing and shoving. One man was overcome in the crush and a doctor hurriedly sent for. At length, order was sufficiently restored so that the Academy's normal business could be attended to, and several papers read. The minute the clock struck four, the regular session was closed. Ushers advanced with the ballot boxes, the dignified elderly academicians queued up, and amid a hum of expectation, the voting began.

The atmosphere was electric as everyone eagerly awaited the results. Marie tallied twenty-eight, Branly twenty-nine, and Brillouin one. There was no clear majority, so a second tally was mandatory. Members conferred in whispering groups, and friends scurried around, trying to get stubborn partisans to desert their favorites. A careless photographer's magnesium light flared, quickly filling the hall with its acrid smoke. Momentarily blinded, the assembly voted once more. This time Marie still had twenty-eight, but Branly had picked up one. He had thirty.

Marie learned the results by telephone in the small office off her laboratory. She promptly rejoined her already alerted, crushed staff, just as a huge congratulatory bouquet to *fête* "la patronne," which they had confidently bought with next week's lunch money and hidden under the table where the precision balances sat, disappeared ignominiously out the opposite door. If she saw the flowers, Marie did not let on. Nor did she mention her phone call. It was work as usual.

Marie was convinced that politics and the press were responsible for her defeat and resolved never again to trust journalists or a world where, one day, she was a heroine, the next, a villain. The fact that Marie let more than ten years elapse before she again permitted any of her research papers to be included in the Academy of Sciences's *Comptes Rendus* eloquently demonstrated her displeasure at its snub.

Marie's inability to win the desired seat was hardly the end of the world. But the timing was poor. Her failure focused the glaring spotlight of the press once more upon her, at a moment when Marie could least afford to submit to public scrutiny her private life, which she had rigorously and successfully shielded—so far.

X
1911–1912

The Langevin Affair

IN THE SPRING MARIE took her two daughters to Italy, where she attended a scientific conference. And when Irène had summer vacation, Marie sent the pair with one of their Polish maids, Manusia, to visit Bronya and Casimir Dluski at their sanatorium at Zakopane. This gave the girls a chance to become acquainted with the rest of their mother's family and to experience firsthand some of the pleasures of growing up in Poland that Mé was so fond of relating—the horseback riding on the plains at the foot of the Tatras, the picnics, swimming in the nearby streams. But study was not forgotten. Irène had a half-hour German lesson, each morning, and worked religiously on her algebra and trigonometry. The fourteen-year-old, with a surprisingly mature sense of values, wrote her mother, "I find that it is pleasant, as you say, to be considered by my aunts as the daughter of their sister, but I think that M. and Mme. Perrin and M. and Mme. Chavannes think of me as the daughter of an intelligent, congenial woman and not as the daughter of a celebrated man and woman."[1] But when Irène suddenly fell ill, she was once more a lonely girl who wanted her mother. "Oh, how I would have liked to have you here while I was sick! . . . Ta grrrande Irène."[2]

In the fall, the Belgian industrial engineer and philanthropist Ernest Solvay invited the world's leading physicists to Brussels with all expenses paid and an additional, generous 1,000 francs for each one's personal outlay. The French contingent included Marie, Jean Perrin, and Paul Langevin. Max Planck of Germany, Marie's friend Ernest Rutherford, and Albert Einstein were among the thirty-odd present. The first of numerous Solvay physics congresses, which Einstein privately dubbed "a Witches' Sabbath," was possibly the greatest gathering of scientific brainpower ever concentrated in one room at the same time and performed the useful function of assembling the people who were accomplishing a revolution in physics and helping them to understand more about each other's work. The French Academy of Science might have humiliated Marie by refusing her admittance, but she could justifiably maintain that the stream of international discovery which gushed from the Curies' early work was changing the nature and growth of physical science.

The Congress began October 30 in the Hôtel Metropole with learned, lively, lengthy discussions. Marie complained frequently of headaches and these, combined with her automatic attacks of nervousness whenever she had to address an audience, caused her frequent, abrupt departures from platforms—and even from committees—often at crucial moments. While Rutherford found her somewhat improved from when they last met, the big burly man took special care of Marie and maintained a gentle supportive relationship with her.

Once again, it was the New Zealander who had the unenviable, double task of trying to vanquish her stubborn insistence that the International Radium Standard she was preparing should remain in her own laboratory and she should determine the fees for its use. One evening, he spent until midnight in her suite, spewing tobacco ash and burnt matches all over the rug, as he strode to and fro, drawing on his pipe—and arguing. Striving to control his "By thunder, Madame!", he lowered his booming voice to what would be a normal level for others and bent down to speak in earnest confidence to the small figure in black, sitting ramrod straight on the couch. "For sentimental reasons I quite understand," he reported, "I am sure it is going to be a ticklish business to get the matter arranged satisfactorily as Mme. Curie is rather a difficult person to deal with. She has the advantages and at the same time the disadvantages of being a woman."[3] A compromise was ultimately worked out whereby the radium, sealed in a glass tube by Marie herself, was deposited at the Office of Weights and Measures at Sèvres and, as agreed upon the year before, the name "curie" was adopted for the new unit of measurement.

———— o ————

Today, perhaps the most common question asked a biographer of Mme. Curie by the remaining handful of people still alive who knew her is: "How are you going to treat her? Panegyrically? Or honestly?" To most of them, Marie was a normal, flesh-and-blood woman who enjoyed men until the end of her life. Many considered this an essential part of her being—perhaps, even, of her drive. And the late twentieth century frankly admits that for women, as well as men, sexuality may or may not have anything to do with love.

While Marie was in Brussels, Paris's *Le Journal* broke the story that Mme. Langevin accused the "illustrious widow" of having an affair with her husband, Paul, and was suing for a divorce. Although the French press of the day could speak of little else, only within the last two decades have any actual details been revealed by those in a position to know. Nothing better illustrates the difference between Marie's two daughters than the way they handled this episode, one of the most significant personal events in their mother's life. Ève, in her romanticized life of Mé that helped establish Marie as a latter-day saint devoting her life to science and humanity, ignored and tiptoed around it. Irène, in the bare-bones style which she employed in the diary she kept from the time she was small, laconically noted: *"Fin 1911—Affaire Langevin*[sic]."[4]

The Langevin story was quickly spread broadside, but the responsible press played it down and kept it off the front pages. No reliable historians gave credence to the spate of continuing articles in contemporary scandal-mongering sheets until the appearance of Marguerite Borel's *Souvenirs et Rencontres,* published in 1968, and André Langevin's life of his father in 1971. Both authors felt the time had come to set the record straight for present-day generations of the Curie and Langevin families. Marie's granddaughter, Hélène, and her late husband, Michel Langevin—Paul's grandson and André's son—might not have even been born, let alone married to one another, were it not, Marguerite Borel pointed out, "for the concerted action of a handful of people connected with the University [of Paris]." And she quotes Jean Perrin: "It is thanks to the five of us [M. and Mme. Borel, M. and Mme. Perrin, André Debierne] who defended her against the whole world and dammed the avalanche of mud that threatened to engulf her, that Marie Curie stayed in France. But for us she would have returned to Poland, and we would have been marked in the future with an eternal shame."[5]

Marguerite Borel—"Marbo," as she would sign her literary endeavors—played a distinguished, leading role on the French literary scene and, shortly before his death, Pierre even wrote an article for *La Revue du Mois,* a magazine she founded with some prize money of her husband's. Marguerite's account of Marie's involvement with Langevin, which deals with events in which she personally participated, rings true, although her memory may be faulty for certain details. Langevin's second son, André, portrays what occurred as a youthful marriage that failed his father was only twenty-two, his mother twenty, when they were wed. Their incompatibility, which was quickly evident, was aggravated with the passing years, and Langevin eventually established a *pied-à-terre* apart from his wife and family. "Why should anyone consider it abnormal," André demanded, "if Paul Langevin considered it his duty to encourage and assist Mme. Curie in her misfortune . . . ?" André concluded, "Isn't it natural enough that this friendship, underscored by a mutual admiration, should be transformed, little by little, over the years into passion and a liaison?"[6] His brother, Professor Jean Langevin, concurs today that this is exactly what happened. Let each interpret the Langevin episode as he sees fit, as a platonic affair, or something more. Either way, for anyone in the 1980s, Marie Curie's reputation does not suffer from a revelation which helps make the brilliant scientist more human. But to understand the furor the disclosure in *Le Journal* aroused and Marie's reactions, the mores of the day must be borne in mind. For in France at the beginning of the twentieth century, the family ruled supreme as a social unit, and the average Frenchman pushed the bounds of decency to extremes where women were concerned.

The first Marie heard of the damning article was en route to still another Solvay meeting, when she was cornered in the Metropole's lobby by several alerted reporters brandishing a copy of *Le Journal*. Asked for comments on the paper's description of her as a "husband-snatcher," she was too stunned to reply. Waving away the persistent newsmen, she brushed past without so much as a glance at the offensive sheet which had been thrust into her hand. Fernand Xau, the paper's founder, had made a fortune as the first Parisian to deliberately aim for a female audience, and he knew how to retain his seven hundred and fifty thousand readers. On page one he plastered a two-column article entitled "A History of Love: Mme. Curie and Professor Langevin." An interview followed between the journalist F. Hauser and Mme. Langevin's mother, Mme. Desfosses, at the Langevin home at Fontenay-aux-Roses. Mme. Desfosses maintained that letters existed to prove her statements, and, while she erred in stating that the present whereabouts of Langevin and Marie were a mystery, her account, for all its inaccuracies, contained the essentials as they came to be known.

It was late in the afternoon before Marie had time to think about what had occurred and to decide what to do about it. In a handwritten note she gave to the Brussels correspondent of the Paris *Le Temps,* Marie stated categorically that she attached no importance to rumors based on "pure fantasy" and, as if to emphasize the absurdity of the whole article, she pointed out: "It is well known in Paris where I could be found." Going on the assumption that attack is the best defense, Marie may have hoped to put the story to rest. *Le Temps,* with its customary discretion, buried on an inside page her reply, reprinted verbatim, together with that conservative paper's own version of the matter.

Not to be outdone, *Le Petit Journal,* a competitor of *Le Journal* but with a circulation that was one hundred thousand smaller, flooded the French capital with "A Laboratory Romance—The Adventure of Mme. Curie and M. Langevin," and included an interview with Jeanne Langevin herself. Paul's wife declared that the affair had been going on for several years, but she had remained silent in hopes of a reconciliation. She possessed no actual proof until eighteen months ago and, then, more recently. This evidence her lawyer was reserving for the court. The last straw, she reported, between sobs, was a violent scene one recent noon. The gourmet Langevin was so outraged at a poorly cooked compote of fruit that he slapped her face and stalked out of the house, taking their two sons with him. The trio had disappeared and, according to Mme. Langevin, had not been heard from since. Her statement was quickly refuted. For Paul spent August in England with the boys and stayed most of September with the Borels, who affirmed that his wife was well aware of his whereabouts at all times.

Scientists—like other men—are not immune to the joys of gossip, and the sedate Solvay Congress was soon abuzz with whispers and raised eyebrows. Langevin and Marie disappeared—separately —from sight. "Rubbish," Rutherford snorted when he heard the rumors, and he received a little farewell note from Marie before she slipped off, ahead of schedule, in order to escape the press. She was touched by his various attentions and would have liked to shake his hand before leaving, she wrote, but she was too ill to do so.

On November 6, after a third paper, *L'Intransigent,* entered the fray, Marie sent a stronger rebuttal to her champion, *Le Temps:* "I consider the intrusions of the press and public into my private life abominable . . . I will undertake vigorous action against the publication of writings attributed to me. At the same time I have the right to demand, as damages, important sums which will be used in the interests of science." And when she received an apology from Hauser of *Le Journal, Le Temps* published that, too.

When analyzing human nature, two and two do not always add up to four. Marie Curie was complicated but she was never devious. So one is prone to accept her vehement denials at face value. It is important to remember that it is the letters she denied having written—not necessarily that she was having an affair with Paul. And it is perfectly true that she may not have written any part of the letters in question. Or, if she wrote Paul letters, she expected him to destroy them and, therefore, she could not possibly be the author of those now produced and attributed to her. But, in light of the testimony made available in recent years, it is almost impossible to dismiss out of hand all of Mme. Langevin's accusations. So it is hard to equate Marie's character as we know it with her reactions to the press stories. For she did not reply to either paper's accusations on the spot, but took time to answer them. It would be interesting to know if she discussed the matter with Paul, who was also at the Solvay. And, of course, there is no way of determining whether Marie thought she could suppress the publication of the letters—authentic, doctored, or forged, as the case might be—by taking so strong a stand.

What is not out of character is her revulsion at the public intrusion into her personal affairs. While she was not impervious to the opinion of others, paradoxically she was always a law unto herself. She mistakenly and naively believed that her personal relationship with Paul, whatever its nature, could remain just that—a private one. This was an even greater miscalculation than her misreading of her colleagues' anticipated reactions at the time of the bruising Academy fight. Marie failed to realize that that battle had once more thrust her into the foreground of public scrutiny at a time when she could least afford it. This would have been a painful experience for anyone, but it must have been excruciating for ultra-sensitive Marie.

Marie was only thirty-nine when Pierre was tragically killed. After his death, both academic work and a long-standing family friendship kept Marie and the brilliant Langevin, five years her junior, in close contact. With his long, curling mustache and little goatee, his wide, warm smile and velvety dark, bedroom eyes which he knew how to use, Paul was the personification of masculine charm. A ladies' man till the end of his days, he delighted in boasting that throughout the twenty-five years he taught at Sèvres he was never given a key to the little private door at the upper end of the school's park. Although this constituted a considerable shortcut to the main buildings, Paul was considered too "dangerous for young girls" to be entrusted with it. And with ample justification. For, despite this wise precaution, he later fathered a child by Elie Montel, one of Marie's former "sèvriennes," at an age when he should have known better.

In 1910, Paul was named assistant director at EPCI, where he had originally started as Pierre's successor, and he automatically received the attractive live-in quarters that went with his new position. But because of his wife's violent temper, which made Mme.

Langevin *persona non grata* with his associates' wives, Paul did not move his family there, apparently heeding Marie's advice. To relax the day's tensions, Paul, like Jean Perrin and others, regularly stopped in after classes for late tea at the Borels'. Marguerite, who had a soft shoulder to lean upon, had developed a reputation for resolving difficult social quandaries. Settled before a cheerful fire in her hospitable little salon with its striped yellow silk walls, she listened sympathetically, day after day, to Paul reciting his litany of woes. What was he to do, he moaned, setting down his delicate Limoges cup so his hostess might refill it, and rubbing his hands over his face and temples. He could not go on any longer. He was so unhappy he had developed stomach ulcers. With three small children and a baby in arms, his small salary was woefully inadequate. His wife could not make ends meet and failed to understand why Paul preferred to dedicate himself to pure science, rather than accept one of the lucrative posts that private industry was forever dangling before him. Matters were not helped, Paul added, by the acidulous interventions of his mother-in-law who lived with them. When Langevin got so nervous and tense that even his students commented, the Borels and the Perrins tried to distract him by dragging him off to see a play at the Odéon or Le Vieux Colombier, or even to the Opéra.

As for Marie, widowhood brought round-the-clock hours of loneliness. Paul reawakened enthusiasms of her Warsaw youth, with his lively interest in politics and people, in literature, the arts, music and good food; he opened new windows for her. An activist like Jean Perrin, he had taken a prominent part in the League of the Rights of Man, which was one of the first groups of intellectuals to take up cudgels to free Dreyfus. Marie had sufficient background in mathematics to keep abreast of the latest developments in physics, and Paul served as an excellent bridge to new theories coming to the fore.

What was equally important in Marie's relationship with Paul—whatever its nature—was the fact that she, more than most, could understand and sympathize with his desire to remain in teaching and research. And, like their intimates the Perrins and Borels, she felt Mme. Langevin was a handicap to his career.

In mid-July 1910, a good year before the press broke the Langevin-Curie story, Paul rented in his own name at no. 5 rue du Banquier, near the Sorbonne, a tiny fourth-floor apartment comprising two rooms and a kitchen, which he converted into a dressing room. He subsequently furnished the flat when he renewed the lease under the assumed name of "Grosnier." Characteristically, Marie made no attempt to conceal her identity, and neighbors reported that she did the marketing and the pair ate there daily. Since Marie left as little to chance as possible throughout her entire life, it is hard to imagine that she participated in this arrangement with her eyes shut. But how she read the future is anyone's guess.

According to Marguerite Borel, Marie's friends never thought twice about the pair being together. Why should they? Paul had been an intimate of both Curies for years, so what was more normal than that he should continue as a close friend of the widow entombed in her grief. Then, one evening some time in early 1911, the Borels had dinner at the Perrins', and Marie appeared at the coffee hour in a white dress with a rose at her waist. She sat down and remained silent as always. But, Marguerite noted perceptively, "something signified her resurrection like the spring, following a frozen winter, suddenly announces its arrival by a series of details." The next day, Jean Perrin stopped by the Borels' to compare observations. "What has happened to her?"[7] he asked. Marguerite, who had never before seen Marie in anything but somber clothes, was equally mystified.

This incident is the only one in Marguerite's account of the Langevin affair that might be questioned. She apparently places it at the Boulevard Kellermann when, at the time in question, Marie lived in Sceaux and was no longer a next-door neighbor of the Perrins. This does not, of course, rule out Marie's appearance there as related. It should be borne in mind that Marguerite was writing

personal memoirs, not history. And the one thing that made a sufficient impression to stick in her mind was Marie's changed appearance, which was sufficiently extraordinary for Jean Perrin to comment on also.

Without trying to read something into chronology that is not
there, it is also worth nothing that Paul's rental of a flat in mid-July
1910, and Marie's changed wardrobe in early 1911, both occurred
after the death of Dr. Curie in February 1910, and one is tempted
to wonder if this might be a case of cause and effect. For with
GrandPé's death, not only did Marie lose her last remaining link
with Pierre, exclusive of the two girls, but her need for close adult
companionship would have been even more acute. On the other
hand, there is nothing to indicate that their intimacy did not long
precede 1910. Marie was very fond of her father-in-law, and she
gave unstintingly of herself to him during the last weeks and
months of his illness, but she was too liberated—and he too worldly
wise—for his presence to constitute a bar to her happiness.

The spring of 1911, Marie, accompanied by Irène and Ève, went
to Genoa to attend a series of scientific meetings. They and the
Borels stayed in the same small hotel at Santa Margherita Ligure. In
the mornings, the five went sightseeing, even venturing by boat to
Rappalo one day. In her slow reflective way, Irène pestered Émile
Borel with questions about everything they saw, and he discussed
mathematics at length with her. Each afternoon, when Marie and
Borel went off in a rented car to their sessions in Genoa, Marguerite kept an eye on the girls as they played on the beach with Walcia
Valentine, their Polish governess. Marguerite had a hard time trying
to cultivate Irène, whom she had seen at the Perrins' and elsewhere. At first, the diffident fourteen-year-old rebuffed her advances, replying stiffly, "I hardly know you."[8] But Marguerite prevailed, and Irène mellowed.

Each evening, while M. Borel prepared for the next day's sessions, Marie, who had already retired, invited Marguerite to come
in for a chat. While the younger woman perched comfortably on

the foot of the ornate iron bed, the older woman discussed her concern about Langevin. As out of character as these confidences seem, this may have been one of the rare moments in her life when Marie felt the need to unburden herself—for whatever reason—and her sister Bronya, that pillar of strength, was not around.

"He is so sad," Marie explained. She was worried that Langevin might yield to his wife's entreaties and, out of weariness and discouragement, surrender to commercialism and be destroyed. She did not want to see that happen. "He is a genius!" Marie exclaimed earnestly, letting the pillows propping her up in bed fall to the floor as she leaned forward to clasp the younger woman's two hands. Perhaps there was also something of the small child in Langevin that appealed to Marie. "I know that he has confidence in you," she continued. Paul was weak. "He must be saved from himself . . . He has need of comprehension, of gentle affection."[9]

By rights the Curie-Langevin story, which broke while Marie and Paul were at the Solvay Congress, should have disappeared from the Paris front pages and been superseded by the news which greeted Marie upon her return to Paris. For on November 7, she received a telegram from Stockholm, informing her that she had won a second Nobel prize. If the French Academy did not want to acknowledge Marie's accomplishments, her international peers did. The Nobel still ranks as one of the world's most prestigious awards, especially in the field of science, and Marie and the American physicist John Bardeen are the sole winners to date—the latter in 1965 and 1972—who have been crowned twice for scientific achievements. As of 1986 only eight women have won it in science. The first time Marie had shared it with Pierre and Henri Becquerel for the discovery of radioactivity. This time she won it alone for the preparation of her one gram of pure radium.

Most foreign scientists were glad to see Marie's own merits rewarded, although a carping few felt her repeat selection was intended more to shame the French Academy for treating her shabbily and to recognize her struggles as a woman in a male preserve than for any other reason. Marie had broken no new ground between 1903 and 1911, even though there was a subtle distinction between the two awards, the first of which was in physics, the next in chemistry. Today most informed people feel that of the two Curies, it is Pierre who was the true giant because of his personal pioneering work in three distinctly separate fields, magnetism, the symmetry of crystals, and piezoelectricity, not to mention his work with Marie. Whereas Marie was limited solely to one—radioactivity. But it's somewhat like comparing apples and oranges because Marie was primarily a chemist, and Pierre a physicist.

Fortified by the honor that this new Nobel reflected on French science, Émile Borel and Jean Perrin were determined to blunt Marie's further exposure to the heinous campaign against her that continued unabashed and had now been joined by xenophobes, antifeminists, and ultranationalists. Accompanied by Raymond Poincaré, an ex-minister who would be Prime Minister within the year and was Marie's lawyer—as well as Paul's—they went to the prefecture of police. There they saw Lepine, the prefect, and demanded the sequestration of the so-called incriminating correspondence which Paul, supposedly, had carelessly left at home in a locked drawer that his brother-in-law had pried open. In addition, Poincaré, who was also the lawyer of the Paris Press Syndicate, asked its president, Jean Dupuy, to telephone the directors of the principal newspapers to place a voluntary censorship on the entire subject.

The more responsible publishers complied. Leon Daudet's *L'Action Française* did not, and *La Libre Parole* interjected a new note with its screaming front page headline: "Will Mme. Curie Remain a Professor at the Sorbonne?" This scandal sheet reported that Mme. Langevin had already instigated proceedings against her husband and "another woman." The customary Sûreté enquiry was under way, and the adultery complaint was due for a hearing on December 7 in the Ninth Correctional Chamber. Then the article lashed out: "Mme. Curie occupies a chair of public instruction . . . Her pupils . . . [and] their families have the right to demand of the professor what the British call *respectability,* [sic, and in English in the French text]."

Marie remained incommunicado at Sceaux upon her return from Brussels. There were too many inquisitive onlookers collected around the entrance to her laboratory in the rue Cuvier to venture there, and she was trying anxiously to protect her daughters as much as possible from the onslaught of adverse publicity. There was little anyone could do for Marie's peace of mind. Even if she was not a scarlet woman having an affair with a married man, the father of four, she had besmirched Pierre's name. And what was worse, in that day and age, the name Curie was about to be dragged through the divorce courts.

This was a difficult period for Irène and her friends—it was over the head of seven-year-old Ève—who did not yet realize what so much commotion was about. Mme. Aline Perrin Lapique still remembers the day when Marie was at the Perrins' and the doorbell rang. Aline's ten-year-old brother, Francis, peered out through the starched lace curtains and reported excitedly to his mother and her guest: "It's Mme. Langevin!" Marie disappeared upstairs, and Mme. Perrin let Paul's wife in. She tried to appease the upset woman. "Be calm," Henriette Perrin soothed. She'd been through this sort of scene so many times with her own philandering husband and learned to look the other way. "Mme. Perrin," Mme. Langevin interrupted, her voice shrill with emotion. "I am not like you. I love my husband." She burst into tears and flounced out.

"But what can you expect?" commented Mme. Lapicque, reminiscing decades later. "Mme. Langevin was a simple soul. Her reaction was typical for someone with her background."[10]

November 23, the day after the Borels returned from an extended absence in Central Europe, Marguerite was roused from a sound slumber by her agitated maid with word that M. Perrin and M. Debierne were below and insisted upon seeing her at once. Marguerite had barely time to reach for the dressing gown at the foot of the bed before the apoplectic men rushed in, each excitedly brandishing a slim periodical. Marguerite recognized *L'Oeuvre* by its traditional red binding.

With a front-page banner shrieking "The Sorbonne Scandals," the weekly's latest edition appearing on Paris kiosks that morning was already sold out. Aggressive Gustave Téry, its editor and author of the lead article, which filled almost the entire issue, was a former École Normale classmate of Langevin. He had abandoned the year before a lackluster career as a philosophy professor at Laon to found this quasi-intellectual gossip sheet. Téry slyly maintained that he was not going to expose the Langevin-Curie epistles, although numerous journalists besides Téry had already seen them. Instead, he published the bulk of the subpoena issued against Langevin by his wife's lawyer, which was tantamount to the same thing but had a far more authoritative ring. Because letters were the sole acceptable evidence of adultery, except *"flagrant délit,"* according to article 338 of the penal code, they were abundantly cited in the writ. But whether they had been tampered with before appearing in the legal document is anyone's guess. The source of Marie's letters is known, but that of Langevin's was never disclosed.

The correspondence was clearly between two people on intimate terms and corroborated Langevin's domestic problems. The subpoena, according to Téry, pointed out that "M. Langevin kept Mme. Curie abreast of his intimate preoccupations, asking her advice and moral direction." For anyone taking the twelve-plus pages of excerpts at their face value, Marie's gravest mistake was to give Paul advice for his failing marriage after first discussing the matter with the Perrins. The three agreed that a separation was the only solution, and Marie relayed this information and matter-of-factly told Paul how to proceed. For his own sake, Paul must not prolong a situation which was keeping him mentally unfit to resume work.

Téry's running commentary highlighted and interspersed the segments and constituted a vitriolic attack on feminism and the purported easy morals practiced in liberal academic circles. Mme.

Curie, "the Vestal Virgin of radium," was not a "dragon of virtue" but "an ambitious Pole who had ridden to glory on Curie's coat-tails and was now trying to latch onto Langevin's." In far-off America, the flamboyant Hearst press summarized *L'Oeuvre*'s article: "Mme. Curie madly in love. The wife in the triangle?—'An idiot,' she declares."[11]

Both Debierne and Perrin had read the venomous piece before bursting in on Marguerite, who later termed it a "series of fragments cleverly separated by ellipses in such a way that the general sense was distorted." And Debierne had already been out to Sceaux. Even at that hour, he reported, a number of surly-looking individuals were gathering in front of Marie's house. "What can we do, Marguerite?" the pair demanded.[12]

While Marguerite hurriedly dressed, her husband was sent for and shown *L'Oeuvre*. "Go out to Sceaux, Marguerite," he ordered, "and bring Mme. Curie and her daughters here. We have two extra rooms where they can stay and be protected from insults."

Debierne accompanied her. By now more people were standing in front of the Curie home, peering around inquisitively. Some were belligerent, others, abusive. Catcalls and cries of "Get the foreign woman out!" "Husband-snatcher!" could be heard even inside the house, and Debierne and Marguerite had little trouble persuading Marie to pack some clothes and accompany them. For once she seemed glad to have someone tell her what to do. Debierne then went off to fetch Irène, who was at a gym class on the rue Tournon with the Chavannes children and Aline Perrin, while Marie and Ève followed Marguerite into another horse-drawn cab. Marie was as white as a statue and as silent. Marguerite longed to take her hand but dared not.

A short time after Marie's arrival at the Borels', Debierne hurried in with Irène. Bewilderment showed plainly on her drawn face. In the hall where they took their work-out, Isabelle Chavannes had spied a copy of *L'Oeuvre*. Seeing the names Mme. Curie and Paul Langevin on the cover, the girl thought the couple had made some new discovery and cried: "Irène, there's something here about your mother!" Too late, Isabelle realized what the story was about. Before she could spare her friend, Irène had snatched the red-bound publication from her, read more than enough in one glance, and fainted. Once at the Borels', she remained glued to her mother's side, her face blotted against the folds of Marie's black skirts. "We must get Irène away," M. Perrin said. "Henriette will take care of her, and she can sleep with Aline."

When Mme. Perrin arrived, Irène, her head downcast, clutched Marie tightly and kept repeating in her grave voice, "I'm staying with Mé." The adults tried to reassure her. When the girl finally consented to go to her friend Aline Perrin, Marie, walking like someone in a trance, allowed herself to be led off to rejoin Ève who was in another room with the Borels' maid.

While Debierne, Jean Perrin, and Emile Borel debated a course of action over the luncheon table, and Marie tried to eat a bite alone with Ève, Marguerite was delegated to answer the telephone. It never stopped ringing. Distressed friends kept calling. No one could believe the story. Marie was so compromised, how could any self-respecting woman ever again be seen with her? Marguerite kept repeating that the allegations weren't true. Marie must be upheld at all costs. She was there with the Borels now. "At the École Normale?" one friend could hardly believe her ears. "Yes, at the École Normale." There was a shocked silence. "Are you crazy?"

After lunch, the Minister of Public Instruction, Théodore Steeg, sent for Borel. Because Borel was its scientific director, he and his wife occupied an official apartment at the École Normale, and Steeg made it clear that by harboring Mme. Curie there, they were bringing disrepute on the entire French academic community. He threatened to revoke Borel, but Borel held his ground. "Mme. Curie will remain with me as long as she wishes."

Marguerite's father, Paul Appell, likewise summoned her. For Steeg had wasted no time in breaking the news of Marie's whereabouts to the dean of the Sorbonne Faculty of Science. When she arrived at no. 32 rue du Bac, Marguerite's mother warned that her father was furious. This was the first scene Marguerite had ever had with him, so it was no wonder that, fifty years later, when she was writing her *Souvenirs,* she could still recall his anger. He felt Marie should resign her post and return to Poland. As the dean accountable for the faculty, he felt it his responsibility to suggest this course of action.

A frantic Marguerite begged him to reconsider and threatened to never see him again should he follow through with his declared course of action.

He reluctantly agreed to "do nothing," as she pleaded.

After having disarmed her father, Marguerite tackled Mme. Cruppi, the wife of the Minister of Justice, while her husband Debierne and Perrin did the same with other influential friends and colleagues. Marie's affair was not the first at the University of Paris. But the others who had been similarly involved were men.

Libel actions were too expensive, so duels still prevailed. But by 1911 dueling had been largely reduced to a ritual; only in rare instances was blood drawn or either participant seriously hurt. The gazette *Gil Blas* declared itself the champion of the dignity of the press—and of Marie—and one of its staff, Henri Chervet, sent his seconds to challenge Leon Daudet of *L'Action Française.* In the ensuing swordplay the latter received a deep gash in his forearm. Because *Gil Blas* also took Téry to task for publishing the Curie-Langevin correspondence, Téry, in turn, fought its editor, Pierre Mortier—with Mme. Langevin's brother as his witness.

It was one thing for Téry to call Langevin a "cad and a scoundrel" and accuse him of hiding "behind Marie's skirts." It was something else to have others duel on his behalf. Early one morning, Langevin arrived at the rue d'Ulm and startled the Borels with his announcement that he was about to challenge Téry to a duel. "I know it's an idiotic thing to do but I must." Borrowing the obliging Marguerite for support, he set off in search of seconds. Paul Painlevé, the mathematician and the second future Prime Minister to be drawn into the affair, and M. Haller, the director of EPCI, agreed, reluctantly, to serve. When the pair stopped for lunch in a little bistro frequented by coachmen and cabdrivers, Marguerite ate heartily but Paul did not touch a bite. They continued on to Chez Gastinne Renette so he might get in some target practice with a pistol, a weapon with which he was unfamiliar. That evening, in order to keep the late editions from her and be sure she got no inkling of what was pending, Henriette Perrin never left Marie's room at the Borels'.

At 10:30 A.M. the next day, the two duelists met in the Parc des Princes Bicycle Stadium—Téry, the tips of his razor-thin mustache waxed stiff; Langevin with his mustache carefully curled and his goatee freshly trimmed. Both were in black, with bowler hats. They took their places, twenty-five paces apart, firearms at their sides as two doctors stood by. Haller and Painlevé wore the *de rigueur* morning coats, while Téry's witnesses were casually attired in jackets and felt trilbies. With the help of a ladder they carried with them for similar emergencies, the resourceful press circumvented the locked gates and high surrounding walls and were seated in the top row of the grandstand. Painlevé began to count, "One, two, three," in unusually quick time and took Téry and Langevin by surprise.

Not a sound shattered the calm. Téry, as the challenged, should have shot first. Instead, he kept his gun pointed toward the ground and looked up at the clouds. Langevin, who was aiming at Téry, lowered his weapon when he saw what Téry had done. He could not shoot at a man who had not fired. The duel was over. Everyone packed up and went home, and Téry explained to his readers: "The defense of Mme. Langevin does not oblige me . . . to kill her husband . . . I could not deprive French science of so precious a brain."[13]

Balladeers and boulevard cabaret reviews seized on the spate of duels. Couplets were sung about "le chopin de la polonaise," as some wit, in a clever play on words, baptized Langevin. ("Chopin"

= a piece of good fortune, especially an opportune conquest by a woman = the famous Polish composer; "polonaise" = a Polish woman [i.e., Marie] = a dance.) But Marie was unaware of all this.

The gathering of the clan Sklodowski—the arrival of her brother, Jozio, and her sisters, Bronya and Hela—increased the pressure on Marie to leave ungrateful France and return to the University of Warsaw, which promised to award Marie her due. But her resolve to stay strengthened with each passing day. The support of Pierre's brother, Jacques, who rushed to her side from Montpellier, was a great comfort. P. Montel, Langevin's friend, brought Langevin's news, but Paul himself did not appear. Marie started seeing a few friends. Paderewski and other compatriots came to call. The extra leaves remained in the Borels' dining room table, and their young cook had orders to prepare for an indefinite number of guests at each meal. The intense activity of the Borels, Perrins, and Debierne bore fruit. If they did not succeed in persuading their colleagues that Marie was innocent, they calmed the academic furor. The University authorities settled on a fact-finding commission—a notoriously time-consuming procedure. And public interest slowly waned.

Marie was no quitter. Besides, taking to her heels might be considered tantamount to a confession of guilt—to an admission that she had tried to break up the Langevin home. Finally she told her family, "I am French. My children are French, like Pierre. I will stay here and continue my work if I am permitted to do so."[14]

Her intimates worried about her health as much as about her state of mind. Marie was beginning to lose weight once more. They wondered if she would be able to make the strenuous forty-eight-hour trip to Stockholm in December to collect her Nobel award. Marie went, however, calling on the same reserves and resolution that had seen her through other difficult periods of her life. Bronya, the doctor in the family, accompanied her for obvious reasons, as did Irène. Marie was concerned about the effects of the past weeks on her two daughters, especially on the elder girl, who had already been greatly disturbed at her mother's failure to win admittance to the French Academy. Irène experienced some difficult moments. But this year of trial served to tighten the bonds between the mother and her rapidly maturing firstborn.

When Marie stood to receive the Nobel medal and leather-bound certificate from King Gustave V in the great Hall of Prizes in the Royal Palace, she was her usual conspicuous self in simple, unadorned black lace amid a glittering galaxy of bemedaled dignitaries and bejeweled women in formal attire. Her pride pulled her through this imposing ceremony organized by the Swedish Royal Academy, the official banquet tendered afterward by the King, and the other formal dinners and receptions where strict protocol was maintained in an atmosphere of great cordiality.

In the lecture expected of each laureate, Marie emphasized that "the discoveries of radium and polonium were made by Pierre Curie and me together."[15] But her speech was carefully worded to underline, once and for all, her own role—both then and now.

The psychological reaction to being in Stockholm under the present circumstances, coupled with the memories the city evoked of her happy past with Pierre, exacted a toll. Only fierce determination kept Marie on her feet, and, by the time she reached Paris, she collapsed and fell into a deep depression. Marie had seen everything through to the end. Her daughter Ève claims that she thought of suicide—as uncharacteristic as this may seem. Bronya and the faithful Debierne hovered anxiously over Marie's pathetic, shrunken figure as she lay tossing in her bed at Sceaux. The Perrins were in daily attendance and Irène and Ève were not allowed in the room. How much of Marie's intermittent high fever and kidney problems could be traced to overexposure to radiation during the past years is hard to ascertain from this distance.

As 1911 drew to a close, Bronya supervised her sister's removal not, as planned, to the new apartment she had rented on Paris's Île de la Cité but on a stretcher to a private clinic. And the Archbishop of Paris convoked a meeting to determine the attitude of his confessors vis-à-vis readers of "disreputable journals."

Some days later, Marie learned that matters were arranged between Paul and his wife. What she most dreaded had been avoided. The writ of separation between the Langevins made no mention of her. No proof was registered officially of her supposed complicity as an "adulteress," and her name would never be dragged into a divorce court. The psychological effect on Marie was quickly evident. Her fever fell and, for the moment, there was no further talk of an operation.

In January, Jean Perrin wrote Rutherford in more detail: "The injuries are attributed to Langevin." Paul assumed the blame because he had not taken the precaution of getting such existing evidence as was available against his wife and which did not, at the same time, involve the use of Marie's name. Perrin included the court orders concerning the disposition of the children: "At 19 the boys can live with him . . . He is keeping the intellectual direction of the children . . . and must naturally pay a monthly allowance to his wife. And now," Perrin concluded with an almost audible sigh of relief, "I hope we shall all be able to get back to work again!? [sic]" In a postscript, Jean added: "Langevin has been most appreciative of your friendship. Mme. Curie has also been very touched by your attitude."[16]

— o —

Poor Paul. He never was very good when it came to money. He picked up one bill, his wife's, that January. Perhaps he was paying another when, in 1923, for an unspecified reason, he assigned to Marie and her daughters a portion of a handsome sum of money he had earned from a patent he shared with Pierre. Meanwhile, when war broke out in 1914, he resumed living with his family.

Paul lost Marie irretrievably—had he wanted her—for in the society of that day, it was impossible for the two to resume any but the most professional relationship, which, of course, they did. Had

Marie wanted Paul, it would have made no difference either. And, of course, the actual extent of her personal involvement can never be known. The only thing certain is that while Paul paid literally, Marie paid figuratively. The year of 1911 left her with deep emotional scars—whatever the reasons for them. Although still a comparatively young woman, no man would ever again play a major role in her life.

XI
1912–1914

Transitional Years

HOME WAS NOW ON THE fourth floor at no. 36 Quai de Béthune on the Île St.-Louis in the Seine; it was within comfortable walking distance of the Sorbonne but was a far cry from their home at Sceaux, where the girls had a large yard and Irène her own private garden, which she sorely missed. This move had been dictated to save Marie the fatigue of her former time-consuming daily commuting and to resolve the needs of better schooling, close at hand, for her growing daughters. The Pont de la Tournelle connected the bohemian and academic world of the Left Bank with this quiet, sedate haven anchored to the past by its gray stone, centuries-old town houses, untouched since Louis XIV's day.

From every point of view except livability the new apartment was superb. Of course, there was no elevator. The acres of shining parquet, on which had once lain magnificent Aubussons of the period, were covered with a few scatter rugs from Polish peasants' looms and served as a vast skating rink for Irène's black cat. The huge high-ceilinged rooms overpowered Marie's humble furniture pieces, which she had inherited from GrandPé, and looked lost amid so much splendor, yet she never added a stick more. And never felt the need to do so. Marie lived here the remaining twenty-two years of her life, and the tall windows, which had formerly been draped in rich damasks, remained bare except for thin net. A mute testimonial to decorating "à la Marie," the overall effect was one of icy discomfort, and the only room that ever appeared lived-in was her own workroom with its clutter of books and papers— and picture of Pierre. Ève's bedroom never looked the same two weeks in a row, because she was forever redecorating it, while Irène never gave two thoughts to where she slept provided there was a bed, and on occasion, she could even dispense with that. But the view from the shuttered windows overlooking the Seine, with its quais and the rear of Notre Dame nestled on the adjacent spur of the Île de la Cité, was unparalleled, and on a warm night when they were opened wide, the river sounds—the silken noise of the *péniches* gliding along, the tugs chugging past, the cries of the seagulls—seeped through the ancient, sleeping town house.

Strong-willed Marie insisted upon coming home from the clinic as soon as possible. Although she had developed some uretal complications, she refused to entertain the thought of a proposed kidney operation until after the February meeting of the Physicists' Congress in Paris. Final stages and details of the International Radium Standard she had been working on since the Brussels meeting had been overseen by Debierne because of her illness, and it was scheduled for formal acceptance when the group next convened.

Marie tried unsuccessfully to have their date postponed because she was determined to be on deck. However, Rutherford confided to a colleague that they would probably be able to finish much more quickly without "Mme. Curie who has . . . a tendency to raise difficulties." To the relief of many attending, she was still so feeble that Debierne, whom Rutherford labeled in his characteristically blunt way, "a very sensible fellow,"[1] represented her. After the sessions were over, Rutherford came to see her for a long chat.

When she was finally operated on at the end of March by the famous surgeon Charles Walther, it was touch and go. A long convalescence followed, and Bronya rented a little house under her own name of Dluska at Brunoy, just outside of Paris in the general direction of Fontainebleau, where she took Marie to recuperate, incognita. In a profoundly depressed state of mind, Marie withdrew further into herself and had a harder time recovering from the notoriety to which she had been subjected than from the surgery.

Irène was sent for her Easter vacation break to visit her uncle Jacques at Montpellier, traveling south with the Borels, who were en route to their country home. Irène missed her adored mother and worried about her. What was even harder for the maturing girl to comprehend was why, exactly, the recent events had so devastated Marie that she insisted her daughter's almost daily letters must be addressed to "Mme. Sklodowska."

The scandal had been extremely hard on Irène, and the final blow was to have to hide, as if in shame, the name she had been taught to adore. She pleaded with her mother to let mail be properly addressed—to "Mme. Pierre Curie." But Marie was determined never to let her name be plastered in the papers again and did not want anyone at Brunoy to know her true identity. One wonders if she ever gave a thought to what this subterfuge might do to her adolescent daughter. It is one thing to try to hide away, another to make such a concerted effort to disguise oneself. Had a sense of guilt prompted her actions? Marie would never have reproached herself for snatching Langevin from his hearth and home, as the public did. Such an accusation was ridiculous. Paul was a born philanderer with a roving eye and would be till the day he died. But what she could blame herself for was to have dragged Pierre's name through the mud. And, since Marie felt she was no longer worthy of bearing Pierre's name, Mme. Pierre Curie was no more.

At Brunoy, Marie could not refuse to receive Poland's greatest writer and Nobel laureate, Henri Sienkiewicz, when he came with a special delegation from Poland to try and persuade her to return and head up a Radium Institute, which the Scientific Society of Warsaw proposed to build for her. But Marie was determined to remain in France because the plans had been accepted for the Radium Institute to be built jointly by the Pasteur Institute and the University of Paris. Even though finalization of some details had been momentarily tabled because of the Langevin scandal, construction was due to start shortly. So Marie did the next best thing. She agreed to direct the Warsaw establishment from afar and sent them two of her best assistants, Danysz and Wertenstein, who were both Polish. From the day she took over Pierre's laboratory, she would always encourage Poles—and women—to work there.

Toward the end of June, Marie suffered a relapse and was taken to a sanatorium at Thonon, in the Savoie mountains, for a month. It is interesting to learn, from Irène's correspondence with her mother, that the girls stopped by to see Langevin on their return from Brunoy for a July 14 celebration with Mme. Perrin and the two Perrin children—a picnic in their Quai apartment while watching the traditional fireworks from the nearby Pont de Sully. Irène's letters are wide-ranging and cover everything from an egg shampoo to the trouble she had reading Minna von Barnheim and *David Copperfield* simultaneously in the originals without confusing German and English; they show her increasing maturity and nice sense of humor. Commenting on the political situation in England, the girl observed: "I have . . . seen that an English Minister is almost killed every day . . . by the English suffragettes, but it seems to me that the[y] . . . have not found a brilliant way of proving they are capable of voting."[2]

Herta Ayrton, the well-known British physicist whom Marie first met when she accompanied Pierre to London, had remained in touch with her ever since. Herta's own recent widowhood and her failure, two years before, to be named a fellow of the Royal Society, Britain's senior scientific body, were additional bonds between them. The moment Herta read about the Langevin affair and learned of Marie's subsequent breakdown, she suggested Marie visit her. Herta's experience as an active suffragette had taught her how to handle both press and police, and she promised complete privacy. Accused, like Marie, of working for, not with, her late physicist husband and tired of seeing British journals recognize Pierre alone as the discoverer of radium, she wrote to the Westminster *Gazette:* "Errors are notoriously hard to kill, but an error that ascribes to a man what was actually the work of a woman has more lives than a cat."[3]

When Marie was well enough to leave the sanatorium, a complete change of environment was in order. So she accepted Herta's invitation, and the press never learned she was there until after she left. The minute Herta knew she was coming, she rented the old Mill House at Highcliffe-on-Sea in Hampshire, located on the edge of the New Forest with nothing but a little wood separating the garden from the seashore. Marie arrived in August, accompanied by her two girls. She was worn out from the trip, and Herta, too, was badly in need of a rest. While Marie slowly regained her strength, Herta endeared herself to Ève by accompanying the eight-year-old on the piano when she sang French songs; she won over solemn Irène by discussing mathematics as one adult to another. Hostess and guest were soon walking along the cliffs daily, a study in contrasts—slender, white-haired Marie more fragile than ever, all in black, and striding alongside, green-eyed Herta, frizzy dark hair flying, in a flowing Pre-Raphaelite robe. When the girls returned home, Marie even ventured, incognita, to London for several days at Herta's home on Norfolk Square before following them across the Channel.

Her health restored, Marie's inherent common sense and pragmatism took over. Notes reappeared in her laboratory book on December 3, 1912; the last previous one was dated October 7, 1911. Marie also resumed teaching when classes began after the holidays. Irretrievably lost was the public's image of her as a widow enshrined forever in widow's weeds. Perhaps it is going too far to say that no man would ever again enter her life, but certainly, no other man would ever again play a major role in it.

Marie had met Einstein at the first Solvay Congress and was so impressed by both him and his work that, shortly afterward, she gave an unsolicited, glowing testimonial on his behalf to officials offering him a position in Zürich. He and his wife stayed with Marie when he came to Paris a short time later, in March 1912, to address the French Society of Physicists at Langevin's request. Paul, whom the German claimed was "the only Frenchman who completely understands me,"[4] was one of a handful of scientists to grasp the implications of Einstein's revolutionary thinking. While Rutherford and Soddy had earlier explained what the actual process of radioactivity was, it was Einstein's famous equation spelling out the disappearance of mass and the appearance of great energy that gave the reason for this. Before the couple left Paris, Einstein and Marie planned a July holiday for their joint families. The walking trip through the Bregaglia Alps and the Engadine was a great success, and the two Curie girls got along famously with Hans, the elder Einstein boy, who was Ève's age. Marie enjoyed herself thoroughly, as did Einstein, who would always refer to her as "the one person whom fame has not corrupted."[5] There was a lot of shoptalk in German, and Einstein was struck by Irène's intelligence; he would become her lifelong friend. Ève was amused at the way he circulated absentmindedly among the boulders, so deep in conversation with Mé that he walked alongside deep crevasses and toiled up the steep rocks without noticing them. One day, the three young people howled with laughter when he suddenly stopped dead, seized Marie's arm, and demanded, peering intently at her: "You understand, what I need to know is exactly what happens to the passengers in an elevator when it falls into emptiness."[6] The imaginary fall in an elevator posed problems of transcendent relativity—there would be no gravitational pull so they would float—and he was struggling with the problem of discovering a mathematical entity with which to represent gravitation.

By fall, Marie felt sufficiently sure of herself to keep an old promise to visit Rutherford at Manchester, where he held the chair of physics at the University, and collect an honorary degree. Irène, who now frequently accompanied her mother on similar jaunts, was not along. She had recently completed the first part of her baccalaureate examination and was studying to pass the second half, in order to enter the University of Paris. In her letter to the girl for her sixteenth birthday, Marie included a new trigonometry problem and the best present of all—word that mail could once more be addressed to "Mme. Curie."

The amount of travel Marie was undertaking now was a far cry from the cloistered life she once led with Pierre, and next, she went to Warsaw to attend, as honorary director, for the ground breaking of the Polish Radium Institute. This was a sentimental trip into the past for Marie, who arrived with her face swollen from a bad tooth, but managed to carry out a heavy schedule. The minute Irène heard the news, she wrote back immediately. She was playing an increasing role in her mother's life, and from now on, her letters voice so much concern for Marie's well-being that it is difficult to tell whether it is the mother or daughter who is writing.

Once work actually started on the French Radium Institute, it was not as easy for Marie to get away. Like another celebrated spouse who spared no effort to build a Taj Mahal to the memory of a loved one, she deemed it only fitting that the Paris municipal government should name the new street created alongside the construction site "Pierre Curie"; on her death, it would be rechristened the "rue Pierre et Marie Curie." She insisted that the original budget include a salary for a gardener, and in the spring of 1913, before the foundations were completely laid, she personally planted willows in the small garden that was to be in the central courtyard uniting the Curie and Pasteur pavilions. Marie believed that laboratories should have big windows and the people working in them should have something green and growing to look out at. She also insisted on an elevator. Nothing escaped Marie's attention. She conducted a daily inspection tour, even climbing scaffoldings when necessary, and on Friday afternoons she participated in the weekly, on-site meeting of the architect Nénot, the contractors, and construction workers. To her dismay, an especially damp winter slowed down certain key installations.

Forming a nucleus of research workers, molding them into a productive team, and keeping them financed and equipped was to absorb the major portion of Marie's remaining life. Unfortunately, the phenomenal success of radium in the treatment of certain malignant tumors caused demand to far outstrip the supply, even from the University of Vienna, where Stefan Meyer was presently producing considerable quantities. The price of any radioactive materials went sky-high, and not unexpectedly, priority of purchase was granted those laboratories concentrating on medical research. The Radium Institute building itself cost only 50,000 gold francs more than a gram of radium, the going price of which was 750,000 gold francs.

Work had been proceeding simultaneously in the atomic field. This year, Niels Bohr, the Danish theoretical physicist who spent a few doctoral months with Rutherford, combined the latter's nuclear model of the atom, which firmly established its nucleus, with Max Planck's quantum theory for a brilliant new description of the atom.

Early in the summer, Marie again sent her girls with Walecia and Jozia, the cook and governess, to L'Arcouest, the peaceful Brittany fishing village that was the summer retreat of a number of Marie's

Sorbonne colleagues. This hamlet of some three hundred fishermen and peasants was discovered at the turn of the century by two
Sorbonne professors, the historian Charles Seignobos and the biologist Louis Lapique. No longer remote but still fairly inaccessible,
"The Port of Science," as some witty journalist nicknamed it long
ago, is inhabited today, near the end of the twentieth century, by
the third generation of the original members. They follow the same
pattern of simple, inexpensive living originally established by
Seignobos, which was so avant-garde for his day. She planned to
join them later, after her duties attendant on the end of the school
year were wrapped up and she made the final move into the new
Institute. Marie was used to staying alone at this season, rattling
around by herself in the big empty apartment on the Quai, with
only the concierge to do some hit-or-miss cleaning and a bit of
cooking. After working late, she would come home to go over the
mail and read Irène's letters full of household affairs—and gossip.
Each letter between the pair, whether from Irène, or to her, ended
on a mathematical note: "The derivatives are coming along all right;
the inverse functions are adorable. On the other hand, I can feel
my hair stand on end when I think of the theorem of Rolle, and
Thomas's formula"—a formula which Irène had previously described as "the ugliest thing I know."[7]

A scant three years after Marie thought her world had collapsed,
her dream of a laboratory dedicated to Pierre's memory and devoted to the study of radioactivity had materialized and was almost
ready for occupancy. Workmen finished glazing the last panes of
glass in the windows of the tiny amphitheater, and the June sun
highlighted the words "Institut du Radium, Pavillon Curie" carved
on the fronton of the building so conspicuous by its newness amid
the old ones all around. The flowers she had planted were bloom-
ing, and Marie was badgering the carpenters to finish installing the
shelves in her new office before the equipment was transferred
from the rue Cuvier and the staff moved in.

The news in *Le Temps* about the assassination on Sunday, June the twenty-eighth, of the Archduke Francis Ferdinand, the nephew and heir of the Austrian Emperor Franz-Josef, and his morganatic wife startled her. A patriotic Serb student shot the imperial couple while they were on an official trip to Sarajevo, the capital of Bosnia, a Turkish province with a large Serb population which Austria had annexed in 1908. Marie had been pessimistically talking with Langevin and other colleagues about a general European war for over a year, and she was worried that the Austrians might seize the occasion to unleash a punitive expedition against Serbia. If a fire were lit in the Balkan tinderbox, where would it stop? By the fourth of July the Paris press concluded that the crisis was over, and by the middle of the month, the bourgeoisie set off on its famed *clôture annuelle*—its sacrosanct summer holiday. The Borels had already left for L'Arcouest; Jean Perrin was about to join his family there, and Marie stopped by the Gare Montparnasse to make a reservation to do the same.

Unexpectedly, the trouble in the Balkans flared anew. On July 23, Austria-Hungary issued an ultimatum, and two days later, the Serbs ordered a general mobilization. Journalists predicted that Russia would not stand by idly and see Serbia crushed, and worried Parisians clustered in the streets around the headquarters of various newspapers, where the latest telegrams and dispatches were pasted up. When Serbia rejected the Austrian ultimatum, Parisian grocers were swamped by housewives stocking up on sugar, and people rushed into shoe stores to buy stout walking shoes. The twenty-ninth, Marie wrote Irène that she felt like she was sitting "on top of a volcano."[8]

On August 1, as Marie returned from the Gare Montparnasse, where she had gone to pick up her train tickets, she saw the poster brigade out, plastering up the white mobilization notices. Less than an hour later, Germany, who was spoiling for another fight with France, started to mobilize also.

Fate took over, unleashing the war that every Frenchman and German thought would be short—and that was to kill ten million men. August 2, German armies violated the neutrality of Luxembourg, and Germany addressed an ultimatum to Belgium, demanding passage for its armies while, at Paris's Gare de l'Est, mobilized men gathered, surrounded by friends, families, lovers. On August 3, the King of Belgium repulsed the German ultimatum, and Germany declared war on France. On August 4, World War I began.

At L'Arcouest, the war assumed an immediacy overnight for Irène and Ève when Aline and Francis Perrin's father was called and returned to Paris at once. Postal service became sporadic, cutting the little hamlet off from the world. Irène, who was as much upset by the uncertainty as by anything else, wanted to rejoin her mother, but Marie advised her daughters that they were not to return unless Mme. Perrin did with her children. She warned: ". . . we shall not communicate easily for some time . . . be courageous and calm."[9]

Poland was invaded, and Marie agonized over the fate of her family, about whom she could get no news. Britain declared war on Germany for violation of Belgian neutrality, and Marie's footsteps echoed hollowly on the floors of her new, deserted Curie Pavilion, accompanied only by those of one elderly laboratory assistant, Razet, with heart trouble. "I would dearly like to bring you back but it is impossible for the moment,"[10] Marie replied to Irène's incessant pleas that she, too, participate in the war effort like some of her older friends. Several L'Arcouest fishermen accused the two sisters of being German because they spoke Polish to their help. So Irène started giving Walecia daily French lessons and took Jozia to be photographed in order to get a *permis de séjour* for travel within France; the Chavannes children were sent to Brittany to stay with the Curie girls. While such multiple charges might constitute a wartime assignment for some, it was not the kind that Irène, who was ashamed of playing tennis and swimming at such a time, had in mind.

Marie genuinely missed her girls. In one of the few times on record, Marie showed her feelings for them: "I am dying to come and hug you. I don't have the time. . . . There are moments when I don't know what to do, I want to hold you close so badly." Lonesome as Irène was, she did not find it strange that her mother should insist on remaining in Paris. She was also old enough to realize that Marie liked to hear from them, so she wrote daily, even when she had nothing to say, and once again, implored: "We must be together in this time of trial."[11]

September 4, two days after the President of France ordered the government to Bordeaux, Marie, too, was headed there, officially charged with putting her radium, "a national treasure of inestimable value," in a place of safekeeping. All the radium that existed in France—and constituted a substantial part of the total world supply —lay at her feet, encompassed by twenty kilos of protective lead which made her cumbersome suitcase even heavier. The train was jammed with men, women, and children, equally laden with heavy baggage and parcels, containing whatever household possessions and valuables were portable, and Marie, who was never one to run away from anything, was horrified lest her fellow travelers think that she, too, was unpatriotically fleeing. The trip was painfully slow, for the train was frequently forced to make long, unscheduled stops in the middle of the abandoned countryside. Arriving at the depot in Bordeaux late at night, Marie was delighted, for once, to be recognized by someone who cried, "But it's Mme. Curie!" She was taken in tow, and a room found for her in the bulging, overpopulated city. In the morning she turned the priceless radium over to Professor Bergonie of the Faculty of Sciences of the University of Bordeaux for safekeeping for the government, and returned by the next train. Few civilians in their right minds were returning to Paris, and the coach overflowed with soldiers; one gallantly shared a sandwich with the frail, white-haired woman sitting alongside when he learned she had come on board with nothing to eat.

The thought of leaving Pierre's dream that was now immortalized in bricks and mortar never crossed Marie's mind. The Germans had already bombed the cathedral at Rheims, a medieval jewel, in an act of wanton vandalism, and she may have reasoned they would be far less apt to plunder and desecrate the empty Radium Institute if the "Madame" herself were there. Still searching for someplace to help her adopted country where her unique qualifications could be employed to the best advantage, prescient Marie foresaw astronomical casualties in the present conflict because of the terrible new weapons employed; to her amazement she discovered that though radiology was a science, few hospitals were aware of X rays, much less had the equipment to employ them. The army health service was in even poorer shape with exactly one transportable X-ray station. Marie had never personally worked with these rays, but she included several lectures on them, each year, in her Sorbonne classes. Their use, she knew, would facilitate the speedy location of projectiles, shrapnel, and broken bones in the wounded, and time could be an important factor in many cases.

Determined to give the Allied troops the benefit of Roentgen's rays, Marie requested to be relieved by the Minister of Public Education from her university obligations so she could devote herself full-time to war work. The Langevin scandal was an affair of the past and Marie was needed. She assumed the directorship of the Red Cross's radiological service, and at the same time, agreed to establish X-ray installations for the National Veterans Association. Marie at once inventoried the X-ray apparatus existing for teaching and research in the various laboratories and on the shelves of scientific instrument manufacturers, and commandeered whatever she found for installation in as many of the city's hospitals as possible. To supplement this, she next browbeat the unconvinced, overworked War Ministry into granting authorization to set up several radiological cars to provide additional service where needed. Execution of her plan was not easy in wartime France, for cars of a certain size had already been requisitioned and suitable ones were hard to beg or borrow. But Marie was nothing if not determined.

September 6, she wrote the girls: "Paris is calm and gives evidence of holding firm."[12] That same day, the Battle of the Marne began and General Gallieni, the military governor of Paris, requisitioned the capital's taxis to rush five thousand men to the front. These five battalions of infantry from the Seventh Division were thrown in at a strategic point and turned the tide. Slowly the Germans withdrew west of Verdun. By the time the French wounded were evacuated into Paris, Marie already had one radiological car in service, shuttling to and fro within the capital. A large Renault, its chassis had been converted according to her specifications by a patriotic car manufacturer, and she had installed in it a Drault X-ray machine, together with a 110-volt, 15-ampere electric generator, which was to serve as a dynamo, using current from the Renault's engine. Total expenses for this first unit were underwritten by the Union of French Women.

Watching September's heavy casualty lists, Marie realized that her specially equipped cars would be far more valuable near the front lines themselves and at the base hospitals, rather than at the capital's hospitals, so the wounded would not have to be transported far to get quick attention. There was only one answer—a fleet of cars transformed like the Renault could assure a rudimentary but effective X-ray system. This staggering endeavor was undertaken, at the start, on her own initiative. Only someone with Marie's prestige could have operated in such a high-handed, individualistic manner, or so successfully. She shamelessly scrounged money to buy equipment, and the government granted her requisitioning power to supplement this.

By mid-September, Marie felt the war situation had stabilized. There was no indication that it would be over soon, but Paris was no longer in imminent danger. So she sent for her daughters. But now that they could leave, Irène was unable to. Three days earlier, while she was climbing on the cliffs along the shore with Charlot, the Lapique nephew, he fell, dislodging some rocks; Irène was so busy helping him that she did not see another rock tumbling down and got hit. Charlot was all right, but Irène's left foot was badly cut, though not seriously. The local doctor had to sew the wound up with metal sutures, and she could not use her foot for at least two weeks until the wound healed. Mme. Perrin was looking after her, but the girl's frustration was so evident at not being able to depart immediately for Paris that she must have been a difficult patient. Marie counseled patience and sent along, as a stopgap consolation, some more mathematics problems.

XII
1914–1918

Les Petites Curies

EARLY IN OCTOBER, THE
girls were back in Paris, suntanned and healthy. Ève was packed off
daily to primary school and learned to knit for the soldiers. Irène
matriculated at the Sorbonne, majoring in mathematics and physics, and enrolled in a nursing course taught by "Les Dames de
France." The two maids kept house, in a hit-or-miss fashion, and
Marie was gone more than she was at home. Whenever Marie had
the time, Irène hired a horse and buggy and helped her transfer
materials from the rue Cuvier to the new laboratory on the rue
Pierre Curie, where Irène had the responsibility of arranging and

classifying the specimens of radioactive minerals and hundreds of scientific journals in the new library.

Irène was a fascinated onlooker as her mother expanded her efforts to bring the benefits of X rays to the men in the field. There had been absolutely no provision behind the lines for war, and at every turn, Marie encountered harassed, bone-weary officials trying to cope with unprecedented situations. Marie also had to struggle against routine and prejudice, and Irène learned an invaluable lesson as she witnessed her mother, her infighting skills honed by the bureaucratic struggle she had recently waged to create the Radium Institute, ingeniously defeat red tape—which the French called in wartime "System D." Marie might be inherently shy, but she was fighting now for the wounded, not for herself, and it was an uphill battle to make the French Army accept civilian aid, let alone from a woman.

Marie kept for herself one big hand-cranked Renault with a truck body and a windshield, but no doors for the front seat. Fully equipped "Radiological Car E's" maximum speed was a lumbering twenty miles an hour. Its color was the only thing that conformed to any known military specifications; it was painted army gray, with a Red Cross and a French flag on either side. The universally poor country roads made riding in it an adventure in discomfort.

In the late fall, by the time Car E was ready, Irène had received sufficient training from Marie and from Les Dames de France to go along as part of her team. Irène's eagerness to participate in her mother's war work overrode any qualms Marie might have entertained about including her. Thrilled to be no longer considered a child, she thoroughly justified her mother's confidence. Irène's baptism of fire quickly matured her and tightened the bonds with Marie, who soon accepted her as an equal. They were no longer mother and daughter but true collaborators, and a special relationship developed which was to continue after the war. Irène attributed this, years later, to the fact that she was very different from her mother, "more like my father and, perhaps, this is one of the reasons we understood each other so well."[1]

For a seventeen-year-old girl to work at the front with the armies of the north was unusual, even in wartime, and the grim, shattering experience inevitably marked Irène. By November 1, on the French side alone there were three hundred and ten thousand dead and three hundred thousand wounded. To experience such tragedy at firsthand and see so many young men disfigured and crippled filled Irène with a lifetime horror of war. Physically, its effects were to prove even more devastating because of the massive doses of radiation she received, working poorly protected as did everyone at the time. Ignorance of the dangers of overexposure was undoubtedly the cause of the leukemia from which Irène eventually died, as her husband, Frédéric Joliot, wrote to Queen Elizabeth of Belgium, who worked on the front near Ypres with her.

The team of the first "Petite Curie"—as the *poilus* would affectionately nickname the twenty-odd cars Marie ultimately put in service—consisted of Marie, Irène, a doctor, a military assistant, and a military chauffeur. On November 1, they set forth on their first field trip to the military hospital in Creil, well within the circumscribed radius where they were allowed to circulate. From time to time, patrols stopped them. Amazed to see Marie in her dusty brown coat, a round battered hat pulled down over her ears, an old leather briefcase alongside, they angrily demanded, "What's a woman doing out here?", glanced at her papers, then waved Car E on.

The minute they arrived in the bomb-damaged building that served as the Creil field hospital, the surgeon, an unshaven man with drawn face and bloodshot eyes, came out to greet them. A nonbeliever where X rays were concerned, he curtly indicated several rows of newly arrived wounded waiting to be examined. Without wasting a minute in idle conversation, Marie and Irène helped unload their cumbersome equipment, which was carried into the room placed at their disposal. The chauffeur, Gagnat, connected the dynamo with a long cable from the car motor to the X-ray machine and established the other necessary electrical connections. Irène showed the local nurses how to hermetically seal the room to be used by blacking out the windows with curtains brought along for that purpose, while Marie decided on the best arrangement for the various apparatus and photographic developing material. Cloth gloves, goggles, and a few metal screens were the only protective equipment used, and everyone present was warned to avoid the direct beam of the rays whenever possible.

The dynamo was started, Irène prepared the radioscopic screen, and within a half hour after their arrival, the first bloody, muddy patient was wheeled in. One after another, the litters succeeded each other. "Will it hurt?" a soldier wanted to know. "Not any more than having your picture taken," Marie replied encouragingly. Most had never heard of an X ray before and did not know what to expect, and Irène marveled at the way her mother, with a few comforting words, was able to put each man at ease. Head wounds predominated because no helmets were issued until the following June. When the War Minister requested them as standard gear, his request had been denied by the Chambre des Députés as being "too German."

That night, the work sheet for Car E noted "30 examinations." Although Marie may not have realized it, her basic detachment and her inevitable, automatic note-taking, as each patient was wheeled in, reduced the gore and casualties to cold, impersonal statistics and must have helped Irène adjust to the harsh realities of so much suffering. Marie spoke little and would write less of the emotional effects of what she saw, while Irène, with the war as a catalyst, matured quickly. Luckily, she had her mother's mental and physical resilience and, like Marie, was equal to whatever shocks and hardships, even dangers, each exhausting day offered. When the pair were in the field they lived like soldiers, traveling in all kinds of weather, sleeping where they could, eating whatever was available. Through it all, the Curie Pavilon was never far from Marie's thoughts, and she was forever filling her worn attaché case with envelopes containing medicinal rosemary, fennel, and other seeds, garnered here and there, to plant in its garden when time and weather allowed. Marie never permitted herself a day off unless she was ill enough to be in bed. Before the war was over, she visited between three and four hundred Belgian and French hospitals. And, once an X-ray station was installed, she continued to return on a tour of inspection to be sure everything was functioning properly.

From the beginning, Marie's greatest problems came from the military medical staff. They resented the intrusion of a woman telling them what to do. Few, if any, of the doctors or surgeons had confidence in radiology, a service which even most civilian hospitals did not yet offer. Fortunately, Marie won most over in record time. By the end of November, the War Minister advised her that he had asked General Joffre, the commander of the military zones, to give immediate consideration to her request for authorization to function directly behind the lines, and before too long, there were a number of hospitals near the front where she set up permanent installations.

Marie had no fixed schedule, never wore a special uniform or a nurse's veil, and worked bareheaded, dressed in an ordinary white laboratory coat. Whenever a phone call or telegram came in, or she received an SOS about some malfunctioning equipment, Marie was off, adjusting a Red Cross armband and stuffing into her pocket her big man's wallet containing her military passes and photographs of her parents. A psychologist might be able to make an interesting case out of the fact that she never carried a picture of Pierre.

The French government returned to Paris from its hasty, undignified retreat to Bordeaux about the time hawkers were setting up their customary little booths along the snowy Paris boulevards with suggestions for Christmas gifts. There were few plush animals for children because most of them came from Germany, and the most popular items were rubber sleeping bags and cork sandals for servicemen. André Debierne and Maurice Curie, Jacques's son who had been working in the laboratory, came home on leave, but when Debierne, who was serving as perhaps one of the oldest corporals in the infantry and had already collected a Croix de Guerre, suggested taking Irène, who happened to be in Paris, to the reopened Comédie Française for a holiday treat, they had to go and come on foot because of the suspension of omnibus service and dearth of taxis.

The girls attached a large map to the dining room wall to better follow the war and chronicled their mother's nomadic life by sticking little flags on it to indicate the various places where she had been, and was presently, working. Irène accompanied her whenever feasible and, at the same time, continued her Sorbonne studies as best she could.

Marie's moments of relaxation were few. This was all to the good. With so little time for morbid introspection, she became good-humored. The end of January, she and Jean Perrin, who was recently transferred, temporarily, to Marie's radiological service, set out for the north in Car E. After a flat tire and twice hitting a tree, they stopped for tea to recuperate at the one hotel in Dunkerque that was open. In that moment of rare relaxation, seated together at a rickety table facing the water, Perrin decided to write Langevin to let him know they were thinking of him. Marie added a few lines at the end, signing with an illegible scrawl, which could be interpreted as "M.C."—or "Marie," unusual as it was for her to use only her first name.

Not until that April in 1915, after the Germans, in defiance of the Hague Convention, used poison gas in the trenches before Ypres did the French Government recall its scientists who were scattered in different units and place them in National Defense Research with Jean Perrin in charge. Perrin perfected an acoustical device to detect night-flying planes by sound echoes. Langevin worked on the growing submarine menace and developed the first effective method to detect them by applying to ultrasonics the piezoelectric phenomenon that Pierre and Jacques Curie had discovered and, then, working out the principle that later formed the basis of modern sonar; André Debierne was in chemical warfare. Marie's friends on the other side of the Channel were equally busy, and Rutherford was likewise involved in submarine detection. Herta Ayrton who, unlike Marie, always emphasized the practical applications of her work in pure science, saved hundreds of Allied soldiers' lives by switching her research with sand ripples and wave motion to air vortexes and by adapting her invention, the hand-operated Ayrton fan, into an effective means of clearing the trenches of poison gas.

When the first zeppelin flew over Paris, around 1:15 A.M. on a moonless but starlit spring night, Marie did not make her girls obey the official injunction to go downstairs in the cold cellar. She never would. Instead, the trio joined the countless other brave souls who were streaming outdoors for a curious look. The capital lay in utter darkness, and in the distance, cannons growled while five searchlights probed for the monstrous invader. Suddenly, sharp claps were heard from the Eiffel Tower, the Trocadero, and the Arc de Triomphe. Incendiary fuses crisscrossed the sky and converged, illuminating what appeared to be a gigantic cigar. Several bombs burst, and planes swept overhead in hot pursuit. Then it was all over.

More zeppelin raids followed, but there was little damage. The offensives in 1915 had little permanent effect and were characterized by an appalling death toll. But with Italy's entrance into the war and the fighting apparently stabilized in trenches along the western front, a more or less normal life resumed in Paris. Bakers were once more permitted to make baguettes, that staple of the French diet; trains were running—but with the shades drawn—and Parisians flocked to Les Invalides to see the latest war trophies.

In spite of the war, Marie insisted that her daughters take a two-month vacation at L'Arcouest and she promised to join them when she could. Of course, she never did, except for a rare day here and there. Ève was old enough now to contribute her share to the war effort, and both girls worked in the Brittany fields for a fortnight. Toiling alongside their friends and other women, they cut and bound the sheaves and worked as thrashers, replacing the men who normally harvested the wheat.

That fall, Marie did not hesitate to leave Irène in complete charge of the X-ray service in an Anglo-Belgian hospital at Hoogstade, a few kilometers from the front. By now Marie knew she was capable of carrying on in her stead, and there was nothing Irène would not do to live up to those expectations. The girl's task was additionally complicated because Van Meeven, the Belgian military doctor there, to whom she must teach the method of locating projectiles with the X-ray equipment, was she informed her mother "the enemy of the most elementary notions of geometry."[2] When one poor wretched soldier was wheeled in with a femur crushed by a piece of shrapnel, Van Meeven, who was old enough to be her grandfather, stubbornly refused to probe for the foreign object through the side from which Irène indicated it was accessible. Ignoring her completely, he insisted upon entering through the gaping wound—and found nothing. Only then was he willing to heed Irène who, for a second time, suggested in her calm serious voice that he explore the region indicated by the X rays. He did so and was able to extract the shrapnel at once.

Irène thrived on the life. She enjoyed sleeping outdoors in a tent like the other nurses and took frequent horseback rides in the evening, when time allowed. The only thing she missed was news from Paris and from her cousin Maurice Curie and André Debierne—in service somewhere.

When the government had a nationwide drive for gold and silver, and Marie offered her various medals, including the Nobel, to be melted down along with other women's wedding bands and equally precious bibelots, the Banque de France wisely declined to accept them. Marie's generosity to the war effort did not stop there. After a consultation with Irène, she used the bulk of her accumulated prize money, which constituted her daughters' sole inheritance, to buy government war bonds. Marie knew they would never be redeemed, but as she told Ève and Irène, the only thing one had to worry about losing was one's honor.

One evening, on her way home from the base hospital at Forges, Marie's Renault skidded and overturned in the ditch. Marie was buried inside beneath cascading, crashing cases and equipment, and badly bruised, but she was more concerned about the loss of her smashed radiological plates than herself. However, she could not help laughing when she heard her chauffeur running around outside frantically, trying to open the jammed doors and demanding in a hoarse stage whisper whether Madame was alive or dead. Toward the end of the war, when there was a crucial manpower shortage and drivers were scarce, she learned to drive herself.

When a call for help came from Amiens, Marie was busy elsewhere so she once more substituted Irène, who had recently finished another solo stint at Montereau. The Amiens military hospital was a big one, and here, unlike at Hoogstade where an X-ray service was already established, she had to start from scratch—an awesome responsibility for any nineteen-year-old. Amiens had been occupied by the Germans and was more than half destroyed before it was finally liberated. The Petite Curie that drove Irène there had a hard time threading its way through the narrow streets crowded with military transports and the ambulances which brought the wounded in daily. Irène went directly to the railroad station to collect her equipment, which had preceded her by train, but the military posted there were not cooperative. Pointing to the sidings jammed with freight waiting to be unloaded, they told her to expect a minimum three-to-four-day delay before she could possibly expect to see any of her X-ray crates and cases. But Irène had learned a lesson watching her mother in operation. Off she drove, routed out a sergeant, commandeered a young medical student to do her bidding, and returned. Assuming an air of great authority, "à la Marie," she employed her mother's high-handed tactics on the railroad employees and guards, and with the help of the pair she brought along, Irène had everything unloaded in a couple of hours. She remained in Amiens a month and was late for the fall 1916 opening of the Sorbonne. But, in the future, she was rarely in the field and, instead, divided the time between her own classes and helping her mother set up a series of six-week crash training courses at the Radium Institute.

Marie decided this was the best way to remedy her own critical shortage of trained technicians and radiologists. So, instead of classes on radioactivity, the first instruction given in the new amphitheater was on radiology. Assisted by Irène, and with the help of a former "sèvrienne" pupil Marthe Klein, and occasionally Mlle. Weil, a laboratory assistant, Marie supervised the training of over one hundred and fifty volunteers, in successive classes of about twenty each. She kept her trainees busy all day, every day, for almost two months, moving from theory at the Curie Pavilion, to practice at the hospital on the rue Vaugirard, which had just been renamed "Edith Cavell" after the recently martyred English nurse. Her pupils might come from widely disparate social and educational backgrounds and included aristocrats as well as chambermaids, but they shared a willingness to learn. Marie was a firm believer in women's common sense and goodwill and was able to explain, in terms simple enough for each one of them to grasp, the bare bones of electricity, X rays, and anatomy that were essential to be able to locate a projectile or take an X-ray picture of a fracture. Patient as well as pitiless, she had no sympathy for laggards or cowards, whom she ruthlessly weeded out.

Meanwhile, Dr. John Joly of Dublin developed a new method to siphon off radon, the gas emanating spontaneously from radium. Not only did radon produce the same biological effects as radium in many instances, but it was easier to use and less dangerous to handle. Since the military required an unlimited supply to cicatrize certain types of wounds, Marie also established at the Institute a regular weekly service to satisfy this crucial need. Her aged laboratory assistant, Razet, assisted in the dangerous milking process, and after verifying the measurements herself, Marie sealed the radon in thin glass tubes which were delivered to the army hospitals set up in the Grand Palais and in the buildings requisitioned up and down the Champs-Élysées as auxiliary medical units. There, doctors slipped these "seeds"—as they were called—into platinum needles and implanted them directly into patients' bodies at the spot where they could be most effective.

Marie erroneously attributed the extreme fatigue she noticed, every forty-eight hours, when she drew off the radioactive gas with an electric pump, to the extreme delicacy of the operation; instead, it was due to inadequate safeguards against the radon leaking into the air she was breathing. But Marie, who had already received more radiation than anybody else working at the Institute and still continued to expose herself daily, had long since accepted perpetual tiredness as part of her body's chronic malfunctioning.

Inveterate note-taker that she was, Marie estimated that during the bitterly cold winter of 1917–1918, the twenty Petites Curies and the two hundred radiological posts that she installed took one million, one hundred thousand X rays. By now, many surgeons had developed such confidence in this new tool that, if time was all-important, they did not wait to have any film developed but operated at once, using the X-ray machine with the plates still in it as their guide.

Early in the morning, on the Saturday before Palm Sunday, Marie and Irène were in the flower market on the Île de la Cité purchasing flowering shrubs to set out in the Institute garden when they heard a whistling and an explosion. Thinking it was a bomb from a lone German plane, they continued their shopping. But the sounds were repeated every half hour, and by the time they returned to the Institute, which was not far away, they learned that the "Big Berthas" now had the city within range of their enormous trajectory. Unperturbed, the pair spent the rest of the day planting. Palm Sunday, as a special Mass was about to start, several bimotored Gothas penetrated Paris's new barrage balloons, which the irrepressible French had already nicknamed *saucissons* (sausages), and scored a direct hit on St.-Gervais, killing seventy-seven worshippers and wounding eighty. The bombings and bombardment became a daily occurrence, and Marie decided to put sandbags around the Institute to safeguard its precious radium. A new German offensive opened in Champagne, and when Marie went to northern Italy for a month to assist the Italian government's search for possible sources of pitchblende, Irène and her sister moved out to the little house at Brunoy which Marie still kept, so they could sleep at night undisturbed by the air raid sirens' continuous shrieking. Even Irène found the German advance nerve-racking, but it was stopped on July 17, and the next day, the Allies attacked.

Pasteur's words, comparing a laboratory to "a temple, a sacred abode . . . where humanity elevated and fortified itself and became better,"[3] which Marie would repeat at the inauguration of the Radium Institute, held as much meaning for Irène as they did for both her parents. Her desire from earliest childhood to emulate Pierre and Marie was so reinforced by her war work that she refused to let her supercharged schedule interfere with the maintenance of her Sorbonne studies. For Irène, research was always the most meaningful aspect of life, and as her daughter, Hélène, would say years later, no matter whatever else Irène might get involved in, she would always return to the laboratory. She could never bear to be away from it very long. That summer, she received her *licence ès sciences physiques*—roughly the equivalent of an American bachelor of science in physics—and was appointed by the University of Paris to serve as her mother's personal assistant, without pay, temporarily substituting for Holweck, who was still in service.

From the moment Marie awoke, on November 11, she kept one ear cocked like every other Parisian for the Invalides cannon to announce the signing of the armistice. When they started to roar, at 11 A.M., she and Marthe Klein rushed around the little shops in the neighborhood searching for flags to decorate the Curie Pavilion.

None could be found, so she bought cloth in three colors—red, white, and blue—and had her charwoman, Mme. Bardinet, quickly sew them together to hang out the windows. Ten million men sacrificed their lives for this day, and Marie was too excited to return to work. With an assistant dragooned from a nearby classroom pinch-hitting as chauffeur, Marie and Mlle. Klein climbed into battered, war-scarred Car E and set off through the jam-packed streets to see what was going on in the heart of Paris. Once across the Seine, the old Renault got stalled in the crying, laughing masses surging into the Place de la Concorde. A number of people clambered onto its roof to be able to see better, and when the car was finally able to inch further through the sea of humanity singing "The Marseillaise," its new passengers went along, cheering at the top of their lungs, while Marie peered out with a broad smile. For her this soon proved to be a double victory. Her lifelong dream of a liberated, united Poland was realized at last, with her friend Paderewski as its President. That night the first sparse reappearance of lighted street lamps spelled the beginning of the end of the City of Lights' long travail.

Irène received a Military Medal for her hospital work, but Marie got none, although this, apparently, was the one distinction the woman who already had so many honors coveted. Probably her granddaughter is correct when she hazards the suggestion that this seeming oversight meant that the Langevin affair was still not completely interred in certain circles. Through an agreement reached with the government health service, Marie temporarily continued her radiological classes. In the succeeding months, the American Army paid $75 a week to have her train twenty American officers in the use of X rays and radiological equipment, while they awaited evacuation home. As an introduction, she showed them the bomb-proof safe-deposit vault in the cellar of a small detached building in the courtyard where the radium was kept, dissolved in water in a minute glass flask. Irène handled their daily laboratory exercises. Any American who used flattery to try and win the favor of the tiny, slight young woman with the green eyes and light brown hair, now worn pulled back from the characteristically high Curie forehead, was met with a cold stare that was fueled by amazement rather than indignation. Irène's lack of makeup and serious expression, her long-sleeved, ankle-length laboratory smock, when the skirts of most contemporaries had already crept up to the calf, typified her no-nonsense matter-of-factness.

This reserved aspect of Irène was a far cry from the one familiar to her L'Arcouest companions, most of whom had known her since childhood and attended the Cooperative together. Irène was comfortable with them, and they with her. She entered into all the activities whenever they were together, exchanged confidences with Aline Perrin, accepted good-naturedly the banter and teasing of her cousin Maurice, and gave as good as she got. She even indulged in the craze for dancing that took Paris by storm that summer and wrote Marie, while the latter was in Italy, that she had rearranged the furniture in the living room to leave a "respectable space for dancing."

At last, with the war behind her, Marie officially inaugurated the Curie Pavilion, the first laboratory she could truly call her own. If, as a memorial to Pierre, it was to become the world-renowned school of radioactivity of her dreams, she must now assemble a staff and furnish the building with the latest equipment.

XIII
1918–1921

"The Radium Woman"

THE POSTWAR YEARS were difficult in France for everyone, including Marie. At fifty-two, the sole means of support for herself and her two daughters was her $160 a month salary as a professor at the Sorbonne, where she resumed teaching; this was about the equivalent of an American professor of the day, and her work as head of the Curie Laboratory was part of that job. For a brief time, Marie continued her radiology classes there for women volunteers, and when Dr. Claude Regaud, the director of the Pasteur Laboratory of the Radium Institute, came back, he made Marie's wartime radon emanation service permanent and expanded it to include civilian hospitals as well. Slowly, other colleagues returned, and within a few years, the Pavilion housed some forty researchers in physics and chemistry, including Marie's graduate students, not to mention technicians and other staff.

With her frenzied wartime activities a thing of the past, Marie was able to devote more time to her daughters. It was a great joy to have Irène in the laboratory with her after so many years alone there, although Ève, who was now fourteen, was more than a little envious of the close camaraderie which had developed between her mother and her elder sister during the war. At no time did she feel as much of an outsider as at mealtime, when the pair were so busy talking shop she could rarely sneak a word in. No wonder, as an older woman, Ève frankly labeled her childhood unhappy. With the passage of time the differences between the two girls, both in temperament as well as in taste, widened. Nowhere was this better illustrated than when Marie gave them both small boxes of candy. Ève gobbled up what she got almost overnight, while Irène stowed hers carefully away in a drawer. Ève was convinced she had forgotten about the present, when she discovered her sister's hoard, sometime later, still almost full. Unlike Ève, Irène was rationing herself to one piece at the same hour, every day, nibbling it slowly, to make it last longer. The same was true with money. Ève spent whatever little she could lay her hands on immediately. Irène let hers accumulate, a franc at a time, until she amassed what Ève considered a fortune, simply because there was nothing she wanted to buy.

That summer, after spending some time with her daughters at L'Arcouest, Marie went to the Midi with Marthe Klein. There she lived a life very similar to her Brittany one, swimming daily in the warmer Mediterranean, working on her book *Radiology and the War,* even sleeping outdoors. Marie was relaxed and felt better. She did not wake up each morning thinking she was going to die on the morrow. As always when away, she wrote home frequently, but for once, her letters were more like those of a mother: "I think also of each of you and of the comfort, joy and affection you give me. You are really both a great source of riches for me, and I hope that life will still give me several good years together with you."[1]

The final demobilization of Holweck, Marie's personal assistant, relieved Irène of those specific duties, leaving her freer to concentrate on the strenuous laboratory work on the long road to her doctorate. Following in her footsteps, Ève enrolled at Sévigné. And Marie, master radiochemist that she was, would devote a large portion of the rest of her life to isolating and purifying polonium, building as big a stockpile as possible of this radioactive element for the Curie Laboratory because it was the best-known source of the strong alpha rays essential for nuclear work.

She kept her Sorbonne classes abreast of the sensational progress being made worldwide in that fast moving field. In November 1919, a formal announcement was made in London at a joint meeting of the Royal Society and the Royal Astronomical Society that the results of a British expedition to the equator to photograph a total eclipse of the sun confirmed Einstein's remarkable geometric interpretation of gravity—his theory of general relativity. The English found that light rays were bent when passing near the sun, exactly as he predicted—with paper, pencil, and an agile brain his only tools. Laymen were dazzled, and Einstein's name became their synonym for "genius." Rutherford, who had recently moved to Cambridge as the head of its Cavendish Laboratory, the number one physics post in England, wryly remarked that the interest of the public was so great in Einstein's theory because no one could offer an intelligent explanation of it to the average man. Seventeen years earlier, Rutherford realized the medieval dream of changing one element into another. He learned that nature was the great alchemist when he discovered that radioactive atoms spontaneously changed their chemical nature in a way that nothing could influence. Now, he found a way to transmute atoms at will, transforming a nitrogen atom into another atom by bombarding the nitrogen nucleus with alpha rays.

Because of the aggravated coal shortage, the strapped French government once again took measures to conserve energy; sugar and other necessities continued to be rationed. And the last thing officials were in a position to do was help scientific research, which had, in past generations, benefited on a limited scale from the generosity of a handful of wealthy private individuals. Since the turn of the century, there was also a modest Caisse Nationale de la Recherche Scientifique—"National Research Fund." With both of these sources under heavy attack by the present rampant inflation, the scientific world was forced to make a far more persistent and forceful drive for funding than ever before. The war's death toll included a disastrous number of potential scientists, and the most brilliant of the survivors accepted industry's siren call of higher wages, in preference to the academic world for, unfortunately, as Perrin remarked, "bright students also have stomachs."[2] Furthermore, as late as 1920, the principle of research as distinct from teaching was still not formally accepted in France. The most prominent scientists of the day sounded the alarm in vain, warning that a nation which did not invest in research was a nation which would decline. England had already taken a page from prewar Germany. But not France.

This was a period of great frustration for Marie. Inflation ate into the small allocation she received annually from the government fund until it barely sufficed to buy two measuring instruments. Because of an inadequate office staff, she wasted a lot of time typing replies to a never-ending flow of mail. Other precious hours were spent chasing after cheap war surplus to fill some of her laboratory's most urgent needs and in similar small administrative jobs that someone else could easily have done for her. Her fierce determination to make the Curie Laboratory a great world center of studies in radioactivity was not in conflict with the basic belief she had shared with Pierre that humanity was the ultimate beneficiary of all scientific endeavor. Already, the prescient British novelist H.G. Wells, in his prophetic 1914 bestseller *The World Set Free,* had drawn attention to an early prediction of Soddy's about the atom's hidden energy. But in the 1920s most physicists were too busy exploring and investigating something more fundamental and far less remote—if ever feasible. They were not concerned with the atom's nucleus, but with its husk or outer covering. Marie's Institute and Stefan Meyer's Institut für Radiumforschung in Vienna, together with the Cavendish under Rutherford, which was the most prominent of the three, were the main European centers devoted to the study of radioactivity—and the atom's nucleus.

Marie was available on Tuesdays and Thursdays at a certain hour for those who wanted to discuss specific scientific questions. Subject matter was equally restricted when, and if, she saw the press, and a request for a personal interview by a visiting American newspaperwoman, in mid-1920, was turned down as summarily as all the rest. But Marie met her match in dynamic Mrs. William Brown Meloney.

As persistent as Marie and fourteen years her junior, the American's career was as unusual for a woman in her field as Marie's was in hers. From a good Southern background, her ambition to be a woman reporter was almost unheard-of for the day, but already at sixteen, "Missy"—as everyone called her—startled the world of journalism by a series of unprecedented interviews with well-known Washington personalities who happened to be family friends. Unhampered by a slight limp resulting from a childhood horseback accident and a frail, tubercular constitution, she was soon the Washington, D.C., bureau chief of the Denver *Post* and the first woman to be accorded a seat in the Senate press gallery. From Washington, Missy moved to New York to her present position as editor of the well-known women's magazine *The Delineator,* and she was in Europe to make a firsthand report on the generous contributions of Butterick's, the magazine's publishers, to European war victims. Over the past twenty years she had interviewed an impressive list of international celebrities including, on the present trip, H.G. Wells and Bertrand Russell, and she hoped to see Mme. Curie.

The word no was not in Missy's vocabulary, and she was as determined as Marie, once she set out to do something. Undaunted after considerable effort and homework, she discovered a mutual acquaintance and returned to the fray. Inexplicably, Marie acquiesced. The novelist Henri-Pierre Roché, the author of *Jules and Jim,* who probably met Marie at Rodin's studio and arranged the encounter, accompanied Missy to the fateful meeting to act as interpreter. This proved unnecessary. While Missy's French was adequate for the occasion, she quickly perceived that Marie was childishly proud of her smattering of English, and Missy got off to a good start when she cannily conducted the interview in English.

Marie might be tiny, but hat included, the petite, gray-haired journalist with the liquid black eyes only reached her forehead. They met in Marie's bare office, which Missy's appraising eye quickly characterized as furnished in pure Grand Rapids, Michigan, style. As she confessed later, Marie's unanticipated timidity discomfited the veteran interrogator, and she found herself apologizing for encroaching on Marie's valuable time. In short order, Missy discovered that while America had about fifty grams of radium—Marie knew the location of each grain—in France only the Institut du Radium had any and that was little more than a gram. Missy was aghast. Marie had only a gram? Marie was quick to correct her. The *laboratory* had only a gram. Impulsively, Missy asked a fateful question: If Marie could have one thing in the entire world, what would it be? The reply was immediate: "A gram of radium for research." The American subsequently learned that the going cost of $100,000 a gram priced it out of Marie's reach; that, at the moment, the chief use for Marie's single gram was to provide radon for cancer therapy; and that Marie's new laboratory was woefully short of essential equipment. To Missy's delight, sufficient rapport was established for her to visit at Marie's Quai de Béthune apartment.

The American, who had previously visited Thomas Edison and Alexander Graham Bell at home and seen their life-style, was unprepared to have Marie, who had never taken a sou in patent royalties, open the door herself because she was too poor to afford a maid to do so. Enlightened self-interest kept the pair meeting. Mrs. Meloney explained that everyone called her "Missy"; Marie did not follow suit. But, after five meetings—four more than anyone else had ever had—the tiny lame journalist knew more about Marie than people who had known her for ten years.

Missy had discovered a wonderful story, and now, she created a mission in which she could play an indispensable role—a noble cause, attached to a great name, which would also make good copy. American women must be awakened to their obligation to help war-battered France in the person of this brave woman who had sacrificed so much to help so many. She could already see the headlines. Indomitable Missy foresaw no problem in finding ten generous American women willing to donate $10,000 apiece to buy a gram of radium. But Marie must come to the United States to accept their gift. Would she do so? Would she also consider writing her autobiography? For Missy was convinced that such a book, if properly promoted—that is to say, by Missy—could make a lot of money for Marie's laboratory. Naturally, Missy's magazine would have first rights to the story.

Marie must have found herself in an excruciating position, terrified of the publicity such a venture would entail, yet eager for the radium and funds Missy promised it would generate. As she learned more about the American, Marie's confidence in her grew proportionately. The fact that they were both small, frail, and prone to chronic ill health which both ignored, was undoubtedly one bond between them; the psychological differences between the extroverted journalist and the introverted scientist seem only to have strengthened the budding friendship which would last till Marie's death. Before Marie could make up her mind whether to accept Missy's terms, a major stumbling block remained, and the fact she already trusted Missy sufficiently to even broach the subject is indicative of the amazing intimacy already existing between the pair. Marie was still haunted by the Langevin affair. Fearful that it might be reopened, she naively demanded that there must be no mention of the taboo subject throughout her American visit. Could Missy muzzle the American press?

Missy understood her anxiety, and from a purely personal point of view, Missy also realized that resurrecting the old Langevin scandal could backfire and upset her whole campaign. America in the twenties was more puritanical than France had ever been. She promised to attend to this delicate matter the minute she set foot in New York, established a code with which to communicate her results, and also gave Marie her private New York telegraph address, which was, appropriately, "Idealism." Never one to waste a minute, even on shipboard, en route home Missy garnered two recruits to her new cause, both of whom were trustees of the Massachusetts Institute of Technology—P.A.S. Franklin, president of the International Mercantile Marine, and Stone, a well-known engineer. Upon landing, Missy immediately visited the leading publishers, as well as the heads of various newspaper chains, and extracted the desired promise. The incorrigible little woman also managed to collect money for the Marie Curie Radium Fund from the most irascible man of the lot, Arthur Brisbane, the columnist and managing editor of the New York *Evening Journal.*

With this problem resolved, Marie had little to lose and much to gain from the proposed trip. Unquestionably, a major plus influencing her ultimate decision, in addition to the anticipated material gains for the Institute, was the splendid travel opportunity the trip afforded her two daughters. These factors far outweighed the terrifying publicity and tiring travel that Marie knew would be involved.

Irène was already tackling a study, the results of which would appear in her first papers in the Academy's *Comptes Rendus.* Marie had suggested this work on chlorine isotopes that involved operations requiring great chemical precision to familiarize her daughter with isotopes, which had been discovered almost a decade before and disproved the previously accepted notion that all atoms of the same element not only had the same atomic number in Mendeleev's Periodic Table—which they did—but also the same weight—which they did not. To determine whether the mixture of isotopes remained in exactly the same proportions throughout the earth's crust, Irène studied and compared the atomic weight of chlorine extracted from salt found in water infiltrating the desert regions of North Africa with that of chlorine taken from the salt in seawater. Irène also got her second mandatory *licence,* this time in mathematics, another rung on the ladder toward her Ph.D.

Marie was anxious that she also pass the *agrégation,* knowing from personal experience how essential this examination was should Irène ever wish to teach in the state-controlled educational system. A curious exchange of letters from this period between Marie, the vice-rector of the Sorbonne, and the Minister of Education, shows that Marie, like other mothers, was not above trying to pull strings when it came to her own child; its existence reinforces later charges that Marie discriminated in Irène's favor when the girl came to work permanently at the Institute. The correspondence also makes Marie a little more human. Irène had only completed two thirds of the classes needed to qualify to take the *agrégation* and lacked the final third, which pertained to the natural sciences. It would be easy enough for Irène to take the required courses, but it was too late to do so in the school year of 1920, and she did not want to postpone necessary doctoral work because she had to wait till the following year to finish these *agrégation* requirements.

Marie took pains to point out that Irène had already devoted two full years to the national defense. As a result, she was behind in her studies, and like those who had been mobilized into the army, she was anxious to finish. Unfortunately, even Marie could not bypass this particular bureaucratic snarl. Rules were rules and no exception could be made.

Meanwhile, in New York, Missy's plans for the forthcoming odyssey were proceeding apace. Contrary to what she had first thought, she was unable to raise the price of a gram of radium from only ten women, so she substituted a nationwide drive for the funds, headed by an advisory committee which included the president of the American Medical Association and leading representatives from a number of universities. Mrs. J.D. Rockefeller, Mrs. Calvin Coolidge, and Mrs. Robert Mead, founder of the American Society for the Control of Cancer, participated actively, and the campaign was rolling into high gear.

As Missy ironed out the details, the flood of letters bombarding Marie spoke now of "1 gram," now of "1 grain." One grain, the equivalent of a fifteenth of a gram, was not enough to justify Marie's leaving Paris. An exchange of cables clarified the matter. Missy wanted Marie for a six-week, coast-to-coast trip. Too long, Marie replied. The King and Queen of Belgium stayed six weeks, Missy countered. Marie was adamant. The Paris press headlined the forthcoming radium as a gift from the United States "to the University of Paris." This was not Marie's understanding. Was she correct? "It's for you," Missy reassured her, ". . . for your personal use, and it is up to you to decide what shall happen to it when you die."[3] Any lingering doubts Marie might have harbored about Missy, or the trip, disappeared. For all her efforts Missy wanted only one thing—to be in complete charge. A reasonable request, to which Marie readily acquiesced: "I won't accept a single proposition without your agreement."[4]

Marie asked also for an appointment with a leading eye specialist —incognita, of course. Marie's ears were buzzing continually, and her eyes had been growing steadily weaker, but it was only recently that she admitted she was having trouble and learned she was facing a double cataract operation. In a letter to Bronya, she confessed a concern that her work might be interfered with or even become impossible. For the first time she voiced a suspicion that must have been gnawing at her for a long period. Could radium, her own child, be responsible? "This cannot be affirmed with certainty . . .

don't speak of . . . [this] to anybody," she begged her sister.[5] Most opthamologists today feel that if Marie had double cataracts at fifty-four—not to mention a buzzing in her ears—radium very probably played a role.

An editorial in the French periodical, *Je Sais Tout* ("I Know Everything"), declared it disgraceful that other nations should honor Marie while her adopted country did nothing. To remedy this, the magazine's administration organized a gala in her behalf at the Opéra to raise money for the Institut du Radium. Marie appeared, amid great applause, accompanied by her two girls and Missy, who had come over to escort her heroine to the United States. Seated in the place of honor, Marie listened with apparent enjoyment to the aging Sarah Bernhardt recite an ode written especially for the event. But it is questionable, even with her thick new glasses, how much of the entertainment, arranged for the occasion by the celebrated actor Sacha Guitry, she actually saw.

Four weeks later, she was on the SS *Olympic,* westward-bound, accompanied by her two girls, Missy, and Harriet Eager, a young, French-speaking American whom she had recently met and invited along at the last moment for unknown reasons. The president of the White Star Line was on hand to escort Marie to the bridal suite, and she had not been in it ten minutes before she examined the heating system and the way the furniture was fastened in place. Her four dark dresses—one more than she ever owned before and which she only bought at the insistence of already clothes-conscious Ève—were unpacked and hung up in the huge closet. The incongruity of this pitiful handful of garments hanging in the cavernous space destined for a trousseau doubtless escaped Marie, who was far more fascinated by the closet light; it shone whenever the door was opened, and she could not locate the switch. When she failed to appear in the dining room at mealtime, Harriet was sent to fetch her and found Marie sitting inside the wardrobe, in the dark, trying to figure out how the light functioned. For most of the voyage, she rarely ventured outside the suite, either because she was a poor sailor or was trying to avoid the others on board. Perhaps it may even have been apprehension about the forthcoming trip. Whatever the reason and whatever lay ahead, Marie had complete confidence in Missy and in her judgment, and she so wrote Henriette Perrin, employing her most prized adjective: "She's an idealist and seems *very* [sic] disinterested."[6]

The $150,000 Missy raised to purchase Marie's radium—a colossal sum for the day—did not come from only the rich, but from women in every walk of life who emptied their pockets for the Marie Curie Radium Fund and would dog her footsteps wherever she appeared.

Her arrival coincided flawlessly with the appearance on the New York newsstands that same morning of the April issue of the *Delineator* which was almost entirely devoted to Marie. Missy's lead article "The Greatest Woman in the World" followed her editorial "That Thousands Shall Not Die" and elaborated on the debt society owed "The Radium Woman."

For someone like Marie who had an almost pathological fear of crowds, the sight of the exuberant, warmhearted welcome awaiting her at the pier from thousands of cheering, waving people must have been appalling—the groups of Girls Scouts; a three-hundred strong delegation from the Polanyi, the Polish-American Society; the blaring brass bands simultaneously playing the American, French, and Polish anthems. A horde of newspapermen and photographers clambered noisily on board, armed with notepads, microphones, cameras. This was Marie's first press conference, American-style, and ignoring Missy's advice to the contrary, she had typed up a declaration to hand out, as was her custom. It was tossed aside unread.

So successfully had Missy emphasized Marie's scorn for gain and her desire to serve humanity that she not only touched America's heart and purse strings, but she transformed this Polish woman into front-page news. Nine massive volumes of clippings at the Radium Institute bear testimony to the awesome results. Avidly looking for copy, the press swamped the frail little woman who peered myopically at them, her snow-white hair brushed uncompromisingly back under a round black hat, seated on deck, with her daughters and Missy hovering protectively alongside. To her right was carelessly dressed, earnest Irène—"peasant-like" was an adjective many journalists applied to her—wearing sturdy, no-nonsense shoes and black stockings like her mother. In stark contrast, on the other side, was effervescent, perfectly poised Ève, who, despite her slender clothes budget, already managed to look like an elegant Parisian, with her silk stockings, high heels, and gaily flowered bonnet. When a reporter good-naturedly teased her about her beauty, Ève blushed and her eyes sparkled so mischievously that one of them promptly dubbed her "Miss Radium Eyes." Attracting and desiring attention rather than repelling it, and always willing to talk, sixteen-year-old Ève would frankly enjoy every moment of the trip. For the first time in her life, she was more useful to her mother than her elder sister because of her ability to satisfy the insatiable media, and she must have relished the situation. Disinterested Irène was not given to jealousy and could not have cared less.

Two limousines sent by Mrs. Andrew Carnegie, whose late husband had been such a generous patron of the Curie Laboratory, whisked the visitors to 31 West Twelfth Street, where the absent John Crane, the American ambassador to China and a friend and neighbor of Missy and her husband, had placed his apartment at Marie's disposal. To reach the door, she had to wade through a sea of flowers sent by a horticulturist who had been cured of cancer by radium treatments, and there were so many more inside that Marie asked Missy if there were not a hospital, preferably for children, where she might send them.

Marie had two days of official ceremonies in New York and visited Smith, Vassar, and Mount Holyoke, where she received honorary degrees. But not all the American scientists put themselves out on her account; many felt she had already done very well, with two Nobels and $50,000 in Carnegie research scholarship money, and were not happy to see any more funds earmarked for science going outside of the United States. Some also concurred with the distinguished former president of Harvard University, Charles Elliot, who maintained that since Pierre's death, Mme. Curie had done nothing of great importance in the laboratory.

By the time Marie, escorted by Vice President and Mrs. Calvin Coolidge, left New York, she carried her right arm in a sling—the victim of too many handshakes from fervent fans. Arriving in Washington late on the eve of the ceremonial presentation at the White House, Missy showed Marie the deed of the gift. Marie was aghast when she learned that the gram was to be given to her, not to the Institute. Furthermore, no provisions had been made concerning the future of her gift. So long as Marie was alive, there was no problem; it would be used solely for scientific work. But what about after she was gone? Marie insisted that the document must spell out her wishes, then and there, that the radium be an outright gift to her laboratory and specifically for scientific use. A lawyer must be found to make this transfer legal at once.

When several of the women from Missy's national committee who had accompanied the party down from New York demurred, politely pointing out the lateness of the hour and suggesting that the changes could be made in the morning, they were startled to discover that they were no longer dealing with a pathetic little old lady in black. With the icy determination well known in international scientific circles, Marie held firm. No. She might die in the interim. A lawyer was routed out of bed, a document drawn up to Marie's specifications, translated into French so she could ascertain whether there were any ambiguities, and witnessed, on the spot, by Mrs. Calvin Coolidge and another. Because of disagreement, no decision was reached concerning the more than $50,000 surplus remaining in the fund because canny Missy had purchased the radium at half price in Russia. The money was temporarily left in the Equitable Trust Company—where it would remain some two years before a satisfactory decision was ultimately reached—but every woman present in the hotel room that memorable evening had the disagreeable presentiment that there, too, Marie would have her own way.

The following afternoon in the East Room of the White House, President Harding slipped over the neck of the same black georgette dress with lace shoulder scarf which Marie had worn at both Nobel ceremonies, a slender moire ribbon from which hung a minuscule gold key. This unlocked the specially constructed, lead-lined casket weighing one hundred and ten pounds that sat on a table nearby. None of the distinguished guests knew that the mahogany-covered coffer was actually empty. For security reasons, the ten minuscule glass tubes containing the radium were elsewhere.

After *de rigueur* receptions at the French Embassy and the Polish Legation, Marie left Washington. The following stops in Philadelphia and Pittsburgh for the customary rites of passage seemed anticlimactic. Limping more pronouncedly than ever, Missy, whose tuberculosis was flaring up, drooped, and Marie was exhausted. But she invariably revived when something scientific was on the program and spent three hours, walking through and inspecting a large mill at Cannonsburg where radium was processed from carnotite, a different radioactive ore that was mined in Colorado.

Back in New York once more, Marie collapsed. Missy's doctor diagnosed hypertension and a kidney infection and ordered complete rest. Her tour schedule was revised accordingly, and most of the Western part canceled. Substituting for the ailing Missy, who had just learned she had a possibly malignant tumor but did not tell Marie, Harriet Eager took over as the trio's escort, and various stratagems were resorted to in order to spare Marie as many mob scenes as possible. Acting as her mother's proxy, Irène received numerous honorary degrees, and her English was sufficiently adequate for her to deliver three speeches on radium which she herself had been requested to give—as Irène Curie, not as a stand-in for her mother.

Largely for her daughters' sake, Marie insisted that the Grand

Canyon remain on the itinerary. Even there, she was recognized and people gathered to stare. From Irène's point of view, visiting this wonder of nature was worth the whole trip. Intrepidly, she and Ève rode sturdy ponies down to the river at the bottom of the canyon while Marie indulged in the purchase of a turquoise and silver Indian necklace, one of the very few pieces of jewelry she ever owned, let alone wore.

They returned east by way of Chicago and Buffalo—to see another tourist attraction, Niagara Falls—then Boston and New Haven. By the end of May, the travelers were back in New York to accept Marie's Columbia University degree. Harvard was one of the few major universities who did not award her one, largely because of its physics department's opposition. Bertram Boltwood, who knew the "Madame" from international scientific meetings where he usually found her intolerable, this time saw Marie in a more sympathetic light and reported to Rutherford, "She is in very poor physical condition . . . and was a distinctly pathetic figure . . . very modest and unassuming, and she seemed frightened of all the fuss people made over her."[7]

When Missy and Marie said farewell, both wept. Once at sea, Marie sat down at her desk. "My dear friend," she began for the first time, instead of addressing Missy with her customary "Madame." "We all love you and want you to be strong and happy . . . We worry a great deal about your health."[8] That said, she pragmatically devoted the rest of the letter to a discussion of what she felt should be done with the remaining Curie Fund money presently in the Equitable Trust. While Marie's trip was so profitable from her point of view, there are some who argue that she set back the cause of women in science in the United States by setting an impossible standard, just as Einstein would do, later, for men.

At Cherbourg, a special police agent was assigned to see that the radium was properly stowed on the boat train, and at the Gare St.-Lazare in Paris, Jean Perrin, Marcel Laporte, a colleague from the laboratory who, according to rumor, was more than a little fond of

Irène, and a few others awaited. The travelers were driven home through streets packed with excited men, women, and children, impatiently watching the star-studded skies for the red or green flare that would signal the winner of the world heavyweight championship being fought that evening. Jack Dempsey won over Georges Carpentier with a knockout in the fourth round, and in a Paris swept by a passion for violent sports, Marie was able to slip home virtually unheralded.

XIV
1921–1924

Irène to the Fore

MARIE'S TRIP PRODUCED results beyond her wildest dreams. Her loot was sufficient to make the Curie Laboratory the worthy equal of its most up-to-date foreign counterpart and thus constituted a magnificent contribution to French physics, in general, in those days of economic hardship on the Continent. Besides her gram of radium, she brought back $22,000 worth of mesothorium and other precious minerals, not to mention gifts of every imaginable type of equipment; and, in addition to the healthy balance from the Cancer Fund Campaign being held by the Equitable Trust, in her purse nestled a check for $6,900, the total of the numerous cash awards received from different American scientific societies, as well as a $50,000 advance on her biography. This was to appear at the end of the book she was writing on Pierre, but in accordance with Marie's stipulations, her life story was only to be published in the United States. "I have a kind of a feeling that in Europe it would not appear as natural as in America," she explained.[1]

The trip also produced an intangible result that was perhaps more important than everything else combined. It taught Marie the power of American-style public relations. As "The Radium Woman," home from a sensational American tour, Marie now realized that her presence, if properly merchandised, was a viable commodity that could spell the difference between success and failure for any cause or undertaking she might deem worthy. She was her own best salesperson, and she learned to make certain accommodations to fame because she found it useful. She was no longer bashful about going around with hat in hand, and she held a trump. For her fame as the discoverer of radium did not then—and still does not—rest, in the eyes of the international general public, on radium's potential as the key to unlock the structure of the universe, but on its proven ability to help in the war against cancer. This was the one area of research that had any popular appeal. Everyone could relate to it, and recent medical successes using radium in cancer therapy, or curietherapy, held out the hope that a cure might be within reach.

At the outset, Marie may have entertained some inner qualms over the begging aspects of her recent trip and wondered if she were breaching her cherished scientific tradition of disinterestedness. However, Marie believed so strongly that there was only one source of progress—science—that she was henceforth willing to represent this idea herself. Missy had a name for Marie's new work, which took her out of the laboratory into the world. "Dignifying science," Missy called Marie's efforts to spare other young scientists, at the start of their careers, the difficulties and hardships she and Pierre had experienced. With this goal in mind, the rest of her life Marie willingly accepted ceremonials and official trips as professional obligations. Armed with firsthand knowledge of the numerous splendid scientific establishments in America, she also willingly accompanied Perrin and Borel, time and again, to call on various education and government officials and lent a persuasive voice to their pleas for fellowships as much as for bricks and mortar.

To recuperate after so much strenuous travel, Marie and the girls went off for a long vacation together at L'Arcouest. Marie always joined the others for a swim, but she spent the rest of her time either correcting the manuscript of Pierre's life, for which she was already under contract and was slowly dictating to Irène, or puttering in the garden.

In September, when Marie left for Cavalaire to oversee a tiny house she was building there, and Ève returned to begin studying for her *baccalauréat,* Irène stayed on. She was enjoying herself with her friends from the Cooperative days; she had a pet raccoon which slept in her room and amused her immensely; and for once she was in no hurry to get back to Paris. She would even take time off later that winter to resume skiing for the first time since the war. An excellent athlete, a tireless swimmer and hiker, when Irène first learned to ski, winter sports were a novelty, and in later years, she enjoyed boasting that she was one of the oldest skiers in France.

In her laboratory Marie was not the commanding, demanding figure the international scientific community knew. She considered those who worked there as her family, and there was an intimate contact between "la patronne," and each one of them. Marie knew in detail each student's and researcher's work, and when she went through the rooms each morning, she would stop with a word of encouragement here—"Oh! What a pretty phenomenon"—or ask a question there, redo a calculation, question a result, or admire a newly made apparatus. In the Institute, the customary sad, firm expression the outside world knew became animated, Marie smiled often and even laughed. But on occasion tempers flared and temperaments clashed even in those sedate surroundings. Colleagues would long remember the day when Holweck, for reasons unknown, shattered the rarefied quiet, pounding on Marie's door—which was locked, for once—and shouting "Bitch! Bitch!" And Marie could be one.

Marie was ashamed of the thick glasses she now wore while waiting for her cataracts to ripen sufficiently for an operation and tried to maintain the fiction of perfect vision. She put color-coded signs on her instrument dial, wrote her lecture notes in enormous block letters, and her staff played along. Even the Swedish research student who proudly rushed in with a spectrum so "la patronne" might admire the doublet—a pair of vertical lines on the photographic plate which was characteristic of the element he was working with—did not contradict her when she talked of a singlet. For he suddenly realized that she could see only one line. To help keep up the comedy, Irène, Ève, or a colleague automatically took her arm and with slight pressure helped her cross the street when she walked home for lunch each noon. At the table one of the girls passed the saltcellar to her the minute she started fumbling for it with falsely assured gestures. When she went to Dr. Moray on the Boulevard Raspail for eye examinations, she once more, as in the past, used an assumed name—"Madame Carré." Whether this policy of subterfuge was dictated by misplaced vanity as much as by Marie's continued desire to hide any evidence of physical deterioration that might incriminate radium is anybody's guess.

The sudden, inexplicable death of Mme. Artaud, a fellow member of the Radiochemistry Society, who had been in the best of health until she spilled a vial of extremely strong radioactive material on herself, once again raised the grim, nagging question of radium's complicity. Not too much later, a New York dentist, Theodore Blum, became suspicious about the cause of a cancerous mouth condition of several of his patients when he discovered that they were similarly employed, painting instrument and watch dials, dipping their brushes in luminous, radium-based paint, then licking them to get a fine point. The physiological effects of radioactivity on the human body were far from being recognized; no experiments were yet available to give any answers. France had yet to follow the lead of the English authorities who, two years earlier, set up a commission to study any possible nefarious effects on healthy cells from the same radiation which was treating certain types of malignant ones so successfully. Hundreds of French workers were still handling radioactive substances in factories, laboratories, and hospitals with only gloves and, perhaps, a rickety screen as any protection. And it was an unwritten law in the Curie Laboratory to shrug off any occupational risks there as negligible, if not nonexistent. If Marie still clung to the fast-waning illusion that radium was not deeply implicated, her hopes must have been crushed by three more successive deaths. Maurice Demenitroux, who had worked with radium and thorium for over two decades, took to his bed with the same symptoms—weariness and aching limbs—that Marie and so many others in the Radium Laboratory complained of, and soon died. So did Marcel Demalander, Demenitroux's comrade and another onetime assistant of Marie. There would later be another victim, Sonia Cotelle, a brilliant Polish colleague who had a polonium tube explode in her face, was already losing her hair and had stomach problems. Leukemia was the contemporary diagnosis in each instance.

These were statistics that Marie could no longer ignore. The subsequent investigation which she ordered at the Institute concluded that the screens of lead and wood available there were adequate safeguards against the rays themselves, together with frequent changes of the workers' white laboratory coats, and that good ventilation was the only way to ensure protection from radioactive gases. She herself wrote in pen across the bottom of this report, the first to be issued from the Curie Pavilion to admit the possibility of hazards, that her personal panacea for any suffering similar to those listed was plenty of exercise in the fresh air. In a letter to Missy as late as 1925, she blamed her colleagues' deaths on a "faulty installation." Irène assumed as cavalier an attitude in the matter as her mother. It is impossible to calculate how much radium either one may have taken into their systems while working in conditions that would be deemed primitive by present-day standards. But no doubt one of the fundamental reasons why Marie stubbornly refused to face up to the facts was because the pair who, between them, had probably handled as much, if not more, powerful radioactive substances than anyone else to date, had unusually strong constitutions that were still holding up remarkably well.

In the early spring of 1922, broad-minded Langevin, who was now considered one of the leading physical theorists of the day in France and was anxious to widen his own understanding of relativity as well as to reestablish contacts between French and German scientists, again brought Einstein, a newly crowned Nobel laureate, to Paris; this time he was to lecture at the prestigious Collège de France, where Langevin had held a chair for more than a decade. Because of lingering bitterness in postwar Paris, it took courage for Paul to sponsor Einstein's talks, originally planned for 1914 and then postponed. Elaborate police precautions were taken, even though Einstein had been a Swiss national since he was eighteen. Nationalism was rampant, and a violent campaign was unleashed, attacking Langevin for bringing "the German Jew" to the city. Barricades were placed around the Collège in anticipation of a disturbance at his opening lecture, but the students in the Latin Quarter behaved for once. The small amphitheater seating three hundred was packed well in advance. Einstein spoke in slow French, and Paul, who chaired the five sessions—three of which were devoted entirely to discussion and took place in a smaller, adjacent hall—sat directly behind him to act as prompter whenever his vocabulary proved inadequate and he had to grope for the proper word. Afterward, the Borels invited Marie, the Perrins, Langevin, and some of the others back to their apartment. Marie saw Einstein again, a short time later, at Geneva. Making a rare exception to her rule never to serve on anything not pertaining to scientific research,

Marie was sufficiently interested in fostering international understanding to sit, together with Einstein, Langevin, Borel, and Perrin, on the newly formed League of Nations' International Committee of Intellectual Cooperation. But Einstein had less patience than Marie, who was elected one of the group's vice presidents, and was quickly discouraged. Within six months he resigned, claiming that "despite its [the Committee's] illustrious membership, it was the most ineffectual enterprise with which I have ever been associated."[2]

Early that summer, Irène joined a new friend, Angèle Pompei, for ten days of serious hiking in the mountains. They had met when Irène joined a group of Sorbonne graduates on a field trip to the Auvergne. A mutual love for long, silent walks, each immersed in her own thoughts, and accompanied by frugal picnics of bread and cherries eaten along the way, was the start of a lifelong intimacy, and this trip was the forerunner of many similar ones with the young Corsican.

Irène took as much delight in transforming a simple cotton frock into one suitable for backpacking—concocting mandatory pockets out of sleeves and belts—as she did in devising an ingenious piece of new equipment for an experiment. She might not be interested in clothes and looked it. But she was always on the watch for lightweight mountain equipment—oiled silk raincoats, a flat, almost weightless purse. Irène spoke little on these outings, but when she did, there was no question where she stood on any given matter. She was nothing if not frank, and Angèle was struck by the clarity with which she expressed herself. Throughout her life, Irène remained faithful to the same republican, socialist, anticlerical opinions she had learned from GrandPé. She already believed in the need to fight for social progress that qualified as the "eternal struggle which advanced thinkers must lead against the reactionaries." This fight must be led effectively, and Irène stoutly maintained that "if a group, not all of whose ideas you approve, seems the best qualified for this crusade, it is necessary to give it your full support."[3] This statement would go a long way to explain her subsequent relationship with the Communist Party. Irène also believed that women had a special part to play in the confrontation and they must obtain the vote so they could make themselves heard.

Irène and Angèle were generally in the mountains two weeks, and Irène, who had inherited Pierre's intense love of nature, thoroughly enjoyed herself. Sometimes they camped out; again, they slept in mountaineers' refuges. Her camera was never out of her hands, and when she got home, the snapshots were developed, carefully classified, and filed in appropriate albums.

Back in the Radium Institute once more, Irène always experienced a tremendous sense of fulfillment and well-being. Like others of her generation, she was fascinated with the rapidly developing study of the atom's nucleus, and while assisting with her mother's Sorbonne students in the laboratory, she was already embarked on the study of polonium that was to be her lifework. She was in a unique position to do so, since she had at hand an adequate supply of this metal, which ever since the war, farsighted Marie was continuing to isolate and stockpile. Furthermore, there was no better qualified radiochemist than Marie to teach her the difficult, delicate task of preparing and purifying polonium for her experiments. Meticulous care, ingenuity, and sometimes speed were called into play, and under Marie's critical eye, Irène was quickly adept at designing and constructing various adaptations of the lightweight bases needed to hold her minuscule, strongly radioactive deposits. She learned how to bombard a screen of matter with alpha rays; then, after closing her eyes to adjust them, like a photographer entering a darkroom to work, she studied the target through a microscope, concentrating on the scintillations that resulted every time the alpha rays collided with the atoms of the screen, counting the flashes and noting down where they hit. A note in the *Comptes Rendus* on the speed of the alpha rays of polonium marked the debut of Irène's in-depth research of polonium's properties that was to constitute her doctoral thesis. Another report on the rays' distribution, and a third on their magnetic deviation, were soon to follow. But, busy as she was, she managed to take five days off to go hiking at Easter in the Juras with Le Club Alpin.

Meanwhile, the efforts of Marie's colleagues to exploit to the hilt her American apotheosis were bearing fruit for the benefit of French science. Edmond de Rothschild donated 10 million francs to establish a foundation to provide scholarships for young people solely interested in research and gave an additional 50 million for an Institute of Biology-Physics-Chemistry, while still more Rothschild—and Rockefeller—money set up the Henri Poincaré Institute of Mathematics and Physical Mathematics with Borel at the head. Both of these new buildings were to be built on the rue Pierre Curie proper. On the land directly behind the Radium Institute, excavation was due to start on the Institute of Physical Chemistry, which Perrin would direct, and an addition, doubling the Radium Institute's original space, was slated to adjoin the Curie Pavilion itself. Within a couple of years the University of Paris also supplied funds to build an annex for Marie at Arcueil to treat hundreds of pounds of raw material.

It would be some time before the Chambre des Députés passed the long-sought mechanism to raise money for research—a small tax on the payroll of French industry. However, at this time, the Chambre made a preliminary gesture, more important symbolically than financially in a bureaucracy where entrenched tradition concerning how money was spent was hard to change, when it finally admitted the principle of pure research, independent of teaching and properly subsidized. The Curie Laboratory was one of the first beneficiaries of this new government largess, and Marie allocated one fifth of the small sum received to support Irène's experiments, to the poorly disguised displeasure of some of the staff who grumbled about nepotism. This was not the first time, and it would not be the last, that Marie showed favoritism at the Institute where her elder daughter was concerned. Scientists are not saints. Marie was perceptibly mellowing with age where her girls were concerned, and Irène's competence in the laboratory was already proven. Unfortunately, Irène carried her father's indifference to people one step further, and she never made any bones if present company was unwelcome. To this day, contemporaries describe Irène's disconcerting habit of reaching under her laboratory smock and lifting up her skirt to pull a soiled handkerchief from a petticoat pocket and blow her nose loudly, an amazing performance that caused more than one unwelcome intruder to stop in the middle of a sentence and retreat nonplussed. Curtness was her long suit, and aside from childhood friends, Angèle Pompei, and family, few ever got to know her well, especially at the Institute where the "Crown Princess" ruffled more feathers than she bothered to smooth.

The summer of 1923, Marie had the first in a series of four cataract operations. It was a success but unexpected complications set in from hemorrhages, and she was in the hospital—under an assumed name—in the torrid heat, with her eyes bandaged, far longer than anticipated. Ève stayed with her the whole time, reading to her, comforting and reassuring her. Ève's assumption of the domestic role with Marie, an outgrowth of the recent American tour, where Ève emerged for the first time as an individual in her own right, counterbalanced Irène's participation with Marie at the laboratory. It made the younger girl feel more secure, more an integral part of the family, and drew the trio closer together.

When the Curies Foundation celebrated the twenty-fifth anniversary of the discovery of radium in December 1923, Hela, Bronya, and Josef came west to participate. The red carpet was rolled out, and the pomp and ceremony on similar occasions was faithfully executed, down to the last detail. Civil and military authorities, delegations from the Chambre des Députés, the great schools, the various student associations, were all present to honor Marie. The President of the Republic, Millerand, presided, and Marguerite Borel's father, Paul Appell, the incumbent rector of the University of Paris, spoke. Later Irène demonstrated some of her mother and father's earliest experiments; she projected onto a big screen the image of gold leaves rising and falling as she charged, then discharged, a gold-leaf electroscope with a sample of radium. The government officially thanked Marie for her many contributions to her adopted country by awarding her, as they had Pasteur, an annual pension that was to be passed on to Ève and Irène on her death.

— ○ —

One day, in the following winter, Irène caught a brief glimpse of a young lieutenant in a blue officer's uniform leaving her mother's office. The next time she saw him was the very end of December 1924, when he rang the bell at no. 36 Quai de Béthune, and she answered the door. He apologized for intruding and explained that he had made a special trip in from Aubervilliers with a letter from his colonel which Mme. Curie had asked him to get. He learned at the laboratory that she had already gone home and was given her Île St.-Louis address.

"One minute, Monsieur," Irène replied. Without giving him a second glance, she promptly disappeared, leaving him to stand hesitantly at the open door.

XV
1900–1926

Prince Consort

THE PARENTS OF FRÉDÉric Joliot were both from *la petite bourgeoisie* and neither intellectuals nor academics. His mother, Émilie Roederer, was born in 1858 in Paris, where her family kept a small bakery. The little brunet's austere manner and appearance bespoke her Alsatian Protestant background, and she was proud of the fact that her maternal grandfather had been Napoleon III's sauce chef, the only servant allowed to be present when the Emperor dined. But she herself was innately republican and liberal in outlook, and astounded others of her milieu by refusing to share the contemporary prejudice about having Jewish friends. As with the rest of her children, Émilie taught Fred the history of the French Revolution and instilled in him a love of liberty and respect for the great struggles of freedom and social justice that remained with him until he died.

Born in 1847, in Briey, Lorraine, the son of a local steelworker, Fred's father, Henri Joliot, moved to Paris before he was twenty and served in the army there during the four months the city was invested. When the Prussian siege of 1870–1871 was raised, M. Joliot, who believed in the rights of the common people, switched uniforms and joined the ranks of those upholding the Commune, a revolutionary municipal council set up in Paris that was one of the first expressions of the class struggle in modern times. A patriotic uprising against the Thiers government, provisionally located in Versailles, which the insurgents held responsible for what they termed a "disgraceful" armistice, it lasted ten weeks. When the regular army crushed them, M. Joliot was one of the last detachment of Communards still fighting fiercely on the hill at Chaillot, which they had been ordered to defend at any cost. Although under heavy bombardment, the men refused to surrender. Joliot was one of those lucky enough to flee through the lines to Belgium and escaped the fate of thousands of his less fortunate comrades. At least twenty thousand Communards were savagely butchered on the spot and a further ten thousand condemned to death or exiled in one of the penal colonies overseas. M. Joliot remained in Brussels until the general amnesty of 1879 brought him back to Paris, where he eventually built up a wholesale dry goods business and married Émilie, who was eleven years younger than he.

Eventually the couple had six children and M. Joliot was sufficiently successful by the time Fred, the youngest, was born to be able to hire someone to run his business for him. He devoted the later years of his life to the things he enjoyed most—fishing, hunting, and music. He was a virtuoso, a teacher, and a composer on the *cor de chasse,* the French hunting horn which was then a very popular instrument, and some of his tunes are still played on those hunts in France that continue to cherish and perpetuate the old ritual.

Fred was born on March 19, 1900, in a comfortable middle-class home on the rue des Marroniers in Paris's 16E Arrondissement. In accordance with a tradition in the Joliot family to add "Jean" to male names in memory of Jean Hus, the bohemian who fought for spiritual reform and died at the stake in the fifteenth century, he was christened Jean-Frédéric, but this first name was never used. Because two elder boys had already died, his parents made a special fuss over Fred, as did the remaining children, Henri, Marguerite, and Jeanne, who was already eighteen and would be like his second mother. Fred was raised in a completely nonreligious family; he never attended church and would be an atheist all his life. Fred was nourished on tales of human suffering and patriotic resistance to Prussian domination in which both parents participated. But, while his father never forgot his youthful sympathy with the poor and oppressed, he was no longer the firebrand of his youth, and whenever his wife brought up controversial political topics at the dinner table, Fred's father would declare them off-limits. Fred adored his mother, who was a strong influence in developing his radical thinking. "Thus I grew up," he wrote later, "in a bourgeois household, but I felt very strongly the contrast between that way of life and the memory of the Commune and my mother's words."[1]

The family was not rich, but enough money was saved to send him, at ten, to the Lycée Lakanal in Sceaux to get an education designed to secure him a good job. He attended for seven years, part of that time as a boarder, and would often cut classes to accompany his father hunting and fishing. His wealthy classmates were not concerned with social questions and considered Fred a "radical." However, this label did not greatly affect his popularity, for at Lakanal, sports were more important than scholastic ability and Fred excelled in soccer.

When his father died, to conserve money the family moved to no. 4 Avenue d'Orléans—today Avenue Général Leclerc—in Montparnasse, near the famous statue of the Lion de Belfort. The Joliots had no tradition of scientific learning in their background, but as a boy, Fred was fascinated with the stories he read about Pasteur and the Curies. He cut Pierre and Marie's pictures out of *Lectures pour Tous,* a popular periodical of the day. When he married Irène, he still had them in the original frames his elder sister Marguerite made for him. For years they had hung in a place of honor in the makeshift chemistry laboratory which Fred rigged up in the family bathroom.

His scientific creativity was hard on the kitchen tile and sink, and more than once when his mother went in to wash the dishes, she could not use the water because he had some mysterious apparatus attached to the faucet. The chaotic disorder in Fred's bedroom also drove her to distraction, but none of the many notes she tacked here and there, admonishing him, produced results. Fred might be as messy as most teenage boys, but he already had sufficient discipline to keep a notebook and write down all the observations from his experiments carefully and chronologically. He became an expert on the blowpipe and made a nuisance of himself shooting pellets from his balcony into the aperitifs and beer of patrons at a sidewalk café on the other side of the street.

Fred had a fight with a milk delivery boy, when he was fourteen, that was traumatic. For reasons he later could not recall, the elder boy taunted him. When Fred sagely ignored the remarks, the other started throwing stones. Fred would always remember his own mounting anger and the continued thud as he sat astride his tormentor and savagely beat his head against the sidewalk. For the rest of his life, Fred was filled with a revulsion and fear of uncontrollable passion and its concomitant violence. In October 1914, when his elder brother, Henri, who had just been mobilized, was reported missing in action in one of the first battles of World War I, he was inconsolable. Fred worshipped Henri, and this tragedy brought home a horror of war that stayed with him always and was underscored in gruesome fashion when Fred, as the sole remaining male in the family, had to identify the corpse when it was recovered well over a year later.

When the time came for higher education, Fred did not have the means to attend either of the two great schools of the day—the École Normale Supérieure and the École Polytechnique. In order to prepare for the equally stiff entrance examinations for Paris's tuition-free EPCI, he entered the École Primaire Lavoisier, which had special classes in the exact sciences for those boys who were getting ready to take them. There was a striking difference between his old and new schools. At Lavoisier there were no spoiled "papa's sons," only boys from the families of day laborers and small merchants, and they studied hard because they knew their parents were sacrificing to give them an education. In the beginning, Fred had a lot of adjustments to make; poor grades his first year reflected the difficulty he had following the stiffer courses. But, by graduation, he was number one in his class.

Because the army needed more men, Fred was mobilized when he turned eighteen in 1918, two years before he was originally due to be called up. Nevertheless, he was allowed to take his entrance examinations for EPCI. The competition was formidable—the previous year only thirty-three out of four hundred and thirty candidates passed and were accepted—and Fred failed. The armistice providentially spared him from front-line duty, and the following June, Fred again sat for the EPCI examinations, and now he passed. Unfortunately, by the time he was mobilized out and able to enter, he fell ill. The family doctor claimed he was another victim of the flu, which reached epidemic proportions that year. When Fred nearly died, his mother called in a distinguished specialist who immediately diagnosed a case of typhoid fever. Gravely shaking his head, that venerable gentleman warned Mme. Joliot that he doubted if he could save her son. Fred did survive, but he was not well enough to enter EPCI until 1920.

EPCI was hallowed ground for Fred because of its close associations with his childhood heroes, Pierre and Marie Curie. It was there in October that he met Paul Langevin, who was the school's director of studies and who was destined to be one of the three main influences in Fred's life; the other two were Marie Curie and Irène.

Paul was the first to recognize Fred's enormous potential and wasted no time in including the freshman with the more advanced students whom he regularly invited to his home. In long discussions in front of the roaring fire at no. 10A Boulevard de Port-Royal, Paul, who was farther to the left than most of his colleagues, talked politics and social philosophy along with a wide range of other topics. From a psychological point of view, the timing for these reflections was propitious for Fred, horrified as he was by World War I's carnage and bloodshed and ingrained from childhood to believe that the essential in life was to fight against injustice. He became Langevin's most ardent, lifelong disciple, both in school and out—even subconsciously copying his mannerisms and the way Langevin moved his hand slowly backward and forward over his head. As head boy from his second year on, Fred had numerous dealings with Langevin on behalf of his classmates, but every time he had to speak to him, he was terrified. It would be a long time before he got over being tongue-tied in Langevin's presence and could talk freely with the older man because he so venerated him.

At the end of his first three terms Fred and his classmates had to choose between chemistry and physics. At first unable to make up his mind, he ultimately switched from chemistry to physics mainly, he told his mother, because he wanted to stay with Langevin. At EPCI a large part of the curriculum was wisely devoted to practical work, and here Fred shone. For he was a born experimenter, brilliant and innovative, with exceptional manual dexterity.

Germany's inability to pay its war debts was one more blow to France's straitened economy. Like the rest of Europe, which was riddled with unrest and mounting unemployment, bitter political and social struggles rent the country; a scission arose between the socialists and those further to the left, who were soon known as "Communists" because they sympathized with the Russian Revolution which had recently swept the Tsar from the throne and promised the establishment of a new order. In 1920, the wave of strikes that began shortly after the conclusion of the war reached a new high with a general strike of transport workers.

To check the trade unions, a right-wing group known as the Civic Union was recruiting strike breakers, mainly among students. Since the majority of the EPCI students supported the establishment side, the school's director, Albin Haller, considered suspending classes so they, too, might help the hard-pressed forces of government and industry. The minority, who were on the strikers' side, sent a letter of protest to the director of studies, Langevin, asking that their right to study, independent of political pressure, be upheld. Although Haller assured Langevin that classes would be available for those desirous of them, the school was closed.

On May 17, *L'Humanité,* the leading socialist daily, published the dissenting students' correspondence with Langevin. His reply, printed verbatim in the same newspaper the following day, made it clear that Langevin had not been consulted about the school administration's final decision, and he broke sharply with Haller's policy. Langevin felt that it was the faculty's duty to see that the school was not diverted from its normal sphere of activity and the youth of the Latin Quarter were not transformed into shock troops against the people. Watching from the sidelines, Fred was impressed by Langevin's concern at the rightists' attempts to arouse class hatred. His latent republicanism, inherited from his mother, applauded Langevin's actions, which taught Fred, at that impressionable age, that a scientist could not be indifferent to the conditions in which people lived but must concern himself with social problems.

That same year, officer André Marty was reduced to the ranks and sentenced to twenty years of forced labor for his part in the second of two Black Sea mutinies. A squadron had been sent to Odessa by France and the Western powers to help support the

White Russians who were trying to overthrow the government that had ousted the Tsar. When the French boats anchored in the Black Sea off Sebastopol received the order to fire on troops of the new Soviet regime on the mainland, the belligerent, thick-set Marty, the son of a militant former Communard, led his unit on board the *France* in a mutiny.

The Marty case aroused a widespread reaction with its two inter-related issues—whether the French government had the right to intervene in the affairs of Russia, and whether an officer had the right to rebel. Even Marie, who held aloof from politics, at least publicly, was sufficiently aware of the case to write Irène that the widespread popular support for the mutineers would "give the financiers and reactionaries something to think about."[2] At the turn of the century, Langevin had taken a strong stand in the celebrated Dreyfus affair, which aroused similar wide-spread emotion, and he, Borel, and Perrin, joined the newly formed League for the Rights of Man to fight and win the innocent captain's ultimate release and rehabilitation. Langevin did the same now for Marty. Fred, with an erstwhile Communard for a father, was not the only member of his generation who was undecided where he stood on this burning controversy. He was present with his friend, Paul's son, André, on December 6 when Langevin presided at a great protest meeting in the Salle Wagram which launched an eventually successful campaign for amnesty for Marty—as well as for the other mutineers, who received lesser sentences.

While most of Fred's friends condemned Marty, Langevin's reasons why the seaman should be exonerated, clearly enunciated that evening in the first political speech that he ever made—and that also marked Langevin's first link with the new French Communist Party—clarified Fred's thinking. He might have been filled with even more admiration for Langevin's courageous, unequivocal stand had he been aware of the official and unofficial pressures on him not to appear. Fred followed Langevin's example now and upheld

Marty, just as he would henceforth follow Langevin's lead in so many other matters, public as well as personal, throughout his life.

In 1923, Fred left EPCI with an engineering degree and a major in both physics and chemistry and went to Luxembourg for a six-week training period at the Arbed—*Acieries Réunies de Burbach, Esch et Dudelange*—steelworks at Esch-on-Alzette. He arrived late in the afternoon, after the mills were closed, and searched the main street for someplace to spend the night. Spotting a sign, "L'Hôtel Frédéric," he turned in there. The dining room proved too expensive for his pocket, so he went up to his room and, before retiring, ate the delicacies Mme. Joliot had tucked into his duffel bag. The next morning he discovered that the "Frédéric" was Esch's highest-priced brothel.

Consequently, when he reported for work, everyone there had a good laugh at his expense. Because Fred was able to laugh with them—and had a grandfather who had been a steelworker in Lorraine—he won quick acceptance from the factory workers. Each night, as he listened to the Belgians, French, and Germans discuss their work and living conditions in the present depressed times, Fred, fresh from the classrooms of EPCI with their textbook examples, found himself pitchforked into the glaring reality of social inequality. For at Esch he saw, on one side, firsthand evidence that France's economy was in shambles, while on the other, incontestable proof of the bloated, war-generated wealth of Arbed's proprietors. Fred developed a lifelong interest in the workers' problems. He also learned a practical lesson from industry that was especially valuable at that stage of his career—how to find workable solutions quickly for whatever problems might arise—and would always boast about his industrial experience, giving the impression that it lasted six years.

When his brief internship was finished, Fred still had to serve out the balance of his military service, and he reported at Poitiers, along with some two thousand others, in the bright blue uniform of an officer-cadet of the artillery reserve. There he was delighted to find his cot in the barracks adjoined that of Pierre Biquard, an EPCI comrade assigned to the same motorized Brigade Seven. At night, after the lights were out, the pair talked at length about the future and what they wanted to do. Although Fred knew he could earn three to four times as much in industry as any scientific fellowship would pay—provided he was lucky enough to get one—he, like Biquard, was more interested in basic research which, with a little luck, could result in practical applications for the peace and welfare of mankind. Unfortunately, such work was still only possible in academic surroundings. Both came from modest backgrounds with no money to continue their studies to fulfill the necessary qualifications for even a poorly paid staff job in the university system. At best, such a position meant devoting many hours to teaching and the necessary, accessory administrative work; only then might any spare time left over be employed in research—to be paid for out of one's own pocket.

When Fred and Biquard learned there was a chance to receive grants from the Fondation Curie, established earlier by Edmond de Rothschild, the latter, because he was due to be demobilized first, wrote Langevin for advice, and the pair went to see him on their next leave. Langevin was sympathetic, but he did not mince words about the problems confronting them. Science was a hard taskmaster, demanding complete self-sacrifice, and Fred and Biquard must be willing to consecrate their lives to it. A *normalien* himself, Langevin also knew the tremendous prejudices of the dominant clique in the scientific establishment against those who did not wear the old school tie of either the École Normale Supérieure or the École Polytechnique: "The academic world is a closed society in France, and you have a tremendous handicap . . . You will find it very difficult to rise. That is, unless you do quite exceptional work."[3]

A few days later he informed the pair that he was willing to take on Biquard. Fred must go to the Radium Institute and talk to Mme. Curie, who also had an opening. Why Langevin made the fateful choice between the two is not known. Presumably he needed some-one to help him right away, and Biquard was due to be mustered out first.

Fred's feelings can be imagined when, at 11 A.M. on November 21, 1924, he was ushered into Marie's austere office. There, before him at her desk, sat his childhood heroine, much smaller than he pictured her and with white hair now, but otherwise looking exactly like she did in the faded magazine picture hanging on his wall. He never dreamt that they might meet one day, and it was not easy for him to talk with her. Marie's own shyness made her even more unapproachable. Fred never forgot that first encounter.

After a brief conversation Marie, who generally accepted anyone Paul recommended and had already made up her mind to take Fred, sight unseen, asked: "Can you begin work tomorrow?" She hoped so because her assistant, M. Cailliet, the man Fred was to replace, would be at the Institute only a short time longer, and Marie wanted him to break Fred in. When Marie learned that Fred still had three more weeks of service, she replied, "I will write your colonel."[4] Perrin had already arranged a modest three-year Roths-child grant from the Fondation Curie so she might hire this new personal assistant; it was approximately one half of what Fred had earned at Arbed.

A short time later, Fred returned to Paris with a letter from his colonel acceding to Marie's request, and on December 17, he re-ported for work in civilian garb. Irène was in the midst of an exper-iment in one of the laboratories when Cailliet was showing Fred around to acquaint him with the Institute. So there is no way of knowing whether she recognized him from their previous encoun-ter at the front door of the Quai de Béthune, any more than Fred could report to Biquard, that evening, on the color of her eyes, for she barely raised her head to acknowledge Debierne's introduction.

Fred had developed into a svelte, *soigné* man of medium height and athletic build; clean-shaven, with a shock of thick black hair ending in a widow's peak and dark eyes, he had the fine clear-cut features that a foreigner might term as typically French. Gay and high-spirited, talkative, and using his hands a lot when he spoke, laughing often in the Institute's normally silent halls, Fred had a friendliness and charm that appealed equally to men and women and thawed even the shiest of the foreign students there, and he quickly made friends with his co-workers. In that rarefied atmosphere, where everyone was "Mademoiselle," "Madame," or "Monsieur," no matter how long they worked together, Fred was quickly known as "Fred" to one and all. He was always ready for a good time, and later, when another colleague Moshé Feldenkrais, one of the few judoists in France, was persuaded to teach a class, Fred, Biquard, and even Irène took lessons in that exotic art.

For someone who throughout his life craved admiration, Fred, from the start, felt a certain basic insecurity in the French scientific establishment which he never completely lost. At home and at the Lycée Lakanal, his environment had been that of the comfortable bourgeoisie. Through his sister Marguerite, a talented painter, he knew some artists and frequented their studios. At the École Lavoisier and EPCI, the students were largely from the working class. Now he entered a still different milieu, the academic world. Acutely self-conscious, he made no bones about this changeover, constantly reminding his colleagues that he was "no intellectual." To make matters worse, from the establishment's point of view, he had trained as an engineer rather than as a scientist. Many in the Paris scientific establishment would always slight him as an outsider; enviously, they wondered how he ever wangled a position in one of the foremost experimental laboratories in the world.

Fred came with impeccable credentials—Langevin's recommendation—and Marie was not long in appreciating his exceptional qualities and great drive, although she would never adjust to the perpetual cigarette hanging from his lip and quickly relegated that activity to the lower basement, Salomon Rosenblum's magnetic laboratory, where she rarely ventured, or outdoors. Since he knew little about working with radioactive material, Marie turned Fred over to Irène to indoctrinate in the techniques she and Pierre had pioneered, as well as to familiarize him with the various apparatus, many of which he had never even seen in operation. Fred was impressed not only by the meticulous care, speed, and ingenuity with which Irène handled polonium, dangerously high in radioactivity; he was equally so by the increasing number of her published articles on alpha rays, the most recent of which—on the rays' distributions—Marie proudly sent to Albert Einstein.

Irène being Irène, it is questionable if she paid much attention at first to her dashing new co-worker, three years her junior, as an individual, although Fred hardly conformed to the stereotyped, ivory tower researcher. Not that Irène was adverse to male company as her long-standing intimacy with Debierne, her cousin Maurice Curie, and the closed circle of L'Arcouestien friends from the Cooperative days attest. She even attended dances at the École Normale with them, staying up till 8 A.M., "which is a record," she wrote Marie, that March. But when Irène was at the Institute, she was there to work and nothing else was on her mind. Socially gauche in the eyes of the rest of the world, she never had, and never would see, the need for useless conversation, including the customary social amenities which she considered a waste of time. Frequently Irène was so preoccupied when she arrived in the morning that she did not even remember to say hello to anyone as she hurried in and slipped on her long white, acid-stained smock, intent on the experiment to set up that day. As the daughter of Marie and Pierre Curie, she was the "Crown Princess" of science and so considered by her co-workers, a number of whom were turned off by her imperturbable calm, which they mistook for coldness, and by her direct manner in answering questions, which was misconstrued as haughtiness.

In fairness to Irène, her position as both daughter and personal assistant of "la patronne" was not an easy one. Colleagues failed to give her own ability its due, referred to her among themselves as a "lump on a log," and grumbled about presumed favors accorded her. With all her proven talents, Irène lacked a cardinal one—the ability to make others forgive her her good fortune. If Irène was ever aware of the impression she created, it would hardly have bothered her. Unlike her mother she was never concerned with her image. She was too sure of herself and she was never one to dissimulate. Once Fred startled her with the question: "What was it like to be the daughter of famous parents?" After a moment's reflection, Irène replied, "Fame was something from the outside. It really had no connection with us."[5] She had never thought about the matter before, but it was as good and as honest an answer as any. Unlike most progeny of celebrated couples who choose to follow in their family's footsteps, Irène was neither intimidated nor discouraged by Pierre and Marie's fame.

The next year was a tough, busy one for Fred. He recognized his good fortune to be working where he was and realized how much catching up he had to do—fast. Intensely ambitious, he plunged enthusiastically into the first research Marie selected for him, quickly demonstrating unusual innovativeness in the creation of new methods of procedure and such remarkable ingenuity in personal modifications of various apparatus that he must have made Marie think of Pierre. This initial project, a comprehensive, micro-electrochemical study of radioactive elements, eventually became the subject of his Ph.D. Following Langevin's advice, which Marie echoed, he also went back and finished the rest of the *baccalauréate cum laude*, humiliating as it might be for an engineer and a former second lieutenant to have to write the same examination as a room full of teenagers in short pants. Only then was he able to register at the Sorbonne for the mandatory courses en route to a *licence ès sciences* and a Ph.D.

At the outset, he shared the impression of most others in the laboratory about the distant, aloof heiress apparent he was working with. In arguments, plain-speaking Irène might be incapable of making the least concession, presenting her point and meeting the world head-on, whereas Fred, while equally unyielding, was more diplomatic; consequently, he was able to put his opponents in a frame of mind to accept his arguments. Opposite as their temperaments were, they did not clash but were compatible and complementary. Slowly, as they worked together daily, the more Fred appreciated her fine mind. Discovering the reality underneath the surface, he realized how much she resembled what Fred had learned of Pierre Curie from those who had known him. "I found in her the same purity, his good sense, his humility."[6]

Fred at first thought she lived only for the laboratory and was surprised to find that, while she was introverted like her father and extraordinarily sensitive, Irène enjoyed a good time as well as anybody and had a delightful sense of humor. It might be hard for Irène to get to know this cheerful, attractive extrovert who was charm personified and whose background and upbringing were so dissimilar from hers. Once she did, she discovered the pair not only shared their work in common but also their love of sports—long hikes in the mountains, skiing, swimming, tennis. Occasionally, when Fred had questions that there was no time to ask at the laboratory, he waited outside at the end of the day, and walked home with her. They traversed the rue d'Ulm, continued behind the Panthéon and in front of the library of St.-Geneviève, where Marie used to study late, and continued on down to the Seine, and finally crossed over on the Pont de la Tournelle to the quiet haven of the Île St.-Louis.

Gradually this turned into a nightly routine, and they did not always go directly to the Curie apartment but lingered along the tree-lined, time-stained quais. As they enjoyed each other's company more, their walks lengthened into excursions on the weekends, to the woods around Paris and at Fontainebleau and Sénart; they discussed the British Nobel laureate Rudyard Kipling, whose writings Irène adored and was reading in the original and, surely, her doctoral thesis on alpha rays. She was editing it, now, and confessed that she hoped it would not be as boring to read as it was to do. She learned that Fred had a deep and passionate sense of justice, and their mutual respect and admiration for Langevin proved another link between them.

His activities were always of keen interest to Fred, and that year, his mentor participated in the founding of the Association of French-Russian Friendship. Under various names, it would play an important role in the diffusion of Marxism in university circles. Langevin felt that intellectually speaking, the Russians had too much to contribute to be excluded from Europe. He was impressed by the advances of Russian science, especially in physics, and became a corresponding member of the Russian Academy of Science.

When the time came for Irène to defend her doctoral thesis, "Research on the Alpha Rays of Polonium," in March 1925, the rumors about the brilliant daughter following in her celebrated parents' footsteps packed the Sorbonne amphitheater with the curious and the fashionable, as well as the usual members of academe. Unlike Marie, Irène, dressed in a plain dark dress, her hair cut uncompromisingly short—Ève never could get her sister to attempt anything stylish with it—did not suffer agonies when speaking before so large a group, and her self-confident voice rang out clearly. It is not known whether Fred was there. But Marie was not. The day belonged to Irène, and she did not wish to detract attention from her by putting in an appearance. So she remained in her office working and, no doubt, reliving her own doctoral examination more than two decades before. For the first time in many months, Marie could hear herself think. Of late, the constant rumble of traffic and heavy trucks passing in the street in front of the Curie Pavilion had multiplied in volume and upset so many of the laboratory's delicate instruments that she high-handedly insisted to the prefect of police that he rearrange the flow of traffic and make the rue Pierre Curie one-way.

Later she welcomed her daughter and the entire staff at tea in the small garden of the Institute between the Radium and Pasteur pavilions. These affairs were Marie's traditional way of celebrating a member of her "family's" special days whenever one of them was awarded a hard-won degree or received a special prize. Several tables were set up under the budding lime trees, chairs were moved outside, developing dishes from the photographic darkroom were filled with cookies, tea made in laboratory flasks over Bunsen burners, and the laboratory beakers and glass stirring rods did double duty as teacups and spoons. Langevin stopped by for a champagne toast and predicted a bright future for the new doctor. A young woman reporter appeared from *Le Quotidien* for an interview:

> —*Had Irène chosen too punishing career for a woman? "Not at all," she replied, with self-assurance. "I believe that men's and women's scientific aptitudes are exactly the same . . . A woman of science should renounce worldly obligations."*
> —*What about family obligations? "These are possible on condition that they are accepted as additional burdens. For my part, I consider science to be the paramount interest of my life."*
> —*When she was asked about the dangers of radium, Irène swept the question aside. She admitted she already had a radium burn, but it was not serious. Here in the laboratory there were less risks than in industry. "We know how to protect ourselves better."*[7]

Like her mother, she had periodic blood checks, which showed nothing abnormal. Perhaps Irène did not know that Marie, whose cataracts were almost ripe, had recently confessed to a new young Polish worker, Alicia Dorabialska, who was guiding her steps as the two walked home in the dark, that she did not fully understand radium's physiological effects.

Next-door neighbors Borel and Perrin also dropped in. The latter, even more the embodiment of a man of distinction now that his curly red hair and beard had turned snowy white, brought the usual bouquet of flowers that he always selected himself, blossom by blossom, for Marie from the flower lady's cart on the corner of the nearby rue St.-Jacques. The continuous, ceaseless efforts for more scientific support from the government that these two men exerted, with the help of the close-knit L'Arcouest group, including Marie—and, whenever needed, Langevin and the socialist politician and writer Léon Blum—would parallel the rise of Fred's career and the crest of French science, from 1925 to 1940.

Because of the growth of industry resulting from the new technologies spawned by scientific progress, a new proletariat, such as Fred had already encountered at Esch, was struggling to advance against entrenched, reactionary men of property. While most academics refused to play politics, Langevin, for one, was increasingly facing up to social issues and the condition of Europe as a whole. Looking east across France's border, where German nationalism had regained a preponderant influence, and southeast, where fascism was coming to the fore in Italy, Langevin no longer had any confidence in international organisms to maintain peace and would increasingly put his hopes for this in a revulsion of the masses against catastrophic war.

Irène was becoming known in her own right outside of France. She turned down a proposition to teach chemistry at St. Lawrence University in upper New York State for one year because, she explained to Missy, with whom she and Ève maintained a warm correspondence, she did not want to be away that long and would only consider teaching radioactivity. Then she hastened to Strasbourg to deliver a lecture at the Physics Society while Marie went to Warsaw.

Borrowing several tricks from Missy, Bronya, who had agreed to be the Polish Radium Institute's first director, also led the money-raising campaign, flooding the countryside with posters saying "Buy a brick for the Marie Sklodowska-Curie Institute," to encourage small donations; she had printed up for sale postcards with excerpts of some of Marie's pertinent speeches, and the government cooperated with suitable commemorative postage stamps. Marie had a triumphal homecoming; sharing cornerstone-laying festivities with the President of Poland and the mayor of Warsaw.

At some point after her summary dismissal of the correspondent from *Le Quotidien'* s question about family obligations as "additional burdens," Irène's relations with Fred turned serious. The first mention of him to appear in her handwriting is in the December entry in her journal: *"Noël—Séjour à Megève*—6 days with Fred, Francis and Colette [the young, newly married Perrins], Jean [Perrin, Sr]."[8] A subsequent postcard, dated February 19, 1926, from the same resort where Fred and Irène had returned for more skiing, this time with Ève, and that Fred wrote to "Dear Mé," ending, "We embrace you tenderly,"[9] bespeaks Marie's acceptance of Fred as a family intimate. Irène casually broke the news of their engagement one morning, sometime later when she came in, as usual, with the breakfast she had made for her mother and herself and sat on the foot of Marie's bed to discuss the forthcoming day's work at the laboratory.

According to Ève, Marie could not have been more astonished. This is hard to believe. She had to have, intuitively, sensed some change in her elder daughter; there were not that many young men in Irène's life for Marie not to be aware of Fred's attentiveness, let alone of his intentions. If Marie was really taken by surprise, it must have been because she refused to admit the evidence under her nose, as with the nefarious effects of radium—a subconscious denial of the facts prompted in this instance by the wrenching realization she was losing her closest associate. But Marie was rarely mistaken in her judgment of people, and by the time of their wedding, she decided that Fred's qualifications, both as a physicist and a husband, passed muster. Secure in her belief that the young couple's mutual interest in science would prove as strong a bond as the one formerly existing between herself and Pierre, she gave the union her unqualified blessing.

When Irène wrote the news to Angèle Pompei, adding, "We have many opinions in common on essential questions," her close friend, unlike Marie, was not surprised. For on their last hiking trip, Irène was constantly humming one special refrain from her growing collection of old peasant songs—"I will make white dolls like others do." And Irène declared, later, in her own inimitable fashion: "I realized that, if I did not have any children, I would never have forgiven myself for having missed the most astonishing experience I could possibly have."[10] However, it is highly unlikely that she married Fred solely to experience childbirth. An inquisitive scientist Irène might be, but every letter she ever wrote to Fred indicates she married for love. It also speaks volumes for the strength of her feelings for him that she evinced no second thoughts about leaving Marie, regardless of their unusually close, dual relationship which she knew could never remain the same once she had a husband.

June 24, their betrothal was official, and both families dined together at Mme. Joliot's in Montparnasse. The scientific community as a whole still refused to see Fred in a favorable light and was shocked at the engagement of the prickly, grave Curie daughter to the captivating upstart. Those who were jealous of the good fortune of this young man "from nowhere" and unable to detect any of his remarkable qualities suggested he was marrying into one of science's "royal families" solely to further his own career. They considered Fred an ambitious opportunist—which he undoubtedly was—and were surprised that Marie had consented to the match. They lost sight of the fact that Irène was far too independent for her mother to dictate to, had she so desired, but their malicious barbs found a target in Fred. The sarcastic title "Prince Consort" rankled, and lay festering. Ten years later, after declaring, "I love my wife," he startled a casual American acquaintance by plaintively, almost apologetically, adding as if he felt explanations were in order, "Why are people so nasty? Why do they claim that I . . . married her just for the sake of my career? But I do love my wife. I love her very much."[11]

This same sensitivity to the question of his marriage and the pressing need he felt to explain it crops up again with another unlikely candidate for a similar confession, Toshiko Yuasa, a young Japanese woman who worked in the laboratory with him in the

1940s and early 1950s. He confided that he suddenly found himself jealous when he saw Irène devoting time explaining experiments to other fellow technicians: "If I hadn't been able to marry her [Irène], I decided to remain a bachelor."[12] Even toward the end of his life, this accusation still rankled sufficiently for him to refute it once again with a colleague, who remembers the painful conversation to this day.

Hard as it is to assess reasons for matrimony given the vagaries and complexities of human nature—not to mention simply sex— after viewing Fred's life as a whole, the feeling persists that at least in the beginning, this was a typical European marriage of convenience from his point of view. A man of tremendous drive and aspirations, Fred's basic insecurity, together with his complementary need to be admired, was never very far from the surface, even after he reached the pinnacle as a Nobel laureate, and it dictated much of his activity. What greater coup, or sop for a battered ego, could there possibly be for Fred, the parvenu who from the day he set foot in the Curie Laboratory was acutely conscious of being an outsider, than to do exactly what he was accused of doing? What he protested—almost too much—that he was innocent of? The fact that the "Crown Princess" of science also happened to be the daughter of "la patronne," as well as of his childhood role models —the Curies—made her conquest triply challenging. Irène's brilliance and the many interests they held in common were so many added bonuses.

One of their intimates related overhearing Fred remark, sometime after they were wed, "No. I have not yet been unfaithful to my wife but, if I am, it will not affect our marriage."[13] Fred was a vain, vibrant ladies' man, full of personality, with a plain-looking wife whose utter lack of interest in her personal appearance must sometimes have been a minor cross to bear—no matter how successful a scientific team they made. So it is easy to understand why other contemporaries still remember him as a "butterfly" who flittered hither and yon but never stayed put any length of time. However, what evidence—and correspondence—is available indicates that theirs was a most successful, satisfactory union for both. And throughout the many dreary months that Irène was later forced to spend, off and on, in sanatoriums, Fred kept the household and their two children on an even keel.

Prior to Irène's engagement, Marie had accepted, at the request of the Minister of Foreign Affairs, to whom she was deeply indebted, a series of lectures in Rio de Janeiro in the interests of better Franco-Brazilian relations. Because she was going so far away, she agreed to what constituted a long tour for her, and she could not leave until her Sorbonne students were on vacation. Irène originally promised to accompany her, before she was engaged, and Marie saw no reason for any change of plans. There was nothing like several months' separation to determine whether she was making a mistake.

For someone who had done so little traveling until she was fifty, Marie was making up for lost time and enjoyed seeing more of the world, trailing glory as she went. Her ground rules were laid out before her arrival—no public speeches other than her specifed lectures; a minimum of official dinners, and no luncheons so she could snatch a few minutes of rest in the middle of the day. The Brazilian trip was to be more like a vacation than an official visit because they were to stay a month and a half, and a number of side excursions were planned. But, if Marie thought—or hoped—that a long absence might cause her daughter to change her mind, she was mistaken. Irène was too deeply in love.

The trip took two weeks each way, and while they were gone, Fred completed *licence* examinations which advanced him further towards his doctorate. Distance made correspondence erratic and infrequent, and Irène was not the first fiancée to worry that the absence of mail meant a loss of interest on Fred's part. Then another long, eminently satisfactory letter would arrive to put her fears momentarily at rest:

What gives interest to life in the lab are the people who animate it. And since your departure I find it empty . . . I shall not return with any happiness until you are there . . . I do not forget you. Stop worrying. [14]

Unfortunately, when his letters did arrive, she had a hard time reading them. Gently, she poked fun at him with a personal deciphering manual:

Letters written in the hieroglyphic language invented in the 20th century by M. Frédéric Joliot, with their translation:

ι	ι	ω
=	=	=
c,r,i,e, l,t	u,n	m

Furnished with these explanations, decipher as an exercise.

[Warning: A word is sometimes cut in two but, in general, two different words are not joined together, according to the Frédéric Joliot rules of penmanship.]

Like with many introverts, only in her letters does Irène reveal the warm, frequently humorous side of her nature known to a handful of intimates and her immediate family. She missed Fred dreadfully and longed "to be pressed close . . . and rub my hands through your hair, mussing it all up . . . [till it stood on end.]" And she worried about him. "You haven't told me whether you were smoking a reasonable or an unreasonable amount. Does such discretion on your part signify that the second hypothesis is the correct one? . . . Try not to smoke like a factory smokestack, go 100 km an hour on your motorbike, and do all the other unreasonable things you are capable of."[15]

The *SS Lutetia* returned September 12, and within the week Irène was at L'Arcouest with Fred. It was his first visit there, and he spent most of his time investigating the fishing potential while Irène attended to details concerning the cottage Marie was about to build. Meanwhile, Marie was at Cavalaire with Ève and Debierne. October 7, the wedding contracts were signed, and Fred and Irène's marriage took place, privately, in the 4 Arrondissement Town Hall at 11:15 A.M., on October 9, 1926, in a civil ceremony. As was to be expected, there was no religious one. Only the immediate families, Debierne, and Biquard were present. After the mayor, who officiated, gave a special talk in honor of Mme. Curie, they all departed by car for a bridal lunch at the Quai de Béthune, which Ève, who cared more about these details than her sister, took pains to see was properly festive. Then the bride and groom returned to their laboratory benches. With a total disregard of anything so conventional as spending their wedding night together, Fred went home to Montparnasse and Irène, back to the Île St.-Louis—for reasons unknown. The next morning, he arrived with a single suitcase at the Quai, and the newlyweds saw Marie off to Copenhagen. She was to be away a week, leaving the empty apartment at their disposal. Later Fred was back at his mother's to supervise the moving of his few possessions—"an armoire, a blue chest, and a little yellow one,"[16] Mme. Joliot scrupulously noted, like the good bourgeois housewife she was.

XVI
1927–1930

A Fast Learner

HE FIRST MONTHS OF married life, always a time of adjustment for any couple, neither Fred nor Irène was well. Fred had his appendix out and was forced to spend two weeks in a clinic, and Irène, who was quickly enceinte, was also suffering from anemia, whether related to her pregnancy or a forerunner of the tuberculosis to come is impossible to ascertain. Fred's recovery was slow, probably because of exhaustion from overwork the past few strenuous years, and Irène would remain wretched for nine months, though she never missed a day's work except when she was away.

In March they went south to the island of Porquerolles for a rest. Irène already had a foretaste of what it was like to be a "fisherman's widow." Some husbands, especially newly married ones, carry a picture of their bride around with them. But not Fred. "Ask him to show you the snap he carries in his wallet,"[1] she challenged a friend. Fred obliged and produced a snap of a majestic pike, the largest one he ever caught. He had the misfortune to arrive at Porquerolles with the wrong kind of bait, but luckily for Irène, he was able to purchase what he needed locally. Otherwise, she confided to Marie, he would certainly have committed suicide or else killed her "in a moment of nervous prostration." Fred added a good-natured postscript, "I believe that with this beautiful sun, the red corpuscles can only rejoice and even produce numerous companions." And he wrote his own mother, "I have an adorable wife."[2]

When Fred returned to Paris, Irène joined Marie on the Côte d'Azur, but she missed Fred:

> *[Mé is forever] telling me what you would or would not like me to do in order to persuade me to do or not to do something. I consider this very disloyal, for what good is it to be away from one's husband, if one is tyrannized by him even from afar?*[3]

Soon after Irène returned, she and Fred moved into an apartment of their own that Marie gave them in a building she bought as an investment with the Perrins, Borels, and Maurains. Nicknamed by the press the "Extension of Fort Science" because so many L'Arcouestiens lived there, off and on, no. 4 rue Froidevaux was an unimposing, six-story building with two apartments to a floor and located south of the Latin Quarter, but within comfortable walking distance of the Institute and near Mme. Joliot's. Across the street was a small park for children to play in. For neighbors, Irène and Fred had at one time or another Francis and Colette Perrin and their family; his sister Aline; Irène's friend from childhood and her husband; Charles Lapique, the painter son of one of L'Arcouest's co-founders; the Borels; and Marguerite's brother, Pierre Appel. Fred and Irène's apartment was a comfortable one on the fifth floor, and because they were always in a hurry, they preferred to race up and down the narrow winding stairs rather than trust the temperamental, rickety cage elevator.

The move consummated the final break with Marie, though it was eased for her by Irène's self-evident happiness. They came regularly for lunch, the mainstay of every French family, three or four times a week and went the other days to Mme. Joliot's. If it seemed strange, at first, to get accustomed to hearing a male voice and male footsteps in the secluded Île St.-Louis household of three women, Marie was comfortable far more quickly with Fred than he with her, and she was soon calling him "Fred" with a special tenderness. But, even now that she was his mother-in-law, the frail elderly woman peering at him through her thick spectacles filled easygoing Fred with a certain awe, and at times, she could be difficult to get along with. By Fred's own admission it was a good year before he felt completely at ease with her. But already Fred felt sufficiently at home, so that heated conversations at the table were nonstop. Institute discussions raced animatedly back and forth between Fred and Marie exactly like the Ping-Pong ball, later, between Fred and Irène when the couple played their daily game in the salon in lieu of dessert. Their give and take was so rapid that an amused Irène could not get a word in and was reduced to the sidelines, exactly as Ève had been when she was small and Irène and her mother's conversation centered around the laboratory.

Ève was now Marie's mainstay at home. She had given her first recital shortly before Marie went south, that early spring, to encouraging reviews. Marie was supportive of her talent and endured countless hours of the girl's practicing on the big grand piano she had purchased for her and installed, as a pendant to the billiard and Ping-Pong tables, at the opposite end of the cavernous living room. Often, Fred and Ève would play four hands on it, or Fred might improvise with sweeping arpeggios. Ève now also had a tiny apartment on the rue Brancion in which to receive her own friends who were from artistic circles, but she still slept at home. Many an evening, Marie would return late, put on her slippers, throw a wool jacket over her shoulders, and come in and stretch out on the couch in Ève's bedroom to chat, as the girl dressed to go out.

She was proud of her younger daughter's attractiveness and many conquests, but she could never get used to the postwar styles ushered in by Coco Chanel with her simple little black dresses cut straight to the knee. At her age, Marie reasoned, Ève should wear color and not show so much leg. As for all those other horrors Ève affected, Marie did not mince words. Those high heels! How could anyone walk on such stilts! And dresses with the backs cut out! Even harder for Marie to get used to was the amount of time Ève spent applying makeup. Marie thought the end results dreadful. When Ève came home, often as not she could see the light still on in her mother's bedroom and would open the door to find Marie sitting on the floor, her graphs and other papers strewn around her, calculating in Polish.

Marie's habitual pessimism still haunted her, and she wrote Bronya that she was thinking about stopping work and going to live in the country to devote herself to gardening and writing scientific books. But this was idle talk. Marie could never find small joys in daily life; she could never live without the laboratory.

Irène worked right up until noon on September 17, 1927, when Fred took her to the hospital. Her daughter, Hélène, was born late that afternoon, and became an instant subject for her mother's ever-present camera. In spite of an inexplicable high fever which developed a few days later, Irène was soon back at work, though still far from well. And every afternoon, whenever Marie was in Paris and the maid, Mme. Blondin, took her first grandchild to the Luxembourg Gardens, "near the lion on the left," Marie appeared. She devoted thirty minutes to the baby, and when the clock struck the hour, she kissed little Hélène goodbye and returned to the laboratory and the infant's parents.

Within a year Irène's life had grown many-faceted. Her responsibilities at the Institute now included complete charge of the work of Marie's new Sorbonne students, while her mother limited herself to selecting and delegating their research projects; she also had a child, a husband, and a household to look after, and Fred was far more fastidious than she would ever be. Like Marie, Irène never learned to cook, but Fred could be a good chef on occasion. With his mandatory second *licence,* which he had just received, Fred was finally able to increase the family income by taking over a class of electrical measurements at the private École d'Électricité Charliat. Meanwhile, he continued work at the Curie Laboratory, honing his research techniques. While Irène had her own laboratory on the ground floor, Fred did not have one. He worked anywhere, but he could most generally be found in the basement room housing the Wilson cloud chamber, which was already Fred's, as well as Irène's, favorite tool. He frequently called the direct, detailed view it provided of the trajectories of rays "the most beautiful phenomenon in the world." "Yes, *mon chéri,"* Irène would correct him with a smile. "It would be the most beautiful phenomenon in the world, if there were not that of childbirth."[4] This marvelous device, for which the Scot C.T.R. Wilson shared the 1927 Nobel prize, was invaluable for the study of radioactivity; it was to the physicist what a telescope was to the astronomer, and was the direct ancestor of the famous "bubble chamber" of the 1960s.

As soon as he thoroughly understood its basic principles, Fred's engineering training enabled him to improve upon Wilson's model. It was a good thing he was very adept with his hands and able to make the modifications he desired himself, because the laboratory only had two mechanics, one electrician, and one glassblower to attend to the wants of twenty–thirty researchers. First, Fred endowed the original chamber with variable pressure. Hitherto, its pressure was roughly that of the surrounding atmosphere, but by redesigning it so that it could be lowered he could now see tracks seventy-six times as long. Then, with the help of a colleague Dmitri Skobeltzyn, a Leningrad scientist who was working at the laboratory on one of Marie's Carnegie grants, Fred drew up ambitious plans and supervised the construction of an enormously improved machine that was also able to photograph—for subsequent study— what could be seen inside the chamber. While droplets of water that condensed around each ion as it passed through a gas saturated with water vapor inside the chamber left a perceptible wake, this telltale succession of beads of condensation—like a rosary— only lasted a fraction of a second. Yet these tracks were characteristic of, and provided unparalleled information on, the different types of particles producing them. Fred's adaptation would likewise prove invaluable because it enabled him to determine the energy of alpha rays by measuring the curvature of their trajectories in a magnetic field. Fred also built an apparatus to detect a radioactive body in solution and to determine its exact weight, even if it was only a question of 0.00000001 gram.

By this intense study, Fred was catching up with Irène and fast arriving at the stage where both of them could be able, almost subconsciously, to notice the slightest irregularities or exceptions in their studies of these rays and their tracks, and draw from them profitable information. Fred had no sense of time where work was concerned so Irène, who was anxious to see for herself how his work was progressing, searched him out, twice a day, at mealtimes. She took the freshly lit cigarette out of his mouth and extinguished it, reminded him to remove his white overalls, and refused to leave until he accompanied her—no easy task. The couple's first paper as a team appeared in the Academy's *Comptes Rendus* in 1928, "On the Number of Ions Produced by Alpha Rays of RaC."

Fred's mentor, Langevin, by now was convinced that all the hopes of humanity lay in the U.S.S.R. and was one of the principal founders of the Circle of New Russia; this was soon transformed into the Association for the Study of Soviet Culture, and especially under Henri Wallon, was to play an important role in the diffusion of Marxism in French university circles.

A pacifist by nature, Paul also participated with increasing frequency in popular manifestations against war and had lately presided at the first great antifascist meeting in Paris at the Salle Bullier, which was attended by over eight thousand people. Marie continued to evince no interest in foreign affairs, politics, or the feminist movement, which she considered an offshoot of the latter. She strongly believed that as a scientist she should stand clear of any such entanglements. However, if her years of travel, especially in America, did not open her eyes to the need for a more activist role in this fields, then it was Fred's subtly increasing influence that did so. He had already shifted Irène from her mother's noncommittal political position, and at Irène's request, Marie acquiesced to sign a petition on behalf of Sacco and Vanzetti. This was only the second she ever signed—the first one was on behalf of Herta Ayrton's jailed suffragettes, years before—and was part of an unsuccessful, last-minute attempt for a reprieve for these two Italian immigrants and supposed anarchists, who became an international *cause célèbre* following their arrest and subsequent condemnation to death in a 1921 killing in Massachusetts.

When Irène and Fred spent their first summer vacation at L'Arcouest with year-old Hélène, Marie's own house, whose construction Irène had been overseeing, was ready for occupancy, although electricity would not be installed for another year or so. Located on an isolated, windswept site on the moor, the cottage was already encircled with luxuriant climbing roses. Tiny, narrow, and undistinguished, like the one she built at Cavalaire, its rooms were badly arranged and poorly furnished, but the view was unparalleled. Fred, too, grew to love the quiet life here with everyone dressed like beachcombers in much-mended bathing suits, cotton dresses, and espadrilles. He soon had a small boat built to his specifications, the *Marsouin*—"the Porpoise"—a whaler with sails and an oar, and later two sailboats, the *Saint-Just* and the *Hélion.* Most mornings, Fred went out early with the native fishermen when they checked and rebaited their lobster pots or went shrimp fishing off l'Île Verte. They quickly accepted him as one of their own, and years later, Fred admitted that he felt more at home with the fishermen there than at scientific meetings, a sentiment that was reciprocated.

In 1929, the couple reported again on alpha rays in the *Comptes Rendus,* and the same year, Salomon Rosenblum, Marie's brilliant protégé, using the Academy of Sciences' big electric magnet set up in its Bellevue laboratory by Aimé Cotton—the husband of Irène's old "sèvrienne" friend Eugénie Feytis—discovered the fine structural lines of these rays. The day of his experiment, Marie got up before daybreak to prepare personally the source of radioactinium he needed. Rosenblum was so excited with his results, which meant that the new quantum laws could be applied to give more information about the internal structure of the nucleus, that he did a frenzied Russian *kazachok* around the magnet. When he returned to the Curie Pavilion and thrust the photograph in "la patronne's" hands, she was overjoyed. In her inimitable fashion, Marie promptly sat down at her bench, exclaiming, "Now I'll make you a really beautiful source."[5]

This pioneering work, the first remarkable discovery of the Radium Institute since its inauguration, resulted in a change of emphasis for Irène and Fred and for other researchers. Henceforth, interest in radioactivity, which had been primarily biological—because of the medical results it produced in the treatment of cancer —switched to an intensive study of the rays themselves. Although radioactive decay was an accepted phenomenon, most radioactive substances, while distinct elements, were available in only the most minute quantities, and many of their chemical properties had yet to be determined and described.

Unquestionably, the direction of Fred and Irène's joint future work was influenced by the availability of Marie's stockpile of radioactive substances. Polonium, a decay product of radium, had complex radiation and physically and chemically resembled bismuth, the next element down on the Periodic Table. Whereas radium emits alpha, gamma, and beta rays whose effects are difficult to disentangle from one another, polonium has the useful property of emitting abundant high-energy alpha particles—five thousand times as much as an equivalent mass of radium—while producing almost no other type of radiation. So it was invaluable to researchers, but unfortunately, nature was stingy. A ton of uranium ore contained only about 0.1 grams, far too little for commercial separation.

Since polonium was largely available only as a by-product of the radioactive decay of radium, and the doctors who used Marie's radon ampoules in the hospitals returned them to her when the radon was used, these "seeds," as they were called, constituted a superb source from which to extract polonium. Marie also collected used ampoules from doctors elsewhere as she traveled abroad, while others sent them to her as an unsolicited tribute. Over the years a good amount of polonium had also accumulated in the stock of radium processed originally by Marie and Pierre. And Marie, who had the final say as to who did what with this precious stockpile, put it all at Fred and Irène's disposal rather than parcel it out, as in the past, in bits and pieces to different researchers in the laboratory for their respective projects. By doing so, she was again subjected to the whispered charge of favoritism—no one would dare accuse "la patronne" to her face—several years, later, when Rosenblum requested permission to use more and was refused.

Whenever they could find the time Fred and Irène, who were doing increasing laboratory work together, also added to this supply of polonium. To do so, they utilized different, new methods that they themselves perfected, employing either electrolysis or evaporation, as the case might be. This was a delicate chemical task, laborious and highly technical; it was also extremely dangerous because of the high levels of radioactivity in the concentrations they were handling, and polonium, which was very toxic, concentrated in the lungs, spleen, and liver if it entered the body.

While the pair were off on a ten-day skiing holiday at Megève, the end of January 1929, with Ève and friends, Missy came through Paris en route home after interviewing Mussolini. Marie, who had lately obtained for her friend the Légion d'Honneur, hurried to consult with her. Marie was anxious to procure a gram of radium—there were still only three hundred grams available in the entire world—for the new Maria Sklodowska-Curie Institute in Warsaw, which was nearing completion and lacked the wherewithal to buy any. Missy had been undergoing radiotherapy for a tumor and was frail and visibly aging, but she was willing, as always, to help a worthwhile cause—and oblige Marie. She promised to do what she could but warned that there was less money available now for everything. Some weeks later, she informed Marie that a gift for Poland had little appeal during an election year in an America in the throes of isolationism. However, it might be possible to raise the sum in Marie's name, if she were to come over once more to the United States.

Marie agreed to a far shorter trip than before and proved much fussier about details. Under Ève's gentle goading, she indulged in one new dress with which Irène hoped she would "dazzle" everyone and set sail in October accompanied by Mrs. Henry Moses of the New York Committee, who came to Paris expressly to escort her over on the *Île de France*.

Once again, Missy had done her homework well. The fund was oversubscribed, and Marie spent the night at the White House as the guest of President and Mrs. Hoover, an unheard-of distinction not normally extended for fear of diplomatic complications. She went to Dearborn, Michigan, as the guest of Henry Ford, to participate in the golden jubilee of the electric light and attended Ford's dinner in honor of her friend and fellow scientist Thomas Alva Edison. She also stayed in Schenectady, New York, with Owen D. Young, the head of General Electric, a company which had donated lavishly to the Radium Institute and whose experimental laboratories she inspected while there. Marie made only one New York appearance and visited Missy's country home in Pawling, New York, before leaving. Marie was now a professional at the art of discrete begging and had learned to enjoy the red carpet treatment accorded her.

Marie's timing could not have been better. Three days after she sailed, with enough funds to buy the desired gram of radium for Warsaw and money left over to put into the Fondation Curie of the Radium Institute, was Black Thursday on Wall Street. Although the stock market crash plunged America into the Great Depression, Missy's friends remained generous. Shortly after the first of the year, she informed Marie that she had persuaded Henry Ford to give her a car "to increase the efficiency of her work,"[6] while Mrs. Moses agreed to provide a chauffeur. Mrs. Carnegie sent additional money, invested in French bonds, to restore to its original level the depreciated income of the scholarships her late husband had established; and other American women sent dogwood trees to Bronya to plant around Marie's monument in the square between the buildings of the Warsaw Radium Institute. Marie received an additional dividend. For the $3,500 yearly annuity which she was presently receiving from the Equitable Trust, from the balance of the funds from her 1921 trip, and which she had been using to rent a gram of radium for Warsaw, was now freed to be used as Missy's Committee had originally intended—for Marie's personal needs and comfort. She also returned with gifts for the family which she purchased herself, including boots for Fred and a cover for Hélène's pram.

No wonder Ève wrote Missy that she had never seen her mother return in better health and spirits. Both she and Irène maintained a warm correspondence with the petite journalist who may, indirectly, have served as a role model for Ève. While Marie's younger daughter had not deserted music, she was doing some translating and working as a music and movie critic for a number of magazines under the pseudonym, "Claude Doré." She wanted to earn enough money to maintain the little car Marie had purchased for her, which she lovingly washed and polished every Sunday.

Conceivably, Marie's repeated success in America was partially responsible for the philosophical mood of her annual New Year's letter:

[I hope 1930 will be] a year of good health, good humor and good work in which you will have pleasure in living every day, without waiting for the days to be gone before finding charm in them, and without putting all hope of pleasure in the days to come. The older one gets the more one feels that the present must be enjoyed; it is a precious gift, comparable to a state of grace. I am thinking of your little Hélène . . . It is so moving to see the evolution of this little creature who expects everything from you with boundless confidence and who believes certainly that you can intervene between her and any suffering. One day she will know that your power does not extend that far and, yet, one could wish to be able to do this for one's children. The least one can do is to make every effort to assure them good health, a peaceful, serene childhood in an ambiance of affection where their wonderful confidence will last as long as possible.[7]

The ending was vintage Marie—a paragraph discussing the tangent of the curve P = function Log x.

Irène's reputation as a scientist worth watching was already established by numerous publications before she met Fred, so after her marriage she continued to publish under her maiden name in order not to lose her professional identity, although "Irène Joliot-Curie" was the correct form for a married woman of the day. Then in February of 1930, she wrote Missy that Fred wanted to join "Curie" to his name and to that of Hélène. "There is nothing officially done in that direction now, but we have the intention to ask for it, and we are already using both names."[8] It is curious that Fred would contemplate this name change because he must have realized that to do so would only refuel previous rumors that opportunism had dictated his choice of a wife. Perhaps he was sufficiently anxious to flaunt his Curie connection not to care. Irène's letter notwithstanding, their scientific reports continued to be signed "Irène Curie and Frédéric Joliot" except for one or two publications in the early and mid-thirties, when it became "Irène and Frédéric Joliot." Numerous contemporaries sensed that Marie herself was not pleased at Fred's appropriating Pierre's name, although it was increasingly evident that Fred could stand on his own feet scientifically. "The boy's a skyrocket," she declared to Perrin with obvious pleasure one day.[9] It may have been amusing to her to reflect how times had changed. No one ever accused Irène of riding to fame on her husband's coattails—and name—as they once did Marie, with Pierre.

The Nobel prize was attributed in conventional fashion to "Irène Joliot-Curie and Frédéric Joliot." But the matter of names does not end there, so it must have been a difficult issue to ultimately resolve. In May 1939, in a tentative uranium-oxide purchase agreement with the Union Minière of Belgium, Fred signed as "Joliot-Curie," yet his signature on the famous *pli cacheté* of October 30 of the same year, involving the possibility of a nuclear chain reaction, reads "F. Joliot." Lew Kowarski, a close associate of the Atomic Commissariat, years later, claimed he pointed out to Fred that there was no need for him to assume the Curie name. Fred replied: "Funny, you have a bee in your bonnet about it. You're like my daughter. She's always telling me: 'Don't call yourself Curie.'"[10] After the war, Fred was known solely by the hyphenated name, which prompted one journalist to remark: "M. Frédéric Joliot-Curie is certainly a great man, but not sufficiently so, it seems, to be called simply Joliot."[11] The one constant in this whole affair is that, socially and academically, he was always Joliot and the couple was always known as "the Joliots."

Spring came early in 1930, so when Fred successfully defended his doctoral thesis, "A Study of the Electrochemistry of Radioactive

Elements," on March 17, it was warm enough for Marie to hold her traditional tea outdoors to celebrate the new Ph.D. on her staff. There was pride and affection in her voice when Marie congratulated him. Debierne, lifting his glass to his Sunday tennis partner, joked that he had come too late to study radioactivity. There was hardly anything left to do except work out to the third and fourth decimal point each atom's characteristics and differentiating qualities. Fred enjoyed a second round of congratulations, and his report was discussed in detail the following Monday at Jean Perrin's weekly tea in the Institute of Physical Chemistry next door, which he directed. Unlike Marie's occasional celebrations to *fête* special events, which were limited generally to Institute personnel, the gatherings in the laboratory of the sociable Perrin were a focal point for all the atomic scientists in the Collège de France and the University of Paris, as well as for those on the staffs of the numerous institutes in the immediate vicinity. These affairs spread the latest news in the field and acted also as informal gatherings. Fred and Irène rarely missed one, and generally Fred or someone else equally vocal was the center of a small group clustered around the blackboard, discussing different aspects or problems of work in progress. Because of his magnetic personality—and his continued weakness for the opposite sex—Perrin's Mondays were an established highlight of the Parisian scene, attracting distinguished visitors passing through, as well as wealthy benefactors like the Rothschilds, and an occasional *grande dame.* As he gallantly offered each of his women guests a cup of tea, he quoted with pretended gravity his own version of Ecclesiastes: "Hasten to succumb to temptation lest it elude you!"[12]

Practical Perrin, whose own children, Aline and Francis, were already married, understood the financial needs of Fred and Irène and now that Fred had his doctorate, got him a salaried position from the Caisse Nationale de la Recherche Scientifique to replace the minuscule Rothschild grant Marie had for him, which was due to expire. As a *maître de recherche,* one of the very first researchers to be financed by that body, Fred could devote himself full-time to research of his own choosing at the Curie Laboratory. While his new stipend was hardly handsome, Fred was saved from the necessity of returning to industry to support himself and his family and could also relinquish his onerous task as lecturer at Charliat. This was the "L'Arcouest network" in action, as opposed to the old-school ties of the establishment. The firsthand knowledge and appreciation that Fred had of the significance of state financial aid at the start of his career would be responsible for many of the decisions he insisted upon later, when he was organizing the development of French scientific resources in post-World War II France.

The substantial increase in government funds, as well as the new statutes received this year by the Caisse Nationale de la Recherche Scientifique, was largely due to the unending efforts of Perrin, the man who dominated French physics between the two world wars, and who had been working tirelessly to improve the role of science and the lot of the scientist. This Caisse, which had been originally established in 1901, would ultimately be superseded by the Centre National de la Recherche Scientifique, an outgrowth of and successor to it. He was aided and abetted in the tedious pioneer lobbying this entailed by Marie, Borel, and others of the L'Arcouest circle. Marie could still wax fierce where something so close to her heart was concerned, and the arguments, not to mention the presence of this legend of self-sacrifice, reinforced Perrin's pleas that the days of the individual scientist working alone in a poorly equipped, ramshackle shed like the Curies' fabled one on the rue Lhomond, must be banished forever. The increasingly leftist Langevin was particularly helpful, because he had already visited Russia several times and could report firsthand on the thorough scientific overhaul undertaken there. Because France was prosperous once more and awake to the stirrings of fascism and German nationalism abroad, construction was about to begin on the enormously costly Maginot Line fortifications, and the government was receptive to their pleas. Bludgeoned by Perrin and his cohorts into the alarming realization that Germany—not to mention other countries—was ahead of France in modern physics and careers as researchers must be opened to young people from every walk of life, the administration proved receptive to the needs of science. Not unexpectedly, the L'Arcouestiens and their friends heavily outweighed all others on the completely restructured Caisse's committees, assuring them, rather than the government, control over financing. This constituted a major victory.

With his finances in better shape, Fred was free to devote himself full-time to the buildup of the polonium supply at the laboratory. Such a hoard played the same role as the big accelerating machines of a later day in the investigation of nuclear structure and was essential if Fred and Irène were to attempt important discoveries in radioactivity. For some of the radioactive phenomena occurred rarely, and experiments had to be repeated over and over in order that these phenomena could be observed systematically. The necessary theories were already in place to try to disentangle and decipher the jumble issuing when elements were bombarded, and Fred's version of the Wilson cloud chamber with its new picture-taking capacity was an invaluable tool with which to study the radioactive process.

Two more preliminaries in the exploration and opening up of the new area in physics being built around the revolutionary theories of relativity and quantum mechanics remained to be resolved: First, the nucleus of the atom where most of its mass and, therefore, its energy was concentrated was considered to be formed uniquely of protons or hydrogen nuclei and electrons or electrically charged particles—a claim that must be substantiated or replaced by another verifiable one; second, the existence of a nuclear particle must be proven. The main European centers still concerned with these matters, besides the Curie, the Cavendish, and the Institut für Radiumfurschung in Vienna, now included the Kaiser Wilhelm Institute in the smart Berlin suburb of Dahlem. By the end of the 1920s, there was a peculiar tension in these circles that signified the possibility of new developments. Only a handful of important scientists and a few hundred adventuresome, imaginative researchers were involved, but their combined efforts would lead to the understanding that man could control the processes going on within the nucleus and eventually transform and utilize them—for peace or war.

In 1930, this small world was startled and puzzled by the lack of proton emission and the very strong radiation produced when a pair of German physicists, Walter Bothe and Herbert Becker, bombarded two elements that were light in weight—boron and beryllium—with alpha particles from polonium. The Germans supposed these were a new type of gamma rays more penetrating than any heretofore known.

— o —

Irène never seemed to fully recover her strength after the birth of Hélène. Her first and perpetual reaction to the ill health that was to increasingly plague her was one of annoyance, and she adopted the attitude that if she ignored her aches and pains they would go away. Following her lead, neither the Curie nor Joliot families ever mentioned or discussed how she was feeling publicly. But her problems did not go away. In January of 1930, Irène went to the mountains for a short stay. Again in July, she was sent to Savoie for a cure, and Marie wrote Missy that perhaps Irène ought to stop work for half a year, but she was not yet convinced of the need to do so. With no contemporary medical diagnosis available, the general assumption is that Irène was suffering at this time solely from tuberculosis, which had probably been transmitted to her from her grandmother Sklodowska by Marie, who suffered from lung lesions when she was younger.

By late summer, Irène was home and well enough to go to Brittany with Fred and Hélène—with, of course, the results of accumulated laboratory experiments tucked into a corner of her suitcase for review and study. The three-year-old was so glad to have her mother back that she came in each morning "to dance like a little devil on top of the bed"—and on top of her mother—and was "shamelessly gaining weight with complete disregard for the normal curve," Irène observed scientifically.[13] Sometime this same year, Fred proudly showed the family friend Einstein the "particle tracks" that Hélène, already alert to the conversation around her, had scratched out with a pencil on a sheet of paper. That gentleman warned, in his usual wry manner, "If you don't watch out, she will become a theoretical physicist."[14] And, of course, she did.

No matter how Irène might be feeling, she was always ready to return to the mountains regardless of the season, and after the Christmas holidays she and Fred were off with Salomon Rosenblum, Biquard, and several others for two weeks of skiing at Megève. In the spring, the pair attended a physics congress in Zurich where they met Bothe and had a chance to discuss with him his recent extraordinary experiments with alpha rays. That summer and fall Irène, who could not seem to shake a cold that kept hanging on, went off again for a rest, once with Angèle Pompei and once with Marie, before rejoining Fred for Hélène's fourth birthday at L'Arcouest. So much moving about sounds strenuous and hardly restful for Irène, who was again pregnant, but it is hard to tell how much was dictated by therapeutic considerations.

That same summer Marie had her fourth cataract operation. Missy came over, limping more noticeably than ever, took Ève along for a jaunt when she went to London, and then returned to Paris to talk to Marie about a possible third trip to America. Herbert Hoover wanted her to visit Stanford, and she was invited to the California Institute of Technology at Pasadena. The trip never materialized, and this was the last meeting of the two old friends. Missy had just gotten over a bout of peritonitis and was in such poor health that Marie wondered if she would ever see her again. There was nothing to indicate that Marie might be the first to go. She rarely published any reports nowadays, but she still continued to lecture at 3 P.M., Mondays and Wednesdays. The reluctant, gradual handing over of the reins at the Curie Laboratory was in process, a difficult transition that was eased somewhat by the knowledge that direction would eventually remain in the family.

XVII
1930–1934

Artificial Radioactivity

BY THE END OF 1931, Fred and Irène had almost quadrupled the amount of polonium available in the Curie Laboratory and purified it until it was almost ten times more intense. This provided them with the largest and most powerful source ever prepared to date of pure polonium, one that was capable of emitting some two million matter-penetrating alpha rays a second, and consisted of two hundred millicurie of pure, powdered polonium on little plates no bigger than twenty millimeters square—scarcely enough to cover the bottom of a laboratory vial. To amass this was a considerable technical achievement that also provided them with invaluable practical experience in complex radiochemistry. Irène worked straight through her second pregnancy, and finally, they were ready to attempt to verify by a series of precise measurements Bothe and Becker's mysterious phenomenon that had intrigued them ever since its discovery well over a year before.

The Germans' experiment was a common type at that stage of nuclear physics. One radioactive substance was placed next to a nonradioactive one and, then, whatever flew out was investigated in an effort to deduce what happened as individual particles from the radioactive substance bombarded the nonradioactive one. More times than not, this was easier said than done. The Bothe and Becker radiation could be studied either by measurement of its intensity or by photographs. Fred and Irène would use both techniques, but they started with the former. The purchase of a Hoffman electrometer, a new model in France and about which Fred knew nothing, was a big event for the Curie Pavilion, where money was not that easy to come by. It took Fred more than a month to install the sensitive instrument. At the outset, the thread holding a mobile needle broke. A new suspension unit was required, but since it would take many weeks to deliver, Fred got a Wollaston platinum thread about three thousandths of a millimeter in diameter and six centimeters long and repaired the damage himself. At his first try, he succeeded in soldering the mobile needle at one end of the Wollaston and the suspension cord at the other. This was no mean feat, as his new assistant Pavel Savel discovered when he attempted the same thing, sometime later, and had to give up after several unsuccessful efforts. Fred also excelled at glasswork, and the two clusters of cadmium mercury batteries which he constructed unassisted aroused the admiration of the laboratory's overworked glassblower, who was too busy to help him.

When the Hoffman was in working order, Fred connected it to his ionization chamber to measure the radiation's intensity by the number of impulses recorded per minute or fraction thereof. Bombarding a plate of beryllium with one of their very strong polonium preparations, Fred and Irène were astounded to find they got a much more intense, secondary radiation from the beryllium—three times that of the bombarding alpha particles—than the one originally reported by the Germans with their inferior, early-model Geiger-Müller counter. Since the mysterious, penetrating radiation that was registering such a high value in the Hoffman did not show up—as electrically charged rays would have done—when they changed procedures a few days later and switched to the Wilson chamber in an endeavor to see, photograph, and identify it, they concurred with the Germans that the rays must be some form of gammas that leave no tracks.

Next, the couple decided to test Bothe and Becker's claim that their mysterious radiation did not produce protons. Here Fred's fertile imagination and instinctive sense of what kind of experiment to try stood him in good stead. The simplicity of what he proposed adds up to genius. Although the Germans' radiation was capable of penetrating ten centimeters of lead, he closed off the opening it had to go through to enter the ionization chamber with a sliver of aluminum that was so thin, only five thousandths of a millimeter thick, that it was very hard to install.

The thinness of the aluminum was the key to the brilliant success of this experiment. Fred used what he had on hand in his laboratory, but had the sliver been a few tenths of a millimeter thicker, he and Irène would have missed what then occurred. Fred began running a series of tests interposing screens of various materials in the path of the radiation between the bombarded beryllium and the aluminum. Only when paraffin wax, often used in physical research, or cellophane, both of which contained hydrogen in chemical combination, were tried did anything happen. When either of those hydrogenous substances were used, something was projected from the beryllium through the wafer-thin aluminium into the ionization chamber. Repeating the experiment in a different form another day, working with paraffin and their Wilson, they were able to observe and photograph proton tracks. By a series of tests, Fred and Irène proved that it was the same protons that were causing the pressure to rise in their previous experiments with the ionization chamber. Apparently the Bothe and Becker rays, after being ejected from the bombarded beryllium, were colliding with the hydrogen nuclei—or protons, as Rutherford had named them —in the paraffin and knocking them out, like boccie balls, to fly through the aluminum into the ionization chamber.

Fred and Irène's report on this newly discovered, fundamental characteristic of the Germans' radiation, "The Emission of Protons of Great Speed by Hydrogenous Substances Under the Influence of Very Penetrating Gamma Rays," was presented by Perrin to the Academy for publication in its *Comptes Rendus,* number 194 of January 18, 1932. Like Bothe and Becker, they thought they were still dealing with gamma rays. They had no satisfactory explanation for how this type of radiation would have enough energy to budge a proton, 1,836 times heavier than an electron and with very little penetrating power, yet which had evidently been pushed out with a lot of force. Perhaps, if events had not been moving so fast in their field, they might have delayed publishing their preliminary results for a few weeks and found the correct theoretical interpretation of what they had discovered. Their haste to rush into print must have brought back a flood of memories for Marie because she, too, had rushed into print years ago when she discovered radium, long before Pierre was ready to publish. Furthermore, like her mother and father, Irène was never very much interested in theory—and neither was Fred.

When he read their report in Copenhagen, Niels Bohr, whose contributions to twentieth-century physics would rank only second to Einstein's, decided that the Joliots' conclusions were inacceptable but the phenomenon itself "prodigiously interesting." Across the Channel, James Chadwick, Rutherford's assistant, had been working off and on throughout the 1920s to discover the long-sought "neutron"—a name Rutherford used to denote a hypothetical neutral particle of a mass approximately equal to a proton, whose presence he first postulated in his "Bakerian Lecture" of 1920. During those years, Lise Meitner generously sent Chadwick some polonium from the Kaiser Wilhelm Institute for his study, but it was not sufficient to permit him to experiment along the lines of Bothe and Becker. Since then, through Norman Feather, a Cavendish alumnus who was spending a year in Baltimore and knew the English physician in charge of the radium supply there, Chadwick had gotten several hundred used radon ampoules.

By 1932, he had separated out and purified almost as much polonium as Fred and Irène had at their disposal. He was ready to begin working with it when he received the latest publication of the French Academy in early February. He felt that it was impossible to assume, as they did, that any particle that was as heavy as a proton could be so easily moved. He discussed this report with Rutherford who burst out impatiently, "I don't believe it,"[1] and asked Chadwick to look into the matter at once.

Starting with an open mind—but with the idea of the neutron haunting the Cavendish air ever since its postulation—Chadwick immediately went to work, convinced that Fred and Irène had discovered something "quite new as well as strange."[2] He had at his disposal an electric linear amplifier that was the only one of its kind in the world at the moment. Connecting an ionization chamber with this new tool, which registered its results on a moving strip of photographic paper and was a definite improvement on the counting devices employed by both the Germans and the French, Chadwick was able to distinguish between nuclear particles and electrons. He confirmed Fred and Irène's observation that protons were emitted from the paraffin. Then he went one step further. He removed the paraffin and bombarded other elements, each time getting protons. Furthermore, the protons' energy was much greater than was possible if the beryllium radiation consisted of gamma rays. Working around the clock and averaging only three hours of sleep nightly over a ten-day period, Chadwick evoked the basic physical law that for every reaction a balance sheet of masses and energies had to be drawn up. No more energy or momentum can come out than goes in. Nothing could explain the Bothe and Becker radiation's high penetrability, lack of magnetic deviation, and inability to demonstrate its presence in a cloud chamber except a neutron. Chadwick had discovered the third elementary sub-atomic particle. The other two were the proton—the hydrogen nucleus—and the electron—the electrically charged particle.

The neutron's name is now so familiar to us and its role so important that it is difficult today to appreciate the collective skills, observation, imagination, and deduction required to establish its existence. In few other instances can the history of a major discovery be so clearly followed, or better illustrate the internationalism of scientific research than this one, which resulted from a series of three experiments, each building on the results of the previous one. Bothe and Becker discovered that certain lightweight elements emitted a very penetrating radiation when bombarded by alpha particles; next, Fred and Irène showed that this secondary radiation could cause hydrogenous materials to emit high-velocity protons; and, finally, Chadwick's momentous results, which appeared only seven weeks after Fred and Irène's original note and in which he gave full credit to Fred and Irène's preceding work.

Since the neutron had approximately the same mass as the proton, it could in any head-on collision communicate all its speed to a proton, whereas in an encounter with a heavier nucleus, only part of its speed would be transferred. Its size, together with the fact that it carried no electrical charge, made the neutron a tool *par excellence* for a detailed examination of the atom's nucleus because it was hardly affected by the nucleus's shell of electrons or by its electrical barrier. Moreover, with a little radon, available on loan from any large hospital, and some beryllium, scientists could get abundant neutrons to make such probes.

By this time, largely through the efforts of Rutherford and Niels

Bohr, the structure of the atom was considered to consist of two parts—a minute nucleus, in which was concentrated the bulk of the atom's mass, and around this, but at an enormous distance, electrons. Fred, who had a penchant for dramatizing the incredible smallness of the world of the atom, liked to point out that if the atom were to be magnified to the size of the Place de la Concorde, the atomic nucleus would be no larger than an orange seed in the center. While the Rutherford and Bohr model of the atom, when understood on the basis of the new quantum theory of the mid-1920s, satisfactorily accounted for most extra-nuclear phenomena, that model failed to account for nuclear phenomena. The discovery of the neutron would go a long way toward achieving that understanding and explain the differences between the nuclear structure of uranium, the heaviest element, and other lighter ones, as well as their isotopes.

Fred and Irène's chagrin when they read Chadwick's letter announcing his results in the February 27 issue of *Nature* can be imagined. It was all too obvious in retrospect. They had come so close. But they had never read Rutherford's "Bakerian Lecture," because there was never time to read everything and they had learned from experience that most similar lectures were invariably a rehash of previously reported work; they were not aware that iconoclast Rutherford's talks, like everything else where that remarkable man was concerned, did not conform to any accepted pattern. Consequently, they were not mentally prepared for the possible existence of a neutron, nor were they looking for it, and they handed a decisive clue to Chadwick, in whose subconscious Rutherford's postulation lay fallow. And the fame of the discovery was his. Years later, when the pangs of disappointment had been erased by their own subsequent revelations, Fred was able to philosophize about this and point out that it was natural, and just, that the discovery of the neutron should be made in the Cavendish, as it was natural, and just, for the discovery of artificial radioactivity to be made at the Radium Institute. "Old laboratories with long traditions have hidden treasures. Ideas expressed in days gone by, by our teachers living or dead, taken up a score of times and then forgotten, consciously or unconsciously, penetrate the thought of those who work in these old laboratories and, from time to time they bear fruit."[3]

As with the birth of Hélène, Irène was at her bench at the laboratory until only a few hours before the birth of her second child, who was born on March 12, 1932, and named Pierre, after her father. Fred explained to his friend Skobeltzyn, who had returned to Moscow when his Carnegie fellowship at the laboratory expired: "We have been working very hard . . . We had to speed up the pace of our experiments for it is annoying to be overtaken by other laboratories which immediately take up one's experiments . . . as was done in Cambridge."[4] Consequently, Irène, who had contracted a painful case of pleurisy and resembled a wraith, was back at the Institute sooner than she should have been. She would not find it easy to mix motherhood and science; while science was her life, she adored her children too.

With two small ones at home, Fred badly needed more income, even though Irène had just been promoted to *chef des travaux* at the Institute with a slight increase in salary. Providentially, another L'Arcouestien, who was also a neighbor in the rue Froidevaux apartment building, the astrophysicist Charles Maurain, came to his aid, unsolicited; as dean of the Faculty of Sciences at the University of Paris, he nominated Fred for one of the junior academic posts of assistant. Meanwhile, Perrin, who was anxious to assure that his many years of endeavor not only to help the lot of researchers like Fred, but also to improve the overall conditions of French science, should never again be stymied by politicians or bureaucrats succeeded in having a Superior Council of Research established. Its purpose was to control funds and wrest the traditional domination of science from the old guard. As the depression in France deepened, the country's move to the left in the 1932 elections brought Herriot to power and reinforced Perrin's efforts.

Since Irène's goal, like that of Marie and Pierre's generation, was scientific progress to benefit all humanity, it was relatively immaterial who made what discoveries where, whether in France or abroad. Some experiments she did for herself alone, and she did not necessarily like those which afforded her the most renown. While she may have been motivated, to a degree, by the favorable fallout for the Curie Laboratory resulting from any successful work, her basic approach was a philosophical one, as she explained in a radio talk:

> *If an explorer tries to satisfy a taste for adventure in Research, it would seem that the tranquil life of the laboratory has little to offer . . . Yet we may find ourselves in the presence of singular facts . . . A task once begun develops in an unexpected fashion, opening new paths for future work. And thus we satisfy our spirit of adventure. Another attraction of scientific life is the almost childish joy one feels while watching natural phenomena, even well-known ones.* [5]

So the couple's present frenzy of activity and grim determination not to be bested again seems to have stemmed mainly from Fred's ambitiousness to make a mark for himself—and Irène's willingness to help him. For anyone as insecure as Fred, to have been so close to a major discovery and miss out on it must have been devastating. Fred and Irène might not be aware of the prevalent gossip, especially at the Cavendish, that they might be included in the Nobel prize Chadwick was sure to receive. But scientists from abroad, who had not found anything of interest in the French Academy's *Comptes Rendus* since Marie's day, once more subscribed and browsed through them to see what Marie's brilliant daughter and son-in-law might be up to next.

Fred and Irène raced to keep up with the increasing number of physicists who had lost interest in studying the electron husk of atoms, once the theory of quantum mechanics was complete, and who were presently crowding into their field. For nuclear physics now had, in the neutron, a powerful projectile to break the atom's nucleus. Nuclear research was, as Chadwick put it, "simply a kind of sport. It was contending with nature"[6]; like solving a puzzle in which difficulties of interpretation were accumulating faster than they were being resolved by the accumulating new knowledge. Perhaps this is one reason why no Nobels were awarded in physics in 1931 or 1934. The next seven years, until the outbreak of World War II, would see the great breakthroughs in nuclear physics, inaugurated by the Cavendish group, that were to transform it from a pure laboratory science into the atomic age of nuclear-power engineering and nuclear weapons. 1932 was to be the nuclear physicists' *annus mirabilis.* Five major discoveries occurred, and Fred and Irène played a varying role in each one.

Experiment followed experiment in rapid succession, and each was published jointly—seven notes in the *Comptes Rendus* alone, between December 1931 and June 1932—as Fred and Irène undertook an exhaustive study of the secondary radiation induced in light-weight elements by a radioactive source. In mid-April, the second great discovery of 1932 also took place at the Cavendish, when John D. Cockroft and E.T.S. Walton produced the first artificial disintegration and transmutation of an element. Marie was present when Fred and Irène gave a report to the venerable French Physics Society on the Englishmen's disintegration of lithium, which also had the consequence of verifying Einstein's famous formula, $E = mc^2$. The pair gave an outstanding demonstration of their own experimental techniques and acute powers of observation, and their enthusiasm recalled for Marie the days when she and Pierre were purifying radium. "Doesn't this remind you of *la belle époque* of our old laboratory!"[7] she whispered delightedly, her usually impassive face betraying the mixed emotions of a widow, a mother, and a physicist.

Reliving, no doubt, the thrill of those first early discoveries, she was silent as Laborde, a former rue Lhomond colleague, walked her home that early spring night. Marie was not well. She had slipped while walking through one of the halls in the Curie Pavilion and fell, breaking her right wrist. It was only a simple fracture that should have responded quickly, but it apparently triggered a host of other ailments. Dizzy, weak, and slightly feverish, she was confined to bed for days on end; the maddening drumming in her ears returned, the radium-induced sores on her fingers were suppurating, and she had a recurrence of her old gallbladder problems. Overnight, she turned into an old woman. Once again she thought of dying, but this time, she was no longer crying wolf when she wrote Missy to make certain that there were no legal loopholes in the agreement regarding the disposition of the gram of radium given her by the women of America; it must remain in the Curie Pavilion after her death. Missy reassured her that there were none. But, for once, the tiny American did not obey instructions when Marie requested that all her letters be destroyed: "They are part of me and you know how reserved I am in my feelings."[8]

Although Marie was tired all the time now, she continued working on a new textbook on radioactivity. At 8:45 every morning, her little closed Ford stopped on the Quai in front, the driver gave three honks, Marie flung on her hat and coat, and was off to the laboratory. As Poland's national heroine, she also went to Warsaw for the gala inauguration of the Marie Sklodowska-Curie Radium Institute, whose cornerstone she had laid several years before and whose patients were already receiving curietherapy with the radium Marie had procured from America.

The end of April, Fred and Irène were off for a fortnight of intense work on cosmic radiation in the Bernese Alps, even though, for any couple who enjoyed the mountains as much as they, this was as much a vacation as anything else. To provide further information on the nucleus, theoretical physicists discovered one promising lead in the mysterious radiation which originated in outer space and subsequently hit the earth. Their base was a well-equipped scientific station located on a plateau thirty-five hundred meters high in the Jungfrauloch. Here they ran a series of experiments on the effects of cosmic rays on the nucleus of the atom and on whether the clouds that came and went absorbed the rays; they skied the glaciers when the weather, and Irène's health, permitted.

Unfortunately, Irène did not recover the way she hoped after Pierre's birth, although she had taken her X rays to M. Palazzoli and he seemed pleased with them. The end of July found her back in the mountains, this time near Chamonix, for a three-week rest. When her mother returned, exhausted, from her Warsaw trip, she joined her for a while, and so did faithful Angèle Pompei. Fred managed as best he could alone in Paris, keeping an eye on his small family, the household, and the laboratory—a triple role which he would be forced to assume more and more with the passage of time. He was having trouble running some experiments at the laboratory because the electrometer kept sticking, and he gently chided Irène, "That's due to the blasted vaseline that you used. That really is a most impressive gaffe, *ma chère.*"[9]

The end of August, when the entire family was reunited at L'Arcouest before Marie went south to Cavalaire, Fred and Irène learned they had lost out once more. The American Carl Anderson, at the California Institute of Technology, found what they were looking for at the Jungfrauloch when he identified the tracks of a new subatomic particle, a positron, which appeared briefly as a result of the collision of secondary cosmic rays. His discovery of an electron with a positive instead of a negative charge was quickly confirmed by Patrick M.S. Blackett and G. Occhialini in England and was the first concrete indication that the universe consisted of antimatter as well as matter. As soon as they returned to the laboratory, Irène and Fred rushed to get out their file of cloud chamber photos. Thumbing through them, they quickly found several plates of an odd phenomenon that they had observed earlier, taken a few notes on, then filed away because they had misconstrued the evidence. These pictures showed the trajectories of one or two energetic electrons in a magnetic field that seemed to be "going backwards the wrong way" and were curved in the opposite direction to that of other electrons from the same source. Examining them now, Fred and Irène realized they were identical to the tracks that Anderson later found and correctly identified as coming from a positron. Once again Fred and Irène had been the first to uncover the evidence of a major discovery, but because they had not recognized it for what it was, they failed to pursue their lead.

———— o ————

From 1932 on, Langevin associated his fight against war with the struggle against fascism. He replied immediately to an appeal from his compatriot, the well-known French writer Romain Rolland, to serve along with Theodore Dreiser, John Dos Passos, Mme. Sun Yat Sen, Einstein, and others on a Committee of Initiative for a World Congress Against the Imperialists' War to be held in Amsterdam that August. In rapid succession he served in a similar capacity with any number of like-minded groups and organizations that were springing up like dandelions in the fertile European soil of the day. Langevin stopped off again in Moscow, en route west from China, and returned home once more filled with admiration for Russian scientists' fine working conditions. With the help of Fred, Jacques Solomon, a brilliant young physicist and his future son-in-law, and others of their age group, Langevin realized a long-standing dream when he established a Workers' University, which held classes a certain number of evenings each week in the annex of the Trade Unions Hall at no. 8 Avenue Mathurin-Moreau. Irène frequently accompanied Fred when it was his night to teach; the orientation of most of the classes there was Marxist. Again, it is hard not to attribute to Fred's influence as a liberal activist the public stand both Irène and Marie had each taken, separately, a few months before, following a heated senate discussion about the continued denial of suffrage for women.

On January 30, 1933, Hitler came to power as Chancellor of Germany. With the subsequent burning and partial destruction of the Reichstag on February 27, which the Nazis blamed on the

Communists, reprisals on them and on the Jews commenced. The opening gun was a national boycott of Jewish businesses, a harbinger of the exodus to follow. Langevin invited Einstein to accept a chair at the Collège de France, but the Institute for Advanced Study in Princeton won out, and he did what he could to help other fleeing Central European scientists to locate in Paris. Langevin continued to sing the praises of the Soviet Republic, with its rise of Marxist socialism, as the one hope in an impossible world. He urged Fred to accept when he, together with other French and British scientists, was invited by the Russian Academy of Science to attend ten days of conferences and lectures in Leningrad and Moscow in the early fall. Irène, who for the second summer in a row spent three weeks in the Haute-Savoie in the Chamonix valley for her health, did not accompany him.

Disappointed by their failure to yet achieve a great discovery that would be uniquely theirs, Irène and Fred were fascinated by the positron, the positively charged electron which Anderson discovered. What produced it? What happened to it when it disappeared? Once more the lights burned late in their small laboratory as they set out to look for these answers. Starting once more with an intense source of polonium and different experimental arrangements, they placed the Wilson cloud chamber in a strong magnetic field, which caused the electrons traversing it to bend, so Irène and Fred could distinguish whether they were positively or negatively charged and measure their energy. As the pair bent over their apparatus, watching intently, the sound of the falling piston provoking the release of gas every four minutes was the only sound. When they bombarded elements in the middle range of the Mendeleev Periodic Table with alpha particles, protons came flying out. When they used the light elements, aluminum and boron, sometimes a neutron and then a positron were ejected, instead of a proton. So it was possible to obtain three kinds of particles—protons, neutrons, positrons. Did this mean that there could be a compound proton, a neutron in association with a positron?

In October they were flattered by an invitation to give a report on their latest work at the week-long Solvay Conference in Brussels, over which Paul Langevin was now presiding and which was devoted, this year, to the structure and properties of atomic nuclei. Nuclear physicists still constituted a relatively small group and, although all the key world figures were present, with the exception of the greatest of them all, Einstein, their meetings at the Université Libre could be easily accommodated in a physics laboratory converted into a lecture room for the occasion. The forty participants, roughly half experimentalists and half theorists, included six Nobel laureates and fourteen soon to be crowned and represented fourteen countries and two generations. Some, like Marie, Langevin, and Perrin, had attended the first Solvay twenty-two years before. W. Bothe, the co-discoverer of the Bothe and Becker radiation, was there, and so was Ernest Lawrence, the American from Berkeley. The previous year, he had invented the cyclotron, a small machine which accelerated particles to a high velocity capable of producing million-volt protons by whirling them around a magnetic field and giving them electric "kicks" as they circled, thereby making them available to probe atomic nuclei.

Even critical Ève would have considered her sister chic in her jumper and striped, short-sleeved blouse that October 21 in comparison with the only two other women present—Marie, in her usual somber gown, and the fifty-five-year-old Austrian physicist Lise Meitner, her thick gray hair pulled severely back and coiled in a bun, her slight figure immersed in nondescript attire. Fred, whose clean-shaven face was almost the only one in the room and made him appear even younger, gave their joint report. He would always do so, at Irène's request. Public speaking was not the ordeal for him that it was for her, but today marked their debut in these exalted spheres and he, for once, was noticeably nervous. Their findings about the neutron were their most dramatic achievement to date, and both were very excited about the possibility of a proton compounded of a neutron and positron, which their experiments seemed to indicate.

Instead of their paper being received with praise, a stormy controversy ensued. Blackett had a different interpretation of their results and remained unconvinced even after Irène took the floor and tried to prove him wrong. Then Langevin recognized Lise Meitner. Fräulein Meitner, whom Einstein would call "the German Marie Curie," was the second woman to have ever gotten her Ph.D. at the University of Vienna and the first to become a professor in the University of Berlin. The head of the physics department at the magnificently equipped Kaiser Wilhelm Institute, she was famous over the years for her work as a team with its director, the renowned Otto Hahn; a formidable researcher, she was highly esteemed for hard, careful work and always listened to with respect. Blunt and tight-lipped, she did not mince words. "My colleagues and I have done similar experiments. We have been unable to uncover a *single* neutron."[10] Then she sat down. Everyone turned, as one, to look at Marie and her children, and bedlam broke out in that sedate gathering as they all started arguing at once. Marie, who had listened to Fred's report so proudly, bristled but did not say a word. Fred and Irène gazed at each other stupefied. To be at their first international conference and have the renowned Lise Meitner, who was famous for the careful precision of her work, disagree with them so emphatically was a catastrophe. And in front of Chadwick, too, who had vaulted over their shoulders to the neutron's discovery.

The session was soon over. Marie stayed behind to talk to several people, and Fred and Irène wandered into the Université's gardens outside, devastated. Their discomfiture might have been slightly relieved had they foreseen that Lawrence would be equally depressed, on the morrow, at the reception greeting his report on a deuterium experiment. It was one thing for Fred and Irène's basic premise to be questioned, and something else again to have the accuracy of their work doubted. They themselves knew that they had made no mistake, for they rechecked their results carefully. That was all that Irène really cared about, but the grim set of Fred's face was commented on and indicates that he was far more affected than she. Delegates who stood around admiring the flowers and talking in little groups avoided the pair because they did not know what to say. It was evident from the way they averted their eyes that most were confident that Lise Meitner was correct and the Joliots had been inaccurate. The young French couple were probably working too fast, which was understandable, considering that they had barely missed out on the neutron and had misidentified the positron tracks which they were the first to observe. Now they were in a hurry to discover something else and did not want anybody to beat them to it.

As a theorist, Niels Bohr immediately realized that if Irène and Fred were correct, the nucleus was more complex than had been envisioned, and theories about it would need modification. A physically imposing man, with an enormous domed head, a long heavy jaw, big hands, and a good athlete in his youth, Bohr was one of the few to approach Fred and Irène that late afternoon. "What you are doing is of the greatest importance," he comforted them in such a low voice they had to strain to hear him. Another theorist, the Austrian Wolfgang Pauli, also strode over with welcome words of encouragement. "Congratulations. Don't give up."[11]

The next day, tall birdlike Chadwick, who hid his unfailing kindness behind an austere facade, was delighted to find his place at lunch was next to Marie. As he sat down, she said the minimum formal words of greeting, turned away, and completely ignored him for the rest of the meal. The snubbed Englishman consoled himself with the observation that the frail, ailing woman seemed to lack sufficient energy to eat her meal, let alone indulge in any conversation. Others present were surprised to realize that even a national monument had feelings where her immediate family was concerned. Fred and Irène remained subdued on the train back to Paris with Marie, Perrin, and Langevin, who emphasized how important it was that the theorists were interested in their controversial report.

If Fred and Irène thought about it, in retrospect, their Solvay debacle produced some good. Because their experiment was so scathingly denounced, no one present took the trouble to investigate their claims for themselves, leaving Fred and Irène without any momentary competition. This was a lucky thing, because the minute news of their discovery of artificial radioactivity reached Berkeley, some months later, Lawrence rushed to his cyclotron; he made a few minor adjustments to the mechanism, and within a half-hour, he and his staff observed the first artificial radioactivity ever produced in America. They hadn't discovered it for themselves almost a year earlier when they first started using the cyclotron because the Geiger counter switched off automatically at the same time as the machine itself; therefore, it could not record the lingering radioactivity.

Still smarting from their humiliating experience, but stimulated to continue by Bohr and Pauli's encouragement, Fred and Irène immediately re-verified their controversial finding that neutrons had been emitted. (Either in December or January, Lise Meitner made the same discovery, and so wrote Fred and Irène.) Their next step was to decide upon, and set up, an exhaustive series of experiments to determine whether the proton was compound, as they had tentatively concluded at the Solvay. By mid-November and early December, their program was in full swing. Fred considered it possible that if they were creating a neutron and positron simultaneously, rather than protons, the process might depend on the amount of energy of the alpha particles bombarding the aluminum. This was a crucial question which they decided to resolve by gradually removing the tiny plate of their polonium source farther and farther from the target. They first ran a battery of tests using a Wilson cloud chamber placed in a magnetic field, photographing and studying the thin line of mist from the ionized beads that indicated radioactive emissions. Then they switched to a different set of experiments and, to determine the intensity of the rays, used the latest-model Geiger counter, which Wolfgang Gentner brought with him from Germany when he came to the Curie Laboratory to work for a few years.

On Thursday afternoon, January 11, 1934, Fred was alone in the basement room where the Wilsons were kept. He bombarded his aluminum target and then slowly withdrew the polonium with its alpha rays. Employing a technique with the Geiger that was new to the Institute and which Gentner, whose laboratory work he was directing, had taught him, Fred noted that neutrons were no longer ejected, but positrons continued to appear. The chatter of the counter indicated that their emission did not die down at once when the source was removed. "Click-click-click," the Geiger went on counting for a few more minutes. Fred was puzzled. Something else was also happening. Not trusting his ears, he repeated the experiment. "Click-click-click," the counter continued as before. Once more it did not die abruptly, but gradually. What Fred had heard the first time and subconsciously recognized, even though he was not expecting it, he heard a second time. Laboratory tradition at the Curie and daily work there had so preconditioned him that every time he heard counters click, it was second nature to use the distinctive, diminishing half-life activity, which was the identifying trademark of radioactive atoms, as a yardstick to measure any new phenomenon. And this was what Fred was hearing now—the sound of the exponential decay of a radioactive element. Barely able to contain his excitement, he rushed up the stairs, two at a time, to fetch Irène. Contrary to the claim of the Joliot children—mythmaking, like their aunt Ève did about Marie in her biography, probably because they did not want their mother robbed of any of the glory of the discovery—Irène was not in the laboratory with Fred at the time but upstairs, working on a related chemical problem.

Fred re-ran the experiment without a word of explanation. He did not need one. Like Fred, Irène immediately recognized the characteristic sound. Together, they reviewed what had occurred.

Probably the counter was malfunctioning. Under the best of conditions, the Geiger was a temperamental, delicate instrument with a mind of its own. A novelty that could not yet be bought commercially, Fred's version, like so many other tools he used, had been made with tender loving care; its amplifier included parts of an old radio set that he constructed many years before. Unfortunately, Irène and Fred had a dinner engagement they could not break— nobody has ever found out where. Before leaving, Fred called his friend Gentner down to the basement and, without telling him why, asked him to check out the instrument before he left for the night and make sure it was functioning correctly.

Irène and Fred must have been too preoccupied that night to make good dinner companions, and undoubtedly, when they got home they stayed up late talking. If they had really stumbled on an entirely new reaction capable of making radioactive material by artificial means, it would have great impact on the study of chemical and biological processes. Until now, physicists agreed that when a particle of sufficient energy bombarded a nucleus, the nucleus could be disintegrated and a different, but stable, nucleus produced, as proven by Rutherford, in 1913, when he transmuted nitrogen. Fred and Irène's phenomenon indicated that, in certain instances, bombardment resulted in the production of an unstable element—a radioactive isotope which, in turn, transmuted into other elements. In light of their recent sorry experiences, if Irène and Fred did not want to lose out a third time they must carefully stake out their observations and have a report ready for the Academy's regular Monday meeting, three days later—provided Gentner gave the Geiger a clean bill of health.

He did. All Friday, the twelfth, and Saturday, the thirteenth, the couple remained at their benches; Irène upstairs, and Fred downstairs. Around 7 P.M. on Saturday, Fred heard footsteps in the corridor. It was Ldislaw Goldstein with his hat and coat on, coming through the underground passage from the annex to avoid a sudden downpour. When he saw Fred, he stopped to say good night.

Fred had arrived at a point where he wanted a third party to repeat the experiment and see if there were any flaws. Without disclosing any details, Fred asked Goldstein to run a check for him, while he took a needed break for a smoke. Goldstein confirmed the results.

After he had done so and, certainly, before they gave their report to Perrin, Fred called Biquard and Langevin to hurry over and come down to the basement cloud chambers room. Biquard arrived first, quickly followed by Irène with Langevin and Marie. Biquard never forgot the disorder or the electric excitement in the room. Fred briefed them and, as was his want, gave credit where it was due. Then he and Irène presented their new experiment. Few words were spoken, except for a couple of questions and answers. It was all over within a half-hour. Fred would frequently reminisce about that day and speak "of his emotion, pride and joy at having been able to offer before these two scientists, to whom he was bound by so many ties, a fresh example of the vital character and ever-widening horizons of science."[12] What a pleasure for Marie, at this stage of her life, to have concrete proof that the work she and Pierre had started would be capably carried on.

Fred and Irène's hurriedly written, historic report "A New Type of Radioactivity" was presented to the Academy on schedule, on the fifteenth, an incredible four days after their initial observation, and appeared in *Nature* on January 19. Rutherford wrote at once, congratulating them and confessing that he had tried a number of similar experiments himself, "but without any success."[13] Coming from that past master, this was true praise. Just as Fred and Irène chided themselves for missing the discovery of the neutron, so Chadwick always regarded it as inexcusable that he missed the discovery of artificial radiation.

Today, it is difficult to realize the magnitude of even the technical aspects of their achievement, given the crude state of some of the equipment they worked with. In 1984, when the fiftieth anniversary of their discovery was celebrated with a special program in the Sorbonne amphitheater, the nuclear physicist Pierre Radvanyi, a former pupil of Fred's, who was then deputy director of Saturne, the French National Laboratory at Saclay, was chosen to repeat Fred and Irène's historic experiment. He had a hard time duplicating their exploit, even though he utilized the most expensive, up-to-date instruments; the university authorities were so worried about possible effects on the audience from the intense radiation of the material to be used that they insisted upon elaborate precautions and, then, at the last moment, made him substitute another source for the original polonium. Yet this was the material Fred and Irène handled daily, often using their mouths to suck it up in pipettes, the way Marie taught them to do, so that the precious grains would not scatter and disappear when they had occasion to transfer them from one minute plate to another.

But Irène and Fred's job was not yet finished. The next step was to provide physical and visual proofs of the creation of the new radioelement, which a chemist would want to see in a test tube. Irène and Fred must identify what resulted from their bombardment of aluminum—a new sort of phosphorus that was never found in nature because, with a half-life of three minutes and fifteen seconds, it was too unstable and quickly transmuted to ordinary silicon. Since the amount of silicon accumulated was so small —"representing at the most a few million atoms," Fred explained in their Nobel lecture—it was impossible to trace it chemically. They would have to work with the unstable radiophosphorus, which could only be identified by its radioactivity; so they had only a little more than three minutes in which to isolate it. When they met a fellow chemist on the rue Pierre Curie one day and asked for advice, he threw up his hands in amazement. He never heard of having to operate under similar limitations. Only a master team, working in close collaboration with complementary skills—Fred with his vivid imagination, ingenuity, and dexterity as a radiophysicist; Irène with Marie's obstinacy and patience and her own ability as a radiochemist—could have accomplished what the couple did within the next two weeks. Their preparations carefully

worked out in advance, one morning, Fred bombarded the aluminum, stoppered the irradiated metal in a vial, and Irène took over.
Employing every trick of radiochemistry that Marie taught her, she
had to add a chemically related element to act as a courier for the
minute amount of radioactive atoms being ejected, and thus got a
mixture big enough to see and handle. Because the pair theorized
that the new product must be some form of phosphorus, she added
hydrochloric acid to the foil and re-covered it. The acid dissolved
the aluminum, producing gaseous hydrogen, which should carry
the phosphorus with it. Irène drew it off, leaving the aluminum
salts behind in the original vial. Once dry, these were no longer
radioactive. The second tube was quickly sealed and transported to
a Geiger counter, whose instant "Click-click-click" proved that
whatever was radioactive was in this second tube. A new, different
test proved it to be the radiophosphorus Fred and Irène had predicted. This entire virtuoso feat was accomplished within the time
frame of its half-life—a little more than three minutes—before its
radioactivity decayed away, leaving only ordinary stable silicon.

Fred reacted to her success like a child, running and jumping
around in the vast laboratory basement, which was empty at the
time. "And," he admitted honestly, "I thought of the consequences
which might follow from the discovery."[14] This is an interesting
commentary, but there is no way of knowing if he was speaking
altruistically, scientifically, or from an ambitious, personal point of
view. Or, perhaps, from all three. And, of course, as he wrote
Skobeltzyn, in Moscow, he got enormous satisfaction from the fact
that their initial observations, given in their earlier Solvay report,
had been proven correct.

From Irène's point of view, the agonizing work must have been
worth it the day she and Fred gave Marie a sample of the first
made-to-order artificial radioelement—the way Marie and Pierre
used to present little tubes of their radium preparation to scientists
they admired. To verify its contents, Marie took the tiny vial in her
radium-damaged fingers and held it near a Geiger counter, and

Fred never forgot the intense joy in her face as she heard the instrument's telltale chatter.

January 29, Fred and Irène consolidated their victory with a second paper to the Academy, "Chemical Separation of the New Elements That Emit Positive Electrons," in which they also announced that they had obtained radionitrogen when irradiating boron. The lifework of two generations of the Curie family dovetailed as if it had been ordained. If the discovery of radioactivity played the same role for humanity as that of fire, it was the role of artificial radioactivity to make matter radioactive by man-made means and make this fire accessible to man. The parents discovered natural radioactivity, which was the property of a few elements, and their study of it led to the penetration of the atom's structure; the daughter and son-in-law discovered how man could duplicate this phenomenon, and artificial radioactivity, in turn, opened up a new understanding of the nucleus of the atom. On the practical side, it would soon prove to be as great a boon to doctors as Roentgen rays were to surgeons. Thousands of new radioactive elements not seen in the earth's crust could be created by artificial radioactivity—a term Fred never liked. He considered the radioactivity he and Irène discovered just as natural as that of the Curies.

XVIII
1934–1939

Fission

FRED AND IRÈNE MIGHT be the French spearheads in this attack to lay bare the inner workings of the atom, but they quickly had plenty of competition. Scientists in Copenhagen, Gottingen, Rome, Berlin, Cambridge, and the United States were soon competing in the same race which was to lead to the liberation of atomic energy. At the same time, the shift of leadership in the field of nuclear physics, from the Cavendish's cramped quarters to the bigger resources of the United States with its multitude of laboratories, began. So the young French pair had their hands full if they wanted to retain their advantage.

They continued to come regularly to the quiet Quai de Béthune for lunch and kept Marie as abreast of the world outside the laboratory as she cared to be. There was plenty to talk about.

This was the beginning of turbulent years for France, a period of great political instability and social unrest; a continuing economic crisis which had broken worldwide in 1929 was also beginning to make small ripples there. Unemployment was on the rise, and the Stavisky scandal, which surfaced with the shady financier's purported suicide that January, bespoke corruption in high places at a time when fascist and semifascist leagues openly challenged the republican regime, and the French Communist Party was unusually active. February 6, a new revolutionary right, inspired by the success of fascism in Italy and the Nazis in Germany, stormed across the Place de la Concorde and tried to seize the Palais-Bourbon, but the Parisian workers put up a fierce resistance and after bloody fighting, literally on the Chambre's doorsteps, thwarted the attempted coup. Less than a week later, Langevin and his son, André, walked proudly under banners proclaiming "Unity Against the Fascist Peril" in the enormous manifestation that socialists and Communists jointly organized.

Early in March, Langevin, declaring that the first task at hand was to defeat the fascists in order to maintain conditions whereby science could continue to exist, launched a manifesto with the philosopher Alain and Paul Rivet, another academic, which heralded the birth of what came to be known as the Vigilance Committee of Antifascist Intellectuals. Mme. Joliot's precept: "One must fight against injustice," which had echoed in Fred's ears since childhood, took on new significance and immediacy for Fred. He felt that only a coward could remain on the sidelines. Telling himself that "things like the attempted February coup happen because too many people remain unorganized,"[1] and shocked by the ruthless way the new Nazi regime was dismantling fine research staffs and sending Jewish professors into exile, Fred followed Langevin's lead and was one of many scientists to affiliate with his group. More than one evening, that summer and fall, he could be found in a small room above the general electricity laboratory of EPCI, assisting Biquard turn the handle of an antiquated printing machine into which Langevin inserted sheets of paper. Fred and Biquard then helped plaster them all over Paris. At some point during this year Fred also joined the Socialist Party.

Because they were so busy preparing the creation of new radio-elements, Fred and Irène took their customary winter ski trip in Savoie later than usual. The young Perrins were along, and Marie joined them too. It was evident that she was far from well, and she gave the family a scare when she did not return one evening until long after dark. Unbeknownst to anyone, Marie had set off alone on snowshoes to catch the alpine glow descend on Mont Blanc. When she returned, very pleased with her outing, she could not imagine why anyone had worried about her.

Irène's constitution was yielding to ill health, although she continued to spend as much time as ever at the laboratory. When Fred remonstrated with her, her stock reply was "There's nothing wrong with me." But this was not true. She had never been able to regain any weight since Pierre's birth, and she was always tired. However, Irène was not yet suffering from any effects of overexposure to radiation.

Marie's own intermittent fever and dizziness continued to plague her. She went out to look over some property she'd recently bought between Sceaux and Antony as house sites for herself and Irène and Fred. Then she took seven-year-old Hélène to the adjacent park. Her granddaughter was learning to skate, and Marie was helping her when she fell and broke her arm; she could only hope it would not take as unusually long to heal as the wrist she had broken in another accident in the laboratory the previous autumn. As if that was not enough, Marie was also troubled with a large gallstone. Still haunted by her father's death after an operation for the same ailment, she refused to consider surgery, but fortunately, a strict diet cured the problem.

The family's efforts to get Marie to slow down and take better care of herself were an exercise in futility. She ignored the minimal precautions now in force at the laboratory and rarely took the periodic blood tests presently required of everyone working there, although she knew that her blood count was abnormal.

Because research on the actinium family was not progressing fast enough to suit her, Marie, personally, lent a hand. The last laboratory work Marie ever did, separating pure actinium X, was a tedious, slow job. She worked at her bench straight through the dinner hour and was still there at 2 A.M. One final operation remained, and Marie stayed seated for another hour alongside the noisy, clanking centrifuge that was whirling around the liquid. Nothing else in the world existed for her as she sat there, willing the experiment to be finished; when she did not get the hoped-for result, she slumped in her chair, her arms crossed, her gaze empty, and lugubriously admitted failure.

Marie did not trudge around the Curie Laboratory as much as formerly. But Irène could always tell the days she managed to make it down to the basement room where the Wilson cloud chambers were kept because Fred invariably came home with a big cigarette burn in his shirt pocket. Fred—and Irène—might, indeed, win the Nobel that year, as Marie proudly prophesized, but no matter how distinguished Fred already was, or might be, Marie's rules forbade smoking on the premises. So whenever Fred and Gentner, who usually worked there together, heard her familiar footsteps, they thrust their cigarettes out of sight in the first place available. Where her laboratory was concerned, Marie still intended to have the final say. And, when the staff complained that the elevator ran much too slowly and a new one was needed, Marie personally conducted a series of tests with a chronometer to prove that the existent service was more than adequate.

For all her empty talk in the past about not having much longer to live, this time Marie was suiting her actions to her words and putting her affairs in order. She expurgated forty-seven dossiers of archives, removing anything and everything which might possibly change the image of herself she wished to present to posterity. The only things of a personal nature that she kept were Pierre's forty-year-old love letters and, surprisingly, those of a rejected, early suitor, a mysterious M. Lamotte. Like someone with a premonition that the end was near, Marie also told Irène where her will was located.

When Bronya arrived to spend Easter, the pair meandered south in Marie's little Ford, with numerous detours along the way to show Bronya this and that, and planned a visit in Montpellier to see Jacques Curie. When they finally reached Cavalaire, the tiny bougainvillea-covered villa was damp and chilly. And Marie, who had a cold and was looking forward to the customary warmth of the Midi, collapsed with a chill. So Bronya brought her back to Paris.

Because Marie was having as many bad days as good ones, Ève succeeded in convincing her that she must see a doctor, something she only did in moments of dire necessity. Marie did not have a regular doctor because no one ever presented a bill, and she felt this placed her in a false position. Professor Regaud, the head of the adjacent Pasteur Pavilion, stopped by to see her, but he could not decide what was wrong. One day, in mid-May, Marie felt well enough to return to the laboratory. But she did not last very long and soon sent for her driver. Walking through the tiny garden en route to the car, she noticed that one of the rose bushes she had planted was not doing well. Calling out to the gardener to attend to it at once, she was driven off, never to return.

Marie did not want anyone to know she was ill because she did not want anything in the papers. On June 6, she went into a clinic for tests. They, too, were unable to diagnose her case, and she returned to the Quai apartment. These were agonizing days for frail Irène, whose own health left much to be desired, as she watched her mother's slow decline.

When Marie showed no improvement, Ève insisted on a consultation by four of the most eminent doctors in the capital. Stumped for an answer, the distinguished quartet hazarded the guess that her old tubercular lesions were acting up and recommended an immediate departure for a sanatorium to conquer her lingering fever. Despite a sudden turn for the worse, Marie departed on June 29, under the assumed name of "Madame Pierre," with Ève and a nurse. The trip to Sancellemoz, near Annecy in the Haute-Savoie, was a nightmare. Marie collapsed at St.-Gervais in Ève's arms and had to be rushed the rest of the way. The X rays taken there, the day after her arrival, unlike those taken previously in Paris, showed her lungs to be clear. So the trip was in vain.

When Marie's temperature rose again, she knew it before the director of the sanatorium. For Marie, like many scientists, insisted on observing her own vital signs as long as she could. But soon the only figures she could read were those on the thermometer. She was even too weak to speak and unable to enjoy the splendid vista of Mont Blanc from her private veranda. Ève insisted on calling in the renowned specialist Professor Roch of Geneva. He was the first to recognize extreme pernicious anemia and held out no hope. Marie remained lucid and did not realize death was near. Rather than alarm her, Ève postponed sending for Irène and struggled to keep the truth from her mother. She wrote Missy that Marie was suffering so much that she "could not bear to look at her and had to go out of the room to cry out of her sight."[2]

On July 2, Fred and Irène arrived, and on July 3, the thermometer in Marie's shaking hand indicated that her temperature was falling. She was too far gone to realize that this was the drop which always precedes the end and smiled delightedly. For the next sixteen hours, Ève and a doctor each held one icy hand. Irène, who was losing not only a mother but a companion and a colleague, was too upset to sit alongside.

On July 4, 1934, Marie died at sixty-seven, a victim of years of overexposure to radiation.

Marie remained a staunch agnostic to the end, so there was no priest and no public prayers when she was buried at Sceaux in the presence of relatives, friends, and co-workers. Her coffin was placed above Pierre's, and a handful of Polish soil thrown on top by Bronya and Josef, who came from Warsaw. A group of newspapermen, kept at bay by the cemetery's locked gates, clambered noisily over the walls for a better view. When Fred walked over and asked that they honor Marie's last request for privacy, they refused.

Five days later, Ève sent Missy Marie's watch, which had once belonged to Pierre, with a little note: "It has no value except that she wore it always and liked it. It was on her table near her bed when she died."[3]

———— o ————

That spring, summer, and fall, the Italian physicist Enrico Fermi announced the discovery of a number of new artificial radioelements; some of these were obtained in even smaller amounts than Fred and Irène's minute initial grains of radiophosphorus and radionitrogen, and their appearance was far more fleeting. Working with the rest of his team at the Institute of Physics in Rome, Fermi, directly following up Fred and Irène's work, discovered that a neutron, when slowed down, was better for nuclear bombardment than alpha rays because it had no charge, so there was no strong electrical repulsion to prevent its entry into a nucleus. Once there, it produced as much havoc as if the moon hit the earth. Using the neutron exclusively, the Italians proceeded methodically to irradiate, one at a time, the entire list of elements in the Mendeleev Periodic Table, and to attempt to identify the results. In common with Irène and Fred and others working in the field, they shared the belief that only one nuclear reaction was possible from this bombardment; no one had any reason to suspect otherwise. When the Italians irradiated uranium, the heaviest and most complex of the known elements, a broth of more than twenty different products resulted, but Fermi's attempt to unscramble them raised as many questions as answers.

In 1940, almost five years after Fermi interrupted his research, because his team was ill-equipped to handle so complex a chemical problem, someone else, using his early work, would receive a Nobel for resolving the uranium puzzle. And the world would never be the same.

Meanwhile, work continued uninterrupted in Marie's subdued laboratory, as she would have wished it. Fred became a guide and mentor to the neophyte Bertrand Goldschmidt, who still recalls the first long conversation the two had together, some weeks after his arrival, and the various pieces of advice Fred gave him, concluding with the necessity of being popular with his co-workers. Fred felt his colleagues were no longer as congenial as in the past. His mentor's sense of uneasiness baffled Goldschmidt. "They hate me," Fred insisted, convinced they were jealous of his success.

That fall Debierne took over as Marie's successor and he and Fred did not hit it off as well as might be expected. Since neither Fred nor Irène were yet academically qualified for Debierne's post, jealousy could not have played a role. Debierne's World War I experiences had been devastating for anyone of André's withdrawn temperament, and many intimates claimed he was never the same afterward. One also wonders what tensions may have been a result of unresolved matters from Marie's day. As close as he had always been to the Curie girls, since their childhoods, there were times when Irène so provoked him that his face and neck turned purple with rage. Whatever the problem, an accommodation was evidently worked out between the trio. Debierne was eminently qualified for his new position, and around Christmastime, Irène wrote Missy that André was being very encouraging and their situation was far better than if they were in charge of the large laboratory. Exactly as during Marie's lifetime, there were forty-odd researchers representing fifteen nationalities and including several women. A point would always be made to retain approximately the same mix. In cold weather, Irène could still be found standing in front of the radiator in the vestibule next to the main entry, her acid-stained white laboratory coat and skirt lifted to warm her rear. This area was a convenient spot for conversation and Irène was never adverse to answering technical queries or participating in a quick discussion of some of the day's burning problems with students or researchers.

Shortly after the first of the year, the doctors ordered her to Savoie for a two-month rest. So she was unable to be in the amphitheater, along with the rest of their colleagues, to hear Fred's initial lecture in his new teaching post as professor on the Faculty of Sciences of the University of Paris. He and the children joined her at Easter, and Irène was well enough to spend considerable time on the slopes with Fred and their friend Émile Allais, who was destined to star in the upcoming Winter Olympics at Garmisch-Partenkirschen. Like everything else he did, Fred was determined to ski well and took great pride in the master's praise for his fast-speed "Allais" turns.

Irène was impatient to get back to her bench, where she was in the midst of an interesting series of experiments. She was presently irradiating thorium and had discovered two mysterious radioactive elements with a half-life of about three and a half hours which she and the students who were working with her were the first ever to see and which she was unable to identify satisfactorily. She thought they were probably actinium isotopes and went on to other matters. Little did she guess that the substance in question was lanthanum and when the results of this irradiation were properly decoded they would prove to hold the key to nuclear fission.

A few months later, in June, she was back in the salutory mountain air, this time at Sancellemoz, the sanatorium where her mother had spent her last days. Irène could get better care there than by staying in a pension on her own, as in the past. While she was gone, Fred moved the children into the house that they were building at no. 76 Avenue le Nôtre in Antony on Marie's two lots adjoining the park of Sceaux, and which was now ready for occupancy. Like Marie, Irène enjoyed working in the garden and did not care for the heat and dust of city life. Their new home was unpretentious but luxurious in comparison with the crowded Froidevaux apartment, which they had long since outgrown. There were separate studies for both Fred and Irène, as well as ample ground for a tennis court and lots of room for Irène's flowers. Antony was within easy commuting distance of the Curie Institute and the Sorbonne—only twenty minutes by car—and, within a year, an electric train would be in service. Equally important, there was a good *lycée* for Hélène at Sceaux, recently renamed "Marie Curie."

With the passage of time Irène's longer and more frequently enforced cures produced inevitable strains on their ménage. These separations were hard on the children, Pierre and Hélène, who were only three and eight and who did not see a lot of their mother, even when she was home, and they were even harder on Fred, for she was his research colleague as well as his wife, and a lot of laboratory matters had to be attended to by mail. Of course, to be gone so much must have been equally hard on Irène, who, at thirty-six, was still a young woman. With these long absences the question of other women in Fred's life cannot be ignored. Contemporaries who knew him well agree that he was most attractive to the opposite sex and not averse to taking advantage of the fact. He was "somewhat of a chaser," an intimate confides, but with one rare exception, no specific names are ever mentioned.

During this difficult time, their star was rising on the world scene, and one young woman, meeting them at the opening of the Palais de la Découverte at the time of the Paris Exposition, two years after they won the Nobel prize, speaks of their being treated there as "demigods." For the dapper, elegant Fred, who was endowed with a charm that the Italian physicist Emilio Segrè likened to that of Maurice Chevalier, to be a celebrity of this magnitude and not succumb to any of the many temptations offered was too much to expect of any man, let alone a French husband of this period when the double standard continued to be an accepted way of life. Irène was a wise woman and madly in love with Fred for as long as she lived, and he was enough of a bourgeois to consider his home and marriage inviolate. Aside from the fact that they made a scientific team par excellence, their temperaments complemented each other superbly, and theirs was a marriage made to endure. One of Irène's oldest friends confided, ". . . [he] once remarked to my brother in front of me, shortly after their wedding, that he had not yet been unfaithful to Irène but, if he should be, this would never affect his marriage."[4] Unquestionably, this was Irène's attitude too. Fred was a good father and surrogate mother; he did not shirk his additional household responsibilities when illness kept her away, and as their correspondence bears witness, their lives together were filled with mutual understanding and great warmth. If Irène was ever jealous of him, it has to date been as carefully hidden as the names of his presumed "passing fancies."

By mid-July, when Fred came to visit, after the move to Sceaux was completed and the mortgage papers signed, Irène's temperature was low enough so that she was permitted a fifteen-minute walk daily, before dinner. Weeks later, when Angèle Pompei came to keep her company, she found her busy doing an article for *Le Journal de Physique,* and in early September, Irène was back in Paris. The newly strengthened Caisse Nationale de la Recherche Scientifique, which Perrin was responsible for welding into a powerful organization for pure research with no precedent outside the U.S.S.R., elevated Irène to a position similar to the one Fred had held there since 1933. This post of *maître de recherches* meant more income which was most welcome with the family's additional medical bills and moving expenses. Irène's doctor told her she could resume work in moderation—a word not in her vocabulary—but must not go to the laboratory daily, and she was supposed to rest each afternoon, wherever she might be.

In March and May of 1934, Langevin presided at two large meetings of the Committee of Antifascist Intellectuals, which he helped found, proclaiming at each one the solidarity of manual laborers and intellectuals, and sometime this year, Fred assumed the responsibilities of an officer of this group. As a scientist, he found it impossible not to get involved in the antifascist movement.

The French Communist Party now recognized that the battle against fascism took precedence over all else and deferred its dream of revolution to make peace with the socialists and its old enemies, the radicals.

On July 14, just before he joined Irène in the Haute-Savoie, Fred participated in the momentous Bastille Day manifestation that gave birth to the Front Populaire and was composed of large delegations of all the parties on the left, including the Committee of Antifascist Vigilance, as Langevin's group was now known. Despite dramatic controversy within the Executive Committee of the Vigilance group, its participation in the event helped assure the Front Populaire's success, and Langevin, as well as the Communist leader, Maurice Thorez, and several others, was conspicuously seated on the roof of one of the two taxis, the one bearing a red flag, not the one with a tricolor, at the cortège's head. Fred, Biquard, and Francis Perrin were prominent in the ranks behind the taxis as the massive demonstration wound its way through an exuberant crowd of some half a million Parisians intoxicated at the promise of a better future.

It was a foregone conclusion in international scientific circles that Fred and Irène would receive a Nobel for their synthesis of new radioelements. Since they did not get the prize in 1934, they could not have been too surprised to receive the wire from Stockholm in November 1935, informing them of their selection. Unbeknownst to Fred and Irène, both Rutherford and Perrin, utilizing their prerogatives as past laureates, had nominated them for the chemistry award. They were overjoyed at this recognition on a worldwide scale, although Irène's pleasure might have been even greater had Marie been alive. Irène clearly recalled the onslaught of the press, thirty-two years before, when her parents received a similar telegram. So she hustled Fred off to the anonymity of the Bon Marché, a big department store not too far from the Institute, to buy a tablecloth they needed. The next day, at the traditional Curie Laboratory tea to celebrate a staff worker's success, Irène artlessly replied, when congratulated, "In our family we are accustomed to glory."[5] Coming from her it was not boastful; it was a statement of fact.

Unlike Marie, Irène was determined to speak out on nonscientific matters when she felt strongly about the issues at stake, a tendency that was unquestionably strengthened under Fred's influence. In a long interview in *Journal de la Femme,* on November 23, she elaborated:

> *I am not one of those . . . who thinks that a woman [scientist] . . . can disinterest herself from her role as a woman, either in private or public life . . . If [the Nobel award] has thrust my name, the name of a woman, a little more in the limelight than on other days, I feel it is my duty to affirm certain ideas that I believe useful for all French women. Therefore, I have accepted the presidency of several meetings where the rights of women are discussed.*

She believed that the government must guarantee equal working rights for women and wanted all women to join in a common fight for civil rights, as well as for political ones.

Some were surprised that neither Irène nor Fred spoke much about Marie in their various interviews at the time of the Nobel announcement. But, she confessed in a letter to Missy, "I do not understand how I could speak of her to journalists."[6] She added that the doctors were again ordering her to hold to the minimum any social obligations and to avoid travel in order to allow her lungs to "consolidate." They only sanctioned the forthcoming Stockholm excursion with the proviso that, on her return, Irène would submit to a complete rest.

Their Stockholm trip must have filled Irène with a sense of *déjà vu*—and satisfaction. She received her leather-bound certificate and medal from Gustave V, the same King who had awarded them not once, but twice, to her mother, and once to her father, a family accomplishment that is still unrivaled. At the time, Marie and Irène were the only women ever to win in physics and chemistry, although several were laureates for literature. But Irène had no intention of doing something she did not wish to do, even in the Royal Palace, and at one point during the official festivities when His Majesty looked around for her, she was not standing in line where she was supposed to be. Irène had already made one concession by appearing in an evening gown for one of the rare times in her life—a long black unadorned taffeta affair with a modest neckline and small puffed sleeves cut away at the shoulders. Enough was enough. And she slipped off to a secluded corner where Fred found her, intently reading something of interest.

As the Nobel winner for physics that year, Chadwick was in the audience the afternoon that Fred and Irène gave their required public lectures. Unlike her parents' joint lecture, Irène and Fred were both on stage at once, and Irène's remarks preceded Fred's. Until their discovery of artificial radioactivity, the development of nuclear physics had been severely hampered by the exorbitant prices of the basic radioactive sources. Now, physicists no longer had this handicap and could go full steam ahead, because they were able to produce, at will, many new radioactive isotopes—over two thousand within the next fifty years. Commenting on this, Fred paused, looked up from his notes and, with his eyes on Irène seated alongside, said, with a sense of emotion that was felt by all present: "It was certainly a satisfaction for our late lamented teacher, Marie Curie, to have seen the list of radioactive elements that she had the honour to inaugurate with Pierre Curie so extended."[7]

He went on to envision chemical chain reactions of an explosive character, entailing the release of inexhaustible atomic energy. Like Pierre, and in words echoing Pierre's, which he had never forgotten, Fred optimistically stated his conviction that mankind would derive more good than harm from new discoveries.

Taking another page from the previous generation, Fred and Irène did not take out any patents. Their newest honors went a long way to persuade many remaining diehards in the French scientific establishment to finally give Fred his due. Perrin was especially pleased they got the prize, for Fred was a shining example of how government support, in the form of the Caisse Nationale de la Recherche Scientifique grants, could help a young person of obscure origins scale Olympus. The repercussions of the Nobel award with its attendant extracurricular obligations marked even more of a turning point in Fred and Irène's lives than it had in Marie and Pierre's. This was especially true for Fred, who was already keenly aware of his responsibilities as a scientist in a world of change, and he would ultimately be forced to make choices that would have tragic personal consequences.

In short order, Fred was elevated to the position of director of research at the Caisse, the highest position available there, and he persuaded that body to buy the old Ampère plant at Ivry. Here Fred gave the first indications of his impressive ability as an administrator when he proceeded to transform and equip Ivry, known henceforth as the Atomic Synthesis Laboratory, into a high-tension laboratory, housing a three-million-volt impulse generator. This was to produce in quantity man-made radioactive elements for researchers, saving both time and money, and before the end of 1937, Fred produced here, for the first time in France, a radiocarbon. Fred was intensely interested in all possible applications of artificially radioactive isotopes, especially in the fields of biology and therapy. The Russian Lew Kowarski, who worked for him, claimed that Fred wanted to be the man who revolutionized biology. True, he had switched and was using Fermi's technique of bombarding with neutrons, but Fermi had only been following Fred's suggestions, as the Italian was the first to admit. Kowarski called Fred "the most ambitious man since Richard Wagner . . . [who] wanted to be Beethoven . . . Shakespeare and Caesar all rolled into one."[8] No matter how many other appointments he might hold in the years ahead, Fred remained Ivry's active director until his death.

The following March, when Hitler denounced the Locarno Pact and marched into the Rhineland, five years ahead of schedule,

France did nothing. In the face of this militant neighbor, antifascism was the cement that held the socialists and Communists together. The country's spring elections saw a decisive vote for the French left; the French Communist Party became a major political force in France, and the socialist leader, Léon Blum, came into power as President of the Council. Anxious to bring women into the government for the first time, even though they still did not have the right to vote, he selected three who were progressive in outlook and universally known—Irène, Suzanne Lacore, a veteran of over forty years in the field of child welfare, and Mme. Cécile Brunschweig, who had devoted her life to improving the lot of women workers—as under secretaries in their respective fields. Women throughout France looked up to the trio as symbols of their long-awaited emancipation.

To the astonishment of her friends, Irène agreed to serve in order "to make it easier for other women to also enter the government." She explained to Missy: "Fred and I thought I must accept it as a sacrifice for the feminist cause in France, although it annoyed us very much."9 Unlike in Marie's lifetime, "disinterestedness" no longer ranked high in the vocabulary of Irène's generation; "responsibility" was their *leitmotiv*. Irène's appointment as Under Secretary for National Education was the first of its kind in France to link science and national development, and both she and Fred knew that if the Blum government remained in power, her functions would be preserved and given to a competent successor. Furthermore, without the prestige of the Curie name, it was highly problematic whether her post would ever have been created. At last there was a chance to realize the dream of Jean Perrin and Marie's friends; with one of their number in power, an unexcelled opportunity presented itself to improve permanently, and on a government level, the lot of scientists and to get more money for laboratories and equipment.

Irène entered office with the tacit understanding she would only remain over the summer, although she knew that by accepting under those limiting conditions she was exposing herself to justifiable criticism. However, to do so under any circumstances represented a real sacrifice on her part, both physically and psychologically. True, her health was good at the moment, but attendance at, or presiding over, any sort of meeting was anathema to her, and now this was destined to be part of her daily schedule, drawing her away from her preferred place on a laboratory bench.

In June, while the country was in the throes of a severe economic crisis and beset with strikes, Irène reported for work and was assigned an office on the upper floor of the Merchant Marine Building. With Blum's sole directive to consolidate scientific research, especially outside of the capital, as a guide Irène started from scratch. She selected Pierre Biquard and Edmund Wellhoff as part of her new staff, a choice dictated not on the basis of their longstanding friendships with Fred but because of their proven capacities. As was to be expected, she was at once attacked for her dry manner and devastating frankness, and the newspapers mistakenly labeled her incredible naïveté and artlessness as haughtiness. Irène was never cut out for her present role. One day, a new secretary brought for her signature a letter of refusal for a government function; noting the omission, which the woman thought was inadvertent, of the conventional phrase "I regret I cannot attend," the typist had added it. Irène refused to sign until this was removed because she was not at all sorry she could not be present. She always called a spade a spade—and felt free to analyze its defects.

By the end of July, Irène was forced to return, briefly, to the mountains. She was to accompany Fred to Moscow in the fall, and he was anxious that she obey the doctor's orders and put on some weight. "I want to have a beautiful Irène with me."[10] When she was finally ready to come to L'Arcouest to rejoin her family, Fred urged her, as she passed through Paris, to buy some elegant, warm clothes for their forthcoming trip. As usual, Irène was equally solicitous of him: "Take care on your motorcycle and with your boat, so I shall find you all in one piece, and don't smoke too much if you want to be my beloved *chéri.*"[11]

In Paris, Irène met with Blum and, on schedule, turned over her portfolio—surely with a sigh of relief—to Jean Perrin, her previously agreed-upon successor. Perrin and Blum were long-standing friends and it had been his suggestion that Blum appoint Irène in the first place. The scientific left was predominantly socialist and solidly behind Blum; since socialism in France was equated with progress, and progress, with science, they, particularly Jean Perrin, were involved in many phases of the forthcoming Paris Exposition of 1937. One of its main attractions was to be a Palace of Discoveries. Conceived by Perrin as a permanent science museum, the Palace was the first contemporary one of its kind in the West. A piece of blatant propaganda, it was intended to arouse enthusiasm for scientific careers in the young and to achieve an understanding and appreciation of science by the general public. Perrin called on all his friends for exhibits; the Van de Graaff accelerator, named for its Alabama-born inventor, which Fred was constructing, was essentially a monumental static-electricity generator and was intended as one of the stellar attractions.

In September, Fred and Irène were in Moscow to attend the first Mendeleev Conference. Fred had been asked to give the inaugural address because the discovery of artificial radioactivity gave new meaning to the Mendeleev periodic classification of the elements. A great fuss was made over the pair, and they were guests of honor at a banquet given by the U.S.S.R. Academy of Science. They were gone about three weeks and also spent some time in Poland, visiting Sklodowski relations and touring various laboratories.

As more and more foreign countries honored Fred, the French scientific establishment reluctantly came to recognize his ability. And that fall, when Langevin proposed his nomination for a recently vacated chair at the Collège de France, the center and symbol of French learning, there was little opposition. These things moved slowly, at best, and it would be almost a year before he finally moved in. The Collège, which was not connected with the University of Paris, had as its main function research, not teaching, and its professors' weekly lectures were open to the public. No degrees were issued. While some might express surprise that Fred should separate from the Radium Laboratory, thereby breaking his intimate collaboration with Irène, a chair at the Collège constituted the pinnacle of success in France and was something no one as ambitious as Fred could turn down. It was only natural that with the passage of time, each might choose to concentrate more on their special fields—Irène in chemistry, Fred in physics. Through Langevin's discreet maneuverings, the chair of the late celebrated orientalist Sylvain Lévi, which happened to be in Sanskrit, was transformed into one for Fred's discipline with its own laboratory and assistants; grafted onto it was an unprecedented second section, with another new laboratory, so that Fred was in charge of both nuclear physics and nuclear chemistry. By the time he was actually installed, in the fall of 1937, Irène had replaced him on the Faculty of Sciences of the University of Paris. Because of their various positions—at the Curie Laboratory, where Irène remained the chief of research projects; the Sorbonne; the Collège de France, with its two nuclear laboratories; the Caisse Nationale de la Recherche Scientifique and its Atomic Synthesis Laboratory at Ivry —it was almost impossible to do any nuclear work in France except through them.

Fred's technical change of address—the Collège de France was located on the rue des Écoles, a short walk from the Radium Institute—brought an end to Irène and Fred's official scientific collaboration, and they only published a few more papers together. In reality, their interests were so closely allied that husband and wife were as *au courant* of each other's work as in the past. They continued to consult on everything, and while never neglecting pure research, they both felt that what they were working on would someday produce important practical benefits for mankind. Fred's engineering training was of great help as he moved swiftly to initiate the development in France of the big equipment coming to the fore in physics laboratories abroad. By the summer of 1937, excavation began on a thirty-foot-deep cellar in the Collège to house his first project there, a thirty-two-inch cyclotron, the newest piece of artillery for physicists. To expedite its installation, Fred sent Nahmias, a trusted aide, to Berkeley, California, for a year's work with Lawrence, who was already building his fourth cyclotron on that campus, and in exchange, Paxton, the cyclotron inventor's assistant, was coming to the Collège on a Rockefeller Foundation grant. Because of his move down the street, traumatic as it was to both Fred and Irène at the time, Fred was soon to have at his disposal various apparatus which the Curie Laboratory had no room for; through them, the next phase of nuclear physics could be more quickly developed.

The Spanish Civil War that erupted shortly before Irène and Fred went to Moscow was a lethal combination of a military rebellion, led by the conservative right-wing General Francisco Franco, against the democratically elected socialist workers' government, and a foreign invasion. The divisions sent there by Hitler and Mussolini, though brazenly described as volunteers fighting for a principle, were regular army troops. The Western democracies, France, Britain, and America, maintained a policy of nonintervention which benefited Franco, and the war quickly developed into a battle of ideologies. The U.S.S.R. was the only power to give support to the Spanish republicans and reaped thanks for its aid, while the West was accused of abandoning democracy in the face of the fascist tide sweeping Europe. Most of the foreigners, including the Americans, who fought in the International Brigades created in the fall of 1936, were Communist. From France alone, where the majority of the left and the masses were heart and soul behind the Spanish republicans, Marty, of the Black Sea mutiny fame, had little trouble rounding up some three thousand French Communists as volunteers. With their courageously spilled blood, they won for the party popularity and sympathizers, including many prominent antifascist intellectuals and, in particular, the famous writer André Malraux. Both Irène and Fred disagreed strongly with Léon Blum and the Socialist Party's policy of nonintervention. They were aghast at the impunity with which Germany and Italy were permitted to bomb and destroy helpless civilians and were so horrified at the devastating raid on the city of Guernica that Langevin had no trouble persuading them to serve on various committees which were working actively to aid refugees from that war-ravaged land.

When Irène returned from Moscow, she started a series of experiments that would occupy her for more than two years and constituted her most outstanding individual work. Since Marie's death she had been irradiating thorium and studying the resultant brew. Now she switched and was irradiating uranium, working with a newcomer to the laboratory, the Yugoslav Paul Savitch. Their working quarters at the Radium Institute consisted principally of Irène's stark office with its table and chair and, in a corner, Geiger-Müller counters, batteries, and a cot Savitch had recently installed. At their disposal was also a sparsely equipped chemistry lab and, on the ground floor, another room with a minute terrace which had once been Marie's office. Here Irène received visitors and rested—to satisfy her doctors—between two consecutive experiments. Irène arrived promptly at 8 A.M. with the program of work for the day. At this period she had a lot of outside engagements, especially to help the Spanish republicans, so it was up to Savitch to make the necessary preparations. Irène returned later to do the actual experiments with him. After irradiation into its components came elaborate fractional precipitations, "à la Marie," to separate the broth of the various elements and their isotopes, which were all transmuting, in virtually invisible quantities, into one another, minute by minute—or faster—and, eventually, to isolate each one long enough to study it chemically. The task was not easy, for all the atoms of a given element are not identical. If a neutron is added to the nucleus, the latter becomes an isotope a little heavier than the same element, with a distinctly different type of radioactivity. The addition or subtraction of other neutrons give still other isotopes. Nonetheless, all the isotopes of a given element behave the same way in chemical treatment.

Most nights, after she went home, Savitch stayed behind on the cot by the Geigers, to watch for and then measure the disintegration of the substances he and Irène had earlier disentangled and which were produced in quantities so small that they were detectable only by their radioactivity. When Irène returned the next morning, he showed her the results and they analyzed them. This around-the-clock schedule of work often left Savitch asleep on his feet; once he was so tired that he dropped and broke a vial, spilling its precious contents, which he felt honor-bound to replace out of his meager personal stipend.

Unfortunately, Savitch had inherited the Geiger counters used by his predecessors, Hans von Halban and P. Prieswerk, who left them behind when they transferred to the Collège de France with Fred, and they were far from adequate for the work at hand. He really needed a counter made of aluminum with far thinner walls, but the overworked laboratory atelier ignored Savitch's request to make him one due to a lack of adequate material. Savitch's eyes lit up, one noon, when a colleague was celebrating the birth of his son by smoking an expensive Havana cigar. Retrieving its metal case, he cut off the rounded ends and took the resultant aluminum tube back to the Curie's technician, who quickly remodeled it to fit Savitch's specifications.

Apparently, Irène's visit to the mountains, during the summer of 1937, when Angèle again joined her, was dictated more by a need for rest than for other therapeutic reasons. She was gone long enough for Fred to confess, "I miss you in spite of your terrible . . . bossiness. Perhaps that is what I miss."[12] Irène knew her husband. "I am glad to know that you are getting a good rest," she wrote, "probably by going out at 4 A.M. to check the fishing nets and going to bed at midnight after having danced, not to mention [having played] tennis in between . . ."[13]

Léon Blum was forced out of power that same summer, in the aftermath of severe economic distress and strikes. He was succeeded by a radical, while the Communist Party, as a sign of its improved status, transferred its main meetings to the gigantic Vélodrome d'Hiver—"the Winter Sports Palace"—and moved its official headquarters to a big modern building. Stalin continued to ship a lot of aid to the Spanish republicans, and the Komintern was openly sending emissaries to the French Communist Party using passports of International Brigade volunteers killed in the Spanish Civil War.

Irène and Savitch were not the only ones who had been studying the uranium broth. Irène's nemesis, Lise Meitner, and Otto Hahn had been doing likewise. When the German team published a paper on their latest results, Irène's findings for the same uranium irradiation were different. She felt it impossible to adequately corroborate the German pair's identification of each of the twenty-plus supposed "transuranians" that they claimed to find. She decided to concentrate, instead, on thoroughly identifying chemically "R-3.5," one of the products she and Savitch had found, and the one that had the most penetrating beta rays—which would make it easier to measure—and a reasonably long existence in which to do their work—a three-and-a-half-hour half-life. The Germans seemed to have missed this isotope entirely. Irène did not remember the mysterious substance with a similar half-life which she and her students had been the first ever to see when they had been irradiating thorium a few years before; nor was there any reason to connect it with their new "R-3.5."

Shortly after the first of the year, Meitner and Hahn wrote Irène giving details of their latest experiment. Since they were unable to find Irène's "R-3.5," they were convinced it did not exist, and they politely suggested that if Irène made a public retraction of this finding, they would not publish their criticism of her work. Either the French or the German team had made a grave error.

Irène and Savitch relocated the elusive substance, whose identification they now thought must be either actinium, number 89 on the Mendeleev Periodic Table, or lanthanum, number 57. The latter was chemically similar but even harder to explain since it was so far down on the table from uranium, number 92 and in last place. Or it could even be a new element, something that would belong after uranium. However, they were prone to rule out lanthanum, for no one had ever heard of a slow neutron transmuting uranium into anything so far down the periodic table from it. Because the radioactivity of the last of the ten necessary fractionations of their quarry was always a few clicks of the Geiger counter higher than the nine preceding ones—probably, Irène surmised later, in the light of hindsight, because they were not testing pure lanthanum— the positive identification of "R-3.5" as an isotope of lanthanum, the same one she and her students had been the first ever to spot in 1935, eluded them.

Many an evening Irène discussed the enigma of "R-3.5" at length with Fred. Unfortunately, few physicists ever thumbed through a publication little used in their profession, *The Journal of Applied Chemistry.* And those who did see the September 1934 issue did not take seriously the suggestion of a respected German chemist, Ida Noddack. She postulated that when neutrons are used to produce nuclear disintegration, a distinctly new and different nuclear reaction was possible than with alpha rays. To date, no nuclear physicist could imagine an atom gaining or losing more than one or two particles at a time. This would change the weight of a heavy element like uranium or thorium only slightly, and the various elements bombarded to date only transmuted into their near neighbor. Noddack, however, thought it possible that the nucleus of uranium, the heaviest element, broke up into large fragments when bombarded by neutrons. These fragments would be isotopes of known elements but would not be uranium's neighbors; instead they would be much lighter elements farther down the table. This, of course, was what happened. But, until the liquid-drop model of the atomic nucleus was applied later to the problem, there was no accepted way to calculate whether the energy involved would permit a nuclear breakup of a uranium atom into several large fragments.

When Fred was in Rome at the International Scientific Congress, he met Otto Hahn for the first time. The German was cordial but frankly skeptical when the two discussed the French team's latest results, pointing out that neither he, Lise Meitner, nor Fritz Strassmann, who had been working on the same problem with him for over two years, had ever observed anything resembling "R-3.5." Fred upheld Irène's work, and later, Hahn was heard to say: "This damned woman. Now I will have to go home and waste six months proving that she was wrong!"[14]

Irène and Savitch replied with a report in the May 30 *Comptes Rendus* that was even more disturbing than their original one. So Hahn wrote Fred, asking that he use his influence on the pair to stop publicly refuting the German results. Otherwise Hahn must contradict her in print, and this would be very distasteful to him. Irène showed Savitch the letter and asked his reaction. "I feel we should continue our work and let Hahn do what he wants," Savitch replied.[15] They did.

Unfortunately, Lise Meitner did not have long to address the problem. In March, Hitler had annexed Austria, her native country, and on July 13 or 14, she fled Berlin, one of the last Jews to cross successfully into the Netherlands. By the end of September, when Chamberlain signed the humiliating Munich accords, Daladier was in office as French Premier. Roiling labor strikes and economic woes had forced the Front Populaire out of the picture. Irène and Fred refrained from any overt political action but lent their names to more than one open letter to Daladier and other authorities, insisting that no more concessions be made to the Italian and German dictators. Irène wrote Missy indignantly about "that traitor . . . Chamberlain: France and the United States are not much better. Sometimes I think that this civilization will really disappear, for fascism is going back directly to barbary, and the democracies

are entirely in the hands of the private interests of capitalism . . ."[16]

War clouds were gathering, and Fred and Irène were further
incensed, after the Munich crisis, when the Council of Ministers
followed the British lead and pressured Prague to yield to the dis-
memberment of Czechoslovakia. Fred openly aligned himself with
Langevin, Perrin, and other French academics and intellectuals
who were against Hitler. Both he and Irène appeared, together with
other prominent scientists, in seats of honor at a large assembly of
intellectuals at the Centre Marcellin-Berthelot, where they heard
the French Communist Party adopt precisely their goals. The Communists' belief in internationalism equated with Fred and Irène's
conviction that, for basic science to flourish, there must be a free
flow of ideas and people; the Communists' appeal for French-Soviet
friendship and aid to Spain echoed Fred and Irène's own sentiments. However, Fred could never claim that he did not know
persecution existed in Russia because, together with Irène and Perrin, he signed a letter addressed to the Procureur-General of the
U.S.S.R., with a copy to Stalin, on behalf of the arrested physicist
Alex Weissberg. In Fred's eyes, certain purges were "necessary in a
country so gravely menaced by enemies both inside and out."[17]

Meitner kept needling Hahn and Strassmann from abroad about
the discrepancies between the German and French results. When
Strassmann tried to show Hahn Irène's team's next report in the
Academy's *Comptes Rendus*, Hahn refused to read it. Strassmann
prevailed, and Hahn returned to the laboratory determined to stop
this sniping back and forth and to prove how hopelessly muddled
the poor French were with their mysterious "R-3.5," which in a
play on words he named "curiosium." For the first time he found
not only lanthanides (atomic numbers 58-71) but also atoms of a
radioisotope of barium [atomic number 56] in the broth that resulted when irradiating uranium. Considered at the time the
world's greatest radiochemist, he was sure of his results and wrote
Meitner on December 19, "Perhaps you can come up with some

fantastic explanation."[18] Her nephew, the physicist Otto Frisch, came to spend the Christmas holiday with her at the little village of Kungälv, and together, they came up with the explanation that the uranium nucleus had fissioned.

The discovery of this phenomenon, with its implication that nuclear fission would release enormous atomic power, was one of the most important milestones of the twentieth century; it was the climax of forty years of fundamental research on the structure of the atom which commenced with the discovery of radioactivity by Becquerel and the two Curies.

Hahn nailed down his find by publishing his "curious results with a certain hesitancy"[19] in the January 1939 *Naturwissenschaften*. Irène read the article the minute the magazine reached the Radium Institute on the sixteenth, and handed it to Savitch without comment. Appalled to have been so close, once more, to a major discovery, it would have been only natural if Irène asked herself whether she and Fred might not have arrived at the same conclusions themselves, ahead of Hahn, if they had still been working together. The same mail brought *Naturwissenschaften* to the Collège de France. Seeing Hahn's name in the index, Fred turned to his report and thoroughly digested the few hints revealed before going home. That evening, he and Irène discussed Hahn's article in detail until late at night, and Fred spent the next several days, incommunicado in his office, studying how to prove the existence of Hahn's new nuclear reaction.

Fred quickly figured out that he did not possess adequate technical equipment to approach the problem by observing the neutrons. So he decided to examine the fission fragments, instead. Some years before, he had briefly experimented with how far a nucleus could travel when charged, and now, within a few days, he deduced that each splitting of a single nucleus should release such an enormous amount of energy that the fragments of the nucleus would fly apart. They could then be collected and identified by the amount of their radioactivity. The next step was to set up the simple, ingenious type of experiment he loved best.

On January 26, Fred erupted into the Radium Institute. He was very excited, stayed only a short while and, without giving any reason, asked Savitch to be at his laboratory at the Collège de France at precisely 3 P.M. Every Saturday, duplicating Jean Perrin's weekly Monday teas, Fred normally gathered together a small group of colleagues in an informal seminar. That Saturday, to Savitch's surprise, only five people were present—Irène; Fred; Pavel Savel, Fred's assistant; Bruno Pontecorvo, who had been Fermi's pupil and was now working with Fred; and himself. But Savitch's memory may be faulty. Indeed, his and Kowarski's accounts of the experiment, which the latter called "one of the most elegant in the history of science" differ widely, and it may have been Kowarski, rather than Pontecorvo, who was present, as others aver. Or they both may have been there and six people, not five, present. Fred shut the door and explained that he had invited them to a demonstration of the phenomenon of uranium fission—"if it is produced."[20] The telltale clicking of the Geiger counter identifying the fragments as the uranium was bombarded spelled success.

Fred did not know that Frisch had beaten him to the draw with a somewhat similar experiment at the Bohr Institute in Copenhagen around January 13. On his return from his Christmas holiday with his aunt, Frisch discussed his and Meitner's interpretation of fission with Niels Bohr, who was leaving the next day for a term of work at the Institute for Advanced Studies at Princeton. Bohr struck his forehead with both hands. "How stupid of us!" he exclaimed. "We ought to have seen that sooner."[21] He divulged the news publicly in Washington, D.C., to the Fifth Conference of Theoretical Physicists on January 26, the same day Fred was doing his experiment and so startled his audience that some rushed off to their laboratories to verify it without waiting for the meeting's end.

At this point, fission was a fact of pure science, nothing more. But Frisch and Meitner estimated that the energy from each bursting uranium nucleus would be sufficient to make a grain of sand visibly jump. And in each gram of uranium there are about twenty-five—followed by twenty zeros—atoms. The next step was to determine how this energy could be harnessed and utilized.

Fred's experiment that Saturday was crucial. Not only did it convince him that fission was real; the timing was perfect for him to throw himself wholeheartedly into this virgin field of research that suddenly opened up before his eyes. While construction of the new facilities and laboratories at the Collège de France and at Ivry had swamped him with administrative duties almost to the exclusion of research for the past several years, they were nearing completion. By now he also had assembled his own trained technical staff and had excellent postdoctoral students to assist him. He selected two to work with him on an equal footing—the Austrian Hans von Halban, an expert on slow neutrons and their absorption in matter, on which subject he already had a substantial body of publications, and the Russian Lew Kowarski, who had only published his thesis on crystals but whose conceptual originality was remarkable. From the start, they worked together as a unit, rather than working separately and then coming together to pool their efforts in a group endeavor.

The trio was in its thirties, with Fred the eldest at thirty-nine, and they were ambitious to excess—an invaluable characteristic for any success. While they worked so closely together that it is frequently impossible to say specifically who suggested what, Fred supplied the drive and was the undisputed leader, always ready to intervene with some unexpected angle when problems arose. His penetrating logic helped clarify their ideas, and his broad scientific background rounded out areas where the other two were weak. He knew how to cut government red tape when necessary, and as Halban later remarked, he "had great foresight concerning the importance of what we set out to do."[22]

Fred's vaunted charm was equally invaluable, for it helped smooth over many rough moments between two rugged individualists—the "Junker," as Halban was called because of his Austro-German background and manners, and the "Russian barbarian," Kowarski's nickname. Lew was a giant of a man whose bulk made an ordinary chair creak when he sat balancing on it. A year older than Halban, blunt and with a mordant wit, Kowarski served initially as Halban's apprentice, then collaborated with him in neutron studies and proved so expert that Halban recommended him to Fred as the third member of the team. The fine-featured Halban, whose name was actually "von Halban" until he dropped the "von," a title of nobility, had some independent means, a cultivated taste, and a love for high society. He studied with Irène and, then, Niels Bohr before settling down with Fred at the Collège de France. A brutal directness, combined with an inflexible, offensive authoritarianism, often made him hard to work with.

For fission to be translated from a laboratory curiosity into a viable source of energy, a divergent chain reaction—one that continues to multiply, once initiated—must be started and sustained. Accordingly, the first problem confronting the trio was to determine whether any extra neutrons were, as Fred suspected, emitted each time a uranium nucleus was bombarded by a single neutron. This would not be easy to detect because of the flood of neutrons used in the irradiation but, if there were, then a chain reaction would be possible. For, if one bombarding neutron produces two— or three—others, then those two could produce four, and so on until the whole mass of uranium was affected. In this fashion an enormous number of atoms would be disintegrated with incredible rapidity, together with the release of an unbelievable sum of energy —energy which Fred hoped might one day liberate man from painful work forever. So it was imperative to find the answer.

Fred went off for his customary ski holiday with Irène and the children, but he remained in constant touch with Paris. When the team's request for additional radium from the Radium Institute went unanswered, one call from Fred to the dragon guarding it released the necessary amount, and the experiments continued un-

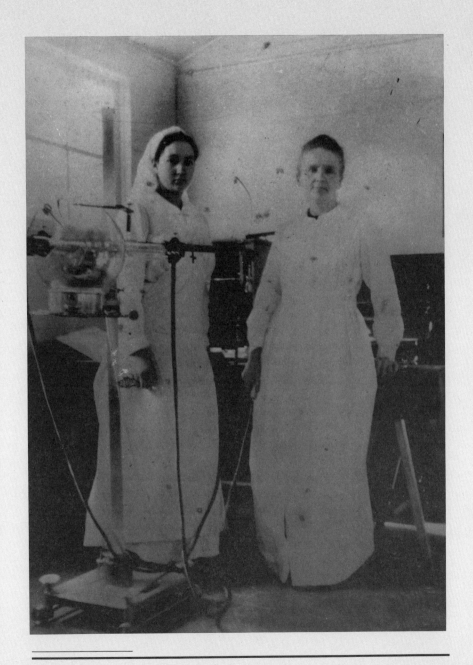

Irène and Marie with part of their X-ray equipment in the Anglo-Belgian hospital at Hoogstade, 1915.

Photographs courtesy of the Laboratoire Curie, Institut du Radium, Paris.

Marie and Irène with the officers of the A. E. F. to whom they taught radiological techniques in 1919.

Marie and Irène in the laboratory at the Institut de Radium, 1923.

Marie with President Harding at the White House, just after the presentation ceremony, 1921.

Fred, Irène (front), Hélène, and Pierre (1934).

Fred, Irène, and Pierre (rear) at L'Arcouest, 1938.

Irène, Marie, and Hélène, 1930.

Solvay Conference in
Brussels, October 1933.
Among those pictured here are
the three women who attended
—Irène, Marie, and Lise
Meitner in the front row.

Irène and Fred at the Nobel ceremonies, 1935.

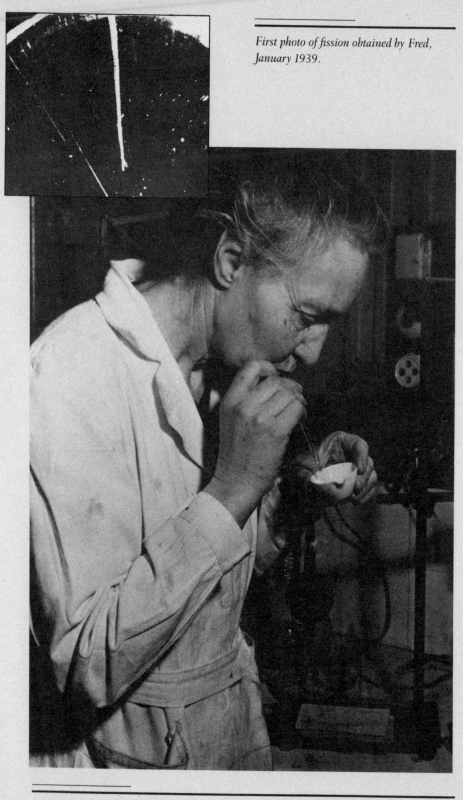

First photo of fission obtained by Fred, January 1939.

Irène in the lab, sucking up fluid with a pipette—a dangerous, difficult technique that Marie taught her.

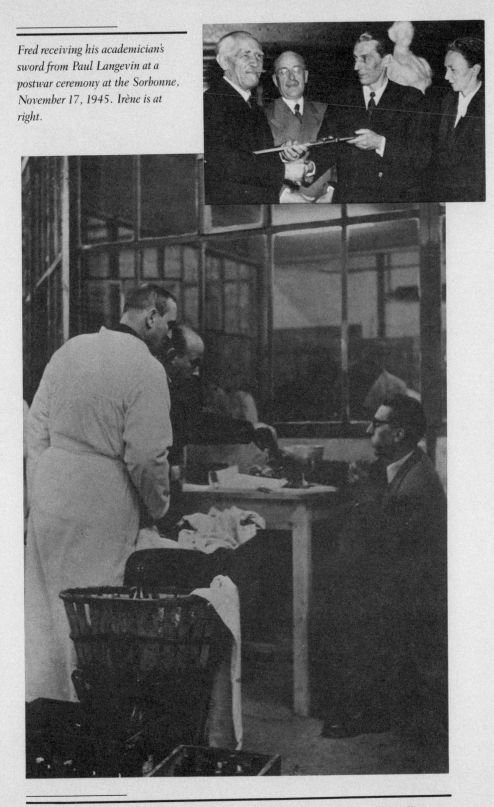

Fred receiving his academician's sword from Paul Langevin at a postwar ceremony at the Sorbonne, November 17, 1945. Irène is at right.

Fred eating a snack while waiting for France's first atomic pile to go active at Châtillon, December 15, 1948. L. Kowarski is on the left.

Irène at the famous World Congress of Intellectuals for Peace in Wroclaw, September 1948.

interrupted. Once the men determined that primary neutrons had a different energy level after fission than the emerging secondary ones, they set feverishly to work around the clock, waiting for irradiations and taking innumerable measurements, before they were able to confirm Fred's hunch about the existence of extra neutrons.

Because Fred was not searching for an instantaneous, explosive disintegration, as with a bomb, but for controlled fission for an energy plant, one major bottleneck remained. How could they slow down the neutrons, when they burst from the bombarded uranium at high speed, in order to provide a better chance of their hitting other nuclei and provoking the anticipated avalanche? Kowarski hit upon the answer while taking a bath—"a situation that was clearly favorable to the idea of neutrons scattering in a liquid environment,"[23] he would chuckle in retrospect. Water could act as the needed moderator.

The men were so anxious to be the first to publish these important results that they decided not to wait for the Academy's next *Comptes Rendus* the following Monday, March 8. Instead, Kowarski personally rushed their report announcing their discovery of the key to the liberation of the atom's vast internal energy to Le Bourget Airport to speed it across the Channel to *Nature,* which could print it earlier. When Kowarski was asked years later why the rush, that bear of a man replied bluntly, "Why not secure priority? Hell, as I always say, it's not vanity—it's bread and butter."[24] Though they did not know it, their only rivals at the moment were Fermi and the Hungarian theoretical physicist Leo Szilard, who got the same results at Columbia a week later.

Central Europe's skies were clouding over fast. On March 16, 1939, the crisis in Czechoslovakia came to a head and what was left of that country was swallowed up by Hitler's Reich. A short time later Szilard cabled Fred to delay further publishing of fission experiments, with their conceivable military potential, as part of a proposed international plan to keep similar information from the European dictators. Halban at first thought the 139-word cable, "the longest we'd ever seen," was an April Fool's joke. But its evident cost convinced Fred that it was not. French physicists as a group despised the anti-Semitic governments that had driven scientists from Italy and Central Europe, and both Halban and Kowarski were part Jewish. Like Fred, who had spoken out repeatedly to condemn French appeasement of the fascists, they expected war within a year or so, but the trio believed a nuclear bomb was not an immediate possibility—should it even prove feasible. As a matter of principle they were against secrecy in basic research, a field where free exchange was essential and had always been complete. Equally important, as Fred pointed out, if they refrained from publishing, Hitler would have succeeded in destroying another precious freedom. Fred was also realistic enough to know that given the present state of Europe, it was, practically speaking, impossible to stop leakage into the Nazi domain.

The final decision was his. On April 7, Fred cabled, "No." He would continue to publish. By that time, actually, whichever way he decided, it was too late. For their second paper had already gone off to *Nature* with the invaluable information that the secondary neutrons being emitted were of the order of 3.5 extra neutrons. Actually this is an error and they averaged 2.5, but this was still sufficient to start a chain reaction.

To hold his lead internationally, Fred intended to investigate the theory of chain reactions methodically. This required heavy funding. Like Perrin, charismatic Fred, lionized as a Nobel laureate, was now moving on his own in high government and even aristocratic circles. He, too, possessed the same extraordinary ability to deal with those who controlled large sums of money. He talked over his needs with Henri Laugier, the director of the CNRS—the Centre National de la Recherche Scientifique—as the restructured Caisse Nationale de la Recherche Scientifique was now called. As a start, Laugier gave Fred what constituted a generous subsidy for the day and, especially, for France—the wherewithal to hire a couple of technicians for one year.

It was one thing to know how to initiate a chain reaction; it was another to be able to sustain one. This called for a theoretical physicist. Jean Perrin's brilliant son, Francis, one year Fred's junior, who worked down the rue Curie from Irène at the Henri Poincaré Institute, joined the team. By May, this wisp of a man, with a nose shortened by a diving accident and a dark pointed beard, produced a rough draft for calculating the critical mass of uranium needed. This information was crucial, for a lump smaller than a critical mass would be inert, while one larger would explode spontaneously upon assembly. In New York, Fermi was making similar estimates. Looking out the window of his office at Columbia one day, at the city of Manhattan spread out before him, he cupped his hands as if holding a ball. "A little bomb like that," he said simply, "and it would all disappear."[25]

As the cool spring sun made the gold inscription on the Collège de France's fronton sparkle, the feverish give-and-take sessions going on in the dark, paneled library inside were reminiscent of a Jules Verne novel; as they talked about changing the face of the map and perhaps diverting the Mediterranean into the Sahara, the quartet sounded like characters in an H.G. Wells fantasy. Unlike a scientist in an ivory tower, studying a phenomenon for its own sake, Fred's team was never allowed to lose sight of the practical aspects of fission. Fred was determined not only to develop the equipment to make the first chain reaction possible, but to set in motion the massive unleashing of atomic energy and to harness it for industrial purposes for the good of mankind. With few minor exceptions, the tradition of the Curies had been to leave to others the problems of practical application, but Halban was convinced that there was a need to exercise some control over the results of the team's recent discoveries, opening up, as they did, a new force of nature. Francis Perrin concurred, and the pair persuaded Fred, confirmed socialist and staunch patriot that he was, that for the good of the many, as opposed to private interests, and to assure France's continuing lead in the field of atomic energy, the four must patent what they could.

On May 1, they took out the first patent anywhere pertaining to nuclear energy and, specifically, for a basic nuclear reactor to contain a chain reaction. The second, on May 2, was for a means to regulate such a machine; the third, on May 4, was for a crude, potential nuclear bomb. Their rights were at once transferred to the CNRS, but the patent applications themselves were kept secret and were not granted until 1950, after the war.

On May 4, Fred also wrote the Belgian Union Minière du Haut-Katanga, the world's largest miner of uranium ore. Marie, as well as Irène and Fred, had had dealings with this firm for years, and several days afterward, Fred went to Brussels to meet with Edgar Sengier, its president. According to one account, Irène went along. The two top executives of the Union Minière then came to Paris and a deal was struck. The first shipment, five thousand kilograms of uranium oxide, a grimy powder resembling charcoal, was quickly delivered to Fred's Ivry laboratory, where there were huge overhead cranes and a big hangar to facilitate its handling; for the oxide, when wet, was denser than solid concrete. By July, the Collège de France's team was installed there. The Radium Institute's annex in the nearby suburb of Arcueil was to assist in the treatment of radioactive materials. But Irène and the Radium Institute's staff were keeping to the laboratory's specialty of radiochemistry and studying the nature of the radioactive products resulting from fission, rather than working on the actual mechanics of the phenomenon itself.

By now, less than one and a half years after its discovery, work on fission was proceeding in different directions in different countries. France was somewhat ahead of the others in the investigation of nuclear reactors and especially in the preparations for important experiments on the mixtures to be used in them. However, Fred and his group were still a number of years away from a working reactor and needed a lot more theoretical work as they moved out of the strictly scientific domain into that of engineering. World War II, while impeding the efforts of the Collège de France team, accelerated the American ones.

On August 2, pushed by Szilard, who was still obsessed with the fear that the Germans might win the nuclear race, Einstein wrote a letter envisaging the effects of an atomic bomb, and by the end of September, this was delivered personally to President Roosevelt by Alexander Sachs, a friend of F.D.R.'s. It was accompanied by a report from Szilard which mentioned that the French work in the field was probably the most advanced of the day. Given the letter's source, Roosevelt set up a consultative committee on uranium to study every possibility for such a weapon.

On the twenty-third, the seemingly impossible happened when a nonaggression pact was initialed by Molotov and Ribbentrop. This gave Hitler a free hand in the West. To rationalize this must have been hard for Irène who, a few short months before, had written Missy extolling communism as "the hope of the future." She, Fred, Jean Perrin, Paul Langevin, and other friends signed a strong declaration of the leftist Union of French Intellectuals, expressing stupefaction at the about-face of the Soviets. This was prominently displayed in *Le Temps* on the thirtieth. A few days later, Maurice Thorez, the head of the French Communist Party, acting on personal orders from Stalin, deserted the French Army into which he had just been drafted and escaped to the U.S.S.R., where he sat out the war.

Ominous as the Nazi-Communist pact was, the 180-degree political turn of the Russians and their invasion of Poland in September, following the German attack there, was even more frightening. Paris was filled with pessimism. The French Communist Party was officially outlawed for supporting the Molotov-Ribbentrop agreement and forced to go underground. Hitler's subsequent invasion of Poland saddened Irène. Her aunt Hela's eldest daughter, eighteen-year-old Ela Szyler, was visiting at L'Arcouest, but the rest of the Sklodowskis were trapped in Poland. Premier Daladier, who, the previous spring, had followed Chamberlain's lead and made a similar promise to support Poland in case of Nazi aggression, stood shoulder to shoulder with London throughout the crisis.

XIX
1939–1940

War

ON SEPTEMBER 3, FRANCE declared war on Germany, five hours after Britain did, and that evening Paris experienced its first blackout. The next day when Irène wrote twelve-year-old Hélène, who remained at L'Arcouest with Pierre, surely she must have recalled an almost identical letter which she, too, received at L'Arcouest, at the beginning of World War I, from Marie:

What is happening is sad, but you have heard us speak often enough of these matters to know that we are not surprised . . . It is possible that we may be separated for some time . . . Paris is very calm and it is hard to imagine that there is a war. I have seen . . . groups of children . . . being evacuated. Pinned on their clothes is a large ticket on which is printed their destination . . . (They look) like small packages waiting to be shipped. We are busy organizing the laboratories to work for National Defense. Study your music . . . do your gymnastics daily so that I will once again see a very erect little Hélène. Also see if you can not do some work in the fields . . . Naturally, if you go to help with something, you must do so very seriously and not drop out as soon as you have had enough. Je t'embrasse, my beloved little girl . . . P.S. Make your little brother go into the water while you watch. [1]

Irène's letter to Missy was uncannily prescient:

Fred has been put in charge of a group of laboratories to organize them for war purposes. I will also work in that direction . . . We hope very much the U.S. will abrogate the neutrality act. This law is unjust and is contrary to the interests of the U.S. for, if there is finally a fascist victory, it is rather clear to see how fascism would establish itself, first, in the countries of South America, getting to the North afterwards. If the U.S. does not help the democracies, at least by selling arms, I think it will be a crime against our common ideal of civilization . . . it will also be the greatest political fault. [2]

As a captain in the artillery reserves, Fred was quickly called up and at once attached to the Centre National de la Recherche Scientifique. Officially, he was made responsible for coordinating the projects of various groups in different laboratories; certain specific government research was placed under his supervision and, technically speaking, his own laboratories at the Collège de France and at Ivry were requisitioned for national defense. Actually, Fred's main activity was at Ivry, where the Van de Graaff was also available, having been moved there after the Paris Exposition, and his work continued to be focused on chain reactions. As he told his mother, "By working I hope to forget the stupidity of man."[3]

Because Fred's team was once more at a stage where he needed increased support of every sort, he met with Raoul Dautry, the new Minister of Armaments, who had previously made a name for himself by bringing the French railroads into the twentieth century and was now in overall charge of scientific research. Like other École Polytechnique alumni, he did not share the socialist views of Fred's circle, but the wiry, dapper little man respected Fred and listened intently. Dautry, like a majority of the French, anticipated that World War II, like World War I, would be a series of long-drawn-out blockades and trench battles. Since France imported most of her oil and a third of her coal, the country could be in serious danger unless new sources of energy were found for her economy and army. Atomic energy might be the solution and also lead to a powerful new weapon, as well as propel submarines. So he promised Fred whatever was needed. Shortly afterward, when Kowarski, Halban, and Perrin were drafted into the army, Dautry arranged for them to remain with Fred on "special assignment."

Military uniforms made their appearance in the laboratories, where the windows were painted over with black paint because people were working there far into the night. Many gaps were visible as, one by one, colleagues were drafted. Guards were posted, and the staff was warned that everything learned in the performance of their duties constituted a secret.

By now, Fred and his team knew what was needed to make a successful chain reaction of uranium atoms; there was no longer anything to show that this would be impossible. In order to nail down their claim to another "first," and get their scientific due, since the war automatically ruled out the possibility of publishing their findings, they deposited a note for the *Comptes Rendus* in a sealed envelope with the Academy of Science. Its contents would not be read for almost ten years, but as Rutherford's protégé, the English Nobel laureate P.M.S. Blackett, later pointed out, "There was little doubt, had not the war intervened, that the world's first self-sustaining chain-reaction would have been achieved in France."4

The pale clearness of rainy autumnal days settled over Paris. Because of the war, the children were going to spend the winter in Brittany with Fred's cousin, Madeleine Gangloff, and Hélène was attending school in Paimpol. Irène's health was once again a cause for concern; she and Fred went out very little and lived like monks except for rare, special occasions when they might join one or two intimates for sauerkraut at Balzar's. The Métro still worked and the rarity of alerts was falsely reassuring. The only visual manifestations of the war were the blackouts, the mandatory gas masks everyone carried slung over one shoulder, and the sandbags around the statues of the Place de la Concorde and the principal monuments. Most people were leading a normal life.

What Parisians dubbed "the phony war" continued. France was committed to a small professional army and a static defense, and German and French troops, stationed in the cement blockhouses of the Maginot Line, faced each other across the border with no gunfire. People were persuaded that Hitler had been bluffing and did not dare attack. So, as Christmas approached, doting parents sent their boys at the front footballs, checkers, dominoes, and comic books to relieve the boredom. Optimism reigned. By holiday time, soldiers were everywhere in Paris and the Casino de Paris was starring Maurice Chevalier and Josephine Baker. The Joliot children and their cousin, Ela Szyler, were brought into town for a fortnight.

With the theoretical work behind him, Fred and his team were thinking less like physicists than engineers as they struggled with construction problems. The tons of reasonably pure uranium and of a 100 percent pure moderator which they were going to require entailed expenditures a hundred times greater than they had ever needed before. This meant that strong government support was essential, and Fred knew that officials could only be convinced to back him when presented with some physical evidence of the quartet's future expectations. So Fred decided to construct, as fast as possible, an actual working model of a self-sustaining chain reaction, in its slow-neutron mode, which they knew would not be explosive. While not above criticism from a strictly scientific point of view because numerous questions still needed clarification and evaluation, such an approach was realistic and businesslike. It should earn the team the go-ahead to construct the full-scale reactor which constituted the heart of a nuclear power station. Kowarski later termed the approach somewhat "unsporting. It's like the desire to reach the North Pole, rather than to know about the North Pole, or the desire to step on the moon, instead of sending an unmanned device for collecting scientific data. But there was really no alternative. And this was why, when Szilard, at one point, asked Fermi: 'What do you think about [a certain] . . . paper by Joliot?' and Fermi replied, 'Not much,' Fermi was right. From a physicist's point of view, the paper [on the reactor] was not very impressive."[5]

Ordinary water was not working well as a moderator. By trial and error, Fred switched to heavy-water, a rare product in which deuterium replaced hydrogen; present in the ratio of two to ten thousand parts of natural water, it was utilized solely for scientific research. He needed several thousand liters, but one to two hundred would suffice for the immediate task at hand.

In mid-February 1940, when Fred went to Dautry to ask him to procure this for him, Dautry shot back, "We must act fast." French Intelligence had learned the Germans were trying to corner the world's existing supply of heavy-water, as well as an additional two thousand liters the minute it was available, from the Norsk-Hydro *Elektrisk kvaelstoffaktieselskap* outside Rjukan in neutral Norway. This was the only place in Europe that heavy-water was produced. Used to make synthetic ammonia, it was made at the rate of a quart a day by tedious hydrogen electrolysis from tons of ordinary water. Axel Aubert, the company's head, a Norwegian of French ancestry, could not imagine why anyone would want so much and was stalling the sale because the Germans refused to tell him what they needed it for. Dautry had also been mystified by this Intelligence report, but after listening to Fred, he realized that the Germans must be working on nuclear energy.

On February 20, Fred returned to Dautry's office in the quiet elegance of the former Hôtel Majestic. Awaiting him was Jacques Allier, a tall, energetic man with a square, bulldog's jaw, who was presently serving as a lieutenant in French Intelligence but who, in peacetime, was an officer at the Norwegian desk of the Banque de Paris et des Pays Basques, which owned control of Norsk-Hydro. When Bjorne G. Eriksen, a director of Norsk-Hydro, was in Paris on business recently, he confided to Allier the unusual demands from I.G. Farben, the giant German industrial conglomerate which held a substantial portion of the remaining shares of Norsk-Hydro. Allier, in turn, had advised Dautry. Fred explained to Allier the significance of heavy-water and why he must get every drop that was available not only for his work but, now, also to keep it from Nazi scientists. To bring back the heavy-water across a Europe riddled by fifth column traitors would be a dangerous undertaking. Could Allier arrange such a mission?

The three men looked at each other without saying a word—Fred's large black eyes glowing with an inner intensity in his cavernous, pale face; Dautry's inscrutable beneath his short black eyebrows; Allier's invisible behind his glasses. Allier broke the long silence. Since he knew Aubert and other personnel of the Norsk-Hydro, he volunteered to go himself.

The participation of French Intelligence automatically enlarged the scope of the Ministry of Armament's undertaking, so Dautry briefed the Premier. Daladier promised full support. With a venture so fraught with peril, Dautry worried about security leaks, and he was disturbed by the continued presence on Fred's team of Halban, with his Austro-German background, and of Kowarski, with his Russian one. Fred considered the pair indispensable and refused to ease them out of the picture. However, he did agree that until the heavy-water was in safe hands, the two should enjoy enforced vacations under close surveillance. Before the month was out, Halban and Kowarski departed on what was euphemistically termed "geological studies"—the bon vivant Austrian to Porquerolles in the Mediterranean to take a cure; the Russian to the equally isolated island of Belle-Île-en-Mer, where he bicycled about and read *Gone With the Wind.*

Speed was essential, for everything indicated that an attack on Norway might be imminent. On February 28, Allier set off with two sets of orders—one signed by Dautry, the other by Premier Daladier, who also gave him a letter. This he stowed in his black leather briefcase together with a credit for 36 million French francs. Fred briefed Allier carefully more than once, and at the last moment, he handed him a small metal tube of cadmium. "Keep this with you always. If the containers of heavy-water are in danger and you don't have time to empty them, pour a little in each one. The contents will immediately become unusable."[6]

Allier's mission had all the ingredients of the classic spy thriller and was, later, the subject of a popular postwar movie. For the scenario lacked little, from *noms de plume* and secret codes to a futile Baltic chase by German fighter planes. Everything worked according to Allier's precision planning, including a thrilling midnight escape with the prize from the heavily guarded, giant Norsk-Hydro plant built into a sheer fifteen-hundred-foot granite bluff beside a powerful waterfall. A carefully rehearsed, spectacular getaway from the Oslo airport threw the alerted Germans completely off-guard. By March 18, the twenty-six seven-liter canisters, which had been hurriedly custom-made by a trusted Oslo craftsman and contained the world's supply of heavy-water, were secreted away in the cellar of the Collège de France. Whereupon a coded telegram recalled Kowarski and Halban from gilded exile.

Some weeks later, when Dautry sent Allier to London to brief British officials on Fred's progress, he arrived in time to attend the first meeting of the famous secret Maud Committee, which had been set up by the Ministry of Aeronautical Production to study a memorandum from Otto Frisch and another refugee, the German Rudolf Peierls, discussing the feasibility of an atom bomb. This was based on Bohr's latest hypothesis that only the uranium isotope 235, which was found in a mass of uranium in the ratio of one to one hundred and forty, underwent fission. The pair came to the conclusion that no material or structure on earth could resist the force of a nuclear bomb triggered by neutron fission of isolated uranium 235. However, Frisch and Peierls were talking in terms of kilograms of isotopes, while Fred and Irène and other radiochemists were still dealing in milligrams. The problem of isotope separation on that scale raised too many questions about any possibility of success before the end of the war, and most of the Maud Committee were already overextended perfecting the radar which enabled the English to win the Battle of Britain.

While in London Allier learned that on April 9, one month to the day after he signed the agreement in Rjukan loaning the heavy-water free to France for the duration, German sea and airborne divisions invaded Norway. Norwegian resistance was not broken until the end of the month.

Irène's health was not holding up, and now she was also troubled with anemia. She was ordered to take a long rest daily, and the doctors wanted her to return to the mountains for a month's cure. But she did not feel that she could leave, for if Paris was bombed, the Curie Laboratory's radioactive substances would have to be placed in security somewhere.

Fred and his team encountered increasing war-related difficulties with their work, but progressed sufficiently to apply for two more secret patents. Additional sealed reports to maintain France's front-line position in the fields of radioactivity and nuclear physics were placed alongside those already deposited with the Academy of Sciences. During that same month of May, Fred found time to help create, and become the first president of, the National University

Front, an organization which was destined to play a leading role in the Resistance.

If the siren alert early on Friday, May 10, drew more Parisians to their windows than into the cellars, the 7 A.M. radio announcement that German troops had invaded the Netherlands, Belgium, and Luxembourg turned the "phony war" into a real one. No one underestimated the adversary, but the man in the street had confidence in the French military.

Several days later, Irène, who had been watching the European drama unfold with increasing dismay, wrote again to Missy:

> *I feel bitter and cannot help it . . . The events of the past year have made it clear that fascism and communism are international. The fascists in different countries help each other and so do the communists. If the democracies do not develop a notion of international solidarity, they will certainly be destroyed.* [7]

On the fifteenth, German forces crossed the Meuse and started enveloping Sedan in France proper. Consternation spread through government circles. Foreign Office dignitaries in emergency sessions at the Quai d'Orsay could hear the thuds of dossiers thrown down from the landings above onto the lawn to be burned.

The sixteenth was a gorgeous spring day with trees bursting into leaf in the Bois de Boulogne. The official inauguration of the Paris Fair proceeded on schedule, but by 11 A.M., the flood of Belgian refugees and those evacuated from certain cities of the new combat zone was causing traffic snarls in outlying Paris. Movie houses, theaters, and barracks were requisitioned, and straw was brought in for bedding for these swelling numbers. Deficient in armor and aircraft, and ill-trained and ill-equipped for a war of fast movement, the French armies were stunned by the collapse of the vaunted Maginot Line. With a command riddled with muddled incompetence, they could not resist the sweep of the German Panzer divisions and Air Force. Nothing stood between the enemy and

Paris. That afternoon, Dautry, who was one of the few to keep his head amid the bad news being received hourly, telephoned Fred with orders that the heavy-water must be moved to a place of safety at once.

"Henri!" Fred picked up the interoffice phone and called Henri Moureu, his deputy director at the Collège de France's chemistry section. "Henri! Come here at once!"

"It was my boss. The unaccustomed sharpness of his voice made my heart skip a beat," Moureu recalled. "I hurried in . . . The minute I saw his drained face, I knew it was something very serious."

"The front has been pierced at Sedan. Dautry just telephoned. We must take the heavy-water to a safe place in Central France immediately. In absolute secrecy. I am entrusting it to you. You have *carte blanche.*"[8]

It was no easy task, with the Third Republic disintegrating, to find a home for a mysterious product named "Z" whose use was a military secret. However, two hours later, after considerable arm-twisting and flag-waving, Moureu was assured that the Banque de France's Clermont-Ferrand branch would act as depository. Rather than run the risk of something going wrong in broad daylight, he waited until 10 P.M., then parked the laboratory's little Peugeot service truck in the blind alley which ran along the back and loaded it. With a hard-to-come-by authorization to carry a pistol and accompanied by the eighteen-year-old lab assistant, Delattre, he set off.

While Moureu was driving south through the night, Churchill and his principal chiefs of staff flew across the Channel to meet with Paul Reynaud, who had succeeded Premier Daladier; and the Germans gave Paris an unexpected respite by wheeling and driving toward the Channel. At dawn Moureu arrived at his destination and stowed away his irreplaceable cargo the moment the bank opened its vault.

On May 18, the news of the evacuation of Brussels and the

installation of the Belgian government at Ostend gave Parisians a better idea of the situation. On the nineteenth, a German communiqué announced that all Holland was occupied. The military situation deteriorated daily, and five days after he accepted it, the nervous bank manager in Clermont-Ferrand notified Fred that he must find another location for "product Z."

Moureu headed south once more. This time he was accompanied by a friend, J.J. Trillat, a native of Clermont-Ferrand who, because he knew the region well, was charged with placing the radium from the Radium Institute in a secure place also. The pair ruled out a military installation because of the risk of bombardment. Similar reasoning eliminated most civilian establishments, and they settled on the Central Prison at Riom. In a code agreed upon beforehand, Moureu checked with Fred on the phone from the office of Fontanel, the subprefect of Riom, and he approved their choice. That afternoon Moureu drove into the Central Prison courtyard, where prisoners quickly unloaded the heavy-water and transported it to an isolated, well-barricaded cell normally reserved for a dangerous criminal.

The twenty-eighth of May, the capitulation of the Belgian army opened the road to Dunkerque. By the end of the first week in June, it was clear that the Germans would soon reach Paris. The quarters around the ministries were covered in a rain of ashes and soot as records were burned. Kowarski and Halban set forth from the Collège de France in an army truck loaded with the team's Geiger counters, amplifiers, spectrums, and the special lead bricks so essential for every experiment to set up a makeshift laboratory in the villa Clair-Logis, on the rue Étienne Dollet in Clermont-Ferrand. Fred and Moureu remained behind, going through their papers, saving only those that were indispensable, destroying any which might give the Germans some idea of the status of their work. They might have saved themselves the trouble, for a short time later every one of Fred's progress reports that he sent regularly to the Minister of Armaments was captured—through negligence or sabotage—as they lay in a railway car shunted to one side at La Charité-sur-Loire.

On Sunday, June 9, the Reynaud government fled in confusion to Tours. The tenth, Italy declared war on France and England. Thousands of Belgians, Dutch, Luxembourgeois, and French from the Ardennes, the Vosges, and the Marne headed south in the broiling sun before the advancing Panzer units.

June 11, Paris was declared an open city, and its streets assumed a deserted air as Parisians brought up the rear of the sinister caval-cade. Fred, Irène, and Moureu were the last to leave the empty Collège de France laboratories. They departed under a sky shrouded with black smoke from the bombed refineries that were burning west of the city. These days were more haunting for Irène than for Fred, who had never seen World War I at close range. She did not know what to expect from one day to the next. Or what awaited her at the end of this sad, difficult trip. For the moment, her children were safe in Brittany. But Fred was a captain in the reserves. Would he have to leave her?

By taking the back roads and country lanes wherever possible, Moureu avoided congestion and German strafing. In Clermont-Fer-rand, a modest Center of Nuclear Studies awaited them, impro-vised by Kowarski and Halban. Without a glance at her surround-ings, Irène, with her usual simplicity of behavior, coupled now with normal fatigue aggravated by another bout of illness, lay down on the floor and promptly fell asleep.

On June 13, Churchill and Reynaud met again, this time at Tours. The fourteenth, the day the first Wehrmacht troops passed through the Porte de la Villette into Paris, Ève, who was back from the United States, where her biography of Marie was enjoying an enormous success, followed the retreating government to Bordeaux —and would then proceed to London. The fifteenth, Paris was occupied. On the sixteenth, eighty-four-year-old Marshal Pétain succeeded Reynaud as the head of the French government. Adored by millions of Frenchmen as the hero of Verdun, he was one of the few remaining symbols of French victory in World War I.

Late that same afternoon of the sixteenth, Fred was trying to momentarily forget his worries and enjoy the superb countryside and fine weather by taking a walk high above Clermont-Ferrand with Moureu. Suddenly a Simca drove up. Lieutenant Allier jumped out and beckoned Fred aside. Dautry had notified him that the army was disintegrating and the French scientists were to leave France with the heavy-water. Fred returned to Moureu: "We must proceed to Bordeaux."

Fred spent the night talking to Halban and Kowarski, first together, then separately, about fleeing the country. In reality, the pair did not have the luxury of a choice, for both were part Jewish. Fred gave them instructions how, with the cooperation of the English government, they must continue their work and carry out the unfinished, crucial experiment with the heavy-water in the name of French science and in the joint interests of the Allies.

By dawn of the seventeenth, "product Z" resumed its exodus in the same Peugeot 402 in which it had come south, along with the two men, their wives, and small children. Lying on top of the canisters, partly because the little truck was crowded and partly to conceal them, the giant Kowarski complained that his "stomach was scrambled and [his] muscles broken"[9] by the time they arrived in Bordeaux shortly before midnight.

The city was a sea of confusion. Its docks were encumbered with supplies; its streets overflowed with more than half a million refugees. Kowarski and Halban located the school provisionally housing the Ministry of Armament with difficulty. There, orders from Dautry awaited them to sail on the British collier *Broompark*, which was docked at nearby Bassens and, once in London, to present themselves at the French Mission, Westminster House, 2 Dean Stanley Street.

Fred, Irène, and Moureu left Clermont-Ferrand within hours after Halban and Kowarski did. The men deposited the ailing Irène

at Clairvivre, a small sanatorium town in the Dordogne near Péri-
gueux, and continued on to Bordeaux, where they arrived just before noon on the eighteenth. As the pair rushed up the steps to
Dautry's office, a broad-shouldered, thick-mustached man came
dashing down. Recognizing Fred, he stopped abruptly, wheeled,
and hurled himself at him. It was the Count of Suffolk, the British
liaison officer attached to the French government from the British
Directorate of Science and Industrial Research. Suffolk was
charged with rescuing certain specific scientists—he had already
rounded up twenty-five—and was one of the few who knew the
importance of Fred's research. "You must come to England with me
at once. Don't worry about your wife or children. I will be responsible for taking her to Brittany tomorrow and, from there, across the
Channel with the children." His fluent French was tinged with a
raw British accent. "Everything has already been arranged for
Halban and Kowarski. They should be on board the *Broompark*
with the heavy-water by now."[10]

Fred shook his head. "I must stay." He hurried off with Moureu
for a last meeting with Halban and Kowarski, but the Germans had
been bombing the docks, so the *Broompark* had been moved. No
one seemed to know where it was. The eighteenth of June was also
the day de Gaulle broadcast his famous declaration from London:
"The flame of French resistance . . . will not be extinguished.
France has lost a battle but France has not lost the war."[11] If Fred
did not hear de Gaulle then, or when the general repeated his
impassioned plea, a few days later, he surely read it when it was
printed up and disseminated broadside as a proclamation.

On the nineteenth the *Broompark* sailed, the last cargo ship to
leave Bordeaux, with the heavy-water and $15 million worth of
industrial diamonds lashed to a raft in case the ship was bombed. It
arrived safely in Falmouth Roads. Halban and Kowarski ultimately
settled down in Cambridge at the Cavendish, working for the
Maud Committee. The heavy-water was hidden in the prison at
Wormwood Scrubs and, little by little, discretely transferred to the

royal librarian at Windsor Castle. Fred would have no further contact with either man until the end of the war.

The British collapse at Dunkerque had accentuated France's feeling of being all alone in the struggle; even those most bitterly opposed to an armistice felt that nothing could destroy the German Army and France's chances of resisting much longer were negligible. Pétain's first official act was to sue for peace before France's total collapse in order to salvage what he could. An armistice was signed, on June 22, in Marshal Foch's former railroad car in the forest of Compiègne, and Pétain went on the air to announce that the negotiations had been concluded "in dignity and honor." Two days later a similar document was signed with Italy. To the eternal shame of those listening—and Fred probably was—his speech ended with the playing of "The Marseillaise." The country was split into Occupied and Free zones and, with the exception of the Mediterranean littoral, the Nazis possessed all the coastal areas.

The day that Pétain signed, Fred returned with Moureu to Irène at the sanatorium in Clairvivre. Whether his mind was already made up to stay when he parted company with Kowarski and Halban in Clermont-Ferrand, as the pair later claimed, or not until he saw Suffolk, is impossible to ascertain. So, too, are his exact reasons for remaining. Kowarski, like Fred's daughter Hélène and his lifelong friend Biquard, would maintain that from the start Fred never had any intention of leaving. Irène was ill, his children were in Brittany, his mother in Paris, and his mentor, Langevin, in Toulouse. A staunch patriot who was keenly pained at the national humiliation, Fred had an extensive family history of resistance to aggression, and as parochial as most of his countrymen, he could never conceive of life away from France. To remain meant to trade his bright future in atomic research for an unknown, dangerous struggle against his country's enemies who, many felt, had already won the war. But not every scientist could desert France, as Bichelonne, Dautry's chief of staff, pointed out when he saw Fred and Moureu in Bordeaux. Fred was a standard-bearer for French

science and scientific independence, and it does not seem presump-
tuous to imagine that, with his reputation and the mystique surrounding the name of Curie, Fred felt he could carry on in some
fashion. He meant to keep his laboratory at the Collège de France
functioning as a research and training center to help French science
survive what he had already predicted to Kowarski, in their last talk
at Clermont-Ferrand, would be a long Occupation. He also intended to organize resistance. On a personal level, Kowarski also
mentioned Fred's lifelong need to be surrounded by collaborators
whose deep attachment to him supplied him with a sympathetic
ambience.

Other factors may have entered in. Bertrand Goldschmidt, one
of Fred's close postwar associates, felt that his inability to speak
good English, his fear that he might not be treated as he merited,
and that he might not receive the technical assistance he needed to
continue his work also prevented his leap into the unknown.

Irène's attitude was characteristically straightforward. She had
only contempt for the Nazis. She thought them "degrading and
degraded" and had no idea of fleeing. She was convinced that they
would not dare lay a finger on a Curie, and she decided to ignore
them. That, Irène reasoned, was the proper attitude for a Curie to
take. "My mother," Francis Perrin once heard her remark, "would
never have abandoned her laboratory."[12]

After a brief visit the men returned to Bordeaux to consult once
more with Dautry. Moureu then continued on to Paris and Fred
rejoined Irène.

At 7 A.M. on June 24, Hitler entered the French capital. The
following day, hostilities officially ended and Hitler paraded his
troops under the Arc de Triomphe. A shocked France wallowed in
stupor, discouragement, and disarray, with more than one and a
half million Frenchmen prisoners of war and more than eight million people uprooted. Pétain and his administration left Bordeaux
under the protection of German troops for Vichy, which was chosen to be the new seat of the French government. There, on July

10, the Third Republic expired when the National Assembly, skill-fully manipulated by Pierre Laval, abolished its institutions and voted full authoritarian powers to Pétain. The marshal declared himself the chief of the French state, prorogued the Chambres, and, forty-eight hours later, designated Laval his vice-premier. Many Frenchmen who grossly underestimated the continued capacity of English resistance and the formidable power of the United States rallied around, profoundly ignorant of what Nazism entailed.

Fred went to Vichy briefly for instructions from the relocated Ministry of Armaments and learned that the administrator of the Collège de France, Edmond Faral, had returned to his post. Shortly afterward, Fred heard from Charles Maurain, the dean of the Collège's Faculty of Science, who was also back in Paris, that the German authorities had shown particular interest in his laboratories at the Collège and at Ivry, and that a number of German officers who seemed to be familiar with his work had asked about him. They were especially interested in the nearly finished cyclotron because Germany did not yet have one.

By the end of July, Fred advised his mother that he had been ordered to return to his laboratory, which was partly occupied by some German scientists. But there was no cause for worry because one of them was his old friend, Wolfgang Gentner, the Geiger counter expert who had worked with him at the Curie for three years.

By August 9, Fred was in Paris. Since Germans were living in the family home in the suburbs, he was staying at the Hôpital Curie, around the corner from the Radium Institute. Shortly afterward he wrote Irène:

Here all is calm and Paris is a big, agreeable city, for there is no longer that insupportable traffic and those disgusting odors of gasoline . . . Debierne is back and has brought good news about our children. I hope that you are serious and are taking your cure correctly. Don't take walks that are too long because I wish to find

*my wife in perfect health again so I can work with her this winter
. . . I am going to the city hall in Antony today to announce my
return and will try to move into our house . . . All goes well at
the Radium Institute . . .*[13]

XX
1940–1944

Occupied France

THE TWO MOST IMPOR-
tant issues and questions involving the rest of Fred's life—his attitude toward the Germans, especially those working in his laboratory, and his role as a Communist—are inextricably intertwined
and stem from the years of the German Occupation. For most
events in France during this period the true story will never be
known, not only as regards Fred but as regards many others. Not all
Frenchmen who remained in France—in fact, very few—were collaborators, and not every member of the Resistance resisted from
the beginning; many jumped on the bandwagon toward the

end, after the Russian victory at Stalingrad, when an eventual Nazi overthrow seemed more than wishful thinking.

From the outset, for the average Parisian, it was life with its daily constraints, with the German Army present but ignored by almost everybody. However, for Fred and a handful of prominent people, it was a different story because their positions kept them in the public eye. In any attempt to evaluate their individual actions while the Germans held sway, it is essential to remember that nothing was all black or all white, but shades of gray during this period about which so much remains to be uncovered. Little was what it seemed to be on the surface; many were playing dangerous games —with their own lives and those of their dear ones at stake—in a perilous, volatile situation for a variety of motives and reasons. But few are anxious to relive those tragic days and bring culprits to trial in order to ferret out and lay to rest the insidious, malicious rumors that still abound in numerous specific instances.

In Fred's case, there are certain documented and known facts and these, together with what is only hinted at, must be presented side by side and so labeled. Beyond that, nothing can be ascertained except for two indisputable things. Fred made a conscious decision to remain in France and returned to Paris when he was in an enviable position to leave the country, well armed with excellent reasons to do so. And, for Fred, patriotism and science were inextricably intertwined. Whatever his subsequent actions, wherever they led him, these two points must be retained and everything else weighed against them—whether he was a genuine member of the Resistance from the start or only intended this role as a cover-up for his collaboration—or vice versa. Or, whether like Talleyrand, he succeeded in keeping a foot in both camps. Whatever he did, patriotism was unquestionably the underlying motive. Fred was determined to keep French science alive during the Occupation to ensure the survival of French nuclear physics as well as the education of the next generation of scientists after the Germans departed. At a time when it was Hitler's policy to treat the French leaders with respect in the hope, not unfounded, that many would collaborate in integrating France into a German-controlled continent, Fred, a Nobel laureate and the standard-bearer of French nuclear physics, was an ideal target.

Hitler's initial arrangement with the Vichy government was a stopgap measure until England was defeated. To achieve victory, the Nazis were anxious to restart the crushed French economy and utilize its factories and laboratories to the fullest. One of the things they were most interested in was Fred's cyclotron in Paris. Norwegian resistance had been broken earlier that summer and Rjukan, with its heavy-water plant, was in Nazi hands. By now they also had access to thousands of tons of uranium ore in Belgium and in the Belgian Congo, but they lacked a cyclotron for measuring nuclear experiments.

Fred's laboratory was one of the first places visited by the officers of the Heereswaffenamt, the administration of armaments for the German Army; they were accompanied by Wolfgang Gentner, who had recently been sent to Berkeley to study Lawrence's cyclotron on the spot. But he still lacked sufficient knowledge to get the cyclotron finished and, then, utilized to its maximum. Without Fred there, nothing could be accomplished. No one knew if, or when, he would come back, so they sealed the doors of the lower basement laboratory where the cyclotron was located and left. As soon as Fred reappeared, so did the Heereswaffenamt with Gentner as interpreter. General Erich Schumann, who was a physicist himself, as well as a descendant of the composer Robert Schumann, was filled with the traditional German respect for a "Herr Professor," let alone so distinguished a one. He assembled the personnel, praised Fred to the skies for his many achievements, then ushered him into a nearby office and shut the door.

A rapid barrage of tough, direct questions ensued—"On what boat did Kowarski and Halban flee?" Three vessels left Bordeaux the day they sailed on the *Broompark*. The other two were sunk by the Luftwaffe, so Fred named one of them. "Where was the heavy-water?" Fred did not have to pretend; at the moment he did not know its exact location in Britain. "Where was the uranium?" Fred knew his stock had been sent to Morocco, but he feigned ignorance as to its whereabouts. A few cursory inquiries concerning the cyclotron were equally adroitly fielded. Scarcely the wiser, the officers clumped out, followed by Gentner, who trailed behind long enough to make a secret rendezvous to meet Fred, around 6 P.M. that evening, in the back of a small bistro they used to frequent together in happier days.

Because of their long-standing friendship, the conversation, when they met, was a painful one, at least for Gentner. The cyclotron was almost ready for its trial runs, and he told Fred that the Heereswaffenamt, who had tried unsuccessfully during Fred's absence to work with it, planned to ship it east. The Heidelberg group of nuclear scientists, for whose use it was intended, warned of the impracticality of doing so. Because of its heavy magnets, it would be an almost impossible task to ease the twenty-seven-ton apparatus out of its lower basement cocoon, some thirty feet underground. By the time it was dismantled, reassembled, and the necessary finishing touches added, the war would undoubtedly be over. It was far more practical to leave the cyclotron where it was and have it attended by the French technicians, who did not need to be trained, as their German peers would, to handle the delicate machinery. Gentner had been asked to head the group in charge of the machine, if it remained in Paris. Should he accept, Gentner would also be held responsible for the entire laboratory; this meant surveillance of Fred's entire personnel and their output as well. Gentner wondered if he would be acceptable to Fred in this capacity? The cyclotron, with its ability to produce the intense sources of radioactivity needed for further research in the field pioneered by two generations of the Curie family, was the cornerstone of any future work at the Radium Institute. Since one of Fred's avowed aims was to assure the continuity of what Pierre and Marie had started, it was imperative that this equipment not leave. He also infinitely preferred Gentner's presence in his laboratory to that of any stranger.

The next morning, Gentner reported to his superiors that if the Heereswaffenamt agreed in writing that the cyclotron was not to be used for any experiment connected with war work but only for basic research, and if Fred was kept abreast of what specific projects the Germans tackled while working with it there, Fred would cooperate and see that the cyclotron was properly maintained. "What will my friends in England and America think of my decisions? That is my only concern,"[1] Fred would repeatedly ask Toshiko Yuasa in the months ahead. The young Japanese woman was already en route to Paris to study with Fred when the war broke out, and he took an almost paternal interest in her, especially during the Occupation.

By the end of September, the Joliot home at Antony was restored to the family in reasonable condition. Irène was back and resumed her normal schedule, coming in as regularly as her health permitted. The children also returned as the Occupation forces had evacuated the entire Western littoral. Everywhere the German presence was increasingly evident. It was harder to get permission, let alone gas, to move about freely. The black market made its appearance and did a land-office business throughout the war.

October saw the initialing of the Rome-Berlin-Tokyo pact, as well as Hitler and von Ribbentrop's ominous Montoire meeting with Pétain and Laval. The word "collaboration" entered the French vocabulary. Those who participated in the start of the new academic year in Occupied Paris are never likely to forget the extraordinary atmosphere; others will find it hard to imagine. Beneath the daily activity and normal preoccupations, everyone was questioning himself, and once the staff and students were back, the first stirrings began spontaneously in those circles where resistance traditionally has its roots. Letters from several militants were read and various possibilities of how to save French intellectual life were discussed. After attending one of these gatherings with the physicist Jacques Solomon, Langevin's brilliant son-in-law, Fred, Solomon, and one or two others who shared with them the need to no longer remain isolated, set up the nucleus of what was to blossom into the Front National Universitaire, the first full-fledged cell of resistants in the Faculty of Sciences and the Collège de France. As soon as anti-Nazi tracts appeared on the Left Bank, the Germans discarded their masks of "peaceful cooperation," and swept dozens of professors and students into jail.

On Wednesday, October 30, on the eve of the Toussaint—"All Saints' Day"—vacation, two Gestapo cars drove up before no. 10 rue Vauquelin and immediately sealed off the entrances to the EPCI administration building. They had come to fetch Langevin and deliver him to La Santé jail. There the distinguished, sixty-eight-year-old man was searched, his personal effects confiscated, including his fountain pen, shoelaces, and belt, and he was placed without any reading matter, paper, or pencils in a cell with petty criminals. Langevin was held incommunicado and it took his family and Fred three days to find out what had happened to him. Finally they were informed that he was being held because of his antifascist work before the war, especially in Spain. Fred's reaction can easily be imagined, but he was hamstrung in his many efforts to free his mentor.

Langevin's arrest, which was intended to strike terror into the heart of the embryonic Resistance, only spurred its growth. As the news spread, protest poured in from everywhere, even from abroad. Many of his former "sèvriennes" hastened to write to him, proudly signing their names, as did the rest of his friends—an act of defiant courage because to do so automatically placed each one on the Gestapo's dreaded lists.

Early on Friday, November 8, the day when Langevin was scheduled to give his first fall lecture, tracts were distributed by young Communists in front of the Collège de France, calling for a demonstration that evening. Anticipating trouble, the Gestapo promptly ordered the doors of the amphitheater, inside, locked. Students who were registered for Langevin's class, one of the most popular there, swarmed around the corridors, frustrated, wondering what was going to happen. Would there be a substitute? At the appointed hour, Fred arrived. Elegantly attired as always, he brushed past the Germans so authoritatively that none dared to stop him. Startled at his unexpected appearance, the crowd in the packed passage recognized him and made way. Fred proceeded to the locked doors, drew a key from his pocket, dramatically opened them, and strode down onto the stage. Every seat was quickly taken and there was a large overflow impatiently waiting outside to hear what he had to say. His voice breaking with an emotion that added eloquence to his words, Fred announced that he was closing his laboratory and suspending his classes until Professor Langevin, "the glory and pride of France," was released from prison. His audience sat stunned. It was one thing to courageously challenge the Nazis as publicly as Fred had by opening the amphitheater; by closing his laboratory and withdrawing his technicians, he was also paralyzing the research of the German scientists there.

Long before Langevin's arrest, both the German and French authorities had, for obvious reasons, forbidden any celebration on Armistice Day, including the traditional parade on the Champs-Élysées. However, a group of students had already planned to go up to the Étoile and leave some flowers on the Tomb of the Unknown Soldier, and Langevin's unjust detention swelled their ranks to some five thousand. The German police brutally dispersed them with gunfire; eighteen were killed, a number wounded, and the many who were arrested were soon sentenced to long jail terms. This bloody melee was a prominent factor in pushing further resistance underground.

When Gentner, who was momentarily in Heidelberg, returned and learned what had transpired at the laboratory during his absence, he was understandably upset. The latest model of an essential component that he had ordered from a German army depot had just arrived to replace the one presently in the cyclotron. The

French original was one of the many "do-it-yourself" parts in the apparatus and had been resurrected by Fred from a radio set which he had built as a teenager. It had been installed by some unidentified technician whom Gentner scornfully characterized as "a well-intentioned amateur." Gentner was convinced that the faulty item was the reason why the balky prima donna was functioning so unreliably and was anxious to see if he was correct. This he could not do with the laboratory closed.

To demand the freedom of a French prisoner was a risky, tricky business, even for a German and, especially, in this instance where two separate Nazi authorities were involved. The Gestapo had Langevin in its clutches, while Gentner and his crew came under the jurisdiction of the Heereswaffenamt. Once he was able to determine that there was no specific, valid reason for Langevin's arrest, Gentner successfully persuaded the Gestapo that holding up work on the cyclotron any longer was harmful to the war effort, and a compromise was eventually negotiated that was also acceptable to Fred. Forty-seven days after he was first picked up, Langevin was transferred to Troyes, a small town some one hundred and fifty kilometers east of Paris, where he would remain under house surveillance until shortly before the war's end.

In the interim, before Langevin was moved, the first issue of L'Université Libre appeared and was almost entirely devoted to him. Edited and printed up by Jacques Solomon and one or two others, it was destined to be one of the Resistance's principal clandestine organs.

Fred's present preoccupation with the effects of radiation on humans and animals was the sort of work he was about to undertake before he heeded the siren call of nuclear fission, and he had long since established a biological section at Ivry but been too busy to work there. Assisted by a dozen or so researchers, he was likewise using radioactive tracers to do studies of biological and chemical processes, especially in the functioning of the thyroid gland. He was also collaborating with Dr. Antoine Lacassagne, the director of the Pasteur Laboratory of the Radium Institute, in an effort to provoke cancer of the liver in a rabbit irradiated by neutrons.

These various projects were enough to keep him more than busy, but even taking into consideration the additional hours his lecturing required, Fred's scientific and academic activities together hardly justified the increasing amount of time he was away from home. Sometimes he left early in the morning and did not return until late at night. Or not at all. He never explained these absences to Irène, and she was wise enough not to ask. Nor did he ever introduce her to the occasional visitor who appeared on the threshold at Antony. Generally he never knew their names himself. Fred's work with the twelve-odd members of the Resistance Committee he helped set up earlier at the Faculty of Sciences involved many secret meetings, and rarely in the same place, although he often used his artist sister Marguerite's atelier.

By November, a *modus vivendi* was established in Fred's Collège de France laboratories. In accordance with the terms of his agreement with the Heereswaffenamt, both the Germans, who established themselves on the second floor, and the French, who were on the other seven, abstained from anything to do with what was then referred to as "the uranium question." Fred had access to the intruders' rooms, and he secretly verified what they were up to each night. A handful of the German physicists, entirely wrapped up in their own world, lived in the ivory tower of pure science; the others, together with the various technicians and assistants accompanying them, were by and large younger men with less restricted interests. As 100 percent Nazis, they looked down upon the French with contempt. With a keen curiosity about everything going on in the other parts of the building, they represented the potential for a dangerous situation. Fortunately, the presence of a few collaborators among Fred's forty workers acted as a safety valve by evincing sufficient pro-German sentiment, so that the rest of the French were able to maintain an air of passive indifference and sink into anonymity. One of the Führer's more ardent admirers, a big blond

Lorraine woman, made an excellent, unwitting cover for Ligon-nière, a technician there who has left an account of his personal Resistance activities. He took this chemistry assistant regularly to a tiny restaurant on the rue Jean-Gujon that was a favorite of many German officers and, accordingly, served as an important source of information concerning Occupation troop movements.

Gentner was responsible for the building's overall surveillance, but his primary aim was to maintain the cooperation of Fred and his staff in order to keep the laboratory functioning smoothly. So in order to eliminate friction, he forbade any German to set foot in the French part unless personally authorized by Fred to do so. And to avoid, if possible, any disruptive, surprise visit from one of the many overlapping branches of the Occupation administration on patrol around the capital, Gentner instructed the concierge that he wanted to be warned immediately upon the arrival of any German, in mufti or out, and told him to advise visitors that no one was admitted under any circumstances without a *laissez-passer* from Gentner. Superior officers of the Wehrmacht paid an occasional official call. With German punctiliousness, they could be relied upon to always appear at the same time and, no doubt, they chose the noon hour because that was when most of the staff was at lunch. They could not have picked a better time, according to Ligonnière. "It was preferable that as few people as possible witness what ["le patron"] . . . had to endure without lowering himself too much. The few pro-Germans who might have been present would have [been delighted and] made a great to-do . . . while the others would have considered M. Joliot, as a result, a collaborator."[2]

Certain contemporaries might later accuse Fred of outright collaboration with the German fission program because the Nazi physicists were working on problems of fundamental nuclear physics. And one Curie technician was heard to mutter, at a ceremony shortly after the war, when Fred received France's highest Resistance medal: *"Eh bien, mon brave!* If the Germans had won, you would have fared just as well."[3] But it is important to remember that Fred—and, for that matter, Gentner himself—remained convinced that a nuclear bomb could not be built until after the war. Because hostilities erupted before he was able to make any conclusive tests with the Rjukan heavy-water, Fred did not even know if a chain reaction was feasible. And he would not learn, until after the liberation of Paris that Halban and Kowarski did successfully carry out in England the interrupted, crucial heavy-water experiment which they had not had time to finish in Paris in December 1940.

Whatever went on of a Resistance nature within the laboratory walls, Gentner saw nothing. Or did not want to see anything. On several occasions, he even went so far as to warn Fred if he learned that one of the French staff was under Gestapo surveillance. The situation prevailing between Gentner and Fred was unique in those troubled times when suspicion and doubt gave free rein to every sort of false interpretation. So it is not surprising that Fred, who exclaimed more than once to Ligonnière, "What one must endure to keep the laboratory open!"[4] should have been tarred and feathered in many quarters. Gentner's actions are verified by his own postwar interviews, including one with Fred's daughter Hélène, in which he adds he saw to it everyone working in the laboratory was provided with supplementary food coupons and cigarettes.

Not every piece of the puzzle concerning Fred's wartime activities fits neatly into place and rare are the documented ones. But those who never lived in an occupied country cannot, especially in retrospect, pass judgment on those who have. A good example is the compromising, exceedingly lengthy interview he gave, February 15, 1941, to the pro-Nazi Les Nouveaux Temps. In the article Fred lashed out against the graduates of the elite École Polytechnique, whom he blamed as "largely responsible, among others, for our industrial bankruptcy and deficiency in war materials." He laid the blame not on the "technicians" themselves, but "on the spirit of this institution . . . It is this spirit which we must correct." This was a typical view of the liberals of the day who, like most Frenchmen, had been brooding over their country's shortcomings ever since the Nazi juggernaut rolled over France. In purple prose, Fred continued: "We others, French scientists passionately attached to our country, must have the moral courage to draw the lesson from our defeat. What do we see? A fall in the quality of the men who became our leaders." But this was neither the time nor the place to call for a removal of all class privileges and barriers to entering a scientific career, and the damning article prompted one of Fred's most distinguished contemporaries to comment on it years later: "One should not wash one's dirty linen in the pages of the Occupants' newspaper."[5]

Gentner's appearance with the distinguished physicist Professor Bothe, who was presently the director of the Institute of Physics at the Kaiser Wilhelm Institute of Medical Research at Heidelberg, at Fred and Irène's on a Sunday afternoon is easier to explain; but it caused enough of a stir at the time for their daughter Hélène to remember the day long afterward. Patriotic Frenchmen rarely socialized with the Nazis, but Irène was Marie's own daughter where convention was concerned, wartime or no. She had a long-standing acquaintance with both men, and she may have been interested in seeing the elderly visitor simply as a fellow scientist whose work on alpha rays with Becker had been the point of departure for the Joliots' discovery of artificial radioactivity. Even throughout the war years, Fred and Irène maintained their regular Sunday open house, for which no invitation was ever issued and at which all generations mixed. It was greatly appreciated by their apartment-dwelling Parisian friends in those days of heavily restricted travel, especially in the summertime. Fred still had no dearth of tennis partners, and like everything else he did, he played to win on the court, declaring the score, point after point, in a loud, triumphant voice.

Fortunately, Irène kept at home the telephone number of the small hotel near the Étoile where Gentner was living, which he had given Fred in case of an emergency. For on June 29, either before or after she received him as a guest at Antony—it would be interesting to know exactly when—a worried Irène called to advise Gentner that Fred had still been at the breakfast table when two Occupation officials in civilian attire called at their home. They picked him up on the suspicion that he was encouraging resistance among the University students, and the three drove off in an unmarked car. Gentner was more angry than alarmed. To avoid such an eventuality and any work stoppage that might ensue, like the one following Langevin's arrest, he had specifically requested that his superior, General Schumann, notify all pertinent authorities that the Heereswaffenamt was doing secret work at the Collège de France, and it alone was responsible for the laboratory there and its personnel. To be of any help to Fred, Gentner must know who ordered his arrest. The pair who came for him had not said, and this would not be easy to determine since most offices were closed on Sunday. Gentner promised to do what he could; he would not leave his room so that Irène could keep him posted on any further developments at her end. Irène next called her long-standing hiking friend, Angèle Pompei, who hurried over, and the two sat down to wait. Even for calm, cool, collected Irène, this must have been the longest day in her life.

Only one other person was sitting in the unswept waiting room in the almost deserted police headquarters on the Île de la Cité, and there was a single uniformed agent on guard when Fred arrived. The other man, who had also been brought in for questioning, knew Fred by sight, and when he introduced himself Fred recognized his name. Maurice Bataillon was also a member of the Committee of Antifascist Vigilance and the two decided that they were probably apprehended because of their membership in this organization. Its head had been seized, a few days earlier, in a general roundup of numerous people with questionable political affiliations. To their surprise, a secretary appeared with some newspapers which she deferentially offered them to read. Neither one did so.

For a man who was never at a loss for words, Fred was strangely silent and only talked in fits and starts. They discussed their chances of going home again, and Fred mentioned his laboratory. "I will never forget," Bataillon said later, "the assurance with which he told me that the German physicists working at his side would intervene in his favor. It was plainly inconceivable to him that scientific camaraderie would not manifest itself, regardless of nationality, in this situation."[6] As president of the International Scientific Workers of the World, Fred would work hard in the postwar years to further the materialization of this ideal, but to nourish such a thought under his present circumstances seems naive, when viewed retrospectively. However, the Germans were not yet sweeping everyone up—the more important, the better—and shipping them off to concentration camps for the flimsiest of reasons.

Toward the end of the morning, the pair were ushered into the office of the courteous Alsatian inspector general. Their joint interrogation ended up as a pleasant conversation with no hint regarding the immediate future. About 1 P.M., someone remembered that neither Fred nor Bataillon had eaten and offered to send out for something from a nearby restaurant—at the men's expense. But they did not have time to finish the food, when they were ordered into a bus with two police agents and taken to the Gestapo's sinister general headquarters in the former French Ministry of the Interior on the rue des Saussaies. Here, only Fred was ordered out; Bataillon continued on to an unknown destination.

Late that night an exhausted Fred, his face white and drawn, returned to Irène on the little electric car that serviced the Luxembourg line. Thanks once again to Gentner's timely intervention, he had been only briefly examined and then set free. The Gestapo official who took the phone call ordering his immediate release obsequiously offered to send the "Herr Professor" home. Fred politely declined. The last thing in the world he wanted to do was to be chauffeured out to Antony in an official Nazi car. Then people really would think he was a collaborator.

On June 22, 1941, the Sunday before Fred had been apprehended, Hitler had astounded the world by wheeling on his ally, Stalin, and ordering his armies to open hostilities on the two thousand-mile Russian front. The French Communist Party's position had been greatly weakened ever since the fall of 1939 when it had been declared illegal, following the Nazi-Russian nonaggression pact. But it promptly heeded Moscow's orders to make life so difficult for the Germans in Occupied France that they must keep more troops in the West. Direct liaison with Russia was quickly broken, however, except for an occasional parachutist, and Jacques Duclos, the spokesman for international communism in the three-man Secretariat that ran the French Party while Thorez remained in Moscow, at once came out in support of the Allies. Now it was clear to the French Communists why they must fight—not because of some of Stalin's convoluted policies, but for their children to have bread and a future in a free France. No longer considered a band of vulgar terrorists, the Communists would eventually be endowed with a patriotic halo and regarded by both the Germans and Vichy as the most dangerous part of the Resistance. Although there were always individuals of every hue in the underground, the Communists played a dominant role through the different Resistant cells they set up or infiltrated.

Up until now, the various small university groups, like the Antifascist Intellectuals, which had all been forced into clandestinity after the ill-fated Armistice Day massacre of the previous year, did little more than try to keep each other's spirits up. They stayed in mutual contact largely through Jacques Solomon's illegal *L'Université Libre,* and the many imitations his leaflet spawned. Once the French Communist Party joined the fray, it instigated the creation in the Occupied Zone of a National Resistance Organization for the Liberation and Freedom of France. It was the type of assemblage which the party, with its tight discipline and its membership already forced underground, was in a commanding position to quickly dominate. Fred, who was disillusioned with the socialists ever since Blum's policy of nonintervention in the Spanish Civil

War, already knew a lot of Communists, largely through Langevin, and now he was thrown into contact with many more. As the recently chosen head of the small knot of resistants in the University of Paris, Fred was one of the few non-Communist members appointed to the governing committee of the new National Front, as it was popularly called. Proud of so outstanding a recruit, the Communists soon elevated him to its presidency, a post he would keep throughout the Occupation, although Pierre Villon, a Communist architect, was actually in charge overall.

The National Front was an umbrella organization that soon had a counterpart in Unoccupied France with which it later merged, and it expanded slowly. Rather than confine its units to definite geographic locales, it differed from other resistant clusters by setting itself up by specific professions throughout the country, consciously positioning itself for power in postwar years. If there were University personnel—teachers and students—in all the groups of the Resistance, it was only in the National Front that a special section was reserved exclusively for them. This academic entity, like the others in the National Front, eventually produced and disseminated its own newspaper and literature. Until 1942 the National Front was really only a skeleton of its future self, making contact with other similar bodies, some of them quite conservative politically. A loose union was formed which papered over the peacetime quarrels between them, and gradually, the National Front became the largest, best-organized, and most belligerent of the lot and assumed a commanding position; however, the National Front never succeeded in reaching its goal of encompassing every resistant. As president of its executive committee, Fred's most important decisions were primarily political ones, involving negotiations with other Resistance groups, relationships with leaders abroad, and the manipulation of public opinion.

Normal life in France was paralyzed. Ration stamps were needed for clothing, tobacco, and shoes, and lines formed for everything. At Antony, Irène and Fred had sufficient land to grow their own produce, with plenty still left over to help other less fortunate colleagues. Irène's daily fare, however, was far from adequate for anyone suffering from tuberculosis or anemia.

On the pretext that she wanted to pick up some laboratory equipment that she had left there during her stay in the tiny sanatorium town, following the evacuation of Paris, Irène got permission to return to Clairvivre. Actually, she wanted to retrieve the radium which Marie had received as a gift from America, as well as the gold, platinum, and other valuable metals from their joint laboratories that she and Fred managed to cache there at the time of the fall of France. Because Fred was refused a permit to leave Occupied France, she was accompanied by two of her technicians. Later that summer, when her chronic indisposition necessitated a return to pure mountain air, Gentner intervened and got permission for her to go to a sanatorium where Swiss friends had invited her. Since there were no diplomatic relations between Occupied France and Switzerland, Gentner's wife acted as intermediary for Fred and Irène's correspondence. At the end of a ten-day stay in the sanatorium proper, Irène moved into a nearby pension, while still remaining under the care of the same doctor. The physical plant might not be as sumptuous, but she was supposed to gain weight, and the food at the pension agreed with her better. Although she sent home a picture to prove that she had put on five pounds, and she got out of breath less easily, Irène was there well into October. She kept busy working on a complete history of the radioelements and tried to console herself "hunting hazelnuts" while Fred took the children camping overnight in a tent at Soisy-sous-Étiolles, where he kept a small boat for fishing on the Seine since he could no longer go to L'Arcouest.

The income from the balance of the Marie Curie Fund from her mother's first trip to the United States was still being deposited regularly in Geneva and proved a godsend to help defray Irène's expenses. Missy, in New York, and Ève, who was in London, were working together to try and find a way to get the four Joliots out of France. But Irène and Fred were not interested. Irène wrote Missy:

Til now nothing is changed in our intentions. We think we have a mission to fill: to prevent the dispersal of the scientific workers from our laboratories and the loss of the radioelements needed for our work that were collected by my mother and ourselves. If we find that, for some reason or other, we cannot be useful any more, then we will try [to leave] . . . If there are no other reasons than the hardship of life, next winter, it is not so very dangerous for [my health.]

A short time later, on August 30, Irène wrote again:

Fred is happy to know that it would perhaps be possible, by way of exchange [for another couple] . . . to go to the United States. We both think that we must not do it now, but if the circumstances would compel us to change our mind, we will arrange [to let you know.][7]

Because the United States was not yet at war, the American ambassador was still very active in France. He had already helped Jean Perrin and Pierre Auger, another L'Arcouestien, cross the Atlantic, and later that fall, possibly as a result of Missy's and Ève's efforts, he made the same offer to Fred. Fred turned him down "because," he told Gentner, "he felt obliged to remain in Paris near his colleagues who were unable to leave France."[8]

That spring, fellow physicists in the United States were already working on the problem of separating the isotope uranium 235 in quantity, and at Berkeley, Glenn Seaborg demonstrated that the isotope 239 of the new element, plutonium, which he had lately discovered, fissioned with slow neutrons even more readily than did U 235. Then, in June, a brilliant report by Britain's Maud Committee, based on Peierls and Frisch's findings of some months past, moved the possibility of constructing an atomic bomb from the realm of pure scientific conjecture into the realm of the possible. Since Peierls and Frisch's work was based on public knowledge, there was every reason to assume that Nazi scientists had arrived at a similar conclusion. If the atom bomb was now feasible, someone would surely make it. But who? Since the British were fighting alone, and the United States was still neutral, the Maud Committee report was sent there posthaste. F.D.R.'s exploratory committee, set up under Vannevar Bush to study the matter, grasped its importance immediately. Aware the Germans might already have a head start, the President had the immense Manhattan Project already on the drawing boards before Pearl Harbor, that December 7. Without the report of the Maud Committee, it is questionable whether the war might not have been over before an A-bomb was dropped.

That same summer, Fred's Collège de France colleague Henri Moureu was appointed director of the Paris Municipal Laboratory of the prefecture of police. Since the police were responsible for any acts of sabotage in the city, Moureu received all the unexploded devices seized by the Germans. This proved an unintentional windfall for the underground. For Moureu, instead of destroying these explosives and detonators after he made his official report, passed them on to Fred. They would then be recycled and used once again by the Resistance. Moureu was also a regular Sunday visitor at Antony and brought invaluable detailed information for the saboteurs.

As the Resistance slowly grew, sabotage, while still sporadic, rose, and the Germans had the army post guards around the clock at a number of important buildings in Paris. They intended to do the same to protect the cyclotron, but Fred persuaded them to let his personnel take turns, on a night-shift basis, to guarantee its security. Whether he intended it to work out the way it actually did or not, Fred's arrangement was, like Moureu's appointment, providential for the Resistance activities beginning to be conducted there. It permitted Ligonnière and two cohorts to return after supper and even spend the night there, if they did not have time to get home before the midnight curfew, without anyone getting suspicious.

Because the BBC was generally badly scrambled by the Germans, news was hard to come by, but Ligonnière successfully concocted a makeshift gadget, small enough to hide inside a purse, that could cut through the static. He and his two fellow conspirators turned out so many that their workbenches resembled an assembly line. Then the Germans garbled London even more. Since it was imperative that the coded Resistance information coming in over the air from England be clearly heard, Ligonnière, with considerable ingenuity, built a permanent listening station that could function under every circumstance, right there in the laboratory.

The Japanese attack on Pearl Harbor on December 7 changed the war picture by catapulting the Americans into the fray. December 8, the United States and Britain declared war on Japan, and on the eleventh, Hitler and Mussolini did the same on the United States, making the war worldwide. However, the Wehrmacht's impressive string of Russian victories only underlined the general French opinion of its invincibility, as it steamrolled over Smolensk, Kiev, and Odessa to arrive at the gates of Moscow. In the interim, General Charles de Gaulle set up the National French Committee in London to further establish himself as the head of the Free French, and his representative to the Resistance, Jean Moulin, repeatedly crossed the French-Spanish border.

Shortly before the end of the year, long after Irène was back in Paris, one of the Curie Laboratory's chief researchers, the brilliant Fernand Holweck, who started his career there as an assistant to Marie, although he never worked with her, was arrested as he passed through the grilled fence to enter the Radium Institute. A member of a small, isolated Resistance team, which was primarily concerned with helping downed British aviators flee to Spain and had been infiltrated by a police agent, his shocking death from torture was the first in scientific circles and spread ripples of fear throughout the entire academic community. Others of Fred and Irène's circle were picked up; Marguerite Borel's husband, Émile, was imprisoned for six months.

The winter of 1941–42 was so severe, weather-wise, that Parisians' main fears were chilblains and missing the last Métro. The most important news item to be read in the paper, first thing each morning, was what different food coupons were good for. Nine-year-old Pierre had rubella and mumps; fourteen-year-old Hélène, rubella. Irène could not shake bronchitis and, the end of February, noted in her journal that it was one degree Centigrade—about thirty-four degrees Fahrenheit—in their bedrooms, but they were able to keep the dining room at eight to nine degrees. Small wonder the adjectives "cold and sad" made their initial appearance in her handwriting. She was not well enough to come to town daily, as in the past, and even slim Fred was slimmer. Parisians were warned not to eat cats because they ate rats, and the latter were full of bacteria often fatal to man. Tobacco was rationed, so one of Fred's assistants picked up butts on the street, emptied out their contents, and carefully re-rolled them into new cigarettes for "le patron." Whether chain-smoking Fred was desperate enough to use them is not recorded.

Not surprisingly, Resistance activities, while still sporadic, were growing and required specialized supplies. So Ligonnière and his two accomplices switched to building radio transmitters and receivers for different Resistance units. Later, when false identification papers were required, they persuaded a young doctoral candidate in the laboratory to neglect his thesis and prepare them. Someone else working there also joined forces with Ligonnière's small band and agreed to use his address at the Collège for a mail drop. If Fred was aware of these varied, increasing activities, he never let on, but he knew his own phone was bugged and was afraid there might be hidden microphones in his office. So one day, to play it safe, he called Ligonnière out into the Collège courtyard. There Fred warned him to be careful. "The laboratory's whole existence could be compromised." And, at the war's end, Ligonnière flatly declared that all his activities "had always been supported by M. Joliot, who had known and done everything possible to help us."[9]

After Fred's death, when his quarters were being prepared for his successor, Pierre Radvanyi, a nuclear physicist at the Collège de France after the war, and Roger Mayer, Fred's secretary during his final years, both found incriminating papers stuffed—presumably in haste—behind cumbersome pieces of furniture which were so heavy that several men were required to move them. These were given to his daughter Hélène and included a map of importance to the underground, a false card of identity with a blank space for the name of the bearer to be filled in, and a complete series of documentations regarding Occupation troops, as well as lists of clandestine journals.

Accused by some of being a collaborator, watched suspiciously by others as a dangerous patriot, Fred's ambiguous position must have doubled the tremendous nervous strain being in the Resistance posed. As one member of the underground so aptly expressed it: "The front was nowhere and enemies everywhere."[10] To escape the omnipresent Gestapo—and the Vichy police who worked hand in glove with the Germans—Fred and the other members of the National Front Committee met in little bistros, a dentist's waiting room, in the Museum of Natural History, even in the *allées* of the Palais-Royal. Possibly to allay suspicions, he gave an important lecture on radioactivity to a parterre of prominent Vichyites, as well as Germans, in the Collège de France amphitheater.

Langevin, still living under house detention in Troyes, with his mail automatically opened, represented to the world outside France a living symbol of intellectual resistance. Scientists as far apart, geographically and politically, as Einstein in America, and Kapitza in the U.S.S.R., tried to win him freedom. It took courage for Fred to slip away to visit him, and when he did, the indomitable old gourmet managed to observe his lifelong custom of personally brewing his guest a cup of real coffee—a minor miracle in those days of ersatz foods, especially in a small provincial town.

The rigors of life in Occupied Paris were hard on everyone and, unfortunately, Irène was again far from well. Fred was so distressed by her weakness that he once more got permission, through Gentner, who was now back in Heidelberg, for her to go to a sanatorium in the Swiss High Alps, where she spent April and May. As soon as her legs got stronger and her breathing improved, Irène was allowed to take a few walks. It was hard, under any circumstances, to be separated from her family for these long periods, but in wartime deep concern about the children's safety—and Fred's—also entered in.

For the situation had altered vastly at his Collège de France laboratory. Sometime earlier that spring, a high-ranking Berlin visitor who came to see the cyclotron disliked the entire atmosphere there; he found Gentner too accommodating to Fred and his staff and denounced him roundly to the Heereswaffenamt. Gentner was promptly recalled but recommended his successor, Wolfgang Riezler of Bonn, to Fred as "a man of great courage and tact." According to an interview Gentner granted after the war, Riezler "continued the work there in the same spirit of [mutual] confidence."[11] Riezler may have, but before Gentner finally left the cyclotron was functioning satisfactorily. After his departure, it was plagued by a host of unpredictable problems which always managed to arise at the most crucial moments, frequently destroying weeks of carefully prepared experiments. Overheating was an acknowledged shortcoming of these early models, which were still as unreliable as the Geiger counter, but the other woes that now beset the Collège de France apparatus caused the veteran French technician in charge to scratch his head in mock despair. If he did not know that it was the night watchman who was systematically sabotaging the machine, he must have at least been suspicious.

Frenchmen, in general, were increasingly unsympathetic to Pétain, whose Vichy regime had from the start chosen collaboration as the only way to shield France from a harsher fate; but few were yet ready to throw their lot in with the Resistance. And it is important to remember that the Resistance in France always represented a minority of the population and, until almost the end, only a very tiny percent of that.

Jacques Solomon and his two original colleagues, who were still turning out the *L'Université Libre,* were arrested, tortured, and on May 23, shot at Mont-Valérien, on the outskirts of Paris. His wife, Hélène, Langevin's favorite daughter, and his mother, who had both helped in the operation of the clandestine press, were jailed the following day. Six months later, as they were shipped through Troyes in a cattle car en route to Auschwitz, Hélène managed to slip through the slit serving as a window a note which was delivered to her father by a sympathetic railroad employee who found it lying on the tracks; she survived the ordeal but her mother-in-law did not. Others picked up where the Solomons left off, and *L'Université Libre,* with its circulation of four thousand, did not miss a single issue; at some point during this somber period another member of Langevin's family, his sixteen-year-old grandson, Michel Langevin, only two years older than Fred's daughter Hélène, whom he eventually married, was picked up for distributing subversive material and spent six months in jail.

Fred was so shocked by the Solomon family tragedy that he asked himself: "What should I do, now, as a patriot?"[12] There was a war to be won. Life in the underground was fraught with peril; there was always the risk of betrayal, and so far, he had survived only because of loyalty. Fred had always felt as one with the people, and he found he could rely on the Communists. It was well known that not all the bourgeoisie or farmers were pro-Ally, and British Intelligence's advice to troops who got cut off from their units and fliers who had to bail out was to search for Communist workers or Catholic priests as the only two reliable havens. Fred told Henri Wallon, another Collège de France professor with whom he worked closely at this period: "If we are both captured, you will be shot because you are a Communist. If I am going to be caught, I want to be caught and shot as a Communist because the Communists are true patriots."[13] He also observed that in the intimacy of dangerous secret meetings, it was the Communists who gave the most satisfactory answers to the troubling moral questions he continually faced. So he applied for membership in the French Communist Party—the PCF. And was accepted.

This was one of the bleakest periods of the entire war, for the German armies were plunging deeper into Russia, and to be a Communist in France was to invite death at German hands. Fred's fateful decision, which he knew would affect the rest of his life, was triggered by the Solomon catastrophe, but it was not the sort to be made on the spur of the moment. Indeed, given his background and associations, especially since he was an adult, there was almost a certain inevitability surrounding this move. It is also hard to ascertain if he actually felt, at the time, that he was helping to shape a new France—if one could look that far ahead—a country in which liberty, equality, and fraternity would be based on social justice and in which science, removed from its class trappings, could truly serve all the people. Some of Fred's contemporaries today consider, in retrospect, that Fred joined largely as insurance against his future, hoping to create a new, improved public image to eclipse the whispered one of collaborator. But his stand must be taken in the context of his day, not that of a later one.

Fred's decision to shed the easy conformist life must have come as no surprise to Irène, who was back in Paris sometime around the end of May. They were too close not to have discussed it in depth. Many who knew Irène well claim that she was an even more ardent Communist than Fred. But Irène never became a card-carrying member herself, probably because, unlike Fred, she was too independent to ever submit to party discipline the way he was willing to do. One colleague also suggests that, as a Curie, she felt she was above joining any party.

On November 8, most Parisians went out for their customary

Sunday stroll, beaming at the report from the forbidden BBC of Brazzaville, which told of the successful Allied landings in North Africa. Everyone realized that this news marked some sort of turning point in the war. Three days later, the Germans invaded and took possession of Unoccupied France, brutally destroying the myth of a Free Zone; before the end of the month, as Nazi Panzer units neared Toulon, the French scuttled their fleet, which was based there, and aroused from their stupor those anti-Germans who had been giving lip service to Vichy. By now the Resistance, which was slowly achieving some degree of unity and showing signs of being a force to reckon with, attained sufficient reciprocal recognition with de Gaulle's Free French abroad to be of political and international benefit to them both.

That same fall, Winston Churchill took a personal interest in Operation Swallow, which the British successfully mounted to knock out of operation the Norsk-Hydro plant at Rjukan, Norway, after word was received that it was once again producing significant amounts of heavy-water. The Germans were nowhere near resolving the secret of the atom bomb, but at the time, neither Churchill nor anyone else realized this. Months after Allied scientists had established beyond a shadow of doubt the feasibility of making such an awesome weapon, the Germans still did not know how to produce a chain reaction in a uranium pile or how to get plutonium. With typical Teutonic arrogance, they were confident that if they could not make an atom bomb, neither could anyone else. In America, however, the Manhattan Project had already been entrusted to the American Army's Corps of Engineers with General Leslie R. Groves in charge. And on December 2, the second day of gas rationing in the United States, "the Italian navigator . . . landed in the new world."[14] Enrico Fermi, in a laboratory especially built in the doubles squash court under the football stadium of the University of Chicago, and using as a moderator carbon in the form of graphite, got a self-sustaining chain reaction. The next week, Roosevelt gave the go-ahead to pass into the industrial stage, with the first bombs scheduled to appear in the beginning of 1945. Meanwhile, Niels Bohr escaped from Denmark, and by the end of the year, he was visiting Los Alamos.

The unusually piercing cold toward the year's end, together with the poor quality of the inadequate food supply, augured additional trouble for Irène, whose health was again deteriorating. Luckily, Fred once more obtained permission for her to go to Switzerland. She went in early November, and this time she remained six months. Stopping first at a hospital in Zurich for a thorough examination, she proceeded to the sanatorium at Leysin with a nurse. Upon her arrival, Irène luxuriated in a beautiful new bathrobe and indulged herself, eating buns made of real white flour, but she was forced to admit that "these advantages cannot completely replace a husband and children. But, still, they are better than nothing. I kiss you tenderly, *mon grand chéri;* and also, *mes petits chéris.*"[15] Her days were spent lying in bed on the terrace, but she was allowed to dress and come down for dinner. And, on the whole, the time passed as well as could be expected. But she missed Fred.

Christmas was sad for the divided family. Fred wrote: "It is the first time since our marriage that we have not been together for this holiday . . . I had a lot of black thoughts, and so did Hélène. But we tried not to show them."[16] And the fact that Irène was serious, this time, about taking care of herself more than compensated. Fred was also concerned about Pierre's poor grades; these he attributed to carelessness, and he was working with Pierre to try and correct this.

For once the mail came through quickly, without the usual long wait between letters, and Irène promptly replied:

". . . I see that I certainly have an 'Ideal Husband' [This is the title of a play by Oscar Wilde.][17] . . . He takes care of the finances, [as well as] Pierre's homework, and he does not forget his wife. His wife does not forget him either . . ."[18]

She was delighted that Fred was working at home two days a

week, as she had so often suggested he do, and was able to devote more time to both Hélène and Pierre:

> *I believe that is excellent for them, partly because I am not there and, partly, because you can be good for them in certain ways that I never can. Their education is also an object of collaboration to which we both must contribute. Unfortunately, at the moment,* mon pauvre chéri, *I am letting everything fall on your shoulders, scientific work, children, household affairs . . . I hope that this will change soon. Meanwhile, I have at least gained two kilos.* [19]

Irène also wrote chatty letters to her children in which she tried hard to be cheerful and to conceal her condition as much as possible from them, especially from the younger Pierre. She did not want either one to share the sense of depression and loneliness she admitted feeling during Marie's many illnesses. She was less successful in this regard with Fred, perhaps because she had a harder time hiding her own emotions: "How I would like to be with you . . . and be able to help you instead of being a burden like I was before I left." [20]

Fred and Pierre Villon met frequently to plan the monthly meetings of the executive committee of the National Front. According to Villon, Fred never gave mere lip service at these meetings but forcefully voiced his opinion on every matter under discussion. His job was in many respects largely a political one; he received emissaries sent in secret from London, issued public statements through the organization's various clandestine newspapers, and consulted with Villon on issues the latter was to bring up with other resistant groups, including a movement to unify the various anti-Vichy groups under the exiled government of General de Gaulle. Fred also received and passed along informers' tips about police activities and anticipated raids, as well as information for the Allies concerning the effectiveness of recent bombings. And, according to Villon, when the National Front had to execute traitors, the final decision was said to have been Fred's.

On February 2, 1943, the capitulation of the German Army before Stalingrad marked the opening of an important new phase of the war, proving, as it did, that the Germans were not invincible. But nothing since the armistice gave France a greater shock than the law promulgated by Hitler himself, two weeks later, after he was forced to start drafting into the army as many of his own industrial workers as possible. The infamous *relève*—an agreement worked out with Laval the preceding June, whereby one prisoner of war was to be released for every three technicians who volunteered for work in Germany—had failed wretchedly; of the one hundred and fifty thousand needed, only seventeen thousand had materialized. The purpose of the Führer's dreaded *Service du Travail Obligatoire*—the "STO or Obligatory Work Decree"—was twofold: to replace the newly drafted Germans quickly; to remove from France as many as possible of those capable of aiding an Allied landing by causing an insurrection.

The STO affected every Frenchman between the ages of sixteen and sixty, regardless of infirmities; some women, too, were finally called up, but not for deportation as much as to replace men who were being shipped east. Frenchmen were faced with the dilemma of either submitting and going off to Germany as slave labor, or going into hiding. The entire underground press campaigned against acceptance of this mass deportation. The Allies did not want the Germans to have this extra labor, and the Resistance would need as many combatants as possible whenever Liberation Day arrived. Aided by false papers furnished by the underground, some one hundred thousand dodgers were eventually funneled into the *maquis,* as those clandestine groups who hid out in secluded regions, aided by the local peasants, came to be called.

Fred worked hard to keep young scientists from among those being shipped off. With the help of Professor Léon Denivelle, an old friend who would work closely with Fred in the Atomic Energy

Commission after the war, he set up Sedars—La Société des Études des Applications des Radioelements Artificiels ("The Society for the Study of Applications of Artificial Radioelements"). The money the pair raised from French capitalists to support this dummy company, which supposedly was to help find nonscientific uses for the cyclotron, enabled Fred to provide additional technicians with indispensable work certificates. Sedars was never very large, but setting it up furnished Fred with firsthand experience that proved helpful later, when he had to work out an effective collaboration between science and industry as head of the French Atomic Energy Commission.

The necessity of handling so many more people in the Resistance created a logistics problem, and France was crisscrossed with underground networks. Arms were a major problem, as these could only come from outside France, and unfortunately, de Gaulle had little funds. In order to get more, he saw a growing need for a National Resistance Council to affirm in Allied eyes that he had total support from the French mainland. Such a group was formed and entrusted de Gaulle with "the management of the nation's interests" a few months later.

At about the same time, word reached the West of the dissolution of the Cominterm, which had been organized in Russia in 1919 to propagate and direct communism abroad. This was welcome news that helped make the French Communist Party more attractive since it was now, supposedly, autonomous. Ever since the siege of Stalingrad, the party's image and the prestige of the U.S.S.R. and Stalin had grown enormously in the eyes of non-Communist resistants. This was helped by the Communists' systematic penetration of various Resistance groups and the subsequent placement in them, at the highest levels, of some of their most capable, devoted members. The legendary bravery of the Communists also made a big impression on outsiders and added luster to the party and to the ideals which could mold such heroes. Even the newly formed National Resistance Council's permanent steering committee of five had a decidedly pro-Communist tint. While, for foreign consumption, the council, as a group, supported de Gaulle fully, it was fairly independent of the general; there would be a great deal of friction between its Communist members and the Free French abroad over everything as D day approached.

A rare glimpse behind the brave facade Fred maintained regarding family life at Antony without Irène is afforded when he informed her that he was permitting Hélène to visit a friend over Easter vacation:

I don't like separations at this time but the trip will do her a lot of good. She needs to relax in another milieu that is gayer than our home. She has worked so hard. I have not let on that I will be unhappy not to have her with me over the holidays. For her part, she is very sorry to leave me, and I had to insist that she go. I knew how badly she wanted to. [21]

Fred apparently missed Irène greatly. She sent him a picture of herself to prove that she was putting on weight and no longer resembled an elephant full of wrinkles. "Bravo!" he replied. ". . . I authorize you to gain some more. I love plump women. [One will suffice.] . . . Your [round] cheeks fill us with admiration, and I am going to be jealous because mine are pitiful." [22]

The end of May, she was back home, in time to savor Fred's victory in the first round of voting for the Academy of Science seat of the late Édouard Branly. Piquancy flavored his success for Irène because it was Branly who years before had won out over Marie in a bitter, tight contest. Langevin insisted on being Fred's sponsor and so functioned, by remote control, from Troyes.

The Allies were flexing their muscles on the war front. Two weeks earlier, a string of Tunisian victories saw the end of Axis power in North Africa; July 10, Sicily was invaded, and shortly afterward, the Russians launched their own first big offensive. By fall, the Resistance was brazenly stealing food tickets for the *maquis* in Paris itself and was strong enough, after Italy capitulated on September 8, to free Corsica single-handedly. Thanks to the arms now being flown in to them, sabotage of the railroads, telegraph lines, and factories was far more effective.

From January 1944 on, there was not a single kilogram of coal for all Paris, and by spring, clothes and shoes were nonexistent unless one had the money to buy on the black market. Yet, with it all, the stepped-up arrests of the Jews and the massive deportations, there was still a supercharged air in Paris. Everyone was holding his breath, momentarily expecting news of Allied landings on the Continent. The Resistance sent small coffins to the most prominent collaborators, and in the rooms of the Collège de France laboratory dangerously close to those of the Germans, Pierre Savel, the assistant director of Fred's laboratory, started to assemble clandestine radio transmitters like Ligonnière had been doing all along.

By May the increased tempo of events made Fred worry about Langevin's safety. Afraid that the Germans might seize him as a valuable hostage and cart him off to Germany, Fred planned his escape into Switzerland with the help of Henri Moureu and Professor Denivelle. The Langevin family was finally able to persuade the seventy-two-year-old to flee. Armed with false papers which Fred brought to Troyes, he crossed the frontier on foot with the help of a team of four Franc-Tireurs Partisans ("Partisan Sharpshooters"), a predominantly Communist group which was responsible for a lot of the most dangerous activities of the Resistance.

Sometime in late spring, Fred was picked up again by the Gestapo. No details are available about this second arrest, other than that he was questioned and released the same evening. Soon afterward, he was dismissed from his teaching post, exactly as Langevin had been before he was thrown into jail. Clearly the time was at hand when Fred, too, must disappear. But, first, he had to assure the safety of Irène and the children.

This was easier said than done. Hélène, who was now seventeen, did not want to leave until she took the *bac* examination for which she had been studying so long. Irène felt she was entitled to do so and Fred concurred, provided a place where she might take it could be found near the Swiss border. Again Denivelle came to the rescue; he not only discovered that the Académie de Besançon gave the *bac* examination in several towns close to Besançon, including his own native village of Montbéliard, but also uncovered a local Montbéliard family by the name of Joliot. This was equally important—to help shield the girl's true identity. The fifth of May, Fred, Irène and the two children were at a family wedding in Paris and then Irène and her brood disappeared from sight. Fred would soon do likewise. Because of the sudden bombardment of the Peugeot works in Montbéliard, the Academy farmed out its *bac* students in the environs. When Hélène took her written examination, she passed so brilliantly that the professor in charge suspected she must be Fred's daughter. The next day, to help preserve her anonymity, he gave her her orals ahead of the others, and she wrote her father: "I am proud as Artaban"—the hero of a seventeenth-century novel—"with my *bac* result. It's you who taught me."[23] On June 5, she rejoined her mother and brother, who were waiting for her in the vicinity.

The same team of Franc-Tireurs Partisans was to take them across into Switzerland, and that night, one of the men appeared and advised them to be ready to set forth the next morning at dawn. A truck took them partway and they continued on foot, knapsacks on their backs, following the ridge of the Juras; they were accompanied by several of the team's small sturdy children, to tool any lurking patrols into thinking that they were a large family group off on a day's outing. Although Denivelle did not know it when he oversaw the final arrangements for their departure, June 6 turned out to be D day on the Normandy beachheads. The resultant shock and confusion reigning among the frontier guards, though short-lived, made slipping over easier than usual; a day later, controls were tighter than they had been in months. Once on the other side, the Franc-Tireurs Partisans exchanged the trio's false identification papers and passports for their own and handed them over to the alerted Swiss Patrol, which was waiting for them.

Irène and her children were taken to the detention center in a pleasant manor house in Porrentruy where escaped prisoners of war and anyone else entering the country illegally were temporarily detained in accordance with Swiss law. After they were disinfected —like everyone there—Hélène and her mother settled down with their books while Pierre was allowed outside to play with the local boys of his own age. Some days later, the prefect of the district, Colonel Victor Henri, happened by and was horrified to recognize Irène, sitting on the floor on one of the straw mats that did duty as a chair, studying a book of logarithms. He had not known she was there and had considerable difficulty persuading her to move into the prefecture with his own family until she could be released. Eventually the three Joliots settled down in Lausanne. The physical and emotional stress of the past weeks would have taken their toll on anyone with even a strong constitution, let alone on Irène with her weakened one. But the peaceful environment, the nourishing food, and the presence of her two children, together with a brief but heartwarming visit with Paul Langevin, wrought miracles. Irène's subsequent three months' stay in Switzerland would have been a real holiday for her if she had not been so worried about Fred.

XXI
1944–1948

The Commissariat of Atomic Energy

EXACTLY WHEN FRED went underground is not easy to pinpoint.

On May 27, the first day of the academic Whitsuntide vacation, he announced at the laboratory that he was going away. Sometime between then and the evening of June 26 he disappeared. The sole personal diary he ever kept—and it was very brief—starts around 10 P.M., that night, when he left Marinette and Jo Ségal's after dinner and plunged into the anonymity of the Métro. Mme. Ségal's name is the only one ever hinted at when questions are posed concerning Fred's rumored, here-today, gone-tomorrow mistresses, and the entire Joliot family were in the habit of dining regularly, every Wednesday, year around, with these L'Arcouest neighbors. Fred descended at the Place des Fêtes, in the working-class neighborhood of Belleville in northeast Paris, a district he knew nothing about, but where he had at some previous date rented an apartment under the name of Jean-Pierre Caumont, an electrical engineer from Lyons. Apparently, this was the first night he spent there. A few weeks later, Pavel Savel, his assistant, who was the only person kept abreast of Fred's whereabouts, was called in by the administrator of the Collège de France, Edmond Faral, who very confidentially told Savel that he had just learned that "le patron" was in Switzerland. Savel thanked him and that same evening repeated their conversation to Fred, who still spent the night at Savel's several times weekly. For there were far too many arrests at the University of Paris not to be afraid of some weak link, and Fred no longer went to his laboratory but was dividing his time between the city and the country, changing places where he slept nightly.

With a frontier separating them in those parlous days, affectionate letters crisscrossed under the pseudonyms of Jean-Pierre Caumont and Gabrielle—Fred's, urging Irène to gain some weight: "You know that I love you a little plump and not just skin and bones . . . Jean-Pierre"; Irène's, missing him dreadfully: "I think of you often . . . When shall I be in your arms where I love to nestle? . . . Gabrielle."[1]

Fred's new abode was the ground floor of a two-story maisonnette, one of many similar ones lined up and down Belleville's dreary streets. His first inspection of his new quarters chilled him —a dining room, bedroom, and a sort of lean-to serving as both kitchen and washroom, with a communal lavatory on the floor above. Like in other similar working-class homes thereabouts, the bed was the biggest piece of furniture in the place. Tense with strain, unaccustomed to his strange surroundings, the first night he was there Fred read *Paris-Soir* and tried to sleep. There was an alert in the middle of the night; then, a half-hour later, an "all-clear."

Fred wrote Irène cryptically: "I remain in the big city where I keep busy usefully . . . I get around on my vélo . . . [and] am perfectly safe at the moment. I am doing a lot of work with the reforms that shall be needed for research in the future. Don't get upset worrying about me. I like a fracas, and I am being prudent, for I want to see the end of the adventure and I love you very much."[2]

That same early summer, when de Gaulle was on a whirlwind trip to Canada, a worried Goldschmidt, accompanied by two other French physicists in exile, the physicist, P. Auger and Jules Guéron, a chemist, wangled three precious minutes of the few hours the general spent in Ottawa to anxiously brief him about the Allies' work on an atomic bomb and its probable date of achievement. Guéron spoke alone to de Gaulle in the trio's name and called his attention to the military and political implications of such a weapon. It was imperative, they emphasized, that Fred's war-interrupted nuclear research be resumed as soon as possible and the scarce uranium deposits in France proper and in her overseas colony of Madagascar be protected.

Fred often had underground rendezvous on the banks of the Seine below Notre-Dame. There he mingled inconspicuously with numerous other Parisians anxious to augment their slender food supply, a fishing rod in his hand and, in his pocket, formulas for explosives, designs for grenades and primitive antitank mines. For under the aegis of the directors of Paris's various chemistry, physics, and biology laboratories, small teams were forming to make whatever supplies possible, with the limited means at their disposal, for the hard fighting that lay ahead.

Rather than declare Paris an open city, Hitler intended to fight there, block by block, in order to delay and hold up the Allied tide. "Paris must be defended at all cost,"[3] were his orders to General Dietrich von Choltitz when he sent him there to take charge. The beginning of August, the Americans began to move inland from Normandy, and by the sixteenth, Choltitz was secretly mining bridges, railroad stations, post offices, telephone centers, the Palais du Luxembourg, where the Senate sat, and the Chambre des Députés. But he stalled setting off the charges, claiming that to do so would raise the city up in arms. Choltitz's subsequent admission of the lengths which he went to avoid an all-out fight in the streets of Paris—and why—bolstered by subsequent revelations of others, dispels the myth that Paris was ultimately liberated by the Parisians themselves.

Meanwhile, twenty-nine-year-old General Chaban-Delmas, who was in France, had been ordered by de Gaulle to retain absolute control of the armed Resistance in the city and to permit no uprising without de Gaulle's explicit orders. De Gaulle represented four years' continuity as a Free French authority, and he expected to assume control over a free France. Unfortunately, the PCF—French Communist Party—which was not the most important single political organization in France, controlled the Resistance in Paris and was determined to force an uprising in order to seize power before de Gaulle could arrive. Afraid of either scenario—the one with Choltitz in charge, the other, with a victorious PCF securely entrenched in command—Chaban-Delmas made a hurried trip to London to try and persuade the Allied High Command that its divisions must head straight for Paris and seize the capital themselves.

Unfortunately for Chaban-Delmas, the Allies were anxious to steer clear of this internal struggle and did not want to impose de Gaulle on France. An even more important consideration, from General Dwight Eisenhower's viewpoint, was the logistics sheet from SHAEF—Supreme Headquarters Allied Expeditionary Forces —emphasizing that to capture Paris would require the equivalent of "maintaining eight divisions in one operation."[4] Accordingly, Eisenhower chose SHAEF's alternate plan, to enclose Paris in a gigantic bag and temporarily bypass it, and Chaban-Delmas failed to get him to change his mind. De Gaulle's goal, nonetheless, continued to be the control of Paris, for whoever controlled the capital controlled the country. So he decided to return to France, with or without Allied approval, and to take possession of the city before the PCF did.

The PCF, whose leadership had survived the war intact, was well aware of de Gaulle's intentions and was determined to thwart him. The head of the underground army for the Paris section was a PCF member; the PCF dominated the unions and the clandestine press and was daily reinforcing these positions, planting agents everywhere in key posts; its Franc-Tireur Partisans was the single most important armed body in the Resistance. The PCF strategy was to prove that Paris's fate depended, not on the de Gaullists, but on the masses of the city and the PCF ability to mobilize them. Most Parisians were patriotic Frenchmen who only wanted the privilege of fighting the Occupants and not much would be needed to get them to rise up.

August 15, the Assumption holiday, Parisians sat around the Place de la Concorde and the Étoile, enjoying the spectacle of dusty German army wagons, tanks, and armored cars fleeing eastward.

Rumors of every sort were rampant, and conditions ripened for an uprising. By the eighteenth, strikes were spreading from the railroads to the Métro, to the post offices and telephone centers. The Parisians sensed that the moment of revenge was near—the insurrection which de Gaulle and the Allies did not want. The only thing lacking was someone to shout, "To the barricades!"

Saturday, the nineteenth, the PCF called the Parisians to arms, and soon, the tricolor floated from several public buildings. Alerted by his friend Moureu, Fred slipped into the Paris prefecture of police, the most important public building in Paris, which was on the Île de la Cité, not far from the Collège de France. Staggering under two heavy suitcases containing the necessary chemicals to make Molotov cocktails, he went directly to Moureu's laboratory in the basement. A team of three, which he assembled on the spot, was soon pouring the private stock of champagne of the just-ousted Vichy prefect of police onto the basement floor and refilling the bottles as fast as possible with acid and gasoline. These were wrapped with paper soaked in potassium chlorate, then rushed by relays to the upper floors.

When the German tanks assaulted the building, Fred's home-made explosives, the prefecture's most deadly weapon, knocked out several. The attack failed. Leaving the bare-chested, sweating trio still at work, Fred hastened back to his laboratory, a repossessed German revolver on his hip.

The insurrection grew so fast that the Gaullist leaders realized there was no chance to stop it. All that was left was to try and control it. And the Gaullist Charles Luizet, who was parachuted in, took command of the police prefecture. During the early hours of Sunday, the twentieth, the day de Gaulle secretly arrived in France, the Swedish consul general negotiated a brief truce with General von Choltitz to pick up the dead and the wounded. However, under PCF prodding, the truce slowly unraveled, and by Monday, the twenty-first, barricades were going up everywhere.

Throughout the subsequent days, as the two-tiered drama continued—the power struggle among the French, between the Resistance groups themselves, who were not unanimously united behind the PCF, and between the PCF and the Gaullists; the military struggle between the Parisians and the German Occupants—Fred and his colleagues stayed at the Collège de France, eating and sleeping there. Like others in the various laboratories scattered about the city, they worked around the clock and managed to keep a steady flow of crude but effective explosives streaming to the prefecture of police, which quickly became the central bastion of the French insurrection.

Early Tuesday, the fighting resumed in Paris. This same morning Eisenhower, briefed on the desperate Paris situation, yielded. General Jacques Philippe Leclerc, known as the "impatient lion" by his American superiors, was ordered to take his second French armored division, the only French unit on the Normandy front, and proceed into the city at full speed to liberate it.

Wednesday, the street fighting continued. Ammunition was running low, and casualties high, for the insurrectionists. Upon receipt of orders from Hitler, Choltitz stepped up his mining operations of the city's principal buildings and, shortly before noon, executed the first minuscule destruction by blowing up the St.-Arnaud telephone exchange.

Thursday, the twenty-fourth, dawned dull and gray. The besieged police prefecture was still barely holding and at 9:22 P.M. three of Leclerc's second armored division tanks rolled up to the Hôtel de Ville, Paris's City Hall. Parisians poured into the streets to greet them, and the steeple bells started ringing.

Bright and early Friday, the twenty-fifth, the Feast of St. Louis, the patron saint of France, the tricolor again flew from the Eiffel Tower, and that afternoon, General von Choltitz signed the capitulation of the German garrison. Hard on the heels of the arrival of the rest of Leclerc's division, the civilian Alsos team, the first American unit to enter the liberated capital, rolled up to the Collège de France and jumped out, eager to talk to Fred. The more progress the Americans made toward an atomic bomb, the more anxious they were to determine how advanced the Germans were along these lines; they were worried that this might be the mysterious secret weapon Berlin was continually boasting about on the radio— and which ultimately turned out to be the V-2 rocket. The Alsos Mission—its code name was Greek for "grove"—was specifically set up by General Groves to find out what the Germans had achieved in the development of nuclear weapons, and Colonel Boris Pash, who was in charge, had taken time to stop by L'Arcouest and Antony to bring Fred welcome firsthand news from both places.

Fred greeted them warmly. Although there was little to eat, and the Alsos team only had their army rations, they pooled what they had, and Fred produced a bottle of champagne to toast victory. Afterward, the weary Americans promptly went to sleep on the spot in their own camp beds. As indicative of the mistrust with which Fred, as an avowed Communist, was viewed in official Allied circles, they had been warned to be very careful what they said or revealed to him; when they interrogated him, the next day, they noted in their reports that he seemed "idealistic" and was not convinced an A-bomb could be built. Spending any more time than absolutely necessary around a dump of homemade explosives, with pyroxylin-treated cotton still spread everywhere to dry, held little appeal, and the team spent the second night bedded down elsewhere, before proceeding eastward.

Saturday, Paris had her first full day of liberty, and it belonged to de Gaulle. After depositing flowers on the Tomb of the Unknown Soldier at the Étoile, he marched down the length of the Champs-Élysées on foot, amid waving flags and a sea of humanity, followed by Fred and other prominent members of the Resistance who fell in behind him spontaneously.

The end of August, most of its sixty-odd members were present at the first meeting of the PCF Central Committee in liberated Paris. It was held at party headquarters, a still-sandbagged, six-story building at the Carrefour Châteaudun, no. 44 rue Le Peletier. Fred is also reported to have been there, seated next to Marcel Cachin, who presided. Presumably he was there as a trophy, for he publicly announced his party membership on August 31. The PCF was confident that the time was at hand to claim the price for its four hard years of service and spilled blood—more than that of any other Resistance group. But de Gaulle had the upper hand, and he had different ideas, as he quickly demonstrated.

Inside France, two major problems faced the general, aside from the ongoing military operations—first, the roundup and punishment of traitors, and second, emergency measures to normalize everyday life as much and as quickly as possible. Within a fortnight, de Gaulle, who had only now been officially accepted by the United States as the head of the French Provisional Government, announced his first Cabinet, which consisted of a mixture from the old political parties. With Machiavellian cunning, two Communists were given posts, although they had clearly expected several more. Aside from their prominence in the Resistance, which made it impossible for de Gaulle to exclude them completely, their presence in the government would keep the exasperated working class patient and as manageable as possible.

The country would be convulsed by the jockeying for power between de Gaulle and the PCF until February 1945, when the French people were supposed to elect a Constitutional Assembly with sovereign power. This was a strange competition between de Gaulle, an old-fashioned conservative with little or no sympathy for the working class, who incarnated the nation and was backed by the official French Army, which had been formed largely outside of France, and the PCF. The PCF enjoyed an extraordinary popularity at the moment, not only because it was the Soviets who had first defeated Hitler with their magnificent triumph at Stalingrad; the Communists also represented the wave of the future. As Robespierre's heirs, the PCF was the party of change that was about to begin a new revolution toward a world of real equality and no injustice.

It is almost impossible to get an exact idea of the size of the party membership at the time, but it was unquestionably swollen by the adhesion of those who had been in the Resistance from the beginning of the Occupation, as well as those who had remained on the sidelines until almost the end, then jumped on the bandwagon to be on the winning side. Also there were some long-standing party members who had done nothing during the Occupation, and a stream of young intellectuals who followed into the fold: Picasso, the writers Paul Éluard and Louis Aragon—and Paul Langevin. On his return to France from Switzerland, the seventy-two-year-old scientist emotionally joined the PCF to take the place of his slain son-in-law, Jacques Solomon. Despite the influx of new blood, it is interesting to note that Duclos, after the Liberation, did not chose any officials or cell captains from among the men who fought as leaders in the Resistance; they were too independent and not as apt to follow party discipline. Instead, he fell back on older party members, who may not have been so active between 1940 and 1944, but who could be relied upon to obey orders.

A new facet, that of war hero, was added to Fred's already formidable reputation when he was elevated to commander of the Légion d'Honneur and also awarded the *Croix de Guerre,* with palms, for his work during the Occupation and Liberation. As part of the huge reconstruction job required in every field, he was immediately appointed head of the Centre National de la Recherche Scientifique, which, as the "Caisse," had been so helpful to him financially, early in his own career. Comfortably familiar with its headquarters at no. 13 Quai Anatole France, Fred seized the opportunity to introduce important changes in scientific research. He proposed an ambitious plan in the direction previously opened up by Jean Perrin, which Fred had been working on with Langevin during the Occupation. Fred felt that the Centre National should play a central, coordinating role like that of the Soviet Academy and take responsibility for applied as well as basic research; its basic ordinance would give it the responsibility to develop, orient, and coordinate all French science. Furthermore, the laboratories established by the Centre National were to provide full-time research careers outside the traditional university structure.

A France where political life was more embittered than ever, where Parisians, if they were not devoting themselves to locating something to eat—perhaps a few potatoes on the scandalous black market—were avidly reading about the arrests and trials of tens of thousands of collaborators, seemed an unlikely place for a reorganized and renascent science. But no one understood better than Fred that science represented a great untapped source of strength for France, and his personal reputation and authority were such that few sought to thwart him when he outlined the tremendous effort entailed to put French science back on its feet internationally.

As the war continued, the Centre, under Fred, set up groups to do military research and sent others into Germany behind the advancing Allied armies to bring back, as booty, two hundred and fifty tons of sorely needed scientific equipment, for even simple laboratory glassware was hard to come by in Paris; they also procured invaluable technical information. For the next six years, until 1950, Fred was the dominant figure when planning for science was considered at the highest administrative levels. Not all the reforms he set in place would hold, but the visionary program of scientific organization set up, originally, under Perrin in the 1930s, was now embodied in a permanent institution. The structure Fred set in place, during a twelve-month tenure as the Centre's director, would continue a good thirty years with little modification.

In September, Irène was back with the children, and she was once more able to return on a nearly normal basis to the Curie Laboratory and research. The recent rest in Switzerland, together with new American antibiotics for tuberculosis sent by Missy, had largely restored Irène's health. As always, no one in the family was ever allowed to discuss this subject with her or within her hearing; she paid no attention to how she was feeling until she was ready to collapse and detested taking care of herself.

Despite the heavy administrative duties his new job on the Quai Anatole France entailed, when the academic year opened, Fred did not neglect his obligations as a professor at the Collège de France. Close associates, who had sat out the Occupation abroad, found Fred thinner and looking his forty years. There were other changes as well that may have been produced by life under the Occupation and his work in the underground. Both Guéron and Goldschmidt felt he talked more than ever—if that was possible. They decided, independently, that he must have a complex about joining the PCF, because he was forever seeking to defend this step, even when there was no need to. He expatiated *ad nauseam* "on the fraternity and closeness of relations in the Party, like a man who had at last found a family."[5] He used the same rather uncomplicated arguments, over and over, to explain why he was a member. "It was difficult," Goldschmidt later remarked, "to know if this was to justify himself, to boast of what he had done or to convince himself."[6]

Fred was obsessed with the idea of starting up fission work and of funding a broad nuclear program as soon as possible. He got his first intimation of the walls of secrecy shutting him off from any knowledge of wartime work abroad in this field when Halban came to London from America on a visit at the end of the year. Fred would have had an even better understanding of the roadblocks in his path had he known that, as a condition for his crossing, Halban, for security reasons, had to promise to reveal only the barest facts concerning his nuclear work.

General Groves also insisted to the British that all Halban's talks with French scientists in London must be secretly monitored and recorded. The Americans were wild, when contrary to their express wishes, and through a misunderstanding, Halban was permitted to continue on to Paris briefly. The British, in turn, felt it unrealistic to expect Halban, once he was there, not to discuss with Fred the results of the heavy-water experiment he and Kowarski carried out at the Cavendish their first December in England, in accordance with Fred's explicit, detailed instructions; or not to talk about what he, Halban, had been doing along similar lines since then. But the British did give Halban a text of what revelations he might and might not make, emphasizing that any mention of the military aspects of his British work was strictly taboo. The British later telegraphed Washington that, to their great distress, the meetings between Halban and Fred occurred in surroundings where the two could talk freely—without eavesdropping microphones.

Halban was anxious to talk about the French patents concerning atomic energy which he, Fred, and the others of the Collège de France team had taken out, in 1940, on behalf of the Centre National. Subsequently, once the pair was safe in London, at the outbreak of the war, Halban asked Kowarski to draw up British patents duplicating the French ones. Fred, when he now saw Halban at the end of November 1944, flatly refused to honor any patent arrangements that did not include a general French-British collaboration in nuclear energy work.

How much Halban also revealed to Fred about the progress being made in North America along these lines is not known, but he would have had little to say about the A-bomb because none of the French scientists working overseas with the Canadian-British efforts had anything to do with that specific phase. It is interesting to note in this regard that Bertrand Goldschmidt would later comment when he saw Fred for the first time, after spending the war years abroad, that Fred asked him very little regarding the progress made in the nuclear field he himself had pioneered, almost as if it were painful for Fred to talk of matters from which he had been excluded. He must certainly have felt a certain frustration at the secrecy and ignorance in which he was being kept. However, since Fred, as director of the Centre National, was, at the moment, in charge of all government-funded research in France, atomic energy did not fill his every waking moment to the exclusion of all else, as had been the case in 1940. And later, of course, once the French Atomic Energy Commission was set up, Fred subjected the returning physicists to a barrage of pertinent questions.

Whether Halban, when he was with Fred, actually remained within the guidelines laid out by the British is unknown. The British, General Groves, and the other American officials concerned with the Manhattan Project, which was on a twenty-four-hours-a-day, seven-days-a-week schedule to build the first A-bomb, were afraid that whatever Fred learned he would surely pass on to the U.S.S.R. Both F.D.R. and Churchill were determined, although for somewhat different reasons, including postwar spheres of economic influence, to abide by the August 1943 British-American agreement at Quebec, which was later reaffirmed at Hyde Park, not to share atomic knowledge with any third power. Groves noted that if Fred reacted unfavorably when he learned about these decisions concerning information sharing, his "recommendations, from the security standpoint, would be that Kowarski, Guéron, Goldschmidt, and Halban be placed in confinement in Canada and not be permitted to communicate with anyone."[7] Security-conscious Groves was so disturbed when Fred went to London several times that fall and early winter, 1944, that the American general resorted, successfully this time, to hidden microphones to keep track of Fred's conversation at his happy reunions with several former French colleagues.

This was the start of a trouble-beset American concern with nuclear technology secrecy that would involve the British and American governments at the highest levels for several years. And it directly foreshadowed Fred's dramatic dismissal as French high commissioner of atomic energy in 1950. As it turned out, the Americans, obsessed as they were about the extent of communism in France and the resultant possibility of leaks of scientific knowledge to the U.S.S.R., were looking in the wrong direction. What vital specific information did later trickle out was carried by British and American spies, as the subsequent arrests of Allan Nunn May in 1946, Klaus Fuchs in 1950, Paul Greenglass and the Rosenbergs in 1951, to name but a few, attest. May, ironically, was Halban's successor as head of the division of physics at Montreal, and in the fall of 1945, he stole and smuggled into the U.S.S.R. a fraction of a milligram of the precious uranium radioisotope which Guéron and Goldschmidt managed to isolate.

The same day Halban arrived in Paris to see Fred, November 24, 1944, de Gaulle flew to Moscow to sign an accord with Stalin. Throughout his maintenance of power, the general would always retain the Russian trump to counter any Western pressures or threats to his sovereignty. As part of the price de Gaulle paid for the meeting with Stalin, Thorez, the secretary-general of the PCF, who had deserted the French Army shortly before the fall of France on Stalin's orders and had been living in Moscow, was amnestied by the French military and slated for a Cabinet post, with the agreed-upon proviso that he was to cooperate with de Gaulle. Shortly before leaving for Paris, Thorez was granted the unique distinction of a private interview with Stalin at which the Russian leader insisted that every PCF member must unite behind de Gaulle in order to successfully liquidate Hitler. Back in Paris, Thorez presided, on November 30, at a huge rally at the Vélodrome d'Hiver and presented the latest party line. Without having to give battle, de Gaulle had won over his bitter political opponent—for the short haul. For the long haul, however, he conferred on the PCF part of the national legitimacy that he himself incarnated, and Communists soon moved into positions of importance on local as well as national levels.

As the year ended, the American and British concern with nuclear security leaks was intensified by the projected return home of four key French scientists—Halban, Kowarski, Guéron, and Goldschmidt. To make matters worse another, Pierre Auger, was momentarily in Paris, but like Guéron and Goldschmidt, he, too, had a contract keeping him in Canada till June. Before leaving for the Yalta meeting, February 7–12, 1945, Churchill was briefed on the matter by Sir John Anderson. The Chancellor of the Exchequer, who was politically responsible for the British Atomic Enterprise, Sir John felt a moral obligation to share some technical information with the French because of the heavy-water they brought to England, and Halban and Kowarski's subsequent work with it there. Anderson hoped Churchill might reopen the question with Roosevelt. The only point in Anderson's presentation which carried any weight with Churchill was the possibility that, despairing of being treated as a third partner in these matters, Fred might counsel de Gaulle "to plunge in the opposite direction,"[8] whereas it was imperative to keep France in the Allied camp during the crucial months of 1945 before the A-bomb was ready. "If such a thing were indeed a possibility," growled Churchill, switching his cigar to the other side of his mouth, "Joliot should be detained by force, but comfortably, for several months."[9] Anderson was so upset at Churchill's remark that he wrote in great haste to Sir Anthony Eden, the British Foreign Secretary, who had already left for Yalta, to ask him to be sure that even the barest suggestion of jailing the greatest French savant of the day must never come up for consideration.

As busy as Fred was, he found time, the end of January 1945, to open the four-day convention of the National Front as incumbent president. Although the organization was not 100 percent Communist, sharing the presidium with Fred were three prominent members of the PCF—Villon, Wallon, Laurent Casanova—as well as General Paul Dassault, the grand chancellor of the Légion d'Honneur, and Paul Langevin. Despite bad weather and the difficulties of transportation and communication, almost a thousand delegates showed up. Most of the speeches dealt with souvenirs of the underground, and one delegation offered Fred the standard of the First Company of the Fifth Dordogne Batalion, all of whom had fallen crying, *"Vive la France!* Death to the Invader!" Whereupon the assembled delegates burst into "The Marseillaise."

In a speech in Orléans in March, Fred stressed not only such PCF policies of the day as cooperation among nations and the nationalization of industry, but also the importance of science and technology for the war effort and the renaissance of the nation. The words were hardly out of his mouth when the electric power for the entire city failed. When Fred continued on for over another hour in total darkness, few in that audience would ever again dispute his belief that science and technology had essential work to do.

April 12, Roosevelt died unexpectedly and, within twenty-four hours, his successor, Harry S. Truman, was briefed on the A-bomb and his awesome responsibility for its deployment. Shortly afterward, on May 1, Hitler's death was announced. Midafternoon of the eighth, the deep-toned bells of Notre-Dame mingled with those from every other Paris church steeple and the booming of the Invalides cannon to officially announce Germany's unconditional surrender. It was a beautiful, hot spring day and a wave of humanity streamed outdoors and up the Champs-Élysées. The crowds that spilled over onto the boulevards stayed out late to enjoy the illumination of the city's principal monuments, visual proof that Paris had been saved intact. Three weeks later, on the twenty-eighth, a huge seven-hour parade mixed tens of thousands of workers and avant-garde intellectuals in a joint hommage to the Communists and the Resistance. Featured were those courageous, hardy souls who had been snatched from the Nazi death camps, with Hélène Langevin Solomon, just back from Auschwitz, in a prominent position.

Shortly afterward, Fred and Irène went to Moscow for the two hundred and twentieth anniversary of the Russian Academy of Sciences. The Soviets sent two planes, one of whose pilots was Molotov's personal one, to transport them and other Collège de France colleagues to and fro. This trip, Fred's third, and Irène's first, was climaxed by a great meeting, on their return, in the amphitheater of the Sorbonne, at which the Joliots, Perrin, Auger, and others who had gone along sang the praises of Soviet society. In Russia everyone worked, and higher education was based solely on intelligence and available to everyone, unlike in France, where less than 2 percent of Fred's students were from the proletariat.

The events of the past few years had temporarily broken up the power of France's bureaucracy and directing class, and no one was in a better position than Fred to take advantage of the disarray. When the new Centre National budget came up, Fred asked for a 200 percent increase. "Allocation granted," replied the Finance Minister, who, without another word, rapped his gavel, and went on to the next item of business.

When Fred and Irène returned to L'Arcouest that summer for the first time since the Occupation, they were saddened by evidence of the Nazi presence everywhere. The Joliots' was one of the few summer places left untouched, because it was in the dead center of a mine field. The whole coastline had been heavily mined, but because the Germans, with characteristic thoroughness, had made a map of each mine's location, German prisoners were sent out to clear them away.

The Brittany calm was brutally shattered when word was

flashed, on August 6, that "Little Boy," a bomb made of U 235 at Oak Ridge, Tennessee, had practically annihilated the whole city of Hiroshima. A few days later, "Fat Man," made from plutonium from Hanford, Washington, was dropped on Nagasaki. This was something that Irène and Fred knew might possibly happen, although they hoped it would not. From the outset, scientists overseas who were involved with the Manhattan Project shared the Joliots' worries about a future worldwide nuclear arms race; some had even tried, unsuccessfully, to prevent what they considered a perversion of their handiwork. At the price of letting the genie out of the bottle, the two A-bombs won a swift Allied victory. The eighth of August, Russia declared war on Japan. Emperor Hirohito then surrendered, and World War II was finally over.

Both Fred and Irène regarded the Americans' use of atomic fission as a great betrayal of science and mankind. They always considered science as a positive factor in human progress, and now, it had become a negative one. Since this change was partly the result of their own pioneering work, part of the responsibility for this desecration was theirs. What was driven home equally dramatically was how far France lagged behind. The day after the bombing of Nagasaki, Fred wrote a detailed article for *L'Humanité*—or "Huma," as the PCF's principal mouthpiece was popularly nicknamed—pointing out: "It is also true that the immense reserves of energy contained in the uranium devices can be liberated slowly enough to be used practically for the benefit of mankind. I am personally convinced that . . . it [atomic energy] will be of inestimable service to mankind in peacetime."[10]

It would be logical to suppose that the mushroom-shaped clouds of destruction over Hiroshima and Nagasaki finally goaded de Gaulle into taking action along nuclear lines simply because he wanted France to have her own bomb. But, at the moment, such weapons were beyond the means of the ravaged country, which had far more urgent needs. France was one of the poorest among the major powers in native sources of energy, with limited coal reserves and less oil, as Fred had pointed out, several months before, in May, when he had a second interview—the first had been to set up the CNRS—with de Gaulle to press home the desperate need to explore the potential of nuclear technology as a new source of industrial power. Auger, who accompanied him, reminded the general that he and Goldschmidt had Guéron already mention this to him when the latter saw the general on the trio's behalf in Ottawa, the year before. Dautry, who was presently serving as Minister of Reconstruction and Urbanism in de Gaulle's Provisional Government, had recently made a similar recommendation to de Gaulle. But, as France walked a precarious tightrope between East and West that summer, the general had other things to absorb his attention, both at home and abroad. Now the time had come for action.

De Gaulle asked Fred and Dautry to draw up a plan for an atomic energy program. With the help of Irène, Auger, and Francis Perrin, they submitted a draft in early October. With a speed seldom seen in government circles, an ordinance and specific law for a Commissariat of Atomic Energy—the CEA—were promulgated into law by the general on October 18, 1945.

Unlike the British and American leaders, who were paranoid on the subject of Communists, when the general selected a head, he chose the most qualified man, regardless of his political affiliations, and he nominated Fred as the high commissioner. "I have confidence in very few men. Joliot, I have confidence in you."[11] While its enabling charter charged the CEA with conducting "scientific and technical research with a view to utilization of atomic energy in the various fields of science, industry and national defense," Fred's avowed objectives were entirely peace-oriented, and his policy statement to that effect was adopted by the government without question or change.

Some people, in retrospect, like to point out what seems a puzzling paradox in peace-loving Fred's position from the start. For he knew by the time of Goldschmidt's return from overseas that it was impossible to have a uranium and heavy-water reactor of the type he was proposing, built with anything except the most limited capacity, and not have it eventually, automatically, produce used uranium rods from which plutonium, one of the essentials for an A-bomb of the Nagasaki type, could be extracted. But what these critics fail to take into consideration is the fact that from Fred's point of view, this built-in potential for the manufacture of nuclear weapons was irrelevant. He was confident that international controls would be in effect long before any French reactor would have this capacity. Furthermore, certain physical factors substantially narrowed the present range of practical alternatives to plutonium, if one were to go the nuclear weapon route, so the new CEA's stated policy was the only realistic one possible in terms of French atomic potential for at least a decade to come. Where the United States was expending several hundred million dollars on its efforts, France would have to get by with several million; in the United States, tens of thousands of men were involved, in France, only hundreds.

At the top of the CEA was an Atomic Energy Commission, four of whose six members—Fred and Irène, Auger and Francis Perrin —were physicists and L'Arcouestiens. Auger and Perrin, *normaliens,* old friends, and brothers-in-law, were under fifty, as were both Joliots. The other two, Dautry and General Dassault, were past sixty. Fred, as high commissioner, was placed in command of all scientific and technical work. And Dautry, convinced of the importance of the new organization, resigned from his present post to assume control, as general administrator, of a separate division of the CEA set up to handle all administrative and financial chores. Dautry had no sympathy with the Communists, and it was not spelled out, anywhere, which of the two heads, the scientific or the administrative, should prevail if an impasse arose. But, in the beginning, there did not seem to be any cause for concern with this arrangement. Denivelle was appointed secretary-general. Since nationalization of industry was a policy of the new government, it was natural for Fred to build this new industrial enterprise entirely under state control, without any recourse to private industry.

Auger commented that the commission's first meetings "were marked by team spirit and mutual confidence . . . [and were like] meetings of the directing group of a club planning the ascent of Mt. Everest or a trip around the world in a sailboat. Proposals which were very audacious for that era could be made and discussed without having their wings clipped by protocol or the budget."[12] And all were united by a common desire for rapid changes in the lives of the masses and their hopes for state science. Unfortunately, none of the six had any firsthand knowledge of recent nuclear work except Auger, who had, for a short period, directed the physics research in Montreal. This was not true with Kowarski, Guéron, and Goldschmidt, the other French physicists from Fred's Collège de France laboratory who were prominently active in the field overseas during the war. Guéron and Goldschmidt were presently in charge of the chemical section at Chalk River, where the latter was already considered an acknowledged authority on plutonium, while Kowarski was responsible for the construction there of the first Canadian heavy-water reactor. When Fred wrote that they were badly needed, the three, who were all under forty, agreed to return as soon as possible. Halban was not invited because the others found him too prickly to work with.

The commission could hardly design an up-to-date, detailed program until the trio arrived, but their departure posed a serious problem for General Groves. He still viewed Russia with suspicion and was afraid that whatever France learned might then become known in Moscow. "You've heard about the Communist Party in France?" he asked a reporter. "I read the PCF is disconnected from the Russian one, but I notice they go to Moscow all the time."[13] So Goldschmidt went to Washington, D.C., to discuss this delicate matter with him. Actually, the French trio knew almost nothing about the A-bomb itself. Finally, the British and the Americans worked out a gentleman's agreement with each one whereby it was agreed they must not publish anything, but they might bring home a "packet of notes" and what they could recall—which posed no problem for Kowarski, who had a phenomenal memory. They were also forbidden to reveal information about anything except what they themselves had worked on, and this knowledge would only be disclosed, one step at a time, as needed in France. Men of honor, the trio, who lacked any PCF sympathies, abided by this ruling, even though upon their return Fred gave them broad authority, and they were quickly submerged in technical problems. There is also no evidence that helpful information ever seeped across the Channel from Britain. But Goldschmidt's team was adept at putting two and two together, and they learned, by chance, the name of the top-secret solvent being used in the chemical plants at Windscastle, in England, where some of the British work was being conducted, from a salesman who had just received a large order for it.

At the end of January 1946, de Gaulle unexpectedly resigned as President of the Provisional Government because he felt reduced to powerlessness in disputes with the Constituent Assembly. His successor, the socialist F. Gouin, like the general, worked to keep France from getting frozen within either of the two spheres of influence that were beginning to solidify abroad. Fred, an ardent nationalist, concurred.

As a faculty member of the Collège de France, Fred still directed the physics laboratory there, and his lectures on nuclear chemistry, which were automatically open to the general public as well as to students, were the Collège's greatest attraction of the 1946 season. After Hiroshima and Nagasaki, Parisians, old and young, ascribed supernatural powers to every physicist, and they flocked to see Fred, elegant as ever, if somewhat slimmer and with more deep furrows creasing his narrow face, scribble unintelligible equations on a big blackboard. He also continued to maintain a strong influence over the CNRS, whose direction he had recently turned over to the biologist George Tèssier, a loyal Communist friend, and he continued to direct the CNRS's Laboratory of Atomic Synthesis at Ivry—and always would.

Irène, too, did more than her share and continued to be as much of an activist as her precarious health, and other responsibilities, would allow. In March, she was in London as a principal speaker at an International Women's Day, and on Debierne's death, that year, she succeeded to his post as director of the Curie Laboratory, a role she had more or less filled for some time as that difficult man became increasingly withdrawn. Out from under the strong personalities of her mother and husband, Irène blossomed there on her own, with a team of twelve *chefs de service* and sixty researchers under her, and was elevated to a full professorship at the Sorbonne. However, the august, tradition-bound Academy of Sciences was no more ready to accept a woman member now than it had been during the lifetime of Marie Curie. Whereas Marie had felt keenly humiliated upon rejection, Irène took it in stride and remarked ironically, "Well, at least they are consistent in their thinking!"[14] She would repeat her try twice again, not because she had any illusions about her chances of success, even if women had just gotten the vote, and despite the fact that she and Fred now blanketed, with their various appointments, the French field of nuclear physics and were probably the best-known couple in the country. Irène intended to remind people that sexual discrimination still existed under the Coupole.

At Fulton, Missouri, that same March, Winston Churchill coined the expression "The Iron Curtain" in a speech, one of the opening declarations of the Cold War that was soon to embrace the world in its freezing grasp.

From the start, the CEA had a unique, elevated position in the French hierarchy. This not only assured scientific leadership and control within the CEA proper; Fred also wielded sufficient influence and authority in the top echelons of government to permit scientists to share policy-making, for the first time, with the great bodies of state and to have a strong role in determining the CEA's direction. Since it was to be directly responsible to the President of the Council of Ministers, rather than being placed under any specific ministry, the CEA also had administrative autonomy, especially during its formative years when France had a bewildering succession of Prime Ministers, few of whom took any interest in nuclear physics. The CEA was also not accountable to the Minister of Finances, an enormous advantage. It was on its own, and Fred considered it his personal fief.

This was most clearly manifested at the policy-making level within the CEA and can be explained by the fact that most of the problems that had to be met in its formative years required specialized scientific knowledge. There was a strong bond uniting the four scientists on the commission of six, and Fred's aggressive personality, as well as capability, strengthened his position as high commissioner and assured him of their support. But it would be erroneous to conclude that Dautry, as administrator-general, was powerless, had he not approved of any steps being taken. For he possessed the authority to call on the Prime Minister in the event of a major dispute at the Commissariat level. In the early years he never did.

But neither the CEA's special status nor his enhanced status as a war hero made Fred's task of developing atomic energy on a large scale and assuring French independence in this domain any easier. His energetic leadership and proven capacity to forge and inspire a team, as well as his skill as an entrepreneur, stood him in good stead, while the efforts of a generation of French nuclear physicists, beginning with the Curies, gave Fred a strong base. However, this was only the beginning. The most pressing problem was recruitment. He must build a strong cadre of young scientists and technicians, but unlike most others in France who were hiring badly needed personnel, Fred would not tolerate the presence of anyone who had wholeheartedly collaborated with the Vichy regime. Nor did he favor the graduates of the elite schools. At the beginning of 1946, the CEA had 12 employees; at year's end it had 236. By

1950, the number had grown to 1,610, but only 7 of the top 200 employees were polytechnicians.

Fred also had to get an adequate supply of heavy-water and uranium. Dautry was able to tie up the Norwegian supply of the former, which was once more being produced at Rjukan, but during the war, the United States and England had set up a world monopoly of uranium. His one hope was to locate sufficient deposits of this on French soil, either at home or in France's overseas colonies. Equally important was finding a suitable location for immediate occupancy, in which to set up shop. Last but not least, Fred must perpetually convince the government, which had other more immediate necessities crying to be financed, of the need to maintain, if not increase, its major commitments to the CEA.

The CEA's administrative headquarters were set up in the confiscated former home of a collaborationist, Louis Renault, the automobile manufacturer—two extravagant apartments on the same floor at no. 41 Avenue Foch, at the corner of the rue de la Pompe. As if to symbolize the commission's split personality from the start, one side was given over to the scientists, the other to the administrative services. Dautry borrowed a few typewriters from American war surplus, and as the CEA soon mushroomed, secretaries were overflowing into kitchens and bathrooms.

The lugubrious, moss-covered fort of Châtillon, part of the dilapidated old fortifications surrounding Paris which had been built after the Franco-Prussian War of 1870, was chosen as the temporary site of the CEA's operations, because it was located close enough for easy monitoring. Up to, and including, the very morning the CEA took possession, Châtillon's deep moats remained the execution site for numerous jailed collaborators, whose fate was being sealed daily in the concurrent trials of prominent Vichyites. Hundreds of tons of explosives were also still stored there. The makeshift laboratory that had the double mission of applied as well as fundamental research resembled a molehill because so much was underground. Fortunately, most of the staff were young and so eager to work with someone of Fred's international stature that their surroundings made little difference; their enthusiasm and faith in the ambitious work that lay ahead saturated the dank dungeons.

The commission's plan consisted of three stages: to construct and build a uranium and heavy-water pile—or reactor—in which, hopefully, they might realize a controlled, divergent chain reaction by the end of 1948. This was in the nature of a scientific experiment. The cooling of a pile was very complex technically, but since the one they contemplated building would only give off several kilowatts of heat, no system of extraction was immediately needed. It would, however, generate sufficient energy to provide French scientists with their own source of radioactive isotopes, so they would no longer have to import them. The second stage, to be accomplished by the end of 1953, was the construction of one or two piles of medium power, as well as the establishment of a large nuclear center. The third stage, which had no time frame, entailed building the first big nuclear power station in France; this was intended to be the forerunner of a network of atomic energy stations to furnish energy for the entire country.

Luckily, sufficient uranium was left over from Fred's original prewar Belgian purchase and had escaped the Nazi clutches, so the group was not held up as they set to work on the first reactor. Irène, because of a lifelong fascination with mineralogy and geology, was a natural choice to be charged with the program of prospecting for more. The crash course she set up in the mineralogy laboratory of the Museum of Natural History turned out more than three hundred adequately trained prospectors by the beginning of 1947. Equipping them was another headache, for even tools as basic as Geiger counters were nonexistent and had to be either specially constructed from scratch or improvised. Bicycles, motorized and otherwise, pinch-hit for transportation as they fanned out over the countryside, and their first strike of importance, in the west central department of Haute-Vienne, would suffice for a considerable time.

Early in June, Fred and Auger were sent to New York. The first of a series of rotating scientists to be chosen from the CEA, they were to serve as delegates to the United Nations Atomic Energy Committee set up to study the problem of international control of atomic energy; they were also to double as experts assigned to Alexander Parodi, the French ambassador to the United Nations. Fred was impressed with New York and wrote Irène: "It reminds me of Christmas time in Paris when I was a child . . . all those things in the windows that I would have liked."[15]

Fred was back in time to attend meetings held in London, the end of July, to coincide with the presence there of many overseas scientists at the Newton Tercentenary Celebration. Representatives from fourteen of the countries present were in unanimous agreement to set up a World Federation of Scientific Workers for the purpose of rallying the scientific world against atomic warfare and the ill effects of secrecy where basic research was involved. The first major association of its kind, after the war, to seek to link the application of science to the needs of an impoverished and insecure world, its avowed concern with scientists' social responsibilities echoed the philosophy of Langevin and other earlier leftist colleagues. Because its aim was so close to Fred's heart, it was inevitable that he should accept its presidency, a post he held for over a decade.

During the Cold War days ahead, the World Federation would provide the only link between various nations, and Fred would be quick to utilize it, although savants, heretofore, rarely stepped into the arena of international politics. Filled with a sense of guilt about his own role in the creation of nuclear weapons, he was aware that the prominence of his new position at a policy-making level in the CEA gave him added leverage to help ban them. Because the World Federation was quickly identified as a left-wing organization, many refused to join, so it never unified scientists as Fred had hoped.

However, it provided a useful forum, and Fred would go wherever he felt he might be helpful to preach the gospel of world peace. He was indefatigable in its pursuit, yet he still managed to take a few seconds off to check the box of minnows, which he frequently carried along, to be sure they did not die before he was able to snatch time for a little early morning fishing.

Fred returned to the United States in September, accompanied by Irène. Her old friend Einstein was the honorary head of the committee that had invited them to participate in the celebration of Princeton's two hundredth anniversary. They were home in time to vote in the first election, under the new French Constitution, for members of the Lower House, which had been rechristened the National Assembly and remained the center of power. The PCF's coherent ideology and its call to selfless struggle contrasted strikingly with the ambiguous programs of most of the other parties. By getting a surprising 30 percent of the vote, it elected more than one hundred and eighty Communists. The PCF emergence as the number one party caused alarm and despondency in Washington. Less than a week later, following a meeting between Truman, British Prime Minister Clement Atlee, and Canadian Prime Minister Mac-Kenzie King, on the presidential yacht on the Potomac, the White House announced its new postwar policy to continue to keep nuclear information from France.

November 17, Fred received his academician's sword from Langevin in the presence of a distinguished assembly in the great salon of the Sorbonne. His acceptance by the Academy of Sciences had been masterminded by his old mentor while he was under house arrest in Troyes, but the traditional, formal induction into the Institute had been waived at the time of his election because of the Occupation. Langevin's obvious frailty made the ceremony even more moving for Fred. Within the month his old friend was dead.

Choked with heartfelt emotion, Fred declared at Langevin's funeral, "He determined my destiny when he said he had a job for me with Mme. Curie."[16] Although Langevin was buried that day at

Père Lachaise Cemetery, he and his lifelong intimate, Jean Perrin, who died in exile while teaching at Columbia during the war, were transferred in a double ceremony, some years later, to the Panthéon, where France reverently keeps her greatest countrymen.

Conditions were slowly improving within France with the help of German war prisoners in coal mining and agriculture. Nonetheless, enormous difficulties were piling up for the government, at home and abroad, and the maldistribution of wealth, which had been bad enough at the time of the Liberation, was far more serious by the end of 1946. The winter was a severe one; prices were sky-high; serious strikes would paralyze the country during the next two years, with the unions split between the socialists and the Communists. The PCF, which was the leading Communist party in Western Europe as well as the number one political entity in France, remained loyal to Stalin as the wartime alliance between the Western powers and the U.S.S.R. slowly broke up, while most of the other French groups leaned farther and farther in the opposite direction.

The increasing inadequacy of Châtillon was one of Fred's major worries at the CEA. Electronic, mechanical, and chemical workshops were jammed into every nook and cranny, and makeshift wooden buildings were thrown up as the existing space became overcrowded. Naked light bulbs dangled from the vaulted stone ceilings of tunnels where technicians worked, literally elbow to elbow. Space was nonexistent for pure research, which entailed work with a particle accelerator of far greater power and sophistication than the one being constructed there. Going ahead with the second stage of CEA's plan, Fred and Dautry settled on the great agricultural plain of Saclay, some fifteen kilometers southwest of Paris, not too far from Versailles, as the site for the desperately needed new plant. And, while the postwar revival of French science was not due to Fred and his collaborators alone—other scientists also survived the war and were organizing notable laboratories—Saclay, the chief French center for basic research, played a preponderant role.

Once the land had been bought, Irène, like her mother before her, insisted on having some five thousand trees planted there where there had been none before. Even so, the local farmers, with visions of Hiroshima haunting them and alarmed at the mere mention of the word "atom," were not happy at the prospect of such a neighbor. So Fred came to the Saclay schoolhouse to allay their fears. Armed solely with a blackboard, he persuaded the hostile group to have confidence in him. As had been often demonstrated, he was readily able to establish a rapport with simple people, and he drove away exhausted but exhilarated, as he always did after talks before responsive audiences.

The winter of 1947–48, the PCF, whose handful of Cabinet members had been ousted that May, led a general strike which, for a time, seemed to endanger the Republic. The government broke it, leaving the party in isolated, bitter opposition and in such great disrepute that, in retrospect, it may seem surprising that any PCF was still permitted to hold high office. But Fred did not conform to the average man's stereotype of a Communist, and he was still considered in many circles only a "parlor pink"—a distinguished, world-renowned physicist who lived well, had a comfortable home in substantial Antony, a summer place at L'Arcouest, and took annual ski vacations, yet who supported publicly those parts of the PCF policy with which he was in accord. Because, like the PCF, he opposed nuclear armament, which he saw as a prostitution of science, and was against American dominance of Europe, Fred was one of some thirty, including other former resistants, to now form Combattants de Liberté to fight these two evils.

Almost concurrently, the successful Communist coup in Czechoslovakia in February 1948, liquidating the legitimate government and installing a Communist dictatorship, fired an anti-Communist crusade in France. The succession of trials in the satellite states with classic confessions as in a Koestler novel, the propaganda of books like that of Kravchenko, the Soviet official who fled to the United States, eclipsed for the average Frenchman the heroic Russian stand before Stalingrad. But it was the numerous, authenticated articles about the millions in *gulags* that shook the left-wing intellectuals the most. Anticommunism grew stronger and louder, lending power to the conservatives in the administration.

The link between the government and the CEA that had been tenuous from its inception was made even more so because of the rapid turnover of administrations—twelve between January 1946 and December 1950. But, now, as France's first reactor emerged from the blueprint stage, the deputies' growing uneasiness at the presence of members of the PCF honeycombing high-ranking government posts was evident. In the early months of 1948, lawmakers unsuccessfully proposed first a symbolic reduction of a million francs in the CEA budget, then later, a more sizable cut as a protest at its Communist head.

Irène had already left for America before the second attack, and Fred wrote her indignantly that the reactionaries were after his scalp: ". . . because I must, as a communist, communicate all I know to the Russians! I thought I had given enough proofs of attachment to my country so they would never invoke this argument . . . But, indeed, they know very well that I am not in the pay of . . . the Russians . . . but am a French citizen. My communist comrades are like me, which does not prevent us from admiring the socialist development in the U.S.S.R. and even to admire what is good in the U.S. . . ."[17]

This was Irène's third and last visit to the United States. She went alone, at the request of the American Joint Antifascist Refugee Committee, on a fund-raising tour on behalf of Spanish refugees from Franco's Spain. It was a long trip for the frail woman, even though she never learned to spare herself, but the cause was so close to her heart that she could not refuse. Her crusade got off to a bad start upon her arrival in New York. To her surprise and indignation, she was forbidden entry, although she had a valid two-week visa. Her sponsors were on the Attorney General's list of supposedly subversive organizations. Goldschmidt, who was in

New York for his stint as an advisor to the French UN delegation, was at the airport to meet her, but all he could do was to wave at her through the glass partition separating them. He was not allowed to speak to her and could only watch helplessly as she argued with the immigration officials and then was bundled off in their car, bound for Ellis Island, where undesirable aliens were kept. He was powerless to do anything that night because it was already after 5 P.M., and the French Embassy in Washington and the New York Consulate were both already closed.

Always adaptable in a crisis, Irène spent the rest of the evening placidly mending her stockings in a room shared with four others, and with the help of the justice department, the French Embassy managed her release at noon the next day. By then she was a *cause célèbre*. She declared to the press that it was true she sympathized with the PCF "on many matters. Yes. But not always . . . not on everything." Irène, who was never a card-carrying member, although her sympathies were staunchly pro-PCF, could give as well as she could take. When one enterprising reporter asked what her reactions were to her detention, Irène answered, "I am not surprised. I am here to aid the antifascists. This is not always as favorably considered as aiding the Nazis." "Americans," she replied to another, "look with much more favor on fascism than communism . . . Americans think fascism has more respect for money."[18]

A good indication of the American temper of the day was shown by the subsequent *Time* magazine article, which suggested that she had been better treated than she deserved, since "all communists in a democracy are potential spies and traitors." The rest of the trip, which included four stops up and down the West Coast, Chicago, Boston, and Philadelphia, went off without a hitch, and she even managed to do some work on a paper on ionium rays somewhere in between. Irène wrote Fred: ". . . the press conferences have gone off better than I'd believed. Apart from a few journalists in New York, I have not had an impression of hostility and, on the whole, what I said has not been too greatly distorted." And, before she returned home, she confided: "Press conferences have positively become my element and I wonder how I shall be able to do without them when I return to France."[19]

Not surprisingly, there was widespread French indignation at her treatment. Fred informed her: "This incident . . . has . . . taken on a very big significance. It is . . . a supplementary drop which for many has caused the vase of accumulated criticism to overflow about the dangers of present-day American policy. They are going too far . . . All the same, we must hope that the American people whom we love, will know how to react in time."[20]

The acceleration of the Cold War and the tension it produced emphasized for conservative Frenchmen the necessity of Western solidarity. Fred, who was speaking increasingly at political manifestations, disagreed. He condemned the Atlantic Alliance and the Marshall Plan's European Recovery Program, which Congress passed on April 2. According to the PCF's simplistic, present view of the world, there were now only two camps, "ours" and "theirs" —"the good one" and the "evil one." And a new PCF slogan: "The French people will never make war against the Soviet Union" appeared everywhere. But, in May 1948, the first chink in the monolithic East appeared when Tito broke with Stalin. And the Berlin Blockade started soon afterward.

Construction continued at a feverish pace on France's first reactor. Its shell of concrete and steel was growing at bulging Châtillon, not in the crowded fort proper, but in an immense hangar built alongside expressly to accommodate it. Here it was also easier to control cleanliness, which constituted one of the main engineering problems, for even the natural oils of fingerprints or the normal humidity of the atmosphere were unacceptable impurities. Kowarski, who liked to have a name for everything he worked on, facetiously christened it "The French Low Output Pile"—FLOP—until someone told Fred what "flop" meant in English. Never at a loss, Kowarski promptly renamed the uncooled heavy-water reactor that was to produce a few kilowatts "Zoë"—for *"Zéro énergie Oxyde,* and *Eau lourde* (heavy-water)."

Fred established the practice of having a summer meeting of the six-member Atomic Energy Commission and whoever else was needed at L'Arcouest to review and check schedules and plans. As their correspondence shows, working at the CEA was not always paradise. Some of their weekly sessions were stormy, especially the last year, when everyone was under great tension to have Zoë go active on schedule. Kowarski was even more outspoken than Irène, and Denivelle could not stand the way he talked to her, but claimed Fred kept Kowarski on because he was needed. Tempers were fraying, and others had equally unpleasant things to say about their colleagues. But Fred was a superb leader and everyone under him at Châtillon pulled together as a team. The commission realized that if any mistakes were made, the entire program could be set back two or three years. And while a small reactor of Zoë's size had only limited technical value, the psychological importance of its impact, once finished, on government ministers and on the general public would be incalculable.

In August, a large French contingent headed by Irène and her friend from childhood, Eugénie Feytis Cotton, Marie's former "sèvrienne"; the artists Picasso and Fernand Léger; and the writers Vercors and Paul Éluard attended the Stalin-approved World Congress of Intellectuals for Peace in Wroclaw—formerly Breslau—Poland. Fred did not go. The ruins of the bombed-out city, which had been more than 80 percent destroyed, provided a thought-provoking backdrop for this meeting of over seven hundred delegates from forty-five countries. It was out of this meeting that the famous World Peace Movement was shortly to evolve. The French group was the largest of the Western ones there, and Irène shared chairing the opening day's activities with Julian Huxley, the British biologist who was presently holding an important UNESCO post. Some of the language used was too strong for many Western left-wingers, who were finding it hard to distinguish between genuine pacifism and mere subservience to the Moscow line. Huxley got so disgusted with the political atmosphere that he flew home at the end of the second day. Irène apparently shared his feelings and, after a bitter Soviet attack on Sartre, was about to do likewise until Jerzy Borejsza, the organizer of the congress, hurriedly got Fred on the line in Paris, and he persuaded his wife to remain.

Hélène had become engaged that spring, and an early winter wedding was in the offing. Given their heredity, it was not unusual that both Joliot children should become scientists, and like "Papachou," as Hélène always called Fred, twenty-year-old Hélène was now attending EPCI. Nor was it surprising, considering how close-knit the family ties were, that her fiancé should be a fellow classmate of the same age—Michael Langevin, Paul's grandson. His father, André, had been a friend of Fred's since both attended Paul Langevin's EPCI classes together.

There was so much hardship in the strikebound mining communities of the Pas-de-Calais region that fall that the Joliots, like many others, took some of the strikers' children into their homes to get them out of the depressing, devastated North. Two little girls, aged nine and five, were still with them in November when Hélène and Michael were married at Antony, with Thorez prominent among the guests.

The next day Irène was in the hospital for a painful mastoid operation, which she had postponed in order not to put a damper on the wedding festivities. Always readily accessible to workers and staff at the Curie Laboratory, she was hardly out of the anesthetic and able to sit up before she was discussing a new process of making radiographs with Mlle. Faraggi, one of her advanced students, who had come to the hospital for this purpose at her request.

Dockers went out as well as railroad workers in support of the miners. But the government held fast. Tanks arrived; over forty thousand soldiers were called in, as well as five thousand police, and the strike was broken. The bourgeoisie won a great victory over the proletariat, and the ground was well prepared for a major anti-Communist propaganda drive.

Fred was beside himself with excitement the last few days before Zoë went active. Although it was only intended to produce five kilowatts of energy, what a colossal difference from the early days when all that was employed to get energy by splitting an atom was a few minuscule grains of a radioactive substance. Everyone at Châtillon was at the point of exhaustion and filled with nervous anticipation. Kowarski arrived at 6 A.M., December 15, attired in a brand-new fire-blue suit. It did nothing for his ample proportions but would make him, as master of ceremonies, stand out more prominently in the official pictures of the day's events. For reasons known only to himself, Kowarski did not include Francis Perrin among the handful of special guests.

Actually, there was nothing to see, as everything transpired within a thick concrete cube. Fred was about to participate in his sole experiment at the CEA—and the most important one there to date—and as high commissioner, he was assigned the task of keeping the logbook. Kowarski's twenty-some technicians took their posts. At 6:30 A.M., Zoë started to fill with heavy-water. About 9 A.M., Fred noted: "Kowarski says that the pile should begin to show activity."[21] But nothing happened. As time passed, the wait and the anxiety made everyone hungry. Kowarski managed to munch a banana, although at regular thirty-second intervals, he had to push the button controlling the pump that regulated the input of heavy-water into the great recipient containing oxide of uranium. Fred nibbled cherries distractedly and refurbished his black cigarette holder with one Gaulois after another. Suddenly the dials began to quiver, registering activity, and the Geiger counters around the concrete pile started chattering.

Shortly after noon, the hangar doors opened. A beaming Fred and Dautry stepped out to announce victory to the anxious crowd of Châtillon personnel gathered there. The personal satisfaction that Fred felt was reflected in the telegram he sent to M. Henri

Queuille, President of the Council of Ministers, announcing that at 12:12 P.M., the first French atomic pile went active. As Fred expressed it later: "There is something profoundly moving, when one builds a machine and engraves on it the date, December 15, 1948, to be able to say that, thousands of years hence, barring corrosion, an earthquake or other accidents, this machine will continue to give almost the same amount of energy."[22]

Now it was only a question of time, money, and manpower, before France could have the big models necessary to provide the power and electricity the country required. Perhaps Zoë's success meant the most to the working people. For them it was a symbol of France's phoenix-like rise from the ashes, proof that their country might one day again rank among the world's great powers.

Especially pleased was the Communist press. While it was aware from a prior Molotov announcement that Russia possessed the secret of the A-bomb, it did not yet know that two years earlier, on Christmas Day 1946, the reactor built by Igor Kurchakov near Moscow reached critical mass. For the world at large, Zoë was the first reactor built outside the English-speaking countries, and L'Humanité, the PCF's principal news organ, reacted accordingly. It saw in its success not only a triumph of one of its most famous members but also a setback to American dominance in France.

XXII
1948–1958

The Jury Is Still Out

FRED'S ACHIEVEMENT, THE breakup of the Anglo-American monopoly in nuclear energy, carried with it the seeds of his downfall; from this time on, the pressure to oust him never relaxed. The tone was set in *Time* magazine, which carried the headline "A Communist Pile." On the nineteenth of December, the London *Observer* commented that it was astonishing that "at the moment when measures of security against Communists are reinforced in England, as in America, the High Commissioner of French Atomic Energy should be Professor

Joliot-Curie." The London *Economist* of the twenty-fifth echoed the same theme and added, "sooner or later, France will have to . . . consider this problem." These and similar articles were believed to reflect official views abroad and, as such, were taken seriously in France. Given the present stage of the Cold War, anti-Communists everywhere felt the Western powers must act fast and stop the U.S.S.R. before it got any more powerful. Unaware of exactly how advanced Moscow already was in nuclear work, they were afraid of the continuation of the French policy of open publication of nuclear research results at a time when the Anglo-American nations were vigilantly pursuing a policy of total secrecy in this field. The lack of any French requirements regarding the political reliability of the CEA personnel increased Allied anxiety over the implications of Fred's accelerating atomic development. Interestingly enough, the spokesman for the British Embassy in Washington, who discussed the possibility of exerting pressure either directly or indirectly on the French to oust Fred, was Donald MacLean, who was later a prominent defector to the U.S.S.R.

On January 5, Fred accepted an invitation to lunch at the Anglo-American Press Association, a weekly affair at which the guest of honor, usually a person in the limelight, was subjected to a barrage of questions. Fred took advantage of this forum to emphasize that in accordance with government instructions, French research and development were exclusively oriented toward peaceful applications. To the charge that Russia might benefit greatly from results obtained in France through the PCF, Fred replied patriotically: "A French Commissioner, like any other citizen holding a post entrusted to him by the Government, cannot honestly think of communicating to a foreign power, whichever it may be, results which do not belong to him but to the community which has allowed him to work. Any Communist is perfectly aware of the necessity for this behaviour. . . . [To do so would be] to commit treason."[1] This is almost verbatim what he had written to Irène in connection with a different matter, on March 22 of the preceding year, when she was in America, and he wrote her now, "I got out of it worthily, telling them the truth."[2] So there is no reason to doubt the sincerity of his feelings. Unfortunately, Irène, who was running a fever and had a persistent cough, had been in Switzerland since just before the holidays, so she was not in Paris to comfort Fred during this difficult period. Her present cure would last two and a half months.

Apparently the Americans were not assuaged, if Drew Pearson is to be believed. On the fourth of February, the columnist reported in the New York *Herald Tribune* that the American ambassador in Paris had received instructions to demand the French government replace Fred. Predictably, *L'Humanité,* which was forever printing every word Fred uttered, did not even mention his Press Association remarks. The PCF was ill at ease with many of the intellectuals it recruited during and right after the war; like Yugoslavia's Tito, they were proving too independent and were unwilling to accept the party's wisdom blindly. Before these incipient renegades could sow any serious doubts among the faithful, they must be dealt with. So a short time later, on the occasion of the twenty-fifth anniversary of the death of Lenin, J. Duclos, the party secretary, declared: "Every progressive person has two fatherlands, his own and the Soviet Union." In other words, a Communist must never have any secrets from the U.S.S.R., which, as the fatherland of every worker, could never be included in Fred's phrase "a foreign power." Someone rash enough to deviate from this or any other party line was apt to find himself viciously reviled in *L'Humanité* and lumped ignominiously with the PCF's worst enemies. For discipline must be maintained regardless of cost.

Goldschmidt recalls that Fred kept him waiting outside his office at the Collège de France till 10 P.M. for a 7 P.M. appointment one evening not too long afterward. He was deep in discussion with one of the PCF leaders, Laurent Casanova, who, when he welcomed Fred into the party during the Occupation, concurred that Fred had been right not to flee France. When he ushered Casanova out, Goldschmidt found Fred "pale with fatigue and unnerved . . .

[He] did not hide from me the agonies he was going through"[3]—presumably after Duclos's public slap in the face. Francis Perrin also speaks of Fred after the war as often a "tormented spirit, plagued by deep self-doubts."[4]

For several weeks, Fred's colleagues held their breath, wondering if he was going to leave the party. Goldschmidt feels the reason Fred decided to stay was because he had such a need to be loved and admired that he lacked the courage to face the calumnious attacks the PCF would subject him to if he left. Perrin's observations, too, bear out that Fred sought and found in the adulation of the crowds compensation for the reserve he still sometimes felt among his peers. Often on Mondays, under the spell of a big meeting over which he had presided on Sunday, and with the crowd's roar echoing in his ears, Fred would tell Perrin and the others "how marvelous it is to feel yourself one with tens of thousands of people as convinced as you are of the justness of their cause."[5]

Meanwhile, the PCF leadership, building on a genuine Communist fear that the United States was preparing to launch a preventive attack against the U.S.S.R., decided that an antiwar campaign had great possibilities for rallying the masses to its side. This would appeal even more if it were tied to attacks on German re-armament and the military alliance with the United States, two government policies that were widely disliked by the French. So it was not by accident when the Bureau of the Women's International Democratic Federation met in Budapest, the preceding December 1948, that its members demanded a big international peace congress be held as soon as possible. Eugénie Cotton, who was an active participant there, was instructed to ask Fred to head this. Considering there were only so many hours even in his day, it was not surprising when he demurred politely, on the grounds that it would be more appropriate for the group to ask a woman. They insisted. Finally, Fred acquiesced because of his conviction that it was necessary to call upon and unite the masses, as well as the World Federation of Scientific Workers, if pressure were to be exerted successfully to halt the drift to war. As he explained: "My proper place *is* [sic] the laboratory not the committee room . . . But I want our movement to spread; it's only then that we'll be able to influence the policy of the West."[6]

He was one of six present when the preparatory committee for the forthcoming congress had its first meeting around a trestle table in a clean, bare office at no. 2 rue de l'Élysée, and in the weeks intervening before its April opening, he organized and directed all its work. Under his guidance the peace congress became more than a simple assembly of people who did not want war; it became a vehicle to create in each country represented an efficient organization to work toward this end. By the time Irène returned, still ailing, she found plastered on walls everywhere posters with Picasso's specially designed dove of peace announcing the meeting. It was to be held April 20–26, at the Salle Pleyel, in the heart of upper bourgeois Paris. Only Communists trained to do what they are told to do, and do it fast, could have organized anything on the Salle Pleyel scale within two months. The congress's timing was important from the Communists' point of view. For on April 4, the North Atlantic Treaty Pact [NATO] was signed in Washington by the United States, Canada, and ten Western European nations, consecrating the division of Europe into two blocs. But France had yet to go along.

Elegant as ever in a gray suit, highlighted by a bright red tie and the rosette of a commander of the Légion d'Honneur in his buttonhole, Fred presided from a dais decorated with the flags of the seventy-two participating countries. He was not a profound political thinker, but his sincerity, as usual, carried the day. His opening address—the best speech of the six days—to the more than two thousand delegates, who represented, conservatively, some six million people, mingled Communist rhetoric with a personal vision of the possibilities of science. His appeal for international cooperation and control of nuclear weapons not only fit the PCF party line and echoed that of a Communist rally the previous month at the Waldorf-Astoria, in New York, but was also repeated by other scientists, around the world, who were advocating similar campaigns. Both the French socialists and the British Labour Party looked on the congress as a PCF- and Moscow-inspired stunt and sharply warned their members not to attend; the worried French government cut the Moscow request for fifty-two visas to twelve, so delegate Shostakovich had to stay home.

No mere figurehead, Fred attended many of the smaller committee meetings as well as the large general assemblies and interested himself in the smallest details. Overnight, the staid Salle Pleyel projected the ambiance of a bazaar, vibrating with as many different tongues as in Babel, and the whole week was so unseasonably hot that the delegates risked drowning in the flood of words mixed with their own perspiration. One meeting was highlighted by Paul Robeson singing in his great bass voice, "Four Generals," a song made popular in the Spanish Civil War, then encoring with "Old Man River"; Picasso, who brought him to and fro in his chauffeur-driven car, limited himself to the announcement that his baby daughter, born on the congress's opening day, was named Paloma —or "dove"—after his dove of peace, which shone down on the assemblage from every available Salle Pleyel wall.

The electrifying news that the Chinese Communists had won a great military victory and entered Nankin ironically interrupted a major pro-peace tirade. It was greeted with wild applause because the fighting in the Far East was a justifiable war of liberation against imperialism. At still another session Fred, totally unaware that within five months the Soviets would release their own first atomic explosion, announced that although the French government was presently directing its nuclear program strictly to peaceful applications, "if tomorrow they ask us to do war work, to make an atomic bomb, we will reply: No!"[7] Others present echoed his sentiments, which were widely reported and quickly appeared as a signed statement on postcards bearing his portrait.

Fred's declaration and, especially, his presence at the head of a congress with an undeclared *leitmotiv* of a fight to the finish against the Atlantic pact, and largely devoted to anti-American propaganda, angered many in France. A journalist in *L'Aurore* demanded that he be fired from the CEA. From the PCF point of view, however, the congress was an unqualified propaganda success, and it ended with a mass demonstration at the Buffalo Stadium in outlying Montrouge, where youth predominated. One of its final acts was to create a standing bureau, the World Peace Council, for the continued promotion of world peace, with Fred as president. Henceforth, until his death, he would devote time and strength to militant action, touring different world capitals indefatigably.

No wonder, when one of his star research students, Toshiko Yuasa, returned in the summer from Japan, where she had sat out the final years of the war, that she commented on the greatly changed air in the Collège de France laboratories. They were not as active as before, and Fred did not appear every day; he still managed to direct the work of each person there, through letters dictated to his secretary—but not in person.

In May, Fred was in London; in October, Rome. Meanwhile, the Berlin Blockade ended and the peace congress's pleas notwithstanding, the Chambre des Députés ratified NATO.

The Atomic Energy Commissariat was right on schedule, and in between Fred's comings and goings, he met with its commission, and plans were approved for the second scheduled atomic reactor. This was to be larger than Zoë and construction would start on it before the end of the year at Saclay.

Because Irène's health did not permit her to take any more strenuous fortnight trips into the mountains with Angèle Pompei, the two old friends substituted motor trips and short walks in the French countryside. Generally, at Irène's request, these included passing by the CEA's new center to survey the progress there.

As guest speaker at the Russian Academy of Science, in a celebration feting the anniversary of the Bolshevik Revolution, Fred made his fourth trip to the U.S.S.R. in November. On Sunday, the day after he returned home, a jubilant Goldschmidt and the team of five who had been working with him came out to present to Fred a small vial containing the first milligrams of plutonium iodate produced in France. It was almost exactly a year since Zoë had started to function. It was long enough for Goldschmidt, France's acknowledged plutonium authority, to be able to finally withdraw the first bar of used reactor fuel and take it to be processed at the workshop in the Bouchet factory, which had been placed at the CEA's disposal. To be sure of no error, Goldschmidt personally carried out the final delicate step. They held their breath—but to everyone's disappointment, there was no precipitate. Then the first man-made element, which does not exist in nature, appeared "like snow."

Although part of the secret of Fred's success as a leader was to leave his colleagues complete freedom once he laid out the general lines of a program they were to follow, his first reaction to the vial Goldschmidt placed in his hand was dissatisfaction. How dare Goldschmidt produce plutonium with its dangerous potential as a key component of nuclear weapons without Fred's approval? But he did not express this feeling and was delighted at the magnitude of the achievement. The following Tuesday, when he gave his semiannual progress report to brief Châtillon's entire personnel and inspire them to further effort, the plutonium samples, together with Goldschmidt and the other five who had worked with him, were the stars of the hour.

Fred's relations with the three "Canadians"—Goldschmidt, Kowarski, and Guéron—were so strained that they had a showdown with him shortly afterward and reproached him for his repeated absences and increasing political activities. The CEA now employed more than a thousand people, for whom the trio was directly responsible, yet Fred was seldom around sufficiently long enough to give them advice or lend them his authority to resolve daily problems. Guéron lost his temper, threatened to resign, and stalked out. The blowup was then settled amicably with the remaining pair. Fred agreed to set aside every Wednesday afternoon to discuss Commissariat affairs with them, and they agreed to no longer criticize openly his extracurricular affairs. Fred went out the door to apologize to Guéron but could not find his office. Although it was some time since the CEA headquarters had moved to the former Hôtel de Clermont on the rue de Varenne, Fred had been there so little that he did not know where Guéron was located. He returned a short time later with Guéron in tow, and the four established what they referred to henceforth as "the spaghetti peace," finishing their discussion amicably over spaghetti at Roger la Grenouille's, Fred's favorite restaurant.

Matters must have reached a critical pass for the men to be so outspoken, and the appearance of plutonium did not help the situation. Rather, it marked a turning point for the CEA, heralding its removal from the bailiwick of the scientists to that of the politicians and the military. Fred was following a parallel course. As Kowarski was to recall, he seemed as if "stranded on a boat that was driven further and further from shore by a strong current . . . Joliot was carried away from us before our eyes."[8] Fred wanted nuclear energy for the betterment of mankind, not for its destruction. Unfortunately, his creation the CEA, fueled by its success, was advancing inexorably toward a fork in the road where a crucial decision must be made regarding its future. For when the CEA achieved its second goal of building a bigger reactor than Zoë, the new one at Saclay would automatically, over approximately a ten-year period, accumulate sufficient used rods to produce adequate plutonium for an A-bomb. Would France then remain steadfast to its commitment of nuclear power solely for peaceful use as it went into phase three and started to build still bigger reactors—with all they entailed? Fred found himself in a dilemma of his own making.

To try and resolve it, the politician won out over the scientist. He devoted still more time both at home and abroad to public action in an effort to save the world from a nuclear holocaust.

Ever since the Paris Peace Congress the preceding April, Fred's reputation had grown enormously in the Far East. When he and

Irène went to India the end of the year, to attend a scientific congress sponsored by Jawaharlal Nehru, the head of the Indian government, a wrong arrival time was purposely given the press in order to avoid a mob scene at the airport. The couple's tumultuous reception and their overcrowded schedule were carbon copies of what occurred wherever Fred went nowadays.

While they were in the Far East, President Truman announced on January 31, 1950, that he had given the go-ahead to work on the hydrogen bomb, despite the violent arguments, pro and con, which split the American Atomic Energy Commission. That body's scientific consultant committee, headed by Robert Oppenheimer, was unanimously against starting a new stage in the nuclear arms race, even though it was triggered by the Soviets' recent successful atomic blast. And Einstein sent an open letter to the President asking him to desist.

The Communists were doing all possible to discredit and impede the present French government, viewing its ties to NATO as a menace to Mother Russia.

In a country already fearful of the threat of another invasion from the East and worried that American belligerence might lead to France's annihilation in another war, the Communists cunningly tied every political and economic issue to the party's stand on peace and nuclear disarmament and adopted the slogan: "The French people will not make war now or ever against the Soviet Union."

During Fred and Irène's absence in India, Fred was the target of the non-Communist press, which predicted that his term as high commissioner would not be renewed when it expired that November. And the government, continuing its haphazard purge of Communists in high places, fired George Tèssier, Fred's choice for successor at the CNRS. *L'Humanité* immediately shouted that Fred was liable to go next, adding if Bidault dared to touch him, this would confirm that the French government was the United States' lackey. The Americans' opinion of Fred had not changed. Wisely wanting to avoid any appearance of directly pressuring France to remove him, they concentrated on doing whatever possible to impede the CEA's progress. As the official in Washington responsible for these matters remarked: "Joliot-Curie's presence . . . made it easier to say 'No' to any French request for cooperation in the atomic field."[9]

Still he kept on traveling. March 15–19, Fred was in Stockholm for a meeting of the World Committee of Partisans for Peace, an outgrowth of the previous year's enormous Paris Peace Congress. Fifteen years before, when Fred and Irène were in this Northern city, the couple were the stars of the hour as newly consecrated Nobel laureates. Fred checked into the same hotel where they had stayed, but when the management found out what he was there for, he was asked to leave. Ilya Ehrenburg, the Russian journalist who came for the same meeting, bumped into Fred on the street, carrying his own suitcase and going from hotel to hotel, trying to find one that was willing to accept a "Red." Some of his committee friends remembered that the nineteenth was his fiftieth birthday and surprised him with a gift when they convened for dinner. "It's a spinning-rod! I can tell by the feel," Fred whispered delightedly to Ehrenburg, who happened to be sitting next to him. He did not like to open the gift in front of everyone, but with childlike pleasure and curiosity written on his face, he bent over and tore a little piece of paper to take a peek. "It's made of some special bamboo," he confided.[10]

The group stayed around the table well past midnight that evening, drafting what became world-famous as the "Stockholm Appeal." The Communists' answer to the American green light for the hydrogen bomb, this new manifesto to ban nuclear weapons was perhaps the shortest the Communists ever adopted and included various phrases from Fred's different talks. Labeled by future historians as the boldest, most ambitious maneuver of the entire Communist peace strategy, even its name was symbolic, as Stockholm had refused to wage war for generations. Fred was the first to sign. Millions of people worldwide ultimately followed suit; others refused to be so manipulated by the Communists. Francis Perrin, Fred's ultimate successor as high commissioner of atomic energy, remarked, "I am a very strong pacifist. But I never signed the Appeal."[11]

After spending Easter at Courchevel with Irène in the new châlet they had just built there, Fred attended the Twelfth National Congress of the PCF. Held in the working-class, "Red" suburb of Gennevilliers, its principal theme was "The Fight for Peace," and above the podium, a huge banner declared: "The French people . . . shall never make war against the Soviet Union." On April 5, Fred gave one of its major speeches. Speaking of the danger of a war fomented by imperialists and of the scientists' struggle for liberty and peace, he asked those present to sign the "Stockholm Appeal" and concluded, echoing the streamer on the wall behind him: "Progressive scientists and Communist scientists shall not give a particle of their science to make war against the Soviet Union. We shall hold firm, sustained by our convictions that in so doing we serve France and all of humanity."[12]

Of course, Fred was referring to the manufacture of atomic weapons, so the whole question was hypothetical, since the French capacity to make one was still a long way down the road. Furthermore, he was not actually stating anything different than he had before on numerous occasions. In a jittery France, where almost every citizen expected war to break out tomorrow, what made his statement suddenly so defiant was the locale and place. This time, he altered his often stated philosophy to fit the occasion by specifically naming Russia as victim.

When Fred's son Pierre was asked years later if his father was surprised when his ouster finally occurred, Pierre replied affirmatively. His father did not formulate policy; he was an administrator. As such, Fred believed he was entitled to be ruled by his own conscience, as long as he was doing his job satisfactorily. The post of high commissioner did not imply any restrictions on its holder's right of self-expression, and Fred, as his letters show, resented any suggestion of betrayal or disloyalty on his part. His daughter Hélène maintained that her father half expected his ouster, yet was half-shocked when it actually came. "Remember," she urged, "our parents evolved in reply to circumstances and events around them. But their basic philosophy never changed."[13] However, both Perrin and Goldschmidt recall that Fred remarked the day following his Gennevilliers speech, "If the government doesn't fire me after what I've said, I don't know what they need."[14] Despite his official position, Fred was again declaring his independence regarding the French government and accepting, without qualification, the Gennevilliers platform of the PCF, which took its orders from the Soviet. Because he was high commissioner, his statement was interpreted by the world at large as a political as well as a personal one.

The consensus among his colleagues at the time was that Fred was the victim of the politics of the day and had been compelled by the PCF, unhappy to see one of its most prominent members still holding a high official position, to throw down the gauntlet before the government. If Fred was left at his post, this would prove its weakness. If Fred was fired at once, he was made a martyr for his political ideas. Either way, the party stood to make political capital at Fred's expense and shore up its contention that the present administration was an American puppet. As one of his close colleagues remarked about Fred: "Never did such a sympathetic man have such an unsympathetic story."[15] And in many respects, the savant was right. For this deliberate, acknowledged provocation of the government does not do him credit. And it is hard to conceive of Fred as politically naive. He not only let himself be used; he helped in the process. While he may secretly have nourished the thought that he would not be fired, even his genuinely felt desire for peace cannot explain his action. And as a pawn, he would be taken away, at fifty in the prime of life, from his own creation, the CEA, and his lifework, atomic research.

If Fred was not complying with party orders, as his colleagues suspect, because he was a good Communist, aware of the need for unquestioning party discipline and putting the needs of the PCF above his personal ones, what prompted Fred to precipitate matters by taking the challenging public stand at Gennevilliers is hard to imagine. It would have been uncharacteristic for him to act out of the arrogant belief that he was too invaluable for the government to touch and that he might remain a good Communist and still retain his post. Of the several possible explanations advanced by those who knew him, the one heard the most frequently is that Fred was blackmailed into doing the PCF's bidding. One contemporary cites a conversation in which Fred remarked enigmatically: "If it wasn't for the children, I'd leave the Party."[16] Had the PCF, a past master at character assassination by prefabricated dossiers, assembled one on Fred, which was easy to do on anyone who lived through the shadowy, gray period of the Occupation, it could easily topple its star. Such a fall from grace would be hard on a man of Fred's vanity and insecurity and, conceivably, on Pierre and Hélène.

In this regard it is interesting to note that, according to Pierre Joliot's mother-in-law, Pierre and his father fought bitterly over politics toward the end of Fred's life. While Pierre is still to this day an ardent socialist, the fact that Hélène, who worshiped her father, is an active Communist speaks louder than a thousand words.

Hard on the heels of his Gennevilliers address, a request in the National Assembly from Deputy Legendre to interpellate the government on Fred's status was tabled by parliamentary maneuvers. However, it was clear that some action must be taken regarding him soon. The New York *Times* of April 10 asked whether Fred's speech had been demanded by the Russians; several Paris papers were busy printing up lists of possible successors. From this distance it is impossible to determine to what extent, if any, supposed interference from abroad, as alleged in the PCF and non-Communist left-wing press, reinforced domestic pressures, when the official decision was ultimately reached to relieve Fred as high commissioner. Certainly there were sufficient internal reasons alone to justify this step. And, perhaps, it was pure coincidence that 70 billion francs' worth of Marshall Plan aid was released three days after the announcement of Fred's dismissal.

Wednesday, April 26, three weeks to the day after his Gennevilliers speech, Fred was in the midst of the regular weekly meeting he had promised Kowarski, Guéron, and Goldschmidt, when he received a phone call summoning him at once to see Georges Bidault, the President of the Council of Ministers. Remarking, "It is either a strong reprimand or dismissal,"[17] Fred hastened across the rue de Varennes to the nearby Hôtel Mâtignon. Bidault, who knew Fred in the underground, wasted no words. "M. le Professeur," Bidault greeted him, his voice charged with emotion, "how I regret that I must dismiss you."[18] Fred was relieved of his functions as high commissioner because of the fundamental incompatibility between the duties of his office and the tenor of his public statements. As he left, Fred pointed through the windows to a century-old tree in the Mâtignon grounds and remarked: "The original gardener is dead, but the tree he planted is still there. Only that counts."[19]

The night of his dismissal, Fred attended a belated celebration of his fiftieth birthday with some twenty close collaborators from the CEA. Bruno Pontecorvo, who was staying briefly with Goldschmidt, a co-worker from Chalk River, joined the group to toast his former teacher. Fred gave no outward indication of what had occurred. But Goldschmidt had remained in Fred's office with the other two members of the "spaghetti peace" until Fred returned from his meeting with Bidault. He had a good gauge of Fred's inner turmoil when he started to say a few words as guest of honor. Famous for conversing in hour-long monologues, Fred outdid himself with such a rambling three-hour discourse on everything popping into his head. Pontecorvo contemptuously remarked to Goldschmidt afterward that no good Communist would ever act like that. He was in a better position to know than his host realized. A few months later, Pontecorvo created an international sensation when he revealed his own Communist affiliation by disappearing behind the Iron Curtain with his entire family.

Goldschmidt and several CEA colleagues were anxious to avoid the risk of a purely political appointment to Fred's vacant post. Two days later when the revocation was public property, they made the rounds of the essential ministries and within twenty-four hours got official assurance that the government would do nothing along those lines until the end of the year, when Fred's mandate was to have expired. Irène was so outspokenly bitter about Fred's treatment that the rest of the Atomic Energy Commission were amazed she did not resign on the spot. She failed utterly to comprehend that Fred as high commissioner could not remain a law unto himself. She finally calmed down and remained at the CEA until December when her term of office ran out. It was not extended.

Fred's revocation, while long anticipated in certain circles, caused great surprise elsewhere, for to the average layman, he was science personified. Numerous protest meetings were called in his behalf, and the young impetuously set out on a door-to-door campaign for signatures for the "Stockholm Appeal" in his name. However, his removal was approved by the general public, with the exception of the far left. A short time later, the National Assembly voted, 399 to 179, its confidence in the government's decision; the Communist deputies' votes were the only negative ones. The non-PCF lawmakers' debates on the termination of Fred's mandate focused mainly on one individual's defiant attitude about an as yet undetermined official policy regarding nuclear weapons, rather than on a matter of general principle involving all public scientific institutions. Nonetheless, Fred's ouster spelled an end to the predominance of scientists as policy-makers within the CEA. His removal was not an isolated incident; other Communists in high places had already been purged, and as the fulcrum in France continued its swing to the right under external pressures, more would be. Nothing resembling McCarthyism ever swept France, however.

Now followed what his son Pierre refers to as his father's "black" period. As Fred commented sadly, and with some amazement, to Toshiko Yuasa, "Even old friends seem to avoid shaking hands with me."[20] So afraid were some former co-workers of being erroneously labeled a Communist by association and being fired that many did everything possible to avoid being seen with Fred. Colleagues who used to scramble to greet him crossed to the opposite side of the street to avoid doing so, and many preferred to walk downstairs five or six flights rather than take the same elevator with him at the Collège de France. Many were the spiteful, petty snubs. The Joliots' traditional Sunday open house at Antony suffered for want of guests, and those who did come found that Fred talked very little of the CEA. A product of his mind and heart, the subject was too painful. He considered it like one of his offspring, and nurturing its development and growth had been a source of great satisfaction for him.

Châtillon and Saclay were off-limits for him, henceforth, which also meant that had he the time to return to research, there was no atomic pile available for him to work with. However, as holder of the physics chair at the Collège de France and director of the CNRS's Ivry Laboratory of Synthetic Analysis, he still had those well-equipped laboratories at his disposal, although he would have a harder time keeping them adequately funded in the future. But Fred had little time to devote to any personal research. He turned with increased ardor to the crusade for peace. More than ever, he thrived on the mammoth audiences with whom he was able to establish an immediate rapport; the knowledge that tens of thousands of strangers worldwide placed their confidence in him was a source of great comfort. Although his work as a teacher and an academic continued, Fred's international activities increased. From then on, the story of Fred's life reads like the travelogue of a person obsessed as he crisscrossed Europe. Nor were Communists the only people similarly involved. Prominent non-Communist scientists elsewhere were equally engaged in sharp controversy over the highly complex scientific, political, and military aspects of atomic energy.

That spring Irène surprised her intimates by knitting tiny booties, like any other prospective grandmother, and on May 21, 1950, Hélène's first child, Françoise, was born. The baby's arrival brought Fred his only real joy of a personal nature in this difficult readjustment period. Still deeper furrows creased his narrow face, while Irène, her hair almost white and thinner than ever, looked older than her fifty-three years.

After having exploited his dismissal to the hilt, the Communist press soon let Fred slide into more or less temporary oblivion, comparatively speaking, a clear sign if any was needed that the PCF considered the whole episode a strategic political ploy. As another indication of cynical Communist duplicity, it is worthwhile to correlate—with hindsight—their blatant setting up of the various peace groups that Fred was so active in, with the feverish, secret work on the Soviet A-bomb as the arms race gained momentum.

That fall, the Second World Peace Congress, which was to be held in Sheffield, was moved, at the last minute, to Warsaw when the British government refused to let the ship bringing Fred across the Channel land. Fred was elected president of the World Peace Council, a new entity of 235 created at the congress's finish. This, together with the World Federation of Scientific Workers, would constitute Fred's two main instruments in the campaign against nuclear weapons. He would remain its president until his untimely death. As with the other groups with which he was connected, Fred was never an inactive honorary president, and his force and influence did not reside solely on his immense authority and reputation, or his powerful, dynamic speaking ability. He always insisted on entering into all the details of the organization's life. At one especially lengthy session of the new Council, Fred, who was presiding, leaned across the large bottle of bicarbonate of soda which accompanied him everywhere nowadays and whispered, teasingly, to Eugénie Cotton, for whom he had as much affection as respect, "When I think how insistent you were for me to become President!" He shook his head in mock seriousness. "That I, so talkative, should be obliged to listen this way to others!"[21]

Irène held up her end of extracurricular activities as best she could, whenever something very close to her heart was involved. Although it was never easy for her to deal with strangers, her earnestness more than offset any lack of graciousness at the mass rallies and conferences she attended at home and abroad, alone or in company with Fred. Early the following March 1951, at a mass meeting in Paris of some thirty thousand women celebrating International Women's Day, she spoke out against the armament race and the continuing war in Vietnam.

In April, *finis* was finally written to the Joliot episode at the CEA with the appointment of Francis Perrin as his successor. According to Perrin, he assumed the post of high commissioner only after much persuasion—and with Fred's explicit approval. But others close to the family still speak of Fred and Irène's initial bitterness at his acceptance. This was understandable, although it made for some tense, painful moments within the close-knit L'Arcouest circle for a considerable time. In the interim, before Perrin took over, the internal structure of the CEA was altered to give the administrator-general top rank and authority within the organization. The lesson of Fred's dismissal was driven home: The government and not the scientists would have the final say over the uses of nuclear fission.

That summer, Fred and Irène visited Poland before going to Moscow, where he received, in the Great Hall of the Kremlin, the first of the Stalin Peace prizes. After a two-week vacation in a *dacha* in the country with Eugénie Cotton, another of the ten prizewinners, a state coach was placed at the trio's exclusive disposal to take them, by train, to Finland for a meeting of the World Peace Council. Several months later Irène could not be invited to the Oxford Conference on radioisotopes because the British government refused to issue her a visa.

War had erupted in Korea, the previous summer, and cholera was rampant in Northern Korea and Manchuria that winter. So the Communist press was widely believed when it reverted to the well-established Communist tactic of attributing epidemics, famines, and other scourges on world capitalism and accused the Allies of waging bacteriological warfare in defiance of the 1925 protocol of the League of Nations. Supporting the PCF condemnation of the West, in early March Fred blasted the United States, citing as his source M. Kuo Mo Jo, president of the Academy of Sciences of Peking and also president of the Committee of the Chinese People for the Defense of Peace, which had recently been set up with Stalin, Mao Tse-Tung, and Fred as honorary chairmen. Kuo's colleague Tsien had for eleven years been one of Fred's best pupils.

There was a strong wave of anti-American sentiment in France at the moment, in part because of constant United States pressure for German rearmament and the installation of an American NATO base in France, and also because the French felt that they were a mere instrument in Washington's hands in the Cold War. A long, bitter public dispute, which the Washington *Post* labeled as his "greatest battle of all" ensued between Fred and Warren Austin, the American ambassador to the United Nations, who accused Fred of "prostituting science" by his stand. Nine Nobel laureates published an open letter asking Fred to retract his accusations about the Allied forces until the International Red Cross, or some other equally impartial group, could make an on-site inspection. But the Chinese and Koreans turned down this proposal on the grounds that it would have a Western bias and fielded another under a Communist. This one, not surprisingly, supported Kuo's stand.

In this unsavory episode, Fred showed, if any doubt remained after his Gennevilliers statements of 1950, that his conception of his duty as a Communist was as strong as that of the most untutored party militant. He seemed to feel that only the Communists could do away with war and the capitalists' exploitation of ordinary man. Whenever orders from on high caught Fred between what his own intelligence and conscience told him and his party loyalty, the glorious end justified the dishonorable means—with rare exceptions. Fred did speak out publicly against Thorez's—and Molotov's

—official line regarding the consequences of a nuclear holocaust. He must also have regarded with great distaste the pseudo-scientific theories of Stalin's favorite biologist, the hack Trofino Lyssenko, that had recently triumphed, on an official party level, supplanting the established Mendelian principle of heredity. But like so many Communist intellectuals he apparently subscribed, in general, to the myth that the PCF leaders knew better than he, and he swallowed their dogma like a religion—the good with the bad.

When it came to the issue of whether any of the peace movements with which he was connected were Communist-controlled, or merely served the PCF strategy of the moment, colleagues felt this was immaterial from Fred's point of view. Banning nuclear war was closest to his heart, so he would have worked for them anyway.

If he was not being manipulated consciously and willingly and wanted to leave the fold, it is surprising that he did not do so either at the time of the Gennevilliers or Korean affair. If he wanted to leave and could not, that is something else again. The jury is still out on that score.

March 5, 1953, mournful singing by a Russian male choir heralded each of the morning's repeated Russian-language broadcasts, over the French National Radio, of Moscow's announcement that Stalin, who had been gravely ill, was dead. In July, the Korean War ended and, in August, the United States detected that the Russians had detonated a thermonuclear bomb, a blast which furnished irrefutable evidence that spying, alone, was not responsible for A. Sakharov's nuclear success. For different materials were used than those in either the Americans' trial run at Eniewetok, the previous year, or in their H-bomb test to come, at Bikini, the following March 1954. Following the 1954 blast, Japanese fishermen on board a small fishing boat some one hundred and fifty kilometers away were coated with a strange white dust. All fell terribly ill and one died. Fred, as president of the World Federation of Scientific Workers, promptly proposed to organize an International Scientific Congress devoted to the dangers of nuclear arms and also wrote the president of the United Nations General Assembly, insisting on the need to take up the questions of atomic, thermonuclear, and biological arms. That he had long-lasting, nagging doubts about Russia's entry into the nuclear arms race and deplored that they had done so was evident when he commented, several years later, at the Fourteenth Congress of the PCF: "Certainly men are not perfect. Mistakes have been made . . . Every person must deplore them and every one can see how we judge these mistakes even when they are the work of a man as important as Comrade Stalin."[22]

The publicity about the stricken fishermen dramatized for the general public the immense potential for destruction of the new H-bomb and aroused it to the increasing dangers of radio fallout even in atomic testing. A new equilibrium of terror was being established between the two superpowers, who would soon have the capacity to annihilate each other. Meanwhile, in the United States, that same spring, an investigation was ordered of Robert Oppenheimer, who headed up the Los Alamos laboratory where the A-bomb was built and felt a strong sense of guilt for having opened Pandora's box. Because Oppenheimer had had connections with the extreme left, many years before, the motives behind his vociferous pleading against the development of the H-bomb were questioned.

Health problems were accruing for both the Joliots. Irène's had deteriorated to the stage where she was home resting on a chaise longue a good deal of the time. She did not complain, permitted no one to discuss her regime, and adjusted her work habits accordingly. Fred, too, was far from well, still suffering from a serious illness and a long convalescence. Because Irène was not strong enough to take care of him and cook the special diet he must follow, three times a day, at home, she had to hire someone else to do so. While attending a scientific meeting in Strasbourg, the previous spring, Fred had been stricken with viral hepatitis, which he presumably caught a few weeks earlier at a meeting in Prague; he was rushed to the hospital there and was quick to insist that his sickness had nothing to do with the effects of radiation. He was worried that if it was believed that he, too, was affected, like Marie, who died from it, many young people might be dissuaded from the study of radioactivity. Today, the consensus is that no one could have been subjected to as much radiation as Fred, and been as casual about taking elementary precautions, and not suffer certain ill effects which probably undermined his whole system. The trauma and strain he had been subjected to since his dismissal must also have taken its toll.

Irène's research was again pushed into the background when she undertook lobbying for a new Institute of Nuclear Physics and Radioactivity. Sweden, Switzerland, and Holland had far superior installations, academically speaking, than the University of Paris, which had long since outgrown its facilities at the Curie Laboratory. The number of researchers there had doubled since the war and in keeping with the tradition started by Marie, Irène as the Curie's director—as well as holder of the Sorbonne Chair of Nuclear Science, like her mother—was anxious to be able to accommodate more foreigners on an exchange basis. The time was past when nuclear research could be done in a few rooms; the Curie did not even have a cyclotron at its disposal, much less space for this important atomic tool.

Although administrative chores were a bore for Irène, this project was dear to her heart, and her efforts were supported by a number of her colleagues on the Faculty of Sciences of the University, the deans of its Faculty, and certain influential functionaries of the Ministry of Education. Fred, too, helped with an important speech at the Society for the Encouragement of National Industry. In this speech he exposed publicly, for the first time since his ouster, his thoughts and preoccupations concerning the future of atomic energy and basic research in nuclear physics in France. After long arduous overtures and endless meetings which did not help her poor health, Irène, who would automatically serve as the new center's future director, obtained the necessary funding and credits. She selected a site at Orsay, a thirty-five-minute Métro ride from Paris, and even went to Holland to inspect, firsthand, the accelerators she was ordering.

After participating in October at a Warsaw celebration of the twentieth anniversary of Marie's death which featured the inauguration of a Curie Museum in the Freta Street house where Marie was born, Irène returned to be fêted with Fred for their own discovery of artificial radioactivity. The brilliant affair was staged by the University of Paris in the amphitheater Richelieu of the Sorbonne, and despite continued government snubs, all officialdom was present and the minister of education presided. Nonetheless, when Irène made a third attempt to storm the Coupole, in an admitted effort to force the issue as a feminist, the Academy of Science once more turned her down; as if to compensate, its distinguished—and stubborn—members awarded the pair the Academy's prized Lavoisier Gold Medal.

The summer of 1955, the construction Irène was overseeing on the first buildings at Orsay ran into unexpected difficulty; special footings were necessary to reinforce the clay soil there in order to support the heavy weight of the great new accelerators and sustain the concrete walls, which were to act as screens against radioactive emanations. It was a good six months after the commencement of work before anything was visible above-ground.

No one ever enjoyed romping with his grandchildren more than Fred, and in August three generations of Joliots were together at L'Arcouest, including the newest edition, Yves. Twenty-three-year-old Pierre was preparing his doctoral thesis on photosynthesis and was especially interested in one of Fred's pet ideas—the possibilities of direct utilization of the energy of the sun's rays. The resultant discussions at mealtime between father and son were so heated that Irène had no chance to put in a word and reminded her of many similar ones between Marie and Fred, on the Quai de Béthune, where she once had the same problem. As usual, Fred won numerous regattas in the tricky Channel waters with his *Marsouin* and the new *Gaby* and frequently accompanied the native fishermen out for a day's catch. Irène had time to relax and indulge in rowing about the bay, a bandanna tied around her head, and as her grandchildren got older, she took great pleasure in teaching them and other L'Arcouest third-generation youngsters how to swim. Regardless of how she felt, she also managed to dance on the village square to the skirling of the Breton bagpipes and violin at the annual church benefit to raise money for the local school.

While there that fall, Fred's continuing campaign against the death and destruction wreaked by atomic warfare exacted a toll of an unexpected sort. He gave up hunting. He had felt for some time that taking life, other than for food, was wrong. Then, one day, in the woods around L'Arcouest, Fred had a bird within range. He watched for a few minutes as it was busy with its young but could not bring himself to press the trigger. "The old hunter in me lost control," he later confessed.[23]

Concurrently, that year, the first Atoms for Peace Conference organized by the United Nations was meeting at Geneva with even the Russians participating. When a foreign journalist expressed surprise during Francis Perrin's press conference at the absence of Fred and Irène, France's Nobel laureates, he replied with embarrassment, "The French Government does not consider their participation necessary."[24] Their names were not mentioned anywhere in the large French exhibit there, although they were prominently displayed in the British one, and the request of a number of scientists that Fred give one of the main public lectures was ignored. Even if the Joliots' wounds from 1950 were healed, it would not have been surprising if they were reopened by this conspiracy of silence. Certainly, intimate relations with Perrin must have been strained. On the other hand, perhaps Fred and Irène were both too busy with Orsay to care anymore.

Fred had never fully recovered from his bout with viral hepatitis in Strasbourg. He was rehospitalized with it earlier this May, and in

October, he was back in the gloomy old Hôpital St.-Antoine for additional long weeks of treatment. When he started to recuperate, he took up drawing and painting and discovered he had some of his late sister's artistic talents. Friends commented on the infinite weariness in his eyes and the dark circles now permanently under them, the thick black hair turning gray. Although his health improved, he was slowly but surely compelled to cut down on his traveling. Forced to spend a lot of time at Antony, he had a small laboratory fitted up at home. There he did research on the comparative strontium content of milk of different dates in order to determine the effects of radioactive fallout due to nuclear weapon tests. He was preoccupied with the thought of dying and felt sure he would predecease Irène.

As always, the sea air at L'Arcouest, the swimming, bathing, rowing, wrought wonders for Irène, and from there she addressed a note to the Congress of Mothers, then in session, approving the "initiative of the International Democratic Federation of Women to convoke a World Congress of Mothers for the defense of their children against the danger of a new war . . . that would be atomic."[25] This would be her last public message.

Back in the city once more, new ailments appeared. Irène's natural pallor increased; she was already thinner than a rail and losing more weight; a low fever came and went. Her tuberculosis was under control, but now doctors diagnosed leukemia. Directly related to overexposure from radiation, Fred would refer to leukemia as "our occupational disease." In Irène's case, her X-ray work with Marie during World War I was the unquestioned culprit.

Except for when she was in a sanatorium, this was the first Christmas vacation since her marriage that Irène did not spend in the mountains with Fred, but he was not well enough for the trip. It was strange to be alone at Courchevel: "I regret, every day, that I have too much room for my personal belongings," she wrote him. ". . . I am even sorry not to have to straighten up your bed, something, however, that I do not like to do. I miss you terribly . . ."[26]

This time, Irène came home without the usual benefits from a stay there. Upon leaving her at the Curie Hospital, next door to the Radium Institute, the taxi driver asked when he should pick her up. She hesitated, then answered, "I don't know." For the first time her body refused to submit to her iron will. "To breathe, to eat, the most elemental functions are painful for me," she confessed to Eugènie Cotton when she visited her.[27]

At the moment, Fred was once more housebound because of recent overexertion, and Hélène was preoccupied with her own small family, so it was Pierre who commuted between the hospital and Antony. When he was finally able to see Irène, Fred made a supreme effort to be cheerful, but he was completely drained, emotionally and physically, once he left the hospital. Every new medication was tried, even one that Toshiko Yuasa ordered rushed from Japan. But there was no hope. Each day Irène was paler and weaker. She was resigned to dying and told her childhood friend, Aline Perrin Lapique: "I don't fear death. You see, I have had a beautiful life."[28] Her mind was clear till the end. She worried that her time schedule for Orsay would not be adhered to, and the day before she died, she discussed in detail with Edmund Wellhoff, who served under her in Blum's Cabinet, a proposed law that she felt would not give any real help to the poor.

Irène died on March 17, 1956. Today leukemia is often treated by injections of one or more of the thousands of radioactive isotopes resulting from Irène and Fred's Nobel-winning discovery. Her coffin was placed in a tiled room in the hospital's lower basement, which fittingly resembled a laboratory, and for two days, people from all walks of life came to kneel and pay their respects to the courageous woman. Then, in accordance with custom, the last twenty-four hours before the services the casket was exposed in the main hall of the Sorbonne, guarded by professors and pupils of the Faculty of Sciences, in fifteen-minute shifts. Irène was given a state funeral, a dignity normally only accorded to statesmen or army heads, although many intimates felt she would have preferred a simple service like Marie and Pierre Curie's. On the other hand, this public acclaim helped the causes so close to her heart—women's emancipation, world peace, and a moratorium on atomic weapons—and the pomp and ceremony made visual amends for the couple's recent years of official oblivion. At the family's request and out of respect for her strong antiwar feelings, the usual military honors and guard were waived. The service in the Sorbonne's great court was followed by a brief graveside one in the cemetary at Sceaux, where her parents were buried.

Her death was a great blow for Fred, who had been sure he would predecease her. His face ravaged with grief; he lost the exuberance that was so integral a part of his nature. Still convalescent himself, it took him a long time to recover any sort of equanimity. Theirs had been a happy marriage, regardless of what Fred's original motives might have been for seeking her hand. He confessed to Ilya Ehrenburg, whom he saw a short time later, "I am not finding this easy,"[29] and wrote Otto Hahn, "I have had some very hard moments, but I have been able to find the strength necessary to resist by working like fury."[30]

Although the five floors and three lower basements of his own laboratory at the Collège de France were already filled to capacity, at Fred's own request he assumed Irène's chair on the Faculty of Sciences and, accordingly, the directorship of the Curie Laboratory with its new Orsay extension. Only twice before had France permitted any one savant the right to occupy simultaneously a chair at the Sorbonne and also at the Collège de France; the physiologist Claude Bernard and the chemist Marcelin Berthelot were the exceptions. But if Fred wanted to see the Orsay laboratories completed, which had meant so much to Irène, this was the best way to assure that they were and, also, to guarantee that a separation be maintained there between fundamental and industrial research. From then on, Fred gave his colleagues the impression of a man racing against the clock; administrative work once again occupied a major portion of his time, as he added meetings with contractors and architects to his already overcrowded schedule.

Living with Pierre at Antony, Fred slowly adjusted to life without Irène. Hélène and her husband were still in the family's old Froidvaux apartment, and they all spent most of their vacations together. When the PCF held its annual congress at Le Havre that summer, Fred, with only 30 percent of his liver functioning normally, was feeling too poorly to attend, but he was elected to a one-year term as a member of its central committee.

By Christmas Fred was well enough to go to Courchevel to ski, and in April 1957, he went to Berlin for a meeting of the bureau of the World Peace Council. But perhaps a better indication of his true state of health was his resignation as president of the World Federation of Scientific Workers, after an eleven-year tenure as president. His friends and children tried to persuade him to relax and return to the laboratory. He claimed there was nothing he wanted to do more, but his conscience would not let him leave to others what he considered his duties. Interestingly enough, his daughter felt that in the long run her father was able to forgo working in the laboratory, whereas her mother never could have.

Although the interior fittings were not yet finished, Fred decided to move the laboratory workers into Orsay that fall; he himself did the same. By October, the accelerators had been installed, and for the first time since his ouster from the CEA, Fred had once again ready access to one. Here he had over two hundred and twenty researchers and technicians, including some fifty *docteurs ès sciences,* all engaged in fundamental research. From his windows he could watch the construction of the rest of the complex that was to perpetuate the great tradition of the Curies—and Joliot-Curies—and which he would not live to see completed.

One day, as he was leafing through some old files of Pierre and Marie Curie's to make a choice for an exhibition at the Musée Pedagogique for the one hundredth anniversary of Pierre's birth, a brisk reflex unexpectedly made him drop the card he was holding.

He had suddenly realized that the material he was handling might so contaminate his hands that he could no longer do any work of his own without throwing out of kilter any delicate instruments he might be using. Checking the *fiche*'s radioactivity with a Geiger counter, Fred was amazed at how high it still was. He was struck by the realization that the radiation that was still registering derived from the original radium that Pierre and Marie discovered and which had initially opened up the world of nuclear physics. Time had indeed marched on. For, with a 180-degree turn, Fred's estranged first love, the CEA, was already setting up a center for experiments with nuclear explosives in the Sahara.

When the academic year resumed, Fred was teaching Irène's classes at the Sorbonne and giving his own series of public lectures at the Collège de France. In May 1958, he made a sixth and last visit to Moscow. He had his first long talk with Bruno Pontecorvo since the Italian scientist defected, and later, on the fifteenth, he had a two-and-a-half-hour private visit with Khrushchev. Only a colleague of the Soviet leader and an interpreter were also present. They were discussing the need to create a world climate for disarmament and peace when, despite orders to the contrary, talk was interrupted by the telephone's strident ringing. Khrushchev ignored it. A few minutes later there was a discreet knock at the door. It opened a crack, someone stuck his head inside and whispered to the interpreter, who took the receiver off the hook and handed it to Khrushchev. As he listened, his face broke into a broad grin. Putting down the phone, he rose excitedly and went over to Fred, struck him heartily on the shoulder, and, with his left hand, made large circles in the air. The interpreter explained to the puzzled Joliot that the third Sputnik was successfully in orbit. The Space Age had begun when the first one was launched the previous October.

On his return, Fred participated in a public demonstration at the Sorbonne in protest against the coup that had just brought de Gaulle back to power. He then put the finishing touches to his last speech, another plea for peaceful coexistence, which was addressed to people worldwide and intended for a Stockholm congress he was unable to attend. The simultaneous meeting of the International Congress of Nuclear Physics in Paris was an important event, the first one held there since 1937. Fred gave the opening address and presided. Those who had not seen him for some time were shocked at his appearance. Fred was bone-weary and looked it; even his familiar smile could not mask his yellow skin, bloodshot eyes, and the thinness of his face. But once he started to talk, his former animation returned, transcending appearances.

After the congress, Fred set off by car for L'Arcouest. But a few days later, he made a special trip back because Jean Berthouin, the Minister of National Education, wanted to visit Orsay. A half-hour before his arrival, Fred called in his secretary and one or two others. "After the visit of the Minister we will know the attitude of de Gaulle and the new government toward us. Will it be one of confidence? Will it mean additional support? We shall see. The Minister's first words will tell the story. If he starts out, 'Monsieur le Professeur,' with a great deal of respect, we can breathe a sigh of relief. If he keeps his distance, this will be a bad sign." M. Berthouin began with "Monsieur le Professeur."[31]

Early in August, Hélène and Pierre, who were at L'Arcouest with Fred, went off on a one-week cruise to see the regatta at Brest. The ninth, Fred spent with his fishermen friends mending nets, and the next day he was off at dawn and returned, delighted with a good catch. In the night of the tenth-eleventh, he suffered a severe hemorrhage. The housekeeper ran for help, and by 9 A.M. Fred was in an ambulance en route to the depot at St.-Brieuc and a Paris hospital. When the train pulled in to the Gare Montparnasse, the waiting ambulance was prohibited by some archaic law from approaching close enough to ease Fred's transfer into it. Lengthy negotiations to remedy the situation were floundering when the engineer, who had been a silent bystander, unexpectedly broke the deadlock. He stoutly refused to unhitch his string of cars and take his engine to the roundhouse until the ambulance for Professor Joliot was allowed to come alongside to fetch him.

Emergency circulatory surgery of a pioneering nature—three years later, it became standard procedure in France—was performed. At first Fred felt better. His strength returned, and he spent a number of days propped up in bed, writing out the last of his course of lectures on radioactivity, and also corrected proof of an article for *L'Age Nucleaire.* His morale and physical condition improved greatly, and he was looking forward to returning to L'Arcouest when a postoperative septicemia set in. As the news spread, hundreds spontaneously offered their blood. The doctors were helpless, and the family no longer left his bedside. On Thursday, August 14, 1958, the shades were drawn on his window in the Peyrot pavilon of the Hôpital St.-Antoine. Fred was dead. His remains were placed in one of the hospital's small halls, which was transformed into a chapel where people might come to pay their immediate respects.

Dr. Raymond Latarjet, the distinguished honorary director of the Institut du Radium, claims that Fred never had viral hepatitis, a diagnosis "uttered to keep him hopeful." According to Dr. Latarjet, Fred suffered "from the first symptoms of liver disfunction until his death, from a cirrhosis produced by overexposure to polonium."[32] So, like Marie and Irène before him, Fred was still another victim of radiation research. In all likelihood the family knew this, and possibly, this is why they did not have the autopsy performed that Fred had specifically requested.

No one can have a true idea of the size of the figure Fred cut in contemporary France—and the world—without glancing, even cursorily, at the massive folios of contemporary press clippings at the time of his death, which are in the library of the Curie Laboratory. The mere bulk is, in itself, overwhelming, even if it was 75 percent Communist-inspired. To get an idea of what Fred meant to the proletariat, one only had to see the slow pilgrimage of thousands of the humblest citizens, men and women who, for two subsequent days, filed by his catafalque in the outer hall at the Sorbonne's main entrance. De Gaulle sent a delicately worded expression of condolences and decreed that Fred, like Irène, should have a state funeral.

An unfortunate wrangle followed between Pierre and Hélène and government representatives, who tried to ignore the children's wishes and make their own arrangements. Pierre and Hélène prevailed, and the services were divided, like Irène's, into two separate ceremonies, the official one and another at Sceaux. Ministers, ambassadors, academicians, senators, the members of the Faculty of Sciences and the Collège de France, and the various dignitaries and representatives from abroad attended the services in the Sorbonne's cobbled courtyard, where Fred's coffin now lay, draped with the tricolor, facing the seventeenth-century chapel, and flanked by the statues of Hugo and Pasteur. Then his body was taken to Sceaux. Friends and colleagues, comrades from the PCF and different peace organizations, as well as his students, and a crowd of anonymous, humble Parisians accompanied the funeral procession in the rain and wind from the train depot to the little cemetery, where Fred now joined Irène.

Acting with such unseemly haste that the conservative press took it to task, the PCF wasted no time, or scruples, in issuing orders to utilize Fred's death to the maximum for propaganda purposes. A neighborhood park in one of the Paris suburbs was promptly rechristened after him, and other similar memorials were soon to follow. The Communist press worldwide urged likewise. The fifth of October, *Pravda* solemnly announced:

To eternalize the memory of the great savant and combatant for peace (1) The Ministry of the Navy of the U.S.S.R. has given his name to one of the boats intended for international service; (2) A group of student alpinists from Tcheliabinsk has made the first assent of an unnamed mountain, 4,650 meters high, and named it after Joliot; (3) One of the craters observed by Luna 3 on the far side of the moon has been named after him.

But it was de Gaulle who had the final say and said what might have pleased Fred most of all—unless that driven man were to have been awarded the Nobel peace prize. When the general visited Saclay, a short time later, he declared: "I am the one who made him the head of the Atomic Energy Commission. I am very satisfied with what I did and I would do it again."[33]

Selected Bibliography

INTERVIEWS

(Any tapes of same that exist are the author's personal ones and are to be found in the Curie and Joliot-Curie Archives of the Laboratoire Curie in Paris, identified henceforth as L.C.)

Auger, Pierre

Biquard, Pierre

Desgranges, Lucien

Frilley, Marcel

Goldschmidt, Bertrand

Gricouroff, Mme.

Joliot, Pierre

Laberrigue, Mme. Jeanne

Labouisse, Mme. Ève Curie

Langevin, Jean

Langevin-Joliot, Hélène

Lapicque, Mme. Aline

Latarjet, Dr. Raymond

Mayer, Roger

Perrin, Francis

Pompei, Mlle. Angèle

Radvanyi, Pierre

Van Hooren, Mme. Denise

TAPES

Decaux, A. Radio program on Marie Curie. November 1984.

Kowarski, L. Oral History interview by Charles Weiner. American Institute of Physics, New York.

UNPUBLISHED CORRESPONDENCE

Correspondence from miscellaneous sources. L.C.

Curie, E., and Curie, I. Correspondence. Columbia University (New York City).

Rare Book and Manuscript Library, Marie Curie Papers.

Curie, I., and Curie, M. Correspondence. L.C.

Curie, I., and Joliot-Curie, F. Correspondence. L.C.

Curie, P., and Curie, M. Correspondence. Bibliothèque Nationale, Départment des Manuscripts, Curie Archives.

Joliot-Curie, F., and Gentner, W. Correspondence. L.C.

Joliot-Curie, F. and I Correspondence. L.C.

Joliot-Curie, F., and Skobeltzyne, D. Correspondence. L.C.

Langevin, P., and Joliot-Curie, F. Correspondence. L.C.

Langevin, P., and Joliot-Curie, I. Correspondence. L.C.

Meloney, Mme., Curie, E., Curie, I., and Curie, M. Correspondence.

Columbia University Library, Rare Book and Manuscript Library, Marie Curie Papers.

(Some of the above has appeared as quotations in other books.)

OTHER UNPUBLISHED MATERIALS

Joliot-Curie, I. Journal, circa 1900–1955. L.C.

Press clippings. 24 boxes. L.C.

MATERIAL IN FILES AT LABORATOIRE CURIE

Biquard, P. Manuscripts of speech on Joliot-Curie at Dennison Hall. London, May 21, 1950.

———. Extensive notes on two-part interview with Professor Denivelle. May 10, 1960, and June 3, 1960.

Cotton, E., and Pompei, A. "Irène Joliot-Curie telle que l'ont connue E. Cotton et A. Pompei." Projet d'un livre sur Irène Joliot-Curie.

Gentner, W. Interviews with F. Joliot-Curie. 1980.

Joliot-Curie, Irène. "Notice sur Travaux Sciéntifique de Mme. Irène Juliot-Curie" (typed).

Joliot-Curie, I., and Joliot-Curie, F. Abécédfaire. Selected quotes.

Laberrigue, J. Handwritten article on Frédéric Joliot-Curie. 1966.

Langevin, A. "Quelques Souvenirs du Temps où Paul Langevin Dirigeait . . . à l'école EPCI . . ."1973.

Ligionnière. "Souvenirs du Temps de Guerre avec M. Joliot." Agent R V A 027.

Mayer, R. Souvenirs de F. Joliot-Curie (typed).

Moureu, H. "Un Épisode Peu Connu de la Bataille de l'Eau Lourde." November 1961.

Myers, W.G. "Memoirs." August 7, 1982.

Perrin, F. "Allocution aux Funerailles Nationales de Joliot-Curie. 1958.

———. Allocution au Congrès Internationale de Physique Nucléaire. July 1964.

———. Speech given at Warsaw on the 100th anniversary of Marie Curie's birth. October 17, 1967.

Perrin, J. Speech given at the Sorbonne on the 25th Anniversary of the discovery of radium. 1923.

Radvanyi, P. "Souvenirs sur Frédéric Joliot-Curie."

Savitch, P. "Ma Collaboration avec Irène Joliot-Curie."

UNPUBLISHED MEDIA MATERIALS

Bordry, P. "Portrait de Marie Curie par ses Amis." Interview for Radio UNESCO on the 100th anniversary of Marie Curie's birth. October 25–26, 1967.

Stengers, L., Gille, D., and Kahane, R. "The Discovery of Artificial Radioactivity." Television script of one-hour show. Fall 1985.

PRE-PUBLICATION EDITION

Goldschmidt, B. *Pionniers de l'Atome.* Stock, 1987.

PUBLISHED PAMPHLETS, BROCHURES, SPECIAL EDITIONS (BY TITLE)

Annales *de l'Université de Paris.* Vol. 37 special number and supplement in memory of the 100th anniversary of the birth of Marie Curie), 1967.

Annales Universitatis M. C. Sklowdowska Lublin. To commemorate the 100th anniversary of Marie Curie's death. Sctio AA, Physica and Chemia, vol. 12, 1967.

Bulletin de Conseil Mondial de la Paix. Special number on F. Joliot-Curie. September 1958.

Document Elle. Fayard, 1981.

Echo. No. 1, Spring 1984.

Echo. "Radioactivité Artificielle." 1934 and 1984.

Exposition sur Marie et Pierre Curie (catalogue). Bibliothèque Nationale, 1967.

50th Anniversaire du Premier Cours de Marie Curie à la Sorbonne. Edited by C. Schulof. Imprimerie Coueslant, Cahors. November 5, 1908.

50th Anniversaire de la Découverte de la Radioactivité par Frédéric et Irène Joliot-Curie. Brochure Commemorative, Palais de la Découverte, 1984.

Heures Claires. "Irène Joliot-Curie: Elle était Notre Amie." (Includes articles by Mme. E. Cotton, Mme. A. Lapicque-Perrin, H. M. Faraggi, and A. Marty Capgras.) No. 130, May 1956.

Musée Pédagogique, Hommage à Pierre Curie. 1956.

Joint Commission on Radioactivity, 4th Meeting of. July 1953

Règards. "Joliot-Curie Tel Qu'il Fut." No. 435 (special number), October 1958.

Union Française Universitaire: "Pourquoi Joliot-Curie a-t-il été révoque?"

PUBLISHED ARTICLES (BY AUTHOR)

Badash, Lawrence. "Radium Radioactivity, and Popularity of Scientific Discovery." *American Philosophical Society,* vol. 122, no. 3, June 1978.

Barrabé, Louis. "Quelques Souvenirs sur Joliot-Curie." *Pensée,* Nouvelle Série, no. 87 (commemorative issue), September–October 1959.

Bataillon, Marcel. "Une Matinée avec Joliot." *Pensée.* Nouvelle Série, no. 87 (commemorative issue), September–October 1959.

Bernstein, Barton J. "The Quest for the Super Bomb." *Stanford Magazine,* Winter 1984.

Biquard, Pierre. "Mon Ami, Joliot." *Pensée,* Nouvelle Série, no. 87 (commemorative issue), September–October 1959.

Boyer, Jacques. "Une visite à M. et Mme. Joliot-Curie (Part 2)." *La Nature,* no. 63, December 15, 1935.

Broglie, Louis de. "Jean Frédéric Joliot-Curie." *Pensée,* Nouvelle Série, no. 87 (commemorative issue), September–October 1959.

Bromley, Dorothy Dunbar. "Two Who Carry on the Curie Tradition." *New York Times Magazine,* January 1, 1933.

Chadwick, Sir James. "Irène Curie." *Nature,* vol. 177, May 26, 1956.

Cogniot, Georges. "Un Homme Véritable." *Pensée,* Nouvelle Série, no. 87 (commemorative issue), September–October 1959.

Cotton, Eugénie. "J'ai connu Pierre Curie." *Horizons,* no. 59, April 1956.

———. "Irène Joliot-Curie." *Pensée,* no. 67, 1956.

———. "Souvenirs." *Pensée,* Nouvelle Série, no. 87 (commemorative issue), September–October 1959.

Curie, Ève. "Irène." From *Marianne* (1936).

del Regato, J. A. "Marie Curie." *International Journal of Radiation, Oncology, Biology and Physics,* vol. 1, 1976.

———. "Joliot-Curie." *International Journal of Radiation, Oncology, Biology and Physics,* vol. 6, no. 5, May 1980.

Ehrenburg, Ilya. "Joliot-Curie." *Horizons,* no. 89, October 1958.

Fabre, Robert. "Une Famille de Savants." *Annales Politiques et Litéraires,* vol. 106, no. 2544, December 1935.

Guillaume, Charles Edward. "Souvenirs de P. Curie." *Écho de Paris,* May 20, 1921.

Haissinsky, M. "Le Cahier Inachevé. *Lettres Françaises,* no. 612, March 1956.

Hugonnot, Jean, and Riou, Michel. "Souvenirs sur F. Joliot-Curie." *France-Pologne,* nos. 165 & 166, Fall 1969.

Infeld, L. "Mes Souvenirs sur F. Joliot-Curie." *Pensée,* Nouvelle Série, no. 87 (commemorative issue), September–October 1959.

Jaffe, G. "Description of the Curies in their Laboratory." *Journal of Chemistry and Education,* vol. 29, 1952:.

Joliot-Curie, Frédérico. "L'Énergie Atomique." *Atomes,* no. 1, March 1946.

———. "La Première Pile Atomique Française." *Atomes,* no. 35, February 1949.

———. "La Première Pile Atomique Française." *Pensée,* Nouvelle Série, no. 23, March–April 1949.

———. Interview protesting against bacteriological warfare. L'Humanité Dimanche, March 10, 1952.

———. "Qui Prostitute la Science?" *Pensée,* no. 33–36, May–August, 1952.

———. "Titres et Travaux (pamphlet)." 1954.

———. "Déclaration" (broadside, as Président du Conseil Mondial de la Paix). January, 13, 1955.

——. "Écrits Diverses." *Bulletin du Conseil Mondial de la Paix,* no. 9, April 1954.

——. Écrits Diverses." *Bulletin du Conseil Mondial de la Paix,* no. 3, February, 1955.

——. "Les Grandes Découvertes de la Radioactivité." *Pensée,* no. 74, July–August 1957.

——. "Écrits Diverses." *Bulletin du Conseil Mondial de la Paix,* no. 22, November 15, 1957.

——. "Le Dernier Discours de Joliot-Curie." *Pensée,* no. 81, September–October 1958.

——. "Discours au Rassemblement Universel pour la Paix." *Pensée,* no. 81, September–October 1958.

——. "La Formation des Ingénieurs." *Pensée,* no. 81, September–October 1958.

——. "Hommage à Langevin." *Pensée,* no. 81, September–October 1958.

——. "Intervention à Radio-New-York." *Pensée,* no. 81, September–October 1958.

——. "Le Savant et l'Artiste." *Pensée,* no. 81, September–October 1958.

——. "L'Université Accuse Pétain." *Pensée,* no. 81, September–October 1958.

Joliot-Curie, Frédéric, et Joliot-Curie, Irène. "Pierre Curie." *Pensée,* May–June 1956.

Joliot-Curie, Irène. "Marie Curie, Ma Mère." *Europe,* no. 108, 1954.

——. "Notes Inédites." *Made in France,* no. 3, May–June 1956.

Jotterand, Franck. "Entretien avec F. Joliot-Curie." *Gazette de Lausanne,* June 29, 1957.

Kowarski, Leo. "Kowarski Raconte . . ." *Sud-Ouest-Dimanche,* July 12, 1970.

Laborde, Albert. "Pierre Curie dans son Laboratoire." Conférence à l'occasion du 50e anniversaire de la mort de P. Curie.

Lacassagne, A. "Frédéric Joliot-Curie, Biologiste." *Pensée,* Nouvelle Série, no. 87 (commemorative issue), September–October 1959.

Langevin, Hélène Joliot. "Gentner à Paris." CERN Publications.

Langevin, P. "Pierre Curie." *La Révue du Mois,* 1906.

Léon, Georges. "Joliot-Curie." *Régards,* Nouvelle Série, no. 388, March 1955.

Marin, Jean. "La Bataille de l'Eau Lourde." Historia, no. 81, October–November 1952.

Maublanc, Réné. "L'Université Française et la Résistance." *Pensée,* Nouvelle Série, no. 15, November–December 1947.

Orcel, Jean. "Joliot-Curie." *Pensée,* no. 81, September–October 1958.

——. "La Pensée et l'Action de Joliot-Curie." *Pensée,* Nouvelle Série, no. 87 (commemorative issue), September–October 1959.

Payot, R. Article on Joliot-Curie. *Journal de Genève,* May 5, 1950.

Perrin, Francis. "Frédéric Joliot." *Dictionary of Scientific Biography VII.* Scribners, 1973.

——. "Irène Joliot-Curie." *Dictonary of Scientific Biography VII.* Scribners, 1973.

Pickles, Dorothy. "The Communist Problem in France." *International Affairs,* April 1952.

Poincaré, Henri. "Les Femmes à l'Institut." *Les Annales,* no. 1438, 1910.

Pompei, Angèle. "Irène Joliot-Curie." *Europe,* May 1961.

Pontocorvo, Bruno. "Un Savant, un Combattant, un Homme." *Pensée,* Nouvelle Série, no. 87 (commemorative issue), September–October 1959.

Powell, C. F. "La Place de Joliot-Curie dans la Physique Atomique." *Pensée,* Nouvelle Série, no. 87 (commemorative issue), September–October 1959.

Prescott, Ann. "Henri Becquerel, Discoverer of Radioactivity." *Laurels,* vol. 54, no. 1, Spring 1983.

Radvanyi, Pierre. "Frédéric Joliot-Curie au Collège de France dans les Années d'Après Guerre." *Pensée,* Nouvelle Série, no. 87 (commemorative issue), September–October 1959.

Savel, Pierre. "27 Années de Collaboration Scientifique avec Joliot-Curie." *Pensée,* Nouvelle Série, no. 87 (commemorative issue), September–October 1959.

Skobeltzyne, D. V. "Joliot-Curie et les Découvertes Fondamentales du XXe Siecle." *Pensée,* Nouvelle Série, no. 87 (commemorative issue), September–October 1959.

Stuewer, R. "Bringing the News of Fission to America." *Physics Today,* October 1985.

Suzor, Francis. "Témoignage." *Pensée,* Nouvelle Série, no. 87 (commemorative issue), September–October 1959.

Teillac, Jean. "L'Oeuvre et la Pensée Scientifique de Joliot-Curie." *Pensée,* Nouvelle Série, no. 87 (commemorative issue), September–October 1959.

Téry, Gustave. [Untitled; story of Langevin affair.]*L'Oeuvre,* October–November 1911.

Thomas, J. André. "Le Martyre de Fernand Holweck." *Pensée,* Nouvelle Série, no. 27, November–December 1949.

Yuasa, T. "Souvenirs of Joliot-Curie." Translated from the Japanese in *Shizen* (Nature), vol. 21, nos. 1 & 2, 1966.

PUBLISHED BOOKS

(The starting point for any life of Marie Curie is the biography written by her daughter Ève. This is the only source for most of Marie's original letters, which were destroyed during the fighting in Warsaw in World War II. The most helpful of the more recent books is the one by Robert W. Reid; see below. —R.P.

Amoureux, H. *La Vie des Français sous l'Occupation.* Arthème Fayard, 1961.

Andrade, E. N. da C. *Rutherford.* William Heineman, 1964.

Aron, Raymond. *L'Opium des Intellectuels.* Gallimard, 1968.

Association Frédéric et Irène Joliot-Curie. *Souvenirs et Documents.* 1968.

Audiat, P. *Paris Pendant la Guerre.* Hachette, 1946.

Bertaut, J. *Paris, L'Opinion . . . sous la 3e République.* Eyre & Spottiswode, 1936.

Biquard, P. *Frédéric Joliot-Curie.* Éd. Seghers, 1961.

———. *Langevin.* Éd. Seghers, 1969.

Blackett, P. M. S. *Biographical Memoirs.* Fellows of Royal Society, vol. 6, 1960.

Chadourne, Mark. *Absences.* Plon, 1945.

Chaskolskaia, Marianne. *Joliot-Curie* (in French; tr. G. Smirnov). Éd. Mir, 1968.

Clark, Ronald. *Life and Times of Einstein.* Abrams, 1984.

Collins, Larry, and Lapierre, Dominique. *Is Paris Burning?* Simon and Schuster, 1965.

Concasty, M. Louise. *Pierre and Marie Curie.* Bibliothèque Nationale, 1967.

Cotton, Eugénie. *Les Curies.* Éd. Seghers, 1963.

Crease, R. P., and Mann, C. C. *The 2nd Creation–Makers of Revolution in 20th Century Physics.* Macmillan, 1986.

Curie, Eve. *Madame Curie.* American edition. Translation by Vincent Sheean. Doubleday, Doran & Co., 1937.

Curie, Marie. *La Radiologie at la Guerre.* Librarie Felix Alcan, 1921.

———. *Pierre Curie.* Macmillan, 1924. (Includes autobiographical notes by Marie Curie. When the book was reprinted elsewhere than in the U.S., Marie Curie refused permission to include her autobiographical notes at the end.)

———. *Radioactivité.* Herman, 1935.

Daniels, C., ed. *Chronicle of the 20th Century.* Chronicle Publishing, 1987.

Desanti, Dominique. *Les Staliniens.* Fayard, 1973.

Destouches, C. *La Lumière Bleue.* Les Éditions du Temps, 1959.

Dewilly, Le Pommelet, Yvonnig. *Paimpol au Début du Siècle: 1900–1914.* Les PresseS Bretonnes, 1984.

Dubois, Edward. *Paris sanS Lumière.* Payot, 1946.

Ehrenburg, Ilya. *Post-War Years.* Vol. 6 of *Men, Years, Life.* Macgibbon & Kee, 1966.

Elsasser, Walter M. *Memoirs of a Physicist in the Atomic Age.* Neale Watson, 1978.

Eve, A. S. *RutherforD.* Cambridge University Press, 1939.

Flanner, S. *Paris Journal: 1944–65.* Harcourt, 1965.

Gilpin, Robert. *France in the Age of the Scientific State.* Princeton University Press, 1968.

Giroud, F. *Une Femme Honorable.* Fayard, 1981.

Goldschmidt, B. *L'Aventure Atomique.* Fayard, 1962.

———. *Les Rivalités Atomiques.* Fayard, 1967.

Goldsmith, M. *The Curie Family.* Heron Books, 1971.

———. *3 Scientists Face Social Responsibility.* Center for Study of Science, Technology and Development (lecture series), CSIR, 1976.

———. *Frederick Joliot-Curie.* Lawrence and Wishart, 1976.

Goudsmit, S. *Alsos, the Failure of German Science.* Sigma Books, 1947.

Gowing, Margaret. *Britain and Atomic Energy—1939–1945.* Macmillan, 1964.

———. *Dossier Secret des Relations Atomiques Entre Alliés: 1935–1945.* Plon, 1965.

———. *Independence and Deterrence: Britain and Atomic Energy—1945-1952.* St. Martin's Press, 1970.

Hausser, E. *Paris au Jour le Jour.* Éditions de Minuit, 1968.

Herriot, Édouard. *Episodes 1940–44.* Flammarion, 1949–50.

Hoffman, B., and Dukas, H. *Einstein.* Éd. Seuil, 1975.

Howorth, M. *Pioneer Research and the Atom.* New World Publishers, 1958.

Joliot-Curie, Frédéric. *5 Années de Lutte pour la Paix.* Éd. Defense de la Paix, 1954.

———. *Textes Choisies.* Éd. Sociales, 1959.

Kedrov, Fedor B. *Irène and Frédéric Joliot-Curie* (in Russian). 1973.

Kendall, Elizabeth. *Where She Danced: The Birth of American Art Dance.* University of California Press, 1979.

Kevles, D. J. *The Physicists.* Knopf, 1978.

Klickstein, Herbert. Marie Curie: *A Bio-Bibliographical Study.* 1964.

Koestler, Arthur and Cynthia. *Stranger in the Square.* Random House, 1984.

Langevin, André. *Paul Langevin.* Les Éditeurs Français Réunis, 1971.

Lot, F. *J. Perrin.* Éd. Seghers, 1963.

Marbo, Camille. *Souvenirs et Rencontres.* Éd. Grasset, 1968.

McKown, R. *Irène Joliot-Curie.* Mesmer, 1962.

Michaux, Baronne J. *En Marge du Drame: Journal d'une Parisienne Pendant la Guerre.* 2 vols. Perrin, 1916–18.

Michel, H. *Histoire de la Résistance.* Presses Universitaires, 1949–50.

Moorehead, A. *Traitors.* Scribners, 1952.

Nobel Stiftelsen. Nobel Foundation, Elsevier.

Pagals, Heinz R. *Quantum Physics as the Language of Nature.* Simon and Schuster, 1982.

Radvanyi, Pierre, and Bordry, Monique. *La Radioactivité Artificielle.* Éd. Seuil, 1984.

Régaud, C. *Marie Curie.* Fondation Curie, 1934.

Reid, Robert W. *Marie Curie.* Collins, 1974. Also: Dutton, 1975.

Reidman, S. *Men and Women Behind the Atom.* Abelard-Schuman, 1958.

Rhodes, Richard. *The Making of the Atomic Bomb.* Simon and Schuster, 1986.

Robrieux, Philippe. *Histoire Intime du Parti Communiste Français.* Vol. 1 & 2. Fayard, 1980.

Romer, A., ed. *Discovery of Radioactivity and Transmutation.* Dover, 1964.

Rose, W. J. *Poland, Old and New.* Bell, 1948.

Rouzé, M. *Frédéric Joliot-Curie.* Les Éditeurs Français Réunis, 1956.

Scheinman, Lawrence. *Atomic Energy in France Under the 4th Republic.* Princeton University Press, 1965.

Sharp, E. *Hertha Ayrton.* Edward Arnold, 1926.

Steed, H. W. *Through 30 Years.* 2 vols. William Heineman, 1924.

Terrat-Branly, Jeanne. *Mon Père, Édouard Branley.* Corréa, 1949.

Thompson, S. D. *Lord Kelvin.* Macmillan, 1910.

Verdès-Leroux, J. *Au Service du Parti—1944–1956.* Fayard, 1983.

Weart, Spencer R. *Scientists in Power.* Harvard University Press, 1979.

Werth, Alex. *France 1940–55.* Hale, 1956.

Wilson, David. *Rutherford.* MIT Press, 1984.

Woznicki, Robert. *Mme. Curie, Daughter of Poland.* American Institute of Polish Culture, 1983.

Ziegler, Gillette, ed. *Choix de Lettres de Marie Curie et Irène Joliot-Curie.* Les Éditeurs Français Réunis, 1974.

Notes

Quotes of less than six words have not been identified, except in rare cases where their sources are vital. Quotes from articles in newspapers, magazines, etc., are not listed when date of same is given in text, nor are page numbers in source of correspondence when date of same is indicated. In the instance of quotes taken from books that came, in turn, from other sources, only the source used here is listed.

The following abbreviations are used:

A.I.P. = The American Institute of Physics (New York City): oral history interview of Lew Kowarski by Charles Weiner

B.N. = Bibliothèque Nationale (Paris), Départment des Manuscrits, Curie Archives

Col. U. = Columbia University (New York City), Rare Book and Manuscript Library, Marie Curie Papers

L.C. = Laboratoire Curie (Paris), Curie and Joliot-Curie Archives

CHAPTER I

1. Quoted material from Ève Curie, *Madame Curie,* trans. Vincent Sheean, Doubleday, Doran & Co., 1937, pp. 20–21.

2. Ibid., p. 72.

3. Quoted material from Ibid., p. 88.

CHAPTER II

1. Marie Curie, *Pierre Curie,* Macmillan, 1924, p. 171.

2. Ibid.

CHAPTER III

1. Marie Curie, *Pierre Curie,* p. 42.

2. F. Giroud, *Une Femme Honorable,* Fayard, 1981, p. 77.

3. M. Goldsmith, *The Curie Family,* Heron Books, 1971, p. 31.

4. Robert W. Reid, *Marie Curie,* Dutton, 1975, p. 64.

5. Quoted material from B.N.

6. Marie Curie, *Pierre Curie,* p. 174.

7. Ibid., p. 67.

CHAPTER IV

1. Marie Curie, *Pierre Curie,* p. 82.

2. B.N.

3. Ibid.

4. Ève Curie, *Madame Curie,* p. 149.

5. M. Howorth, *Pioneer Research on the Atom,* New World Publishers, p. 22, n.

6. Ève Curie, *Madame Curie,* p. 163.

CHAPTER V

1. Marie Curie, *Pierre Curie,* p. 169.

2. Ève Curie, *Madame Curie,* p. 172.

3. Marie Curie, *Pierre Curie,* p. 104.

CHAPTER VI

1. *Écho de Paris* (L.C.: press clippings).

2. L.C.: J. Perrin; speech given at the Sorbonne on the twenty-fifth anniversary of the discovery of radium.

3. L.C.: E. Cotton and A. Pompei, "Irène Joliot-Curie telle que l'ont connue E. Cotton et A. Pompei," Project d'un livre sur Irène Joliot-Curie, p. 2.

4. Robert W. Reid, *Marie Curie,* p. 127.

5. Quoted material from B.N.

6. Reid, *Marie Curie,* p. 123.

7. David Wilson, *Rutherford,* MIT Press, 1984, p. 90.

8. B.N.

9. F. Giroud, *Une Femme Honorable,* p. 158.

CHAPTER VII

1. Ève Curie, *Madame Curie,* p. 216.

2. Camille Marbo, *Souvenirs et Rencontres,* Éd. Grasset, 1968, p. 140.

3. Quoted material from L.C.: E. Cotton and A. Pompei, "Irène Joliot-Curie telle que l'ont connue E. Cotton et A. Pompei," Project d'un livre sur Irène Joliot-Curie, p. 15.

4. Eugenié Cotton: *50th Anniversaire du Premier Cours de Marie Curie à la Sorbonne,* ed. C. Schulof, Imprimerie Coueslant, Cahors, November 5, 1908.

CHAPTER VIII

1. *Nobel Stiftelsen,* Nobel Foundation, Elsevier.

2. *Document Elle,* Éditions Fayard, 1981, p. 7.

3. B.N.

4. Ibid.

5. Quoted material from Ève Curie, *Madame Curie,* p. 246.

6. Ibid.

7. Ibid., pp. 248–249.

8. Ibid., p. 252.

9. Ibid., p. 254.

10. F. Giroud, *Une Femme Honorable*, p. 193.

CHAPTER IX

1. Marie Curie, *Pierre Curie*, p. 92.

2. L.C.: E. Cotton and A. Pompei, Irène Joliot-Curie telle l'ont connue E. Cotton et A. Pompei," Project d'un livre sur Irène Joliot-Curie, p. 20.

3. *Annales de l'Université de Paris*, vol. 37 (special number and supplement in memory of the one hundredth anniversary of the birth of Marie Curie), 1967.

4. Robert W. Reid, *Marie Curie*, p. 160.

5. Ibid., p. 167.

6. Quoted material from R. McKown, *Irène Joliot-Curie*, Mesmer, 1962, p. 32.

7. L.C.: Cotton and Pompei, "Irène Joliot-Curie," p. 20.

8. Quoted material from L.C.

9. A. S. Eve, *Rutherford*, Cambridge University Press, 1939, p. 190.

10. Reid, *Marie Curie*, p. 166.

11. Jeanne Terrat-Branly, *Mon Père, Édouard Branly*, Corréa, 1949, p. 210.

CHAPTER X

1. Gilette Ziegler, ed., *Choix de Lettres de Marie Curie et Irène Joliot-Curie*, Les Éditeurs Français Réunis, 1974.

2. L.C.

3. David Wilson, *Rutherford*, p. 257.

4. L.C.: Irène Joliot-Curie's journal.

5. Quoted material from Camille Marbo, *Souvenirs et Rencontres*, p. 121.

6. Quoted material from André Langevin, *Paul Langevin*, Les Éditeurs Français Réunis, 1971, p. 63.

7. Quoted material from Marbo, *Souvenirs*, p. 109.

8. Ibid., p. 106.

9. Quoted material from Marbo, *Souvenirs*, p. 107.

10. Quoted material from L.C.: taped interview.

11. *San Francisco Examiner*, November 26, 1911.

12. Quoted material from Marbo, *Souvenirs*, pp. 106–119. All quotes, following pages, to "I know it's an idiotic thing to do but I must" are also from Marbo, *Souvenirs*, pp. 106–119.

13. Gustave Téry, [untitled], *L'Oeuvre*, October–November 1911 (second installment), p. 4.

14. Marbo, *Souvenirs,* p. 119.

15. *Nobel Stiftelsen.*

16. Quoted material from F. Giroud, *Une Femme Honorable,* p. 248.

CHAPTER XI

1. Quoted material from F. Giroud, *Une Femme Honorable,* p. 249.

2. Gillette Ziegler, ed., *Choix de Lettres de Marie Curie et Irène Joliot-Curie.*

3. Robert W. Reid, *Marie Curie,* p. 219.

4. "Joliot-Curie Tel Qu'il Fut," *Régards,* no. 435 (special number), October 1958, p. 7.

5. *Annales de l'Université de Paris,* vol. 37 (special number and supplement in memory of the one hundredth anniversary of the birth of Marie Curie), p. 32.

6. Ève Curie, *Madame Curie,* p. 284.

7. Ziegler, *Choix de Lettres;* L.C.: unpublished correspondence.

8. Ziegler, *Choix de Lettres.*

9. Ibid.

10. Ibid.

11. Ibid. (Including quote immediately preceding.)

12. Bibliothèque Nationale, *Exposition sur Marie et Pierre Curie* (catalogue), 1967.

CHAPTER XII

1. Irène Joliot-Curie, "Marie Curie, Ma Mére," *Europe,* no. 108, 1954, p. 110.

2. Ibid., p. 103.

3. Bibliothèque Nationale, *Exposition sur Marie et Pierre Curie* (catalogue).

CHAPTER XIII

1. Gillette Ziegler, ed., *Choix de Lettres de Marie et Irène Joliot-Curie.*

2. F. Lot, *J. Perrin,* Éd. Seghers, 1963, p. 165.

3. B.N.

4. Ibid.

5. F. Giroud, *Une Femme Honorable,* p. 306.

6. Robert W. Reid, *Marie Curie,* p. 259.

7. Ibid., p. 268.

8. Col. U.

CHAPTER XIV

1. Col. U.

2. B. Hoffman and H. Dukas, *Einstein,* Éd. Seuil, 1975, p. 18.

3. Quoted material from Angèle Pompei, "Irène Joliot-Curie," *Europe,* May 1961, p. 232.

CHAPTER XV

1. M. Goldsmith, *The Curie Family,* Heron Books, 1971, p. 88.

2. Gillette Ziegler, ed., *Choix de Lettres de Marie Curie et Irène Joliot-Curie.*

3. P. Biquard, *Frédéric Joliot-Curie,* Éd. Seghers, 1965, p. 28.

4. Quoted material from Franck Jotterand, "Entretien avec F. Joliot-Curie," *Gazette de Lausanne,* June 29, 1957.

5. R. McKown, *Irène Joliot-Curie,* p. 72.

6. M. Rouzé, *Frédéric Joliot-Curie,* Les Éditeurs Français Réunis, 1956, p. 31.

7. *Le Quotidien,* March 31, 1925.

8. L.C.: Irène Joliot-Curie's journal.

9. L.C.

10. Quoted material from Angèle Pompei, "Irène Joliot-Curie," *Europe,* May 1961.

11. Spencer R. Weart, *Scientists in Power,* Harvard University Press, 1979, p. 22.

12. T. Yuasa, "Souvenirs of Joliot-Curie," tr. from the Japanese in *Shizen* (Nature), vol. 21, nos. 1 & 2, 1966.

13. L.C.: taped interview.

14. L.C.

15. Quoted material from L.C.

16. L.C.: taped interview

CHAPTER XVI

1. F. Giroud, *Une Femme Honorable,* p. 365.

2. Quoted material from L.C.: correspondence.

3. Ibid.

4. P. Biquard, *Frédéric Joliot-Curie,* p. 36.

5. Robert W. Reid, *Marie Curie,* p. 299.

6. B.N.

7. Irène Joliot-Curie, "Marie Curie, Ma Mère," *Europe,* no. 108, 1954, p. 119.

8. Col. U.

9. Giroud, *Femme Honorable,* p. 365.

10. A.I.P.

11. Personal communication.

12. F. Lot, *J. Perrin,* p. 110.

13. Quoted material from L.C.: correspondence.

14. S. Riedman, *Men and Women Behind the Atom,* Abelard-Schuman, 1958, p. 144.

CHAPTER XVII

1. Richard Rhodes, *The Making of the Atomic Bomb,* Simon and Schuster, 1986, p. 162.

2. Ibid., p. 404.

3. Franck Jotterand, "Entretien avec F. Joliot-Curie," *Gazette de Lausanne,* June 29, 1957.

4. M. Goldsmith, *Frederick Joliot-Curie,* Lawrence Wishart, 1976, p. 42.

5. Eugénie Cotton, *Les Curies,* Éd. Seghers, 1963, p. 190.

6. Spencer R. Weart, *Scientists in Power,* p. 42.

7. Albert Laborde, "Pierre Curie dans son Laboratoire," Conférence à l'occasion du 50e anniversaire de la mort de Pierre Curie.

8. Col. U.

9. L.C.

10. Weart, *Scientists,* p. 44 (paraphrase).

11. Quoted material from P. Biquard, *Frédéric Joliot-Curie,* p. 44 (paraphrase).

12. Ibid., p. 41.

13. Goldsmith, *Frederick Joliot-Curie,* p. 57.

14. Ibid., p. 54.

CHAPTER XVIII

1. M. Rouzé, *Frédéric Joliot-Curie,* p. 55.

2. Col. U.

3. Ibid.

4. L.C.: taped interview.

5. A.I.P.

6. Quoted material from Col. U.

7. *Nobel Stiftelsen.*

8. A.I.P.

9. Quoted material from Col. U.

10. L.C.

11. Ibid.

12. Ibid.

13. Ibid.

14. A.I.P.

15. L.C.: P. Savitch, *"Ma Collaboration avec Irène Joliot-Curie."*

16. Col. U.

17. J. Verdès-Leroux, *Au Service du Parti—1944–1956,* Fayard, 1983, p. 482, n. 98.

18. Richard Rhodes, *The Making of the Atomic Bomb,* p. 253.

19. Ibid., p. 255 (paraphrase).

20. Quoted material from A.I.P.

21. Rhodes, *Making of the Atomic Bomb,* p. 261 (paraphrase).

22. A.I.P.

23. Ibid.

24. Ibid.

25. Rhodes, *Making of the Atomic Bomb,* p. 275.

CHAPTER XIX

1. L.C.

2. Col. U.

3. L.C.

4. Spencer R. Weart, *Scientists in Power,* p. 150.

5. A.I.P.

6. Jean Marin, "La Bataille de l'Eau Lourde," *Historia,* no. 81, October–November 1952.

7. Col. U.

8. Quoted material from L.C.: H. Moureu, "Un Épisode Peu Connu de la Bataille de l'Eau Lourde." November 1961.

9. A.I.P.

10. Quoted material from P. Biquard, *Frédéric Joliot-Curie,* p. 64.

11. C. Daniels, ed., *Chronicle of the 20th Century,* Chronicle Publishing, 1987, p. 511.

12. L.C.: taped interview.

13. L.C.

CHAPTER XX

1. T. Yuasa, "Souvenirs of Joliot-Curie," tr. from the Japanese in *Shizen* (Nature), vol. 21, nos. 1 & 2, 1966.

2. L.C. Ligonnière, "Souvenirs du Temps de Guerre avec M. Joliot," Agent R# V# A# 027.

3. L.C.: taped interview.

4. L.C.: Ligonnière, "Souvenirs."

5. L.C.: taped interview.

6. Marcel Bataillon, "Une Matinée avec Joliot," *Pensée,* Nouvelle Série, no. 87 (commemorative issue), September–October 1959.

7. Quoted material from Col. U.

8. L.C.: W. Gentner, interviews with Joliot-Curie, p. 5.

9. Quoted material from L.C.: Ligonnière, "Souvenirs."

10. Spencer R. Weart, *Scientists in Power,* p. 166.

11. Quoted material from L.C.: Gentner, interviews, p. 10.

12. P. Biquard, *Frédéric Joliot-Curie,* p. 70.

13. M. Rouzé, *Frédéric Joliot-Curie,* p. 43.

14. Richard Rhodes, *The Making of the Atomic Bomb,* p. 442.

15. L.C.

16. Ibid.

17. Ibid.

18. Ibid.

19. Ibid.

20. Ibid.

21. Ibid.

22. Ibid.

CHAPTER XXI

1. Quoted material from L.C.

2. Ibid.

3. Larry Collins and Dominique Lapierre, *Is Paris Burning?* Simon and Schuster, 1965, p. 55.

4. Ibid., p. 20.

5. Spencer R. Weart, *Scientists in Power,* p. 213.

6. B. Goldschmidt, *Pionniers de l'Atome,* p. 281.

7. Ibid., p. 301.

8. Margaret Gowing, *Britain and Atomic Energy—1939–1945,* Macmillan, 1964, p. 216.

9. Ibid., p. 216.

10. P. Biquard, *Frédéric Joliot-Curie,* p. 108.

11. M. Goldsmith, *The Curie Family,* p. 158.

12. Weart, *Scientists,* p. 219.

13. Ibid., p. 220.

14. L.C.: E. Cotton and A. Pompei, "Irène Joliot-Curie telle que l'ont connue E. Cotton and A. Pompei," Project d'un livre sur Irène Joliot-Curie, p. 22.

15. L.C.

16. Frédéric Joliot-Curie, "Hommage à Pierre Langevin," *Textes Choisies,* Éd. Sociales, 1959.

17. L.C.

18. Quoted material from L.C.: press clippings.

19. Quoted material from L.C.

20. Ibid.

21. M. Goldsmith, *Frederick Joliot-Curie,* p. 153.

22. Frédéric Joliot-Curie, "La Première Pile Atomique Française," *Pensée,* Nouvelle Série, no. 23, March–April 1949.

CHAPTER XXII

1. M. Goldsmith, *Frederick Joliot-Curie,* p. 158.

2. L.C.

3. B. Goldschmidt, *Pionniers de l'Atome,* p. 434.

4. L.C.: taped interview.

5. B. Goldschmidt, *L'Aventure Atomique,* Fayard, 1962, p. 186.

6. Ilya Ehrenburg, *Post-War Years,* vol. 6 of *Men, Years, Life,* Macgibbon & Kee, 1966, p. 184.

7. Goldschmidt, *Pionniers,* p. 434.

8. Spencer R. Weart, *Scientists in Power,* p. 258.

9. Ibid., p. 259.

10. Quoted material from Goldsmith, *Frederick Joliot-Curie,* p. 166.

11. L.C.: taped interview.

12. P. Biquard, *Frédéric Joliot-Curie,* p. 99.

13. Personal interview.

14. Goldschmidt, *Pionniers,* p. 437.

15. Personal interview.

16. L.C.: taped interview.

17. Goldschmidt, *Pionniers,* p. 437.

18. L.C.: taped interview.

19. Goldsmith, *Frederick Joliot-Curie,* p. 234.

20. T. Yuasa, "Souvenirs of Joliot-Curie," tr. from the Japanese in *Shizen* (Nature), vol. 21, nos. 1 & 2, 1966.

21. Quoted material from E. Cotton, "Souvenirs," *Pensée,* Nouvelle Série, no. 87 (commemorative issue), September–October 1959.

22. Frédéric Joliot-Curie, Message to 14th Congress of PCF, *Textes Choisies.*

23. Biquard, *Frédéric Joliot-Curie,* p. 126.

24. Goldsmith, *Frederick Joliot-Curie,* p. 172.

25. Jean Orcel, "La Pensée et l'Action de Joliot-Curie," *Pensée,* Nouvelle Série, no. 87 (commemorative issue), September–October 1959.

26. L.C.

27. Angèle Pompei, "Irène Joliot-Curie," *Europe,* May 1961, p. 241.

28. R. McKown, *Irène Joliot-Curie,* p. 179.

29. Ilya Ehrenburg, *Post-War Years,* p. 186.

30. Goldsmith, *Frederick Joliot-Curie,* p. 203.

31. L.C.: taped interview.

32. Quoted material from personal interview.

33. L.C.: taped interview.

Index

About the Author

Rosalynd Pflaum received the prestigious
French Legion d'Honneur in 1978.
A summa cum laude *graduate,*
she attended Stanford University.
She has won praise on both sides
of the Atlantic for her
biographies of the Duc de Morny
and the Duchess of Courland.
She lives in Minnesota.

BOOK MARK

The text of this book was composed in
the typeface Fairfield with
the display in Robin and Folkwang
by Berryville Graphics,
Berryville, Virginia

Text and insert printing is by
Berryville Graphics,
Berryville, Virginia

BOOK DESIGN BY
CAROL MALCOLM